T0109986

Critical Praise for *Lincoln's Men*

"[*Lincoln's Men*] will be a surprise best seller."
—William Safire, *The New York Times*

"An excellent book. . . . Davis' talent for the details that define the whole is used to great advantage here, and his ability to craft the evidence to support his premise makes the book all the more convincing."
—Ed Malles, *The Orlando Sentinel*

"In William C. Davis' *Lincoln's Men*, Abraham Lincoln rises above the sniping of revisionist historians and retains the towering image that makes him synonymous with freedom and the potential for greatness in the common man. . . . [A] vivid portrayal of how soldiers felt about the soft-spoken 'father.'"
—Richard R. Roberts, *The Indianapolis Star*

"Lincoln becomes a stronger, larger military leader through this book's exposition and research. Davis has written a much-needed chapter of Civil War and military history."
—Bill McLain, *San Antonio Express-News*

"What matters about *Lincoln's Men* is that it is an overview of an always interesting subject."
—Jonathan Yardley, *The Washington Post Book World*

ꞁ "Using letters written by soldiers during the Civil War, Davis offers compelling evidence of the compassion Illinois's favorite son had for the U.S. soldiers."
—Tara Croft, *Chicago Magazine*

"A worthwhile . . . study of the emotional bonds forged between the average Union soldier and 'Father Abraham' Lincoln. . . . His examination of Lincoln from the viewpoint of the average Union soldier confirms 'Old Abe's' undeniable genius as a wartime leader."
—*Kirkus Reviews*

"By examining [Lincoln's] relationship [to his men] Davis sheds new light both on our 16th president and on his epoch."

—*Publishers Weekly*

"Lincoln's relationship with Union generals has overshadowed that between himself and the average soldier, a situation remedied by Davis' study."

—Gilbert Taylor, *Booklist*

"Compelling. . . . Anyone who hopes to understand how and why Lincoln came to embody the Union cause and ensured that soldiers did not die in vain must read Davis's stunning book."

—Randall M. Miller, *Library Journal*

"*Lincoln's Men* is a giant step toward understanding the Civil War as a triumph of the will of the American people. A very important book, *Lincoln's Men* is at once an insightful biography, a story of ideas that have consequences, and a study of leadership. To read *Lincoln's Men* is to spend a long evening with William C. Davis and savor the wisdom of his extraordinary knowledge of Lincoln and his soldiers."

—Emory M. Thomas,
author of *Travels to Hallowed Ground: A Historian's Journey to the American Civil War*

"Despite a plethora of books on Abraham Lincoln, no writer has ever investigated substantially the relationship between 'Father Abraham' and his soldiers in the Union's darkest hour. Now, utilizing thousands of quotations from Billy Yanks, the master storyteller of the Civil War has crafted a narrative as detailed as it is delightful, as revealing as it is refreshing. This is historical reporting at its very best."

—James I. Robertson, Jr.,
author of *Stonewall Jackson: The Man, the Soldier, the Legend*

"Once again, William C. Davis approaches an important topic with the sure-footed grace that makes the rest of us envy him. *Lincoln's Men* is one of the most innovative studies written of the Union soldier."

—Reid Mitchell, author of *Civil War Soldiers*

LINCOLN'S MEN

HOW PRESIDENT LINCOLN BECAME
FATHER TO AN ARMY AND A NATION

WILLIAM C. DAVIS

A Touchstone Book
Published by Simon & Schuster

TOUCHSTONE
Rockefeller Center
1230 Avenue of the Americas
New York, NY 10020

First Touchstone Edition 2000

TOUCHSTONE and colophon are registered trademarks
of Simon & Schuster, Inc.

Designed by Carla Bolte

Manufactured in the United States of America

10 9 8 7 6 5 4 3 2

The Library of Congress has cataloged the Free Press edition as follows:

Davis, William C., 1946–
    Lincoln's men: how President Lincoln became father
to an army and a nation/ William C. Davis.
        p.   cm.
    Includes bibliographical references and index.
    1. Lincoln, Abraham, 1809–1865—Relations with soldiers.
2. Lincoln, Abraham, 1809–1865—Military leadership.
3. Lincoln, Abraham, 1809–1865—Public opinion.
4. Soldiers—United States—Correspondence.   5. Soldiers—
United States—Diaries.   6. United States—History—Civil War,
1861–1865—Personal narratives.   7. Public opinion—
United States—History—19th century.   I. Title.
E457.2.D33   1999
973.7'092—dc21   98-8069
                                                    CIP

ISBN: 978-0-684-86294-1

. . . behold, my covenant is with thee,

and thou shalt be a father of many nations.

. . . thy name shall be Abraham;

for a father of many nations have I made thee.

Genesis 17: 4–5

CONTENTS

ACKNOWLEDGMENTS

THE AVERAGE UNION SOLDIER IN THE CIVIL WAR DID not spend all, or even a great deal, of his time thinking about President Abraham Lincoln. To the extent that the letters and diaries they left behind allow us to judge, those in the eastern theater only commented on him on a few occasions—his four principal reviews of the Army of the Potomac in 1861–63, and a few less extended visits to the army, his relief of General George B. McClellan from command of that army in November 1862, the issuing of the Preliminary and final Emancipation Proclamations, the enlistment of black soldiers from 1863 onward, the 1864 presidential election campaign, and the assassination in April 1865. Other issues brought comment from time to time—the draft, confiscation policy, Northern dissent, and more—but in the main soldiers confined their written musings to these areas. Out in the western theater they commented even less, since Lincoln never visited those armies, and they had no interest in McClellan.

Yet it seems evident from what these Billy Yanks did say that they came to adopt a very definite sense of who Lincoln was, his role in the war, what he meant to them, and how they felt about him. Lincoln's life has been plumbed to almost every depth, from his taste in music to his feelings on religion, yet this vital relationship between him and the soldiers who fought in, supported, and in the end died in his war, remains unpenetrated beyond a few paragraphs here and there, especially in recent works by James M. McPherson, Reid Mitchell, and Merrill Peterson. It cries for a closer look, especially when considering just how the Union soldier maintained his heroic morale in the face of years of failure. Many factors help account for Billy Yank's unyielding resolution. The works of Bell I. Wiley, James I. Robertson, Jr., and most recently McPherson and Mitchell present cogent analyses of the underlayment of what McPherson calls the "sustaining resolve" that saw the Yankee soldier through from defeat to victory. What remains unexplored, however, is the role of Lincoln himself as one of those foundations, and thus *Lincoln's Men*.

Historians always face great danger when they attempt to penetrate the minds of past peoples, even from an era like the Civil War that left behind such abundant raw materials for study. The more than 2 million men who in some form and for some period served the Union during 1861–65 must have written in sum tens of millions of letters and diaries during the war. The majority no longer survive, but what remains is staggering, representing easily tens of thousands of collections, varying from a single diary or a few letters to mammoth correspondences whose letters number in the hundreds. For his recent pathbreaking work *For Cause & Comrades*, James M. McPherson consulted more than a thousand sets of letters and diaries, and might easily have spent the rest of a lifetime trying unsuccessfully to include every known source.

Yet what the historian soon discovers is that, after a while, a pattern emerges. The soldiers everywhere seem to comment on the same events, and with largely the same sentiments. For *Lincoln's Men* somewhere around six hundred manuscript collections were mined, not counting another two hundred or more published sets of wartime diaries and letters. Yet, even though the healthy sampling of eight hundred or more represents a very respectable research base, it is still in no way a meaningful percentage of the 2 million. Moreover, all historians dealing with soldier letters and diaries must be aware that they are hearing only from a segment of the 70 percent or so who were literate, a sampling further refined by the fact that a great many men in uniform who did write letters and diaries chose for whatever reason not to comment upon current events, their leaders, or anything more important than the weather.

What this means, of course, is that, for every soldier voice that remains to tell us of his concerns and feelings, there are hundreds from whom we can hear nothing, whose thoughts can be inferred only from their actions, and that imperfectly. In short, though historians draw their conclusions from those who wrote the documents that survive, we need to remember that the silence of all those others is *possibly* just as eloquent, but of what we cannot say. It may be that their letters and diaries did not survive, or are not available. It may be that they had so little interest in anything other than the weather, their food, and their bowels—the three most common topics of most soldier communications—that they had nothing to say about Lincoln, emancipation, the conduct of the war, or anything else. Or it could simply mean that they vented their opinions around the campfire and not in writing, or even that those who voiced intemperate or adversarial attitudes not consonant with the postwar veneration of Father Abraham, later removed such expressions from their papers. Many a memoir written years after the war reveals an adoration for the president altogether missing from the author's wartime correspondence.

The point is that historians need a fair portion of humility in setting forth conclusions about the feelings and attitudes of a broad population like the Union soldier, and especially where Lincoln is concerned. The samplings that it is practical to use are so small, and with so many built-in qualifiers, that only the foolish or the smug dare maintain that the vocal few whose words remain can speak with absolute authority for the great silent majority. Yet those vocal few are all we have, that and some statistics and perhaps some ingenuity. Thus anyone writing a book like *Lincoln's Men*, and anyone reading it, must remember that much of history is at best an educated estimate. In these pages, so much space is given to direct quotations by the soldiers themselves in the hope that from their own words, even when sometimes repetitive, some truer portrait of their sentiments may emerge.

Several friends and colleagues have contributed generously of their time and knowledge in helping bring this book to fruition. Staff at a number of institutions have, as always, been more than helpful, but the people at the United States Army Military History Institute at Carlisle Barracks, Pennsylvania, were especially patient during extended research. Their manuscripts section contains easily the largest and most comprehensive collection of Union soldier letters and diaries in the nation, representing every geographical region, and virtually all branches of service and shades of opinion. If it does not quite offer "one-stop shopping," there will be no expression of sentiment found elsewhere that is not represented in its staggering holdings. Richard J. Sommers, a friend of more than a quarter-century, gave unsparingly from an unrivaled memory of the Institute's holdings; David Keough and James Baughman in the manuscripts collection, and John Slonaker and Louise Arnold-Friend in the main library, stretched the definition of hospitality. Two more old friends, James M. McPherson and James I. Robertson, Jr., cordially agreed to give the manuscript a reading. Their unparalleled knowledge of the common soldiers of the Union yielded rich benefits. Several people, including Joseph Goodell of Brea, California, and Robert Grunwell of Lynchburg, Virginia, willingly lent access to family papers in their hands. And Dennis Brown provided useful background on Lincoln's film "career." To all of them, heartfelt thanks.

Special thanks are due to Thomas and Beverly Lowry, two true pioneers. They have undertaken the Herculean task of examining all of the more than one hundred thousand court-martial transcripts in the National Archives, a job now at the midway point. Already their findings are being felt in the Civil War community, and in the area of Abraham Lincoln's direct involvement in military justice especially. Even though they plan their own work on the subject at a future date, they have most generously made available their findings to date on the president's hand in every case in which he intervened. Some of the insights gleaned from those actions would be impossible to obtain from any other source.

Like all Americans of their time, the Union soldiers wrote idiosyncratically, their spelling sometimes phonetic, and often unique to the individual. As long as the soldier's meaning is clear, no attempt has been made to correct his spelling and capitalization or to intrude pedantic paraphernalia like "[*sic*]." If the reader spots a misspelled word in a quotation, he or she may safely assume that the author, too, knows it is misspelled but feels no need to make a pointless display of his knowledge. Besides, part of the delight of working with these wonderful young men is to share their wonderfully inventive means of expressing themselves. Whether fighting on the battlefield or scrawling a letter home, they knew how to make themselves understood, their meaning unmistakable. The late Bell Wiley, the first historian to study them comprehensively, often said that no time was so well spent as that which he passed in their company.

It was a sentiment that Father Abraham understood better than anyone.

LINCOLN'S MEN

INTRODUCTION: A BOY AND A BOOK

E VERY BOY WANTED TO BE A SOLDIER. AS HE MARCHED WITH his stick "musket" on his shoulder or fenced with a wooden sword, he became his grandsires wresting independence from the British in the war of the Revolution, his father preserving that freedom in 1812–15, or even his grown brothers mustering to meet the native menace that still threatened from time to time on the settled frontiers. He was the Minute Man, the yeoman abandoning his plow to meet a crisis, sacrificing all if need be, then to return to his humble pursuits when danger passed—the very definition of the new American.

The story of those first Minute Men echoed powerfully in the imagination of American youths in the 1820s. The image possessed irresistible appeal. Writers reinforced its attraction with a stream of exciting and often lurid histories and novels, frequently more fantasy than fact. They were creating the mythology of a new people, and imagination and exaggeration were the tools used to sculpt their infant gods. Books sought not just to inform, or even to entertain, but to instruct, to mold a new generation of Americans by the example of the Founding Fathers, and a public still heady with self-conscious pride in its new place in the world made an eager market. Even out on the frontier of southern Indiana such influences made their mark. Even in the humble log cabin of a semiliterate farmer at Pigeon Creek such a book could make an impression, and even on a boy who had no brothers in the militia, whose father did not fight the British in 1812, though his grandfather had been a soldier of the Revolution.

In this instance the book was Mason Locke Weems's *The Life of Wash-*

ington, and sometime in the mid-1820s a copy found its way to the small but comfortable cabin of Thomas Lincoln, and into the hands of his teenaged son, Abraham, newly—if yet imperfectly—literate after two years of intermittent schooling. The story Weems told was one of the very first books the young Lincoln read, and it impressed him just as it did tens of thousands of other Americans, young and old alike. *The Life of Washington* first appeared as a book in 1809, the very year of Abraham Lincoln's birth, though it had been in print in other formats since the turn of the century. Episodic and heavily fictionalized, it all but deified Washington, and clearly made him an agent and favorite of the Almighty. At the same time, it imbued the Revolutionary cause with a sense of predestination in the face of overwhelming odds, and made of every common volunteer a hero.

"I remember all the accounts there given of the battle fields and struggles for the liberties of the country," Abraham Lincoln would recall more than thirty years later.[1] Certainly Weems covered them all, or at least those in which Washington commanded. At Monmouth the general personally inspired his men to meet the enemy. At Saratoga, again motivated by Washington and "*fired* with the love of *liberty,* the Americans poured out by thousands, eager for the glorious contest." In perhaps the most dramatic battle passage of the book, Weems described the "avenging passions" of the Continentals as they met and defeated the foe.[2]

Yet it was an earlier and smaller fight that stayed with Lincoln, more a skirmish by later standards, and yet one fought in the darkest hours of the Revolution. He never forgot how the genius of liberty followed Washington's army the night it crossed the Delaware and marched on Trenton. "*Pale* and in tears, with eyes often lifted to Heaven, she moved along with her children to witness perhaps the last conflict," wrote Weems. Washington was never more inspiring as he prepared the men for the attack, seemingly imitating the lion as he called "his brindled sons to battle . . . till, kindled by their father's fire, the maddening cubs swell with answering rage." At last the general waved his sword above his head and shouted, "*There! my brave friends! there are the enemies of your country! and now, all I ask of you, is, to remember what you are about to fight for. March!*" By his looks and voice the general "rekindled all their fire, and drove them to the charge."[3] The account of Trenton and the heroism of the men in the face of seemingly certain defeat "all fixed themselves on my memory more than any single revolutionary event," Lincoln remembered. Despite his youth and backwoods ignorance of men and the world, still the story of Trenton struck him with the thought that "there must have been something more than common that those men struggled for."[4]

Moreover, as he read the book, Lincoln saw Weems repeatedly come back to a few central themes. In almost every battle he dwelled on some gallant American who fell gloriously, and much lamented. The dead soldier was venerated, Weems limning a Washington forever haunted by the scenes and the costs of the battlefield: *"There the battling armies met in thunder—the stormy strife was short; but yonder mournful hillocks point the place where many of our brave heroes sleep: perhaps some good angel has whispered that their fall was not in vain."* Through it all, Washington himself remained a man of unparalleled modesty. When he took command of the Continental Army, the Virginian confessed, *"My diffidence in my own abilities was superseded by a confidence in the rectitude of our cause and the patronage of Heaven."*[5]

Yet most of all the imaginative writer returned again and again to an idea founded, no doubt, on Washington's by now universal sobriquet as the "Father of His Country." As a young officer in the Virginia militia during the war with the French, Weems's Washington looked on the British army in which he served under General Edward Braddock as his "family," loved the men under him "as his children," and when angered at them showed "paternal displeasure." Weems rang these familial chimes the more so in dealing with the Revolution and its aftermath. "With a father's joy he could look around on the thick-settled country, with all their *little ones,* and flocks and herds, now no longer exposed to danger," he wrote of the general. When he discussed Washington's farewell address to his troops, he said it should be read "with the feelings of children reading the last letter of a once-loved father." And in the end, when the Virginian died, Weems called for Americans spiritually to "gather yourselves together around the bed of your expiring father—around the last bed of him to whom under God you and your children owe many of the best blessings of this life."[6]

Less than a decade after reading Weems, Lincoln published his very first public political statement in March 1832. He spoke in part of books and learning, and expressed the hope that "every man may receive at least, a moderate education, and thereby be enabled to read the histories of his own and other countries, by which he may duly appreciate the value of our free institutions."[7] Certainly, by the agency of Washington's life, Weems left an impression of the meaning of freedom and sacrifice and citizenship on young Lincoln. Learning by his own experience, Lincoln thereafter advocated the reading of history as a means of instilling patriotism. It was a message deeply impressed on a whole generation. Weems addressed *The Life of Washington* to children, and most of its readers were youths like Lincoln when they read the book, youths reared in a culture that preached reverence for the father. By emphasizing the "father" ideal of Washington, Weems took his young readers into a realm whose relations they understood. They were children who reverenced and obeyed their fathers; Americans were the figurative offspring of Washington and the Founding Fathers, and by extension of their great men and leaders in all times.

This was hardly new with Weems. By the time Lincoln read his book, this paternal view virtually surrounded Americans. His generation grew up in an atmosphere that quite consciously equated the United States with a family, in an effort to inculcate the reverence and patriotism needed to ensure the longevity of the Union. Doing so, in fact, helped make the nation understandable by reducing it to a familiar level, just as Weems made the Revolution meaningful and comprehensible by identifying it with Washington personally. The Union was like a house, its states and people members of a family, and automatically, of course, the president was the father. Already Washington had been enshrined as the Father of His Country, an idea even better illustrated by the Revolutionary financier and patriot Gouverneur Morris when he declared: "AMERICANS! he had no child—BUT YOU." In the prevailing view, the Founding Fathers were truly "fathers" to the nation and its people, and so were their successors, the men chosen to govern. The thrust of Weems's book and prevailing thought implied that, in the present and the future, especially in a time of crisis, the people should look to their foremost leaders for protection and guidance, and accord them the parental obedience and respect that in their own families they reserved for their fathers.[8] Thanks to their background before the Revolution, Americans felt an instinctive distrust of civil and military rulers, but the family and the father on the other hand remained unquestioned and universally acceptable figures of authority, with ancient power undiminished by modern thought. Better yet, ideally, love and reverence bound children to the father and the family out of love and reverence rather than fear, which made discipline and control all the easier to achieve, and the more potent because freely, rather than grudgingly, given.

Though Washington's memory never quite fathered a cult, there is no doubt that the power of his image, and especially as delivered to millions by Mason Locke Weems, generated enormous influence on how Americans saw their nation, their rulers, and even themselves. Certainly Abraham Lincoln absorbed and reflected that feeling. "Washington is the mightiest name of earth—*long since* mightiest in the cause of civil liberty," he would say in 1842. "To add brightness to the sun, or glory to the name of Washington, is alike impossible. Let none attempt it. In solemn awe pronounce the name, and in its naked deathless splendor, leave it shining on."[9]

There was another message in *The Life of Washington*, one implied rather than stated. Not only was every president potentially an heir to the legacy of the Virginian, it seemed to suggest. Any American might conceivably be called upon one day to wear that mantle, and possibly in a moment of great peril critical to the very family, the Union, of which they were all a part. Yet could Americans really expect to see another Washington, another Father of His Country come from their midst? Weems himself asked, "For who among us can hope that his son shall ever be called, like Washington, to direct the storm of war, or to ravish the ears of deeply listening Senates?"[10]

Who indeed?

1

COMMON MEN, UNCOMMON CRISIS

And Abram said unto Lot, Let there be no strife,
I pray thee, between me and thee,
and between my herdmen and thy herdmen;
for we be brethren.

[Genesis 13:8]

WHEN LINCOLN FIRST HEARD THAT CALL TO THE STORM of war, it was not to save the nation, or even a very significant piece of it, but only to put down a minor uprising by the Sauk and Fox, who sought to return to their ancestral homeland in Illinois. Lincoln himself had moved to the new state in the summer of 1831, aged just twenty-two, settling in the village of New Salem. It was there, the following March, that he published his statement about history and education as part of an announcement of his candidacy for the state legislature. Then, just a few weeks later, a chief named Black Hawk led about two thousand of his people across the Mississippi and into Illinois, immediately igniting an uproar across the frontier. While United States Regulars rushed to the scene, the governor issued a call for militia to gather on April 22 at Beardstown. The day before—nine miles from New Salem, at Richland Creek—Abraham Lincoln enlisted as a volunteer for thirty days.[1]

His motivation was that of many of the others who went with him on the road from Richland Creek to Beardstown. He was young, and adventure offered some lure. There was a danger to the community, though a small one. He was out of work, and serving in the military offered at least temporary employment, even if it kept him from campaigning for the legislature. And, undeniably, there was some sense of duty, of obligation to the extended "family" of the frontier community, a place where neighbors of necessity took care of each other. Lincoln hardly expected as he enlisted that those impulses would be enhanced by a special pride soon thereafter, when the volunteers held the customary election of officers. To his amazement, two names were put forward for company captain, one of them his own. Thanks to the illiteracy of most of the men, they voted with their bodies rather than ballots. Lincoln and his opponent stood in an open field, and the men simply lined up by the man of their choice. When they were finished, a substantial majority stood behind Lincoln.[2]

This was something that Captain Lincoln had not expected, and it thrilled him. One of his closest confidants in later years recalled, "He prized it and the distinction it gave him more than any which in after years fell to his lot." Lincoln himself reflected almost thirty years later that no subsequent success of his life gave him as much satisfaction. It was the first time he had been elected to anything, and it gave him a taste for the thrill of public approbation. He met the honor by making a brief speech of thanks that, however modest the circumstances, was almost certainly his first public address before any electorate.[3] In an instant, his willingness to serve his country was transforming him, raising him in the eyes of his peers and in his own.

Of course, there was something of a rude awakening. Young Captain Lincoln quickly learned that the volunteer was not and never would be a true soldier but, rather, a civilian temporarily on loan to the military. The sixty-eight men in his company were many of them friends from New Salem, fellows with whom he had wrestled and swum and played pranks about the village. They knew him too well to be awed by his sudden rank. That and the native independence so prized by all Americans of the time ensured that his hold over them as an officer extended only so far as his ability to *win* their cooperation, for he could never *make* them do what they would not. This became all too apparent the very first time he gave an order. One of the boys responded that he could "go to the devil," then thoughtfully added, "sir!"[4]

Much more learning than just humility went with his rank. Lincoln led the company to Beardstown, and then to Rushville, where the Sangamon County Company formally mustered into the 4th Regiment of the Brigade of Mounted Volunteers. They received their muskets on April 28, and had probably already commenced what little drill instruction the captain could give them.[5] In later years he would himself tell the tales of his hapless attempts at training and discipline. One story alone became legendary, his account of marching his command in a line of twenty men abreast toward a fence and not knowing what order to give to re-form them into a narrow column of fours to pass through its gate. His solution was to halt the company and dismiss them for two minutes, with orders to re-form on the other side. Worse, one evening a soldier stole into an officer's quarters and removed a fair quantity of liquor, the result being that the next morning several in the company were too drunk or ill to march. Lincoln himself bore the punishment for his failure to control them by being made to wear a wooden sword for two days. And when his own youthful enthusiasm got the better of him and he fired his musket in camp despite clear orders to the contrary, his superiors arrested him and took away his genuine sword for a day.[6]

There were many lessons he could draw from such experiences, but the most important of all was that exuberant young men could not make the transition from peaceful civilians to soldiers overnight, and would never make it completely. And when three of his men went absent without leave before the end of their short thirty-day enlistment, he also learned that, coming as they did from a culture with a high disregard for authority, many in the end simply could not, and would not, recognize the right of the military to keep them in service after they no longer wished to stay. Their in-bred high spirits could all too often get the better of their sense of obligation to an enlistment form. It had little or nothing to do with cowardice or laziness, or lack of patriotism, but a great deal to do with a rampant thirst for independence.[7]

Another volunteer in the 4th Regiment recalled that Lincoln's Sangamon boys were "the hardest set of men" he had ever seen. John T. Stuart, a major in the regiment and Lincoln's future law partner, remembered that "he had the wildest company in the world," and added that as a young captain "Lincoln had no military qualities whatever except that he was a good clever fellow and kept the esteem and respect of his men."[8] Indeed, as Lincoln quickly learned, keeping the esteem of the volunteers, even more than discipline, was paramount, for they would only follow and obey a man they respected. Instinctively he knew that good humor, patience, a willingness to share equally in the hardships of the privates, and an absence of self-importance were the best means to bind the men to him. Fortunately, they were already traits of his nature.

Certainly he shared in their privations, especially hunger: the military supply system worked imperfectly at best, and the soldiers often went without rations. When his men went hungry, so did he, on one occasion passing two days without food. Nor did he prove to be above the age-old soldier practice of improving his ordinary fare by foraging among local farmers' chickens and hams.[9] "I can truly say I was often very hungry," Lincoln remembered sixteen years later, and though he never saw a fight with the Sauk or Fox, he well recalled "a good many bloody struggles with the musquetoes," and more than one "charge" upon a field of wild onions when there was nothing else to eat.[10]

Of course, there was more than hardship to bind the men to their captain. Lincoln enjoyed the camp fun of the volunteers, the wrestling, the foot races, the myriad ways of filling the empty hours of the evening when not on the march.[11] Thanks to his six-foot-four-inch height, and the leverage it gave him, he was a formidable wrestler even though lean and sinewy, and he challenged and threw all comers. Already he displayed well-honed talents as a storyteller, a popular commodity on long evenings in camp.[12] He sat beside the same campfire as the lower ranks, sharing with them the hatchet handle they used to grind their coffee beans in a tin cup, joining them in baking their rough bread by sticking balls of the dough on the ends of their ramrods and holding it over the open flames. He fried his meat with them—when he had it—and ate it from the same slabs of elm bark that they used, and he eschewed sleeping in an officer's tent to share one with his men. He showed patience and consideration in dealing with the problems of the men, as when he arranged for one man who had lost his horse to transfer to a foot company by trading places with a soldier from that unit who had a horse and wanted into the Sangamon outfit, even though it required the subterfuge that each would answer to the other's name at roll call, since the transfer was entirely unofficial.[13]

Yet Lincoln did not shun moral or military responsibility in the interest of popularity. One day an old follower of Black Hawk wandered into their camp seeking food, his days of resistance obviously well behind him as hunger, not bayonets, forced him to make his personal peace with the whites. The Sangamon County Company never saw any action or even any hostiles during their month of service, and some of the volunteers wanted to kill this poor old fellow since they had never killed any of his compatriots in battle. Captain Lincoln stood up to them and backed them down, probably saving the old man's life, yet at no cost to his standing with his men.[14] Indeed, the episode taught him two lessons. One was the necessity of making an example of standing for the right, for even men in the wrong respected that. The other, a darker maxim of war, was that the best of men could spontaneously sink to a level of misbehavior or even savagery that would never have occurred to them as civilians. It took a firm but fair hand to lead these citizen-soldiers; there needed to be understanding beneath the glove.

As a result, though their service was brief, the Sangamon volunteers developed a high regard for their captain. John Rutledge of New Salem later recalled proudly, "I was with him in the Black Hawk War, he was my captain, a better man I think never lived on earth."[15] They followed him on a bloodless campaign that took them to Rock Island, but fortunately not to join the nearby command of Major Isaiah Stillman, who met with a bloody repulse nearby on May 14. Survivors of the defeat—which was more running skirmish than battle, with Stillman doing the running—came into the 4th Regiment camp the next day, first reporting that two thousand under Black Hawk had butchered more than three hundred Americans. Lincoln's company, with others, set out to pursue Black Hawk and soon came to the scene of the skirmishing, where they learned that in fact only eleven of Stillman's volunteers had been killed.[16] Right there was a lesson on the reliability of information that came from panicked volunteers.

Lincoln's term as a captain expired without his ever catching up to the foe, and on May 27 he and his company mustered out of service at Ottawa, near the mouth of the Fox River. Yet that very day he re-enlisted, this time as a private in a new twenty-day company commanded by Captain Elijah Iles. Lincoln made no pretense of his reason for remaining in the volunteer service. "I was out of work, and there being no danger of more fighting, I could do nothing better than enlist again," he would tell his later friend and partner, William Herndon.[17] He was footloose and homeless, and he had missed his chance to continue running for the legislative seat. Most of all, he was penniless and needed the modest pay offered by the state militia. Even volunteer soldiering was an honorable, if temporary, profession, and from this time onward Lincoln understood quite personally that pay was a very acceptable substitute for ardent patriotism in attracting a citizen into uniform, or keeping him there.

A Kentucky-born Regular Army lieutenant named Robert Anderson mustered Lincoln and Iles's company into the service, but their enlistment passed without a sight of Black Hawk or a prospect of fighting as the native band far outran the desultory pursuit of the soldiers.[18] On June 16, after Lincoln's second enlistment expired, he joined yet another company, this time signing on for thirty days with Captain Jacob Early's Independent Spy Corps.[19] Only now did he finally see some real vestige of this very little war. On June 25, a small skirmish took place at Kellogg's Grove, in the northwest corner of the state, and five men were slain. Early's company went to reconnoiter the area soon thereafter, and Lincoln and his friend George Harrison went out in advance at dawn one day to scout through the tall prairie grass looking for the dead. As they rode up a small rise to the scene of the fight, Lincoln suddenly saw the red light of the morning sun reflected on the heads of the five bodies, and he saw that "every man had a round, red spot on top of his head, about as big as a dollar." They had been scalped. "It was frightful, but it was grotesque," he later told Herndon, "and the red light seemed to paint everything all over." He never forgot this sight, an indelible reminder that soldiers really did die in war.[20]

Lincoln finally mustered out for good on July 10 and along with Harrison made his way back to New Salem, partly on foot, partly by canoe, and some of the way by sharing a horse with Harrison, John Stuart, and another returning volunteer. "We had a first rate time on this campaign," one of them later recalled. "We were well provided—the whole thing was a sort of frolic."[21] Indeed, in later years, Lincoln actually cast self-deprecating ridicule on his Black Hawk War service, recalling that he never broke a sword or saw a hostile foe, but he had bent his musket once by accident. "I fought, bled, and came away," he boasted, adding that it was mosquitoes and not Sauk and Fox that drew his blood. Yet beneath the humor lay a serious stratum of pride. Herndon saw easily that, for all of Lincoln's joking about his volunteer service, he was nevertheless "rather proud of it after all." Years later, in 1850, when Congress granted to Black Hawk veterans a land bounty of forty acres in Iowa, Lincoln, a prosperous attorney by then, regarded the grant with such pride that he declared he would never sell the property while he lived, even though he never set foot upon it.[22] The land itself meant little or nothing, but what it represented to Lincoln meant a very great deal indeed. Like Washington and the heroes of the Revolution, he had come forth in the tradition of Cincinnatus, forsaking his—admittedly unpromising—civil pursuits to take the musket of a volunteer soldier and share the tedium of the camp and the dangers of the field in defense of his friends and neighbors, his New Salem "family." It hardly placed him beside the Father of His Country. He wore no gaudy uniform, only his own homespun. He may have had a sword as an officer, but it was probably a rude and rusty one from the state armory, and by his own admission he carried a bent musket. No bards or historians would wax eloquent over his service, and yet it was a life's milestone to *him*. He had served his community and country, and his pride and sense of accomplishment in that, modest as it was, made tall Abraham Lincoln stand a little taller. He did not overlook the lesson that what it did for him it could do for any man.

In the years that followed the peace, Lincoln made his way in life, slowly at first, but then with more confidence, and prosperity. He returned again and again to the pride he felt in being a volunteer, and by extension the feeling that all Americans who served their country should have. Just six years after the Black Hawk War, now living in Springfield as a legislator and leader of the state Whig Party, Lincoln reflected on the theme in his first major public address at the Young Men's Lyceum. He looked back on the days of the Revolution, "when nearly every adult male had been a participator in some of its scenes" (a myth that he, like most sons of the Revolutionary generation, already believed, thanks largely to writers like Weems). The consequence of that involvement, he said, "was, that of those scenes, in the form of a husband, a father, a son or a brother, a *living history was* to be found in every family—a history bearing the indubitable testimonies of its own authenticity, in the limbs mangled, in the scars of wounds received, in the midst of the very scenes related." Those Revolutionary forebears had been the pillars upholding the temple of American liberty. Now they were almost all gone, and if the latest generation, and those that would follow, did not "supply their places with other pillars," then the edifice would fall. He enjoined the audience that Americans could have no higher aim than to defend their country, so that, when they came to the final day of judgment and the last trumpet "shall awaken our WASH[INGTON]," they could say, "We permitted no hostile foot to pass over or desecrate [his] resting place." Their hope lay in the law and patriotism. "Let every American man remember that to violate the law, is to trample on the blood of his father," figuratively the same as treading on the grave of Washington. Thus it was the duty of Americans to protect the Union not only against enemies from without, but also from any within.[23]

Whenever Assemblyman Lincoln looked back on the achievements of American volunteers in the past, he praised their virtues, even when, sometimes, he opposed their politics. He was no admirer of President Andrew Jackson, yet he rose in the legislature on the thirty-sixth anniversary of Old Hickory's victory at New Orleans to proclaim his pride as an American in the victory and the military fame of Jackson. When a soldier's politics suited his own, as with presidential contender General William Henry Harrison in 1840, Lincoln could be all the more enthusiastic in extolling a man who went into battle, "where cowards dared not show their heads—where storms of 'leaden rain and iron hail' carried death and desolation in their course."[24]

Yet always his greatest praise, and concern, he reserved for the common volunteers who followed the great men. When he wrote of "the old soldiers of the war of 1812–13 and '14," he reminded people that before that conflict they had had no organization, and yet, when the crisis came, "immediately on learning that an organized foe was invading their land, they too organized—met—conquered—killed and drove the foe."[25] When he was running for re-election to the legislature in 1836, one of his stated concerns was securing proper recognition for men who had served their country in uniform. "I go for all sharing the privileges of the government, who assist in bearing its burthens," he said. Any man who bore arms as a volunteer should have the vote, regardless of the usual property qualifications required. Though not a supporter of paying pensions to volunteers, who in defending their country were, after all, defending their own interests as well, still he unfailingly supported their right to land bounties like the one he received, and frequently assisted some of his old Sangamon Company companions with their claims.[26]

By December 1847, when Lincoln had moved from the state legislature to taking a seat in the United States Congress, the United States was in another war, though by now all its principal battles had been fought and the issue all but decided. Lincoln was no supporter either of President James K. Polk or of his war with Mexico, which Lincoln regarded as nothing but raw aggression. Yet he divorced his opposition to the war itself from his concern for the hundreds of thousands of young men who enthusiastically volunteered to fill the armies led by Generals Zachary Taylor, Winfield Scott, and others. Those young men did not make the war. They only answered their country's call, and regardless of the injustice of the conflict, when citizen-soldiers endured hardships and ran great risks in service of their country, they were entitled to every consideration that Lincoln and others back home could offer. The previous spring, even before winning his House seat, Lincoln introduced resolutions in a public meeting at Springfield rejoicing in Taylor's recent victory in the Battle of Buena Vista, and remarking, "with highest pride, the imperishable honor won by our Illinois brethren, upon that bloody field."[27] Of course, Taylor was already a Whig presidential hopeful, so Lincoln's kudos to him may have had some political motivation, yet, as his subsequent actions showed, his compliments to the soldiers were sincere enough. Once in Congress, Lincoln used his first extended speech in the House to pay tribute to the soldiers who "have given us the most splendid successes—every department, and every part, land and water, officers and privates, regulars and volunteers, doing all that men *could* do."[28]

The conflict—Americans called it the Mexican War, whereas the Mexicans would more subtly refer to it as the "War of American Intervention"—was militarily over when Lincoln went to Congress, and the actual treaty ended it in the summer of 1848, though not before Lincoln had joined other Whigs in vainly voting against a resolution proclaiming the war just. Even in casting his vote, however, Lincoln made plain to friends the distinction he drew between supporting the war and supporting the volunteers and Regular Army soldiers then in Mexico. Repeatedly, appropriations bills came before the House to vote funds for feeding and supplying the armies, and Lincoln emphasized that his position opposing the resolution "has nothing to do, in determining my votes on the question of supplies. I have always intended, and still intend, to vote supplies."[29] In fact, he found it necessary to defend himself repeatedly, then and even a decade later, when Democrats charged that he and other Whigs had sought to undermine Polk by voting against appropriations, starving the armies as a result. "You have constantly had our votes here for all the necessary supplies," he reminded the administration supporters. More than that, he added that even many Whigs—including some from Illinois—were in Mexico with the armies. "Through suffering and death, by disease, and in battle, they have endured, and fought, and fell with you," he said. "I think of all those brave men as Americans, in whose proud fame, as an American, I too have a share." He offered them thanks "for the high, imperishable honor" they had won for Illinois and the United States.[30]

Lincoln did support the supply appropriations, and twelve years later still felt proud that he had voted "for all the measures in any way favorable to the officers, soldiers, and their families."[31] More than that, he tried to look out for the interests of Illinois volunteers in the field, using what little influence he had as a freshman to secure army appointments or promotions, and even trying to get yet another volunteer regiment from Illinois accepted in service before the war officially closed.[32] He sought fair play for the volunteers themselves when they left the army. He kept insisting that all volunteers be treated equally when it came to pay—Lincoln never forgot how important his pay had been to *him* as a volunteer—and if a man died in the army, then he sought to get any arrears for his survivors. With Washington usually behind in paying its soldiers, he had to help some men collect what was owed them, and since the government would augment pay with land bounties for veterans, Lincoln spoke on the floor, introduced a bill, and dealt directly with the commissioner of pensions in an attempt to make it easier for men to get their land warrants. Moreover, he argued that the veterans should be able to claim good public land that they particularly wanted, rather than simply being issued a title, as he had been, and he wanted the bounty-land rewards extended to veterans of the 1812–15 war with Britain as well. *All* veterans of *all* wars should share in the best and most current benefits.[33]

Lincoln's efforts for the war veterans followed him through the next decade. He did not seek re-election to his seat in Congress in 1849, and he spent several years devoted to his growing legal practice and helping launch the new Republican Party that emerged in 1854 out of the ruins of the old Whigs and several other smaller groups, most of them united by opposition to the expansion of slavery. By 1858, even though out of public office for nearly a decade, Lincoln had become one of the leading Republican spokesmen in the nation, and when it came time to challenge his old friend Stephen A. Douglas for an Illinois seat in the United States Senate, the state Republican convention chose Lincoln to make the bid. In the summer and fall of 1858, Lincoln and Douglas electrified not only Illinois but the nation with a series of debates that focused attention on far more than a political race in their state. The growing debate over slavery, chiefly the questions of whether it was to be contained where it already existed, or allowed to expand into new territories, and if so how, absorbed Americans. Besides the moral issue of slavery itself, the question in the end distilled to one of power and the nature of the Union. In order to perpetuate itself, slavery had to expand by the creation of new slave states that would maintain a parity with the free states, at least in the Senate, thus enabling the slave bloc to stop any congressional legislation designed to attack slavery where it already existed. Contain slavery and eventually it must die; allow it to extend itself, and it might last indefinitely. Lincoln himself, in a debate with Douglas, likened the situation to a "house divided," a family at war with itself, in which eventually one side or the other must ultimately prevail or else the house collapse.

In the effort to meet the potent challenge from Lincoln, Democrats used every means, including blatant falsehood. On June 28, the ardently Democratic Chicago *Times* ran a spurious oath supposedly taken by Lincoln in 1847: "I, Abram Lincoln, of Sangamon County, refuse to vote one dollar to feed, clothe, or minister to the wants of the sick and dying volunteers from my own State, who are suffering in Mexico. Let them die like dogs! Let them die for want of medicine! Let the fever-parched lips of my Illinois neighbors crack in painful agony— not one drop of cooling liquid shall soothe them if I can help it." As its blatant language revealed, it was of course a parody, and even some Democrats repudiated it as obviously a hoax that could hurt Douglas rather than Lincoln, yet it still succeeded in reviving in grotesque exaggeration the old charge from 1848.[34] Lincoln was forced to respond, and the vehemence with which he did so revealed just how sensitive he was to any suggestion that he would deny an American soldier the fair treatment he deserved.

Douglas himself hinted at the charge—though far more temperately than did his official organ, the *Times*—when he and Lincoln met at Ottawa for a debate on August 21. The "Little Giant," as he was called, accused his opponent of "taking the side of the common enemy against his own country" in the Mexican conflict, and even though that was a perversion of the truth, Douglas let the matter rest there, no doubt counting on the old stories of the voting against appropriations to be remembered and do their work in the voters' minds without his having to risk personally repeating an accusation he knew to be false. Lincoln, however, refused to let the matter rest on that basis. Only a few minutes after taking the platform, he dealt quickly with Douglas's veiled comment. He pointed out that Douglas "did not make his charge very distinctly but I can tell you what he can prove by referring to the record." Lincoln may have voted against approval of the war itself, he said, "but whenever they asked for any money, or land warrants, or anything to pay the soldiers there, during all that time, I gave the same votes as Judge Douglas did." When his opponent "by a general charge, conveys the idea that I withheld supplies from the soldiers who were fighting the Mexican war, or did anything else to hinder the soldiers, he is, to say the least, grossly and altogether mistaken."[35]

For one thing, Lincoln felt pride in his record of support for the volunteers. For another, he knew full well that thousands of the voters had served in Mexico, and if they believed what Douglas hinted at, it could cost him, for almost all Americans shared his veneration of the citizen-soldier, and they had been brought up, like Lincoln, on the execrations heaped by Weems and others on those in the Continental Congress who allowed Washington's army to go cold and hungry. Being branded an enemy of the interests of the volunteer could ruin any man seeking office.

Thus, when the rumors and repeated charges did not go away after that first refutation, the Republican became increasingly irritated. A few weeks later, the opponents met again in debate at Charleston, on September 18. This time, though Douglas did not mention the Mexican War issue at all, Lincoln was not about to let the matter drop. When he followed the Little Giant to the stand, he allowed only a few minutes to pass before getting to the Mexican War charges, again chiding Douglas for reviving the old falsehood even if he did "not take the responsibility of putting it in a very definite form." After pointing out that some of Douglas's own newspaper backers had repudiated the story, Lincoln turned around on the platform and walked to one of the Little Giant's supporters, Orlando B. Ficklin. Taking him either by the hand, or by the collar "in no gentle manner" according to one witness, Lincoln led Ficklin to the front and presented him to the crowd, saying as he did so that Ficklin had served in the House with him in 1848 and personally knew that the withheld-appropriations-votes story was a lie. "He knows, as well as Judge Douglas, that whenever a dollar was asked by way of compensation or otherwise, for the benefit of the soldiers, *I gave all the votes that Ficklin or Douglas did, and perhaps more.*"[36] Years later, Lincoln's friend Ward Hill Lamon claimed that Lincoln had become so aroused as he tried yet again to refute the old charge that he began shaking Ficklin by the collar as he spoke, and that Lamon himself reached forward to break his friend's grip on the hapless Democrat. Supposedly Ficklin afterward said, "I never had such a shaking in my whole life."[37] Contemporary descriptions, even those by Democratic newspapers, fail to mention any such episode, yet Lamon knew Lincoln intimately, and even if his recollection of the event half a century later is gilded, at its root it may well reflect knowledge gained directly from Lincoln himself of just how deeply he felt the injustice of the slander.

Lincoln lost that election, though the Mexican War accusation hardly played any role in the voters' decision. But the exposure he gained in the national press thanks to the debates helped make him one of the defining figures as the sectional controversy escalated toward 1860 and the presidential contest. The Democratic Party deadlocked at its nominating convention, the hard pro-slavery Southern rights faction unable to swallow the Northern democracy's favorite, Douglas, because he was not solid enough on slavery extension. With every prospect that their opponents would divide and field two candidates, the Republicans who gathered in Chicago for their own convention suddenly found themselves faced with the probability that they were not just choosing a nominee, but the next president. William H. Seward of New York was the favorite, but he lacked support in crucial Pennsylvania and equally important Illinois, where Lincoln's power was unassailable. Though not a true "dark horse" when his supporters put him in nomination, Lincoln was still a far second to Seward on the first ballot. As three other, more distant candidates stepped aside, the bulk of their following went to Lincoln rather than Seward. On the third ballot, he claimed the prize.[38] In November, though he took only 39 percent of the popular vote, Lincoln faced Douglas and two other opponents who so divided the opposition that the Republican easily carried the decisive electoral ballot. But it came at a terrible price. Despite his repeated promises that as president he would not interfere with slavery where it already existed, the leaders of the slave states could only see in his election a mortal threat to their "peculiar institution," their economy and civilization, and ultimately a perpetual relegation to being a helpless minority in the halls of power. Acting out of fear, emotion, pride, and myriad other influences that were just as naturally human as rationally unjustified, they determined that their only recourse was to secede. South Carolina went first, on December 20, 1860, steadily followed by more states, until, eventually, eleven would declare themselves independent.

The house had divided. Ironically, almost everyone seemed to view the catastrophe in the same sorts of metaphor that Lincoln himself so often used to describe the Union. "We have pulled a temple down," crowed one South Carolinian the day the first secession ordinance passed, and a woman in Charleston simply observed, "We are divorced." The temple and the family were both shattered. Worse, immediately upon seceding, South Carolina demanded the surrender of United States facilities and installations, an arsenal, a customs house, and most of all Fort Moultrie and unoccupied Fort Sumter, guarding Charleston Harbor. The army garrison of fewer than a hundred officers and men could hardly hold out against the thousands of Southern volunteers who soon rallied to the city, but if anyone struck a first blow, it could ignite civil war. Lincoln spent an uneasy Christmas as the crisis mounted. It would not be surprising if the situation facing him took his memory back to *The Life of Washington*, and those stirring passages and enduring lessons that remained with him still. Did he remember Weems's closing words, "For who among us can hope that his son shall ever be called, like Washington, to direct the storm of war?" Incredibly, what would have seemed inconceivable to a rough frontier youth more than thirty years before, had happened. The call had come.

Even before his election, Lincoln knew there could be serious trouble. Speeches from Southern pulpits and courthouses and presses all threatened secession if he won the election, and he knew that it would take superhuman forbearance to maintain the peace after that. In late October, a week before the election, he turned his thoughts to the men who would have to try to keep that peace, or else deal with the consequences of a rupture. The auguries from the army looked bad, for many Southern officers promised to resign before recognizing him as commander-in-chief, and a rumor reached Lincoln's ears that the officers commanding at Fort Kearny, in the Nebraska Territory, intended to take themselves and their arms and go south in order to resist the new regime actively.[39]

Then came December 20, the secession of South Carolina, and the immediate fear of a clash over the forts in Charleston. "If the forts fall, my judgment is that they are to be retaken," Lincoln told a friend in the army two days later. "The most we can do now is to watch events."[40] Even while watching, however, the president-elect already knew what he *might* have to do. The day before Christmas, hearing a rumor that incumbent President James Buchanan might actually order the forts to be surrendered, Lincoln suggested that if that happened he would immediately make a public announcement that he would reclaim them by force if necessary once he took office. General-in-chief Winfield Scott "must retake them," of that there was no doubt. "This will give the Union men a rallying cry, and preparations will proceed somewhat on their side, as well as on the other." Shortly after the New

Year, he mused to General John E. Wool that he was uncertain just "how far the military force of the government may become necessary to the preservation of the Union." He would rely on his generals for that, claiming that up to this time "I have given but little attention to the Military Department of government." But his meaning was clear, and indicated that he had thought enough to know one thing. Once more the nation might need to turn to its young men to volunteer, to trade their plowshares for swords.[41]

Events moved so quickly that Lincoln and the Union could scarcely do more than watch. More states followed South Carolina in seceding, and on February 4, 1861, delegates from five of them met in Montgomery, Alabama, with no instructions and no plan of action other than to consult. Four days later, however, they had framed a constitution, formed a provisional government, and chosen Jefferson Davis of Mississippi as the president of their new Confederate States of America. On February 18, even as Lincoln himself made his slow journey to Washington to take office, Davis was inaugurated amid an atmosphere of belligerent euphoria, while the streets of Montgomery teemed with companies of rustic volunteers anxious for the inevitable whipping they would give the Yankees if it came to war. With every new state to secede, there were more forts and federal installations seized, more opportunities for a sudden outbreak of violence. Meanwhile, in Charleston, the Union garrison at Fort Moultrie abandoned the place and took refuge in Fort Sumter, in the middle of the harbor, where they would be safer, and where more than a mile of surrounding water made a potentially disastrous collision the more unlikely. Lincoln remembered the man in command at Fort Sumter, though that officer surely had no recollection of the Illinoisian. He was Major Robert Anderson, the same man who twenty-nine years earlier mustered into the Black Hawk service Iles's company, and with it one now very special young volunteer from New Salem.

All of this, and everything that could happen as a result of it, labored Lincoln's mind as he prepared to leave Springfield for the trip east to answer his call. On February 11, he boarded a train, but before leaving he spoke a few words to a crowd there assembled. In making his farewell to home and friends, the weight of that call oppressed him. "I go to assume a task more difficult than that which devolved upon Washington," he told them. "Unless the great God who assisted him, shall be with and aid me, I must fail. But if the same omniscient mind, and Almighty arm that directed and protected him, shall guide and support me, I shall not fail, I shall succeed. Let us all pray that the God of our fathers may not forsake us now."[42]

From then until he reached Washington two weeks later, he spoke to the people almost daily, sometimes twice a day, and his words revealed that, whatever he had told Wool, his thoughts were very much on the legacy of Washington, not as a president but as a war leader, and on the question of whether this generation of Americans would respond to the need of their country in the same fashion as those whom Weems called Washington's "children" had answered their father's call. The refrain came frequently from Lincoln's lips. Two days after leaving Springfield, he told the Ohio legislature, "There has fallen upon me a task such as did not rest even upon the Father of his country, and so feeling I cannot but turn and look for the support without which it will be impossible for me to perform that great task. I turn, then, and look to the American people."[43]

Before he left Springfield, he had been approached by a group of East European immigrants in Chicago who had formed a militia company and wanted to call themselves the Lincoln Riflemen. He gave them his blessing, and their approach may have reminded him that, in the terrible contest that might lie ahead, there were many kinds of Americans to whom he could look for help in saving the Union. On February 12, his birthday, he told an audience of German-Americans in Cincinnati that working men like them were the backbone of all governments, and hinted that as president he would pursue an open-door policy toward their friends and families still in the old country should they choose to come to the New World. He suggested a liberal homestead law that would allow such people to make a home of their own, but did not go on to say what he may have been thinking, that many of those immigrant men, both in the audience and those yet to cross the ocean, might need to earn their places and their land grants as Americans by first becoming volunteer soldiers. Despite his hope for peace, Lincoln was already starting to prepare his countrymen for what he feared he might have to ask them to do.[44]

For the first ten days of his trip east, Lincoln came down repeatedly on the idea that if they would only stick together they could pass this crisis. "To the salvation of this Union there needs but one single thing," he said in Indianapolis, "the hearts of a people like yours. When the people rise in masses in behalf of the Union and the liberties of their country, truly it may be said, 'The gates of hell shall not prevail against them.'" Three days later, in Pittsburgh, the sight of a cheering throng moved him to declare, "If all that people were in favor of the Union, it can certainly be in no great danger." In Cleveland he told an audience, "It is with you, the people, to advance the great cause of the Union and the constitution, and not with any one man. It rests upon you alone." He reminded an Ohio crowd that those unhappy with his election should not yield to disunion. "If we all turn in and keep the ship from sinking this voyage, there may be a chance for Douglas on the next; but if we let it go down now, neither he nor anybody else will have an opportunity of sailing in it again." In fact, the shopworn "ship-of-state" metaphor got heavy use. "Don't give up the ship!" shouted a man in the throng at Conneaut, Ohio, and Lincoln yelled back, "With your aid I never will as long as life lasts."[45]

Gradually, as he got closer to Washington, a change, perhaps unwitting, came over Lincoln's remarks. More and more he sought to identify himself very personally with the cause of the Union, perhaps recalling the way Weems so completely made Washington and the cause of independence synonymous. At Dunkirk, New York, on February 16, his train for the first time surrounded by local militia, he grasped a flag on the car platform and declared, "*Standing as I do, with my hand upon this staff, and under the folds of the American flag,* I ASK YOU TO STAND BY ME SO LONG AS I STAND BY IT." More and more their active involvement would be needed to preserve the Union. "It is with your aid, as the people, that I think we shall be able to preserve— not the country, for the country will preserve itself, but the institutions of the country—; those institutions which have made us free," he said in Poughkeepsie three days later, and again that day, in Peekskill, he added, "Without your sustaining hands I am sure that neither I nor any other man can hope to surmount those difficulties." The people must sustain him, for he needed not just the Almighty's help but theirs, his statements redolent of the words Weems gave to Washington as he assumed command of the Continental Army: "*My diffidence in my own abilities was superseded by a confidence in the rectitude of our cause and the patronage of Heaven.*"[46]

There was another shift of direction during the final few days of his trip, and this could hardly be unintentional. By now officers of Southern birth were starting to resign their commissions in the army and the navy, and even before Davis took office, the provisional Congress of the new Confederacy created its War and Navy Departments, preparatory to raising a volunteer army. On February 16, Davis told a crowd in Montgomery, "The time for compromise has now passed, and the

South is determined to maintain her position, and make all who op-
pose her smell Southern powder and feel Southern steel." Two days
later, after taking his oath as provisional president, he went further:
"We must prepare to meet the emergency and to maintain, by the final
arbitrament of the sword, the position which we have assumed."[47]
That same day, General David Twiggs surrendered United States military posts in Texas to the secessionists without resistance; more federal holdings in Texas and Louisiana were taken over under threat in
the next two days; and on February 21, word reached Lincoln of a plot
by secessionists to assassinate him before he could take office.

No wonder that he now began to counter Davis's militant words
with some of his own. Speaking to the New Jersey Senate, just a few
hours before learning of the plot against his life, he talked of his youth,
when Weems's biography had so impressed him and perhaps begun his
youthful fascination with being a soldier. "You all know," he told them
cheerfully, "for you have all been boys." But then he turned serious.
"The man does not live who is more devoted to peace than I am. None
who would do more to preserve it. But it may be necessary to put the
foot down firmly," he warned. "And if I do my duty, and do right, you
will sustain me, will you not?" The next day, in Philadelphia, he was
more emphatic. "There is no need of bloodshed and war," he said at
Independence Hall. "I am not in favor of such a course, and I may say
in advance, there will be no blood shed unless it be forced upon the
Government." Yet now he did not entirely repudiate the idea of a clash
of arms. "The Government will not use force unless force is used
against it." The same day, Washington's birthday, in Harrisburg, he
saw several military companies parade, and heard the promise of more
if it came to war. He told Governor Andrew Curtin, "While I have
been proud to see to-day the finest military array, I think, that I have
ever seen, allow me to say in regard to those men that they give hope of
what may be done when war is inevitable. But, at the same time, allow
me to express the hope that in the shedding of blood their services may
never be needed." A few minutes later, he addressed the legislature and
went on to say, "It is not with any pleasure that I contemplate the possibility that a necessity may arise in this country for the use of the military arm." Happy as he was to see those patriotic young men willing
to fight for the Union, "I do most sincerely hope that we shall have no
use for them." If it did come to war, however, he promised, "It shall be
through no fault of mine."[48] Lincoln was not rattling his saber, but he
was letting them know that it sat free in its scabbard.

Even as he spoke at Independence Hall, Lincoln harked back to the "toils that were endured by the officers and soldiers of the army" that fought the Revolution. He wondered what it was that sustained them, and believed that in part it was that, in achieving liberty for themselves, they would be giving hope to the world "for all future time." Two weeks later, when he took his oath of office, he tried to remind Americans—both those now rebelling in the Confederacy, and those who might have to endure toils and risks to restore the Union—of what their Revolutionary forebears had suffered to bequeath. He spoke of "mystic chords of memory, stretching from every battle-field, and patriot grave, to every living heart and hearthstone, all over this broad land." Their ancestors had left *their* hearths to risk and sometimes give their lives to build and preserve the new nation. They had heeded the patriot's call, proud sons sustaining their fatherland. This was a subtle reminder of the obligation of Americans in 1861 to be willing to take the same risks if need be. Even though he closed with an appeal to the "better angels of our nature" for peace and fraternity, it was only after a sterner reminder to those in rebellion. "There needs to be no bloodshed or violence," he said, "and there shall be none, unless forced upon the national authority." Nevertheless, it was his duty as chief executive to defend and maintain federal property wherever it might be threatened. "All the power at my disposal will be used," he said in veiled warning, "to hold, occupy and possess these and all other property and places belonging to the government."⁴⁹ Both Lincoln and the millions of young men in the North knew that he could not achieve this objective by himself.

The next month was dominated above all else by the situation of Major Anderson and his garrison in Fort Sumter. As Confederate volunteers continued to gather in Charleston, ringing the harbor with batteries trained on the fortress, excitement and rapidly dwindling patience increasingly threatened to turn the confrontation into a crisis. The questions were simple. Would Lincoln agree to Confederate demands to evacuate the fort and hand it over, would Lincoln attempt to send supplies and reinforcements to allow Anderson to hold out, and when would the Southerners decide to stop negotiating and simply open fire? From the first he rejected any thought of handing over the fort. He could hardly have forgotten Mason Locke Weems's description of a hauntingly similar situation in the Revolution, when General William Moultrie was asked if he would abandon a fort he occupied on Sullivan's Island, just a mile from Fort Sumter. *"Give us but plenty of powder and ball, sir, and let them come on as they please,"* Moultrie replied in Weems's dramatic prose.[50]

No, Lincoln was not giving up anything willingly. For advice he turned immediately to his aged, corpulent, but still mentally keen general-in-chief, Winfield Scott, a hero of two wars. The president wanted to know how long Anderson could hold out without supplies and reinforcements, and at the same time learned from Scott and other officers that they saw no prospect of effectively relieving the garrison, considering the batteries that controlled Charleston Harbor. Besides the political crisis, Lincoln also felt an immediate concern for the welfare of Anderson and his men, fearing that they faced "starvation, not to mention disease." He told his Cabinet that it would be inhuman to allow them to starve. The government and the president had a duty to care for their soldiers. Thus, relieving the garrison—or at least making an attempt—was not only a political necessity, but a humanitarian obligation as well. After three weeks of wrestling with the decision, he finally determined to attempt a relief.[51]

Even while the relief expedition was being organized, with Lincoln heavily involved in selecting the officers and setting plans, he sent a message to Major Anderson advising him of his intention. He would at first try only to send food and necessary supplies. If the Confederates did not interfere, he would do no more. But if they tried to stop the resupply, then Lincoln would attempt to reinforce Anderson as well, and he knew that could lead to hostilities. He promised the major that he did not wish "to subject your command to any danger or hardship beyond what, in your judgment, would be usual in military life." Nevertheless, Lincoln knew the high risks involved. Already Northern governors were in touch with him proffering regiments of state volunteers if he wanted them. Remembering the smart-looking units he had seen when he spoke in Harrisburg, Lincoln wired to Pennsylvania Governor Andrew Curtin on April 8, "I think the necessity of being *ready* increases. Look to it."[52]

The waiting and uncertainty came to an end on April 12, even as Lincoln's relief expedition arrived outside the harbor. The Confederates gave Anderson an ultimatum, and then opened fire, and by the following afternoon, with part of the fort in flames, the tiny garrison had no choice but to surrender. Stunned by the not wholly unexpected news, Lincoln told people that same afternoon, "In every event, I shall, to the extent of my ability, repel force by force." Two days later, he issued a proclamation calling on the governors of the several states, including slave states like Virginia and Tennessee that had not as yet seceded, to raise and furnish to the national government seventy-five thousand volunteers for putting down the rebellion.[53] Lincoln had every reason to expect a prompt and patriotic response. Even before the firing on Fort Sumter, in the last days of peace, he had heard from individual men in the Union who were ready to take arms, indeed anxious. "Give those South Carolina villians h—l and we will support you," declared a member of the 7th New York National Guard. Immediately after the call, a father in New Hampshire wrote the president, "I have but one son of seventeen Summers, he our only child, a man in stature—We are ready to volunteer, to fight for the integrity of the Union." Soon there would be hell enough for all of them.[54]

In fact, even with the Union in crisis and war staring him in the face, Lincoln did not possess the constitutional authority to raise an army. Only Congress could do that, but the national legislature was not in session and would not be until a special call assembled it on July 4. At this critical moment, the federal government was paralyzed, and in the interim Lincoln was on his own. All he could turn to was an old statute that allowed the chief executive to turn out the state militia temporarily, until thirty days after the assembly of Congress in an emergency, and that at least gave him authority to issue the call for seventy-five thousand whom he could keep in service until August 3. He felt confident that when the volunteers came forth they would be good men. Whichever side of the Mason and Dixon Line they came from, the people of America derived from the same stock, and shared the same traditions. "Man for man, the soldier from the South will be a match for the soldier from the North," he said, "and *vice versa.*"[55]

Thanks to the preparedness of the governors, Lincoln knew even before issuing his proclamation that there were regiments ready and waiting. As the governors telegraphed him asking how many men they were to send, he telegraphed back to them, the press of business sometimes making his responses nothing more than a laconic "Thirteen Regiments."[56] Nor was there any doubt about where they should go. Even as Lincoln issued the proclamation a convention in Virginia discussed secession, and two days later voted to leave the Union. Maryland, too, was a slave state, with deep economic and political attachments to the seceded states. Washington, on the northern bank of the Potomac, thus faced a now hostile Virginia across the river, and had a none-too-friendly Maryland at its back. Lincoln and his capital were isolated and virtually undefended, and that was where the volunteers should come, and quickly.

For two weeks after the surrender of Fort Sumter, Lincoln and his city waited fretfully for relief. At first there were no defenders other than a hastily assembled group of 120 men from Kansas raised on April 14 by Senator James Lane, called the Frontier Guard. On April 18, Scott assigned them as a bodyguard for the president, billeting them in the East Room of the executive mansion, making them almost literally a part of Lincoln's family.[57] Now every day the president could hear the sounds of soldiers in his own house, and see them drilling on the lawn outside. But 120 men were nothing compared with the Virginia volunteers starting to mass on the far side of the Potomac. He needed regiments, many regiments, and soon. Worse, Maryland itself refused to furnish any volunteers, and then promised a dangerous passage for any volunteers from elsewhere in the Union who must of necessity pass across the state to reach Washington. Trains from Philadelphia could bring the volunteers to Baltimore, but they had to get across that city to the Washington depot to continue their journey, and there, on April 19, the 6th Massachusetts met a mob that turned ugly. A riot ensued, and in its aftermath four soldiers lay dead, along with several civilians. The balance of the regiment reached Washington and bivouacked in the Senate chamber in the Capitol, but not before bringing at least a little relief to a very anxious president. "If you had not arrived tonight," Lincoln told their commander, Colonel Edward Jones, "we should have been in the hands of the rebels before morning." Hyperbolic to be sure, but no one knew what to expect just then.[58]

They were hardly enough to relieve Lincoln's anxiety. Though Baltimore was so dangerous, there seemed no other way to get volunteers to the Potomac. "Our men are not moles, and can't dig under the earth," he told a delegation from Baltimore that asked him not to try to come through the city again. "They are not birds, and can't fly through the air. There is no way but to march across, and that they must do." As for the Baltimorians' protestations of wanting to preserve the peace, while they themselves offered no criticism of the forces of disunion in their own state, he chided them sternly. "There is no Washington in that— no Jackson in that—no manhood or honor in that." He would bring his troops through Maryland if he could, but he had no desire to expose them to another riot, and would not require that they pass through Baltimore if another route was available. If attacked, however, he promised to respond, "and that severely."[59]

The waiting became oppressive. The governors of Rhode Island and New York had wired him that volunteers were on the way, principally the 7th New York. One man of the 11th New York even mailed Lincoln a photograph of himself with his head shaved to the scalp, leaving only a patch an eighth of an inch long trimmed in the shape of a bald eagle.[60] There was small comfort in that. One morning, as he sat in his office, feeling all but helpless and deserted, besieged by the belief that even a small force of Virginians could march right into the city, Lincoln heard outside what he thought sounded like a cannon, perhaps betokening the arrival of another regiment. "They are here," he said in relief. But no one else heard the sound, and there were no volunteers parading down the avenues to save the capital. It had been a cruel trick of imagination. On April 21, he heard a drum and bugle, and again his spirits lifted until he found that it was only Lane and his company. By April 24, when he went to the bivouac of the 6th Massachusetts and talked with some of the men wounded in the riot, he gave way almost to despair. "I don't believe there is any North," he grumbled. "The Seventh Regiment is a myth. Rhode Island is not known in our geography any longer. *You* are the only northern realities." Over and over he repeatedly asked, "Why don't they come! Why don't they come!" A young man in the Treasury saw what he called "that peculiar expression I think the saddest ever shown upon the face of man" as Lincoln haunted the rooms of the White House waiting. It was an expression that hundreds of thousands would see in the days ahead.[61]

Finally they came. On April 25, the 7th New York arrived and marched down Pennsylvania Avenue, a band playing, with thousands lining the sidewalks to cheer. Lincoln came outside to watch them as the regiment marched right up to the executive mansion, and the soldiers and citizens thought he was perhaps the happiest-looking man in the crowd. "He smiled all over," said one. The next day the regiment held a grand parade, then stood at attention, their right hands raised, as a magistrate swore them into national service. Lincoln was there, holding his small sons, Willie and Tad, by the hand. The swearing-in done, the volunteers formally went to the "present-arms" position to salute him, and Lincoln responded by simply, and rather awkwardly, removing his tall stovepipe hat, then putting it on again, all the while holding it by the back of the brim. Private Robert Shaw believed the president looked "as pleasant and kind as possible," though a civil servant present thought the soldiers could only appreciate how much their arrival relieved Lincoln if they had seen him two days before, wearing that sad expression. When someone brought a pail of water for the soldiers to drink, Lincoln joined them, then spoke familiarly with the men and officers, and showed his relief by joking with them, almost doubling himself over when he laughed, despite his grip on the two boys' hands. Yet Private Shaw saw more beneath the conviviality. "I couldn't help thinking of the immense responsibility he has on his shoulders," Shaw wrote the next day. "Lincoln knows what he is about. No one would have suspected, who saw him reviewing us, holding his two little boys by the hand that he had so much to think of."[62]

The situation steadily improved over the next few days as more regiments passed through Maryland without mishap. The 8th Massachusetts arrived April 27, and Lincoln met them, too, thanking the men and officers for restoring the sabotaged railroad between Washington and Annapolis. Indeed, as each new unit arrived, he tried to welcome them. Most of these volunteers seemed to feel they had a right to see and be seen by their president, to display for him their patriotic commitment to the Union; for his part, Lincoln instinctively grasped that in the crisis the president needed to be seen, especially since, with Congress out of session, he virtually *was* the government. When, finally, a Rhode Island artillery battery arrived, he watched them pass in review and then spoke, expressing his pleasure "with the patriotism of the noble little State which has come out so nobly in defense of the Union." When the 7th New York band serenaded him on May I, he listened from the portico of the executive mansion, received the applause of the volunteers, then told them he still hoped for a peaceful resolution of the current difficulty, but reminded them that they, and the hundreds of thousands like them throughout the Union, would be more powerful in determining the outcome than he. Nor did Lincoln forget to offer personal thanks to those ersatz volunteers in little companies like the Frontier Guard, who had stepped forward in the darkest hours after Fort Sumter. Lane's group disbanded April 26, after a review at the White House, and in vouchsafing to them his appreciation he reiterated that there was still hope for peace. "But if the alternative is presented, whether the Union is to be broken in fragments," he said, "or blood be shed, you will probably make the choice, with which I shall not be dissatisfied."[63]

Lincoln did more than show himself and say a few words to the volunteers as they mustered in their regiments. He began meeting the sol-

diers individually, sometimes by chance or necessity, and often simply
because they called to visit him. Soon after the Lincolns moved into
the White House, a problem developed with the cooking range in the
kitchen, and at Mary Lincoln's request four men from the 12th New
York Militia marched to the mansion, came into the kitchen and
stacked their arms, and soon had the stove torn apart in the middle of
the room. Just then the president wandered in and half sat, half leaned
on a table, holding one raised knee in his clasped hands. "Well, boys, I
am certainly glad to see you," he said with a grin. "I hope you can fix
that thing right off; for if you can't, the cook can't use the range, and I
don't suppose I'll get any 'grub' to-day!"[64] There was a personal touch
in his openness that disarmed men who might otherwise have expected
a chief executive to be distant or aloof. Men who thus encountered him
felt an instant warmth toward the president that they could pass on to
their messmates. His unaffected charm could even work on some of
the nabobs from New England, who arrived expecting Lincoln to be
uncouth and ignorant. Invariably he surprised them with his manners.
Private Shaw, from a prominent Boston family, called on the president
on April 30, not for any pressing business, but simply because he
wanted to see him and felt that as a citizen and a volunteer he had a
right to expect an audience. Lincoln rose from his work table and met
him with a hearty handshake, then asked him to sit; for several minutes
they talked amiably. "It is easy to see why he is so popular with all who
come in contact with him," Shaw wrote immediately afterward. "He
gives you the impression of being a gentleman."[65]

From the very first, Lincoln never forgot the importance of showing
himself to the volunteers, or of granting them as much access to him as
the mounting pressure of the crisis allowed. He needed them, and he
needed to have them behind him, and with them the uncountable men
at home who might be required before this business was finished.
Every soldier he met made, in a way, an ambassador, not only to others
in the man's outfit, but also to those not yet enlisted. Every new regiment that came from the North left behind the inspiring sight of its
leavetaking, the flags flying, the bands playing, the crowds cheering,
and the reinforced idea that what was happening in America was something demanding the patriotism and sacrifice of its young men. On
May 2—as Lincoln was inviting Major Anderson, newly arrived after
being allowed to take his garrison home from Fort Sumter, to visit him
at the White House—in faraway Toledo, Ohio, a new regiment of
volunteers left the city for Washington. Carlos Colton watched them

march off and felt a surge of patriotic ardor. "I felt just as though I wanted to go with them & put in *another vote* for Old Abe," he wrote that day. "Not in the ballot box but in the heart of one of [the] vile traitors who are trying to plunge our people into Civil War."[66] By whatever mixture of example and inspiration he could concoct, "Old Abe" needed to light that same fire in the breasts of millions.

2

"A PEOPLE'S CONTEST"

And when Abram heard that
his brother was taken captive,
he armed his trained servants, born in his own house . . .
and pursued them unto Dan

[Genesis 14:14]

LINCOLN TRULY BEGAN BUILDING HIS VOLUNTEER ARMY for the Union on May 3, 1861, when he issued another proclamation, calling for an additional 42,034 volunteers, not to serve for a mere ninety days like the first wave of seventy-five thousand, but to enlist for three years. It was his first public hint that the crisis might not be over in a summer, that they could be in for a war of unimagined duration.[1] His slim legal authority for doing so was an almost ancient militia law dating back to 1792. It was hardly adequate for the emergency, but until Congress met on July 4 it was the best he could do.

In the aftermath of the Revolution, Congress sought in 1783 a means of defending the interior of the new nation in a manner consonant "with the principles of our government." The spirit of liberty and independence allowed for no compulsory filling of its military ranks, nor would Americans' native distrust of large professional armies admit the creation of any substantial permanent force. "A standing

33

army would endanger our liberties," protested one leader, and Washington and General Henry Knox, entrusted with preparing the plan, understood that they could only approach the military needs of the country with some kind of citizen-soldier solution. Knox asserted that the volunteer militia represented "the ideas of freedom and generous love of . . . country," and devised a plan for a national militia of men trained at arms but remaining civilians, subject to call to service in an emergency. Even that proved too much when he added that the several state militias should be uniformly armed and trained, for that smacked of centralization. The debate wavered among those who wanted central congressional management of the state militias, those favoring regional legions, and those standing firm for exclusive state control. In the end, Washington recommended to Congress a volunteer system organized under the same rules as the tiny seven-hundred-man Regular Army, but stopped short of proposing that a term of militia service should be an obligation. "Our National Militia," he said, "is to be the future guardian of those rights and that Independence, which have been maintain'd so gloriously, by the fortitude and perseverance of our Countrymen." That was fine, but the plan never got a step further.[2]

Knox tried again in 1786, when, as secretary of war, he drafted his *Plan for the General Arrangement of the Militia.* In it he recognized that republics were inherently less prepared to meet emergencies than autocracies, precisely because they rested on the consent of the governed and were thus less decisive in a crisis than a dictator or monarch. The happiest medium he could devise was a militia system that incorporated the ideals of the Revolution with the national defense. The government must inculcate in American men the belief that "the love of their country, and the knowledge of defending it, are political duties of the most indispensible nature." He wanted near-compulsory militia service for young males, paid for by older men forming a militia reserve, and using summer training camps not only to train the men in arms but also to provide them with ideological instruction about free government. It would make, he promised, "a race of citizens, equal to the dignified task of defending their country."[3]

That plan, too, died in its infancy, though Washington tried to revive it in 1789 with some modifications. "An energetic national militia is to be regarded as the capital security of a free Republic," he argued. Start the young off in the militia now, and within a generation there would be thousands of them well trained and ready. He would teach individuality and democracy at the same time that he produced soldiers skilled to meet any emergency. When such an emergency came, Congress must have the power to mobilize the state militias, making every militiaman subject to being conscripted if necessary, and when actually on duty in the national interest, the militias were to be armed and equipped and paid by Congress. But Congress itself picked the plan apart, diluting it severely in the Uniform Militia Act of 1792, which provided for no systematic training or federal oversight, and made the men provide their own arms and accouterments.[4]

Part of the problem was that Americans learned the wrong lesson from their Revolution. Already evidencing the beginnings of the mythology that so drove Weems in his *Life of Washington*, they overestimated the ability of militia, forgetting that distance from England, French intervention, and a number of other factors played just as significant a role in American victory as the Minute Man and the Continental soldier, who after all actually won very few battles. In the political rhetoric of their brash new nation, they forgot some very practical realities, and instead saw even in Knox's proposals an attempt to militarize the country with a *de facto* standing army. Still, if he misread republican sentiment, Knox fully appreciated the ideal of the militia myth of a Revolutionary army composed of all elements of the community, and therefore constitutionally unable to violate the wishes of that community. The citizen-soldier was the only proper defender of a republic.

Not surprisingly, when the new nation depended on its uncoordinated militia, the results were disastrous. In its very first military engagements as an independent nation, it suffered bloody and embarrassing defeats of small armies led by Josiah Harmar and Arthur St. Clair at the hands of native forces. At least Washington did then get authorization to expand the professional army from a mere seven hundred into the Legion of the United States, with a maximum of five thousand soldiers, and in 1794 it redeemed itself with a victory over the Shawnee and Miami at Fallen Timbers. But then a penny-pinching Congress soon abolished the Legion, and in its place created the new United States Army. Even then the military remained a ball kicked back and forth between Federalists and Republicans. President Thomas Jefferson allowed the creation in 1802 of a military academy at West Point, New York, to train professional officers, but otherwise the army languished. Often as not, the men who enlisted did so because they were destitute and needed the pay and clothing, or were younger sons who stood no hope of inheriting family property and used the service to get themselves relocated on the western frontier, where land was cheap. A sixth of them came from other nations, recent immigrants who brought no other skills with them, and scarcely half of all soldiers could read or write. They served long and tedious duty in frontier outposts, rarely saw their pay and rations on a timely basis, and as a result deserted in alarming numbers, forcing the high command three times to declare general amnesties for absent men who voluntarily returned to duty. By 1812, the United States Army numbered barely six thousand men, entirely unprepared for the war that broke out with Britain that year.[5]

Americans distrusted even that tiny army, showing special scorn for the unrepublican social divisions between officers and enlisted ranks. Any organization that depended upon discipline and subordination instead of free will and independence seemed an affront to Revolutionary ideals. And on a much more mundane level of self-interest, the only contact that most Americans actually had with their professional army was on the edge of the frontier, where the military bore the responsibility of keeping the peace by honoring treaties with the native tribes, and that included preventing land-hungry settlers from moving onto virgin soil that seemed theirs by right of destiny. Furthermore, those on the margins of civilization accustomed themselves to settling their troubles on their own, and felt no doubt that citizen volunteers made far better Indian-fighters than Regulars. What need, then, for an army?[6]

The War of 1812 should have answered the question, for, in the absence of a substantial army, and in the face of the utter failure to organize the state militias in any systematic fashion, the country found itself woefully unprepared. To meet the emergency, Congress authorized President James Madison to call for a hundred thousand volunteers, yet, even after suffering military reverses on all fronts and seeing the British march into Washington in 1814, Congress still refused to take the next step to conscription. Instead it tried to renew recruiting efforts for volunteers, and offered land bounties as an inducement to enlist. Even though a total of 527,000 volunteers enlisted at one time or another during the war, the volunteer army was actually deteriorating by the end of 1814. The Napoleonic threat, not American might, persuaded Britain to cease its efforts to regain its colonies.

In the aftermath of the war, Americans once again learned the wrong lessons. On the one hand, the professional commanders like James Wilkinson, Henry Dearborn, William Hull, and others mostly lost their battles, including the loss of the capital. Only Winfield Scott won any real laurels for the United States Army. By contrast, volunteers led by state militia generals like Andrew Jackson and William Henry Harrison won stunning victories at Tippecanoe and New Orleans. Thus, in the minds of the people, the professionals were discredited and the Minute Man tradition was vindicated yet again. Congress, on the other hand, saw only the difficulties of recruiting volunteers, the cost of paying their bounties, the high rate of desertion, and the utter impracticality of trying to fight a war with state militias with no uniformity of training or arms, and in the face of sometimes independent and uncooperative state authorities. As a result, it decided to do nothing more about the issue of imposing a national militia system, and instead chose to rely on a very modestly increased Regular Army for national defense. In essence, it was no policy at all, and the nation had advanced scarcely a step since 1792.[7]

The Union was still waiting for the next step when the guns in Charleston reminded Americans once more of their unpreparedness. Lincoln himself, knowing the limitations on his actions before the convening of Congress, also appreciated that the interval between March 4 and July 4 gave him some time for unilateral action without having to worry about being second-guessed, as long as he did not overly stretch his powers under the 1792 act. Within a few days of taking office, he drafted a proposal to establish a Militia Bureau with an inspector general to oversee all militia business, establish a uniform system of organization and drill, oversee standardization of arms and equipment, and compile a single set of training instructions to send to the several states. He was proposing very nearly what Washington and Knox had advocated almost eighty years before him, and even turned his thinking to assigning office space, stationery, and furniture to the effort, as well as access to public records necessary for the inspector general to do his job. Lincoln knew he was stepping out of the bounds of the 1792 legislation, and took the precaution of submitting the plan to his new attorney general, Edward Bates, to see if he had lawful authority to take such a step. Bates's response was what the president probably already knew: that, without proper congressional authorization of the plan and an appropriation to fund it, Lincoln risked infringing seriously on state prerogatives, and at a time when he could not afford to risk irritating his loyal governors.[8]

Lincoln simply filed the proposal away, and turned his efforts to what he could do without fear of contradiction; there he managed to go considerably beyond what Congress might have allowed. Even as more ninety-day regiments were coming in, he issued his May 3 proclamation calling out volunteers for three years, and the response proved greatly heartening. The states immediately began raising and sending regiments in surprising numbers. New Jersey turned over a whole division at once, six regiments or more, the very day after the proclamation; in responding, the president offered thanks for "the new Corps of Volunteers" (significant or not, this was the first time he had capitalized the term). Thereafter, he asked people on the scene in New York and elsewhere to keep him advised at the end of every day of the number of soldiers who had left for Washington. From his secretary of war he demanded quick action in the necessary formal acceptance of the state units into the national service.[9]

Almost every state wanted to send more men than specified in its quota within the 42,034. By May 19, some 28,678 men under arms camped in and around Washington, and they just kept coming. Lincoln already had ten regiments from Indiana and was willing to stretch to six more. Then he endorsed New York's forwarding ten regiments beyond its quota. When Pennsylvania filled its call, Lincoln stretched the rules again, even urging Secretary of War Simon Cameron, a Pennsylvanian, to make sure that his friends in the Keystone State came forth quickly so he could continue accepting them. He took an additional regiment from Michigan, and more than asked from Massachusetts. Within six weeks, Ohio not only met its quota, but offered an additional six regiments, and Lincoln took them. Soon he accepted another four regiments from Indiana. In addition to the recruiting efforts of the governors, private citizens were raising and equipping regiments at their own expense. The son of utopian Robert Dale Owen offered a cavalry regiment from Indiana, and Lincoln ordered Cameron to accept it even though the Hoosier quota had already been filled. In fact, he took the 26th and 27th Pennsylvania, which had been raised by private funds, even before he issued his call. Moreover, through confusion—or simply independence—some regiments came forward with enlistment periods other than three years. Ideally, Lincoln should have insisted that they change their enlistments to meet the requirements; instead he accepted a number of units, like the 11th New York and two Indiana units, even though they signed up for only six months. As he told Cameron, his policy was "Present your Regiment in working form, and it will be received."[10]

Then there were the men of foreign birth who answered his call.

New York, especially, offered thousands of Germans anxious to serve the Union. Lincoln himself suggested putting together a regiment of Poles from the several states, and, of course, there were the Irish. Lincoln had spoken to a lawyer from New York about raising a brigade—three regiments or more—of Irishmen, but he replied in protest that he knew nothing about enlisting volunteers, choosing their officers, and all that. "You know plenty of Irishmen who do know all about such matters," Lincoln supposedly replied, "and as to the appointment of officers, did you ever know an Irishman who would decline an office, or refuse a pair of epaulets, or do anything but fight gallantly after he had them?" Within weeks, he had all or mostly Irish regiments like the 14th Massachusetts and the 69th New York lending their own flavor to the increasing ethnic mix of his burgeoning army.[11]

Lincoln also hoped to get soldiers from the so-called border states—Kentucky, Missouri, Maryland—slave states that stopped short of stepping over the brink of secession. Their governors had refused to furnish any volunteers at his first call for seventy-five thousand on April 15, most of them seeing behind his purpose of defending the Union a "wicked" intention to invade and coerce the South. But Lincoln knew how deep Union sentiment ran among the common people of those states, and from the outset he expected to reap some share of volunteers from them. They would be doubly important, even if their numbers were few, simply for the political and moral impact of men from slave states' willingness to put the Union above a sectional interest. He did not include them in his May 3 call, but there were other ways of enlisting their loyal men. He put Kentuckian Major Anderson, now a brigadier general and a national hero, in charge of organizing regiments from the Bluegrass, even though the state had declared itself neutral and enlisting Kentuckians would have to leave the state to do so. He gave every encouragement to the local raising of two Maryland regiments, in spite of the tricky legality of the government's inability to provide for them since their state was not included in the quotas. Lincoln even counted on volunteers from the western counties of Virginia, those beyond the Appalachians, where Unionism ran strong, and he gave Anderson authority to include western Virginians in his Kentucky regiments.[12]

The president involved himself in helping independent companies in Illinois and elsewhere to get into the regiments of their choice. He helped ease the way for ninety-day and six-month regiments to convert to three years' service, while refusing to hold any man to a longer term involuntarily. There were even a few moments to devote to the navy. The May 3 proclamation expanded the naval service, but none of the volunteers sought were to go to that service, so Lincoln was happy to lend his support to the private raising of a naval brigade.[13]

Throughout all his involvement with raising the volunteers, Lincoln was driven by several imperatives. First, he knew that he was better off doing as much as possible before the deadline of July 4 and the convening of Congress, even if he took volunteers far above his quota. Having spent a term in Congress himself, he knew from experience the same lesson that Henry Knox had recognized all those decades before. A single man, using unilateral power, could meet an emergency much faster and more effectively than a representative assembly. As soon as Congress sat, it would be in a position to second-guess him, to deny or slow appropriations. By taking every soldier who came forward now, he could present Congress with a *fait accompli* army that it would be political suicide for the representatives to attack or try to disperse. Then, too, the larger the army he raised quickly, the more patriotic men of the Union who came forth ready to fight, the stronger the message that might send to the Confederates, perhaps dissuading them from continuing on their course.

And most of all, with the patriotic explosion in the wake of Fort Sumter, Lincoln was more than wise enough to know to do nothing to dampen that ardor. Indeed, he tried his best to enhance it, to give every man who wanted to stand up for the Union a chance to be a soldier, to feel in future years the pride that Lincoln felt still in his own long-ago modest days as a volunteer in the Black Hawk War. Because every man must have a chance to take a hand in saving the country, he went out of his way to include as many elements of society as possible, including the foreign-born and, even more potent politically, men from the slave states. It was a way of forging a social as well as a military weapon, a means of binding every element of society to the one paramount purpose. In the interest of achieving that end in the emergency, he made it clear that he wanted no delays. "Why should it not be done at once," he would say. "Lose no time," he told Cameron more than once, "this is very important, and should not be neglected or delayed." Red tape, if it could not be cut, might at least be stretched. When he made a decision to bend the rules, he forcefully reminded officials to "let there be no further question about it." In taking soldiers beyond the quota, he observed that state volunteers, "by their peculiar talent for taking care of themselves, . . . will give us less trouble in supplying them, than will most other troops." In his enthusiasm, the president occasionally stepped on some gubernatorial prerogatives. When a private committee offered fourteen New York regiments to be raised independently of Governor Edwin Morgan's official efforts, Lincoln accepted. Naturally, Morgan protested. The president admitted his technical error, but was unrepentant. "We are on no condition to waste time on technicalities," he responded. "The enthusiastic uprising of the people in our cause, is our great reliance; and we cannot safely give it any check, even though it overflows, and runs in channels not laid down in any chart."[14] Those tens of thousands of the sons of America wanted to reunite the house of their fathers, seeing in the Union but a magnification of their own homes, and Lincoln would do nothing to discourage them.[15]

There was more Lincoln could do. Not only was he anxious to see the soldiers, since every arriving regiment made Washington that much more secure. He wanted the soldiers to see him. Thus he continued the reviews and serenades of April on an even more frequent scale as the three-year regiments began to arrive. Regiment after regiment, on arriving in Washington, made a march down Pennsylvania Avenue past the executive mansion its first order of business. The 1st New Hampshire paraded by on May 29, and the 7th New York yet again the next day. The 2nd Michigan called to pay its respects on June 10, and the 2nd Rhode Island marched past a smiling Lincoln two weeks later. "He looks like a good honest man," one Rhode Islander wrote that evening, "and I trust that with God's help he can bring our country safely out of its peril." Four days later, the 1st Minnesota arrived, and after their review Lincoln spoke with their colonel, who quickly reported the president's compliments. "The Col. tells us that 'Old Abe' has confidence in us," one of the privates wrote that night, "and *we shall not betray it.*" Occasionally Lincoln did not wait for the parade, but went to meet the soldiers, as when he boarded the steamer *Baltimore* on May 12 and was out on the Potomac to see a New England outfit as it arrived by boat.[16]

By the end of June, Lincoln had already been seen by tens of thousands of men, making perhaps just as many impressions. One soldier of the 1st Massachusetts simply walked into the White House—not to see the president, but to sit down and write a letter. Like uncountable others, he regarded it as his right to enter the chief executive's house, and even to make himself somewhat at home in what was, after all, merely the "First Home" in a nation made up of homes and families. "Saw Abe Lincoln," he was able to add to the letter after the president happened to walk through. "Good looking man." Indeed, most soldiers commented on their first sight of the president, and the private from Massachusetts was rather generous. Most found Lincoln either ugly, or at least quaint-looking, but none of them ever saw anything they could take to be unkindness in his face. Now and then a soldier had a much more personal encounter. When Lincoln reviewed one of the new Pennsylvania regiments, he was startled to find a seventeen-year-old private named Mahlon Shaaber who stood six feet six and a half inches tall, even taller than the president. Lincoln called the boy out of line and, speaking from his own experience as a man of abnormal height, proceeded to give him advice about his health. He should avoid pies and pastry in any form, abstain from alcohol, and when he slept keep his head lower than his chest to expand his lungs. Something of a hypochondriac himself, Lincoln was no one to be giving nutritional advice, yet far more important was the impression made on young Shaaber. The president of the United States had, for a few moments, taken a personal interest in *him*. It was the sort of moment a man never forgot, the sort of moment that could bind his loyalty forever.[17]

Of course, there were a few who found Lincoln's unaffected common touch with the men a bit underwhelming, though rarely the volunteers themselves. Some New York soldiers were disappointed in the president's bearing and manners in reviewing them. When Lincoln sat on horseback to review men in their camps, he often turned his head to talk with the officers or other civilians at his side, and some thought he should act like a soldier himself—stare straight forward and say nothing as they passed. Just as bad, some found it offensive that Lincoln often had his two young sons with him, and sometimes paid more attention to them than to the volunteers. "These things dont sound well at all—The influence is bad here," wrote Robert Colby, a well-intentioned civilian who heard complaints. "There is no need of your being so infernally awkward," he continued. "For God's sake consult somebody, some military man, as to what you ought to do on these occasions. . . . You ought to assume some dignity for the occasion even though your breeding has not been military," he said. However much Lincoln may have bristled—or more likely chuckled—at that, he agreed wholeheartedly when Colby went on to say, "It dont require half so much sacrifice on your part to rectify it as it does of the men to go from their homes for the hardship they undertake." Lincoln would use virtually this same argument innumerable times in the days ahead, as he reminded the civilian population that they must do their duty to sustain the volunteers. Moreover, the president could feel nothing but hearty accord when Colby offered some very perceptive thoughts about the soldiers and the people:

> The people here care a mighty lot about the volunteer soldiers—They feel that unless the spirit and loyalty of the soldiers are kept up and encouraged in every way, the country is to suffer immeasurably before these troubles are disposed of—and you, though you were autocrat, can never be popular with the army unless you try your best to lead them to think you appreciate their evolutions. . . . A lawyer in his office can put his feet on a table higher than his head, if he wishes to, but he cant come any such performance as Commander in Chief of the armies of the United States in their presence.[18]

These were the very sentiments that Lincoln had already demonstrated motivated him. Indeed, in the main they were simply in his nature. Yet, contrary to what Colby and some of the New York volunteers thought in these early days of the war, that supremely common touch, the absolute absence of affectation, would in fact win the affection and loyalty of these men more than any amount of military formality.

One of the reasons Lincoln took the time to see so many soldiers face to face was probably that he knew it was inevitable that the time would come when he would have to ask them to risk more. He need only stand at the bank of the Potomac and look across to Arlington and downstream to Alexandria to see Confederates parading their own young volunteers. Even though a secession convention took the Old Dominion out of the Union more than a month before, the question remained to be settled for good by a popular ballot on May 23. The small band of Confederates occupying Alexandria had left on their own on May 5, but Lincoln postponed doing anything about sending troops across the Potomac, to avoid driving wavering Virginia voters over to secession. But when the referendum revealed a heavy margin for separation, the administration decided to act quickly to give the capital a bit of breathing space by occupying at least the ground on the south bank that largely commanded Washington.

The task went to a man very close to Lincoln, young Elmer Ellsworth, who until recently had studied law in the offices of Lincoln and his partner, William Herndon. Though only twenty-four,

Ellsworth organized and trained his own volunteer regiment, now the 11th New York, and, clad in its uniform, accompanied Lincoln on his trip from Springfield to Washington. Now he commanded them as colonel in the growing Washington army. Lincoln's affection for young Ellsworth was so close as to be paternal, and already he had tried to advance his career. The day after he took office, one of Lincoln's first actions, and his very first attempt to use a bit of political patronage, was to see if he could make Ellsworth chief clerk in the War Department. When he made his aborted plan for a Militia Bureau two weeks later, he proposed Ellsworth as inspector general. "Ever since the beginning of our acquaintance, I have valued you highly as a person[al] friend," Lincoln wrote him on April 15, the day he made the call for seventy-five thousand. He was anxious to hand Ellsworth "the best position in the military which can be given you," and gave the young man a statement to that effect to display at the War Department or anywhere else he might advance his career.[19]

The Virginia referendum gave the president a chance to do something more. He directed that troops cross the Potomac and occupy the Virginia bank, including Alexandria, and he gave the job to Colonel Ellsworth. It should have been a bloodless exercise, with the Confederate volunteers long gone. Ellsworth led his regiment over, and boldly they marched through the streets of the town, until they stopped at the Marshall House, an inn with a secession flag flying from its roof. Ellsworth himself went inside and up the flights of stairs to the rooftop, where he took down the flag, only to be met on his way back down by the proprietor of the house. The man killed Ellsworth instantly with a shotgun, and was then himself shot and bayoneted by Corporal Francis Brownell. The Union had its first volunteer martyr.

Lincoln was crushed. He ordered the funeral held the next day in the White House itself, and he and Mary rode in a public procession just behind Ellsworth's regiment. In the anguish of that ride, he may have recalled how, in all those descriptions of battles in Weems's *Life of Washington*, inevitably some brilliant young patriot was cut down in the cause. Now Lincoln knew one personally. That same day, he wrote to Ellsworth's parents, "So much of promised usefulness to one's country, and of bright hopes for one's self and friends, have rarely been so suddenly dashed, as in his fall." His own grief was almost as great as theirs at the loss of "my young friend, and your brave and early fallen child." Lincoln did not let the day close without taking Corporal Brownell aside for a private interview. Three weeks later, he made him a lieutenant in the 11th United States Infantry as a reward for having "stood by Col. Ellsworth at his death."[20]

Lincoln was no fool. He knew that men would die before this business was ended, but the irony that the first to fall was one so young and so close to him tasted bitter indeed. It may have brought home to him, however, the understanding of how serious the war was going to be. Even though the Confederates had pulled back from the south bank of the Potomac, they were known to be massing in thousands only a few miles beyond, building earthworks and emplacing batteries. Lincoln saw a gas balloon make several ascensions from the lawn of the White House itself in June; the aeronauts reported by a telegraph line to the ground the rebel buildup they could see off toward Centreville.[21] Arkansas, North Carolina, and Tennessee had followed Virginia in seceding, and day after day through June there were reports of skirmishes from the lower Potomac all the way to Boonville, Missouri. Seven Union regiments met a small but embarrassing defeat at Big Bethel, Virginia, not far from Fort Monroe, one of the few Union installations too strong for Confederates to appropriate after seceding.

It all made perfectly clear to Lincoln that neither his forty-two thousand nor all the over-quota regiments he had raised would be enough. He faced the prospect of a conflict against eleven Southern states across a front that stretched from Washington to the Mississippi and beyond. Confederate volunteers already equaled, and may even have exceeded, his own forces. This was going to be a war on a continental scale, and it demanded armies of a size never before seen on that continent. As far back as April, after the firing on Fort Sumter, a friend suggested to Lincoln that he must call for six hundred thousand men if he was going to put down the rebellion, but the president then rejected the notion of anything so great. As he prepared for the convening of Congress on July 4, however, he realized that he must now change his perception, and his expectations.[22]

The Fourth of July was a big day. It began with Lincoln, General Scott, and others reviewing the freshest regiments marching down Pennsylvania Avenue. As the 3rd Michigan went by, a private turned his head to look at "the honest and homely face of our good President Lincoln." New Jersey troops passed in review, and then more, as many as twenty thousand from New York alone. Cannon and squads of riflemen fired salutes all during the parades, and despite oppressive heat everyone felt a festive atmosphere. The New York troops tried to get Lincoln to make a speech to them, but he politely declined in spite of repeated calls, and said only a few self-deprecating and amusing words, before introducing Scott and members of the Cabinet to make brief remarks of their own. There were fireworks that evening, and then a heavenly display through the night, for a comet was then passing through Ursa Major, its tail stretching over fifty degrees of the sky.[23]

Lincoln dated his message to Congress July 4 but did not send it until the next day. In it they, and the Union, for the first time heard him speak at length about their situation, and his intentions. He spoke of his first call for seventy-five thousand volunteers, and of how "the response of the country was most gratifying; surpassing, in unanimity and spirit, the most sanguine expectation." Anticipating some complaints, he pre-empted them by going on to confess that his call for an additional forty-two thousand may not have been entirely constitutional, but was "ventured upon, under what appeared to be a popular demand." This was a neat way of suggesting that he had only answered the will of the people, but that was all surely moot now. The crisis had escalated, and it was time for the government to legislate "the legal means for making this contest a short, and a decisive one." He asked for authorization to raise four hundred thousand—at the last minute he raised it from three hundred thousand—and an appropriation for $400 million to meet the costs of the campaigns to come. "The evidence reaching us from the people leaves no doubt that the material for the work is abundant," he said. It needed only Congress's authorization "and the hand of the Executive to give it practical shape and efficiency." Indeed, the outpouring to date had been such that the War Department "had more trouble to avoid receiving troops faster than they could provide for them than from any other cause."

"In a word," said Lincoln, "the people will save their government, if the government itself will allow them." Harking back to the men who won independence in the Revolution, he declared, "Surely each man has as strong a motive *now*, to *preserve* our liberties, as each had *then*, to *establish* them." He saw no question that they would do so. He had only to look about him in Washington. "So large an army as the government has now on foot, was never known before, without a soldier in it, but who had taken his place there, of his own free choice." More than that, these volunteers were the very finest men in the Union, artisans, scientists, professors, and professionals. There was hardly a regiment "from which there could not be selected, a President, a Cabinet, a Congress, and perhaps a Court, abundantly competent to administer the government itself." It was the army of inspired and motivated citizen-soldiers that Washington and Knox had dreamed about.

"It is now for them to demonstrate to the world, that those who can fairly carry an election, can also suppress a rebellion—that ballots are the rightful, and peaceful, successors of bullets; and that when ballots have fairly, and constitutionally, decided, there can be no successful appeal, back to bullets." It was, he said, "a People's contest," and he believed that "the plain people understand and appreciate this." In passing, he referred to the increasing, and embarrassing, number of officers educated at West Point and the Naval Academy who had resigned and gone south even after receiving their military education at the government's expense. "Not one common soldier, or common sailor is known to have deserted his flag," however. "The greatest honor, and most important fact of all, is the unanimous firmness of the common soldiers, and common sailors." This was all the testimony they could ask, if testimony were needed, that the people would see the Union through. "This is the patriotic instinct of the plain people," said Lincoln. "They understand, without an argument, that destroying the government, which was made by Washington, means no good to them."[24]

That same night, in addition to the comet, a blazing meteor flashed across the sky. To a superstitious generation, the heavens seemed full of portents. A superstitious man himself, Lincoln could only hope they augured well for the Union. Congress gave him what he asked, and meanwhile he pressed on with preparations. He involved himself personally in trying to settle problems encountered by his volunteers—especially now matters of terms of service for the original ninety-day men, for some units, like the 69th New York, found themselves held in service an extra month, thanks to an error in dating their enlistments. The time of most of those first outfits would expire in the middle of July, and yet by July 15 the 69th, at least, had yet to be paid, and nearly mutinied in protest. "I have placed as high an estimate upon their loyalty and valor as upon those of any other regiment," he said, and intended to see that they were not mistreated. Meanwhile, he kept on visiting the camps and reviewing the regiments. "I have seen him and he is just such a looking man as I supposed he was as homely as a hedge fence," wrote a boy of the 2nd New Hampshire. With his wife, Lincoln went to the camps of the 1st and 2nd Rhode Island to watch the men hold a dress parade in their honor. As he made those visits, the president knew what the volunteers yet did not. The concern to ensure the security of Washington was long past now. It was time to go from the defensive to the offensive. Led by Brigadier General Irvin McDowell, they would be marching from their camps in Washington and Arlington and Alexandria on July 16, their goal Centreville and, beyond that, the railroad junction at Manassas. It was all a first step on the road to Richmond and that "short and decisive" end to the war. As he looked at all those faces, and hoped by his visits and his encouraging words to boost their spirit of patriotism and determination for what lay ahead, Lincoln might have remembered back to Weems's account of Washington preparing *his* men for the advance on Trenton. *"There! my brave friends! there are the enemies of your country!,"* said the Virginian, *"and now, all I ask of you, is, just to remember what you are about to fight for. March!"* [25]

Washington's march ended in victory. Lincoln's volunteers got as far as the waters of Bull Run. It was a debacle. McDowell met a Confederate army that slightly outnumbered him, but in the end both forces were little better than armed mobs and the battle could have gone either way. Insufficiently trained and hurried to the front, unprepared for what a battle was like, each side was ripe for panic, and the spark struck McDowell's men first. By the end of the day, more than fifteen hundred of them were dead or wounded, and over a thousand more prisoners in the hands of the Confederates; much of the rest of the army streamed back toward Washington with little semblance of order. Lincoln got the news in the War Department telegraph office, where he had anxiously kept up with McDowell's progress for the past several days. "The day is lost," came the shocking word. "Save Washington and the remnants of this army." Lincoln went to his Cabinet room and spent the rest of the night there receiving later reports, some from eyewitnesses. "It's damned bad," he told a congressman. [26]

Indeed it was, and Lincoln would not shirk his share of the responsibility for pressing McDowell to take field before he was ready. But there were more immediate concerns than blame. The day after the battle, Lincoln began visiting the troops now returned to their camps, trying to raise their morale, sometimes taking Secretary of State William Seward with him. He promised the men that he would take care of them, that what had happened was not their fault, that what had gone wrong would be put right. When he met units that had behaved well, he made sure to offer his compliments. "Mr. President, these are the men who saved your army at Bull Run," said McDowell when he and Lincoln visited the 3rd United States Infantry. Lincoln looked up and down their lines closely and said simply, "I've heard of them!" Perhaps he had, and perhaps not, but merely by implying that their behavior in action was well enough known to have reached his ears, he reinforced their pride in their performance. He might very well have said essentially the same thing to every regiment he saw.[27]

Nor did the men indicate that they had lost any faith in him. Five days after the debacle, Lincoln and Seward got in a carriage and rode across the Potomac to see Colonel William T. Sherman's brigade. "We heard that you had got over the big scare, and thought we would come over and see the 'boys,'" Lincoln bantered with Sherman. "I discovered that Mr. Lincoln was full of feeling, and wanted to encourage our men," recalled the colonel. Sherman invited the president to speak to the brigade, and Lincoln accepted, though at first almost unable to be heard over the cheering from the volunteers. "Don't cheer, boys," he said. "I confess I rather like it myself, but Colonel Sherman here says it is not military, and I guess we had better defer to his opinion." In speaking to the men, Lincoln simply stood in his carriage and then gave what the colonel recalled as "one of the neatest, best, and most feeling addresses I ever listened to." He talked of the defeat at Bull Run, reminded them that the reverse in no way reflected badly on them, nor did it lessen the duty they still owed to the Union, and promised that as commander-in-chief he would make sure that they had everything they needed to accomplish the task ahead of them. There would be no more sending half-trained mobs off to fight battles. And if any man, to the lowliest private, felt himself ill-used or denied his due, that man was to come to Lincoln personally. As many of them knew already, the door to the White House stood open to anyone.

In camp after camp Lincoln said substantially the same thing. At Fort Corcoran, an officer actually came forward at the end of Lincoln's speech to lodge his grievance. During a disagreement with Sherman that morning, the officer had so aggravated the colonel that Sherman had threatened to shoot him. Lincoln already knew that the spirit of independence among some, especially the volunteer officers, posed a threat to the military order necessary for the benefit of all, and seemed to sense an example of that before him. He looked at the man, then at Sherman, then stooped down to put his mouth to the fellow's ear, and said in a whisper intentionally loud enough for all to hear, "Well, if I were you, and he threatened to shoot, I would not trust him, for I believe he would do it." The upstart officer left amid the laughter of the enlisted men. It was a risky business offending anyone, but Lincoln had been an enlisted man himself once, and he well knew how a common soldier loved to see "the brass" put in its place. If the president had been trying to win friends, he won many at one officer's expense.[28]

Despite the joking, Lincoln's concern was real. When he visited the camp of the 2nd Wisconsin and made much the same talk, a captain stepped up and said, "Lincoln, look here! here is a specimen of the soldiers," and then showed a man with the seat worn out of his trousers. "Give us good guns and respectable clothing and there will be no trouble." Some of their rifles were defective as well, and the president promised to remedy the problem. He also started the work of persuading men due to go home in the ninety-day regiments to stay on. Some were determined to go, and he could do little other than receive them when they paraded at the White House, thank them for their service, and express the hope that after they got home they would think of re-enlisting to continue the fight until the job was done. On that same visit to Fort Corcoran, he met with the 69th New York, which had been so aggrieved until he took up their complaint, and asked them now if they would re-enlist. They responded that if he asked them to do it they would, then gave him a cheer and promised to stay in arms as long as the war should last.[29]

At every stop the volunteers saw the same expression on his countenance. "There was stamped on his face a fresh, vigorous, healthy and courageous look that inspired confidence," wrote Robert Beecham of the Wisconsin regiment that same day. They had been beaten, and it was dawning on them that there could be a long war ahead. "We certainly needed some encouragement," and that is what he gave them. "It was good to be impressed with the fact that the president on whose shoulders rested this mighty burden of war, with its vast train of results, either for weal or for woe to the people of a hemisphere, was not discouraged with the outlook," wrote the Wisconsin private. Seward spoke to the regiment in platitudes that Beecham dubbed "taffy," but when Lincoln spoke "he only said in a mild, gentle way, that he had confidence in the ability and patriotism of the American people and their volunteer army to meet and overcome every enemy of the republic." When Lincoln stopped speaking, the soldiers rushed his carriage, each wanting to shake his hand. They kept him at it so long that poor Private Beecham finally gave up. "I felt like shaking hands with Mr. Lincoln myself," he lamented, "but on second thought it seemed best not to assist in wearing the poor man's life out."[30]

The shock of Bull Run electrified the nation perhaps even more than the firing on Fort Sumter. Regiments serving west of the Appalachians talked of little else besides what they would do if they were at the Potomac front. "I have no doubt but that if the President, whom we already regarded with much favor, had asked it," wrote a recruit in the 7th Indiana, "the entire regiment would have gone as one man to save Washington City." Though there was never any real danger of the Confederates' advancing on the city—even if Lincoln briefly feared it—he certainly encouraged all who could to come quickly. On the day after the battle, when a Chicago regiment said it could be at the capital within forty hours, Lincoln responded by wire, "Bring the Regiment in 40 hours, or if need be, in a few hours more." The day after that, he drafted a memorandum of military policy that called for the discharge of those ninety-day regiments that did not wish to re-enlist, the reorganization of the rest of the army, and a constant regimen of drill to ensure they would be properly trained before their next battle. Still smarting under the new emergency, he added a directive that "the new volunteer forces be brought forward as fast as possible."[31]

For Lincoln, time remained uppermost on his mind for several weeks to follow. On into the fall, he kept encouraging and accepting regiments under the new four-hundred-thousand call, solving disputes where he could, bending rules where necessary. Continually he rectified delays or inequities in soldier pay, tried to settle problems with the commissions of the officers, and authorized individuals to raise troops on their own, promising that the government would supply them even though they were not part of the regularly summoned volunteers. He also renewed the effort to recruit Kentucky regiments, sidestepped the rules to accept regiments from Missouri for less than three years, and asked General Scott to try to enlist loyal men in the part of coastal North Carolina under Union control, even if he could not get a regiment and had to settle for a mere company of a hundred men. The considerable moral and publicity value of having those men from the slave states, and especially anyone from the seceded states, made the extra effort more than worthwhile. He also continued to welcome ethnic regiments to come forward, and even approved a plan to enlist loyal *Californios,* men of Mexican birth now citizens of California, into a regiment of cavalry. Overall, between Lincoln's efforts and the enthusiastic response to his July 4 call, by the end of the first week in August he had commitments for more than four hundred regiments, completely filling the quota, with still more men wanting to enlist. Indeed, private recruiters actually competed with the governors for men, and to a man who wanted permission to raise a German brigade above the quotas, Lincoln could only point to all the others already committed and plead, "If they *all* come, we could not take yours, if they do *not* all come we shall want yours; and yet we have no possible means of knowing whether they will all come or not."[32]

The president also turned his attention to the equipment in the hands of those volunteers. He recommended getting civilian iron foundries into the business of casting cannon, and instituted the purchase of massive quantities of arms from Europe until government armories and private manufacturers tooled up to meet the army's needs. Lincoln even involved himself in mule procurement for the army. In the first rush to arms, a fair amount of shabby, defective, or just cheap material was pressed into service, and already the War Department was dealing with contractors more anxious to profit from the crisis than to furnish reliable goods. Lincoln himself saw the uniforms that had fallen apart. Soldiers and officers complained to him of defective weapons, and he saw them on his reviews and inspections after Bull Run. Many blamed the secretary of war, who, though not overtly corrupt, was certainly inefficient and given to favoritism in granting contracts. Like a number of regiments, the 14th New York discarded their government blankets during the rout after Bull Run. Regulations required that they pay for replacements themselves, but on getting them they found the blankets to be half the regulation weight and made of inferior material, yet still they were charged full price. "Your soldiers hate this man Cameron," one said in bringing the problem to Lincoln's attention, "and will soon learn to despise the government that keeps him at it." In fact, there were so many complaints about Cameron that he became a liability; Lincoln would replace him just after the New Year.[33]

But there was something more than guns and animals and uniforms that Lincoln had to supply his volunteers. He needed to find them leadership. McDowell deserved very little blame for the Bull Run fiasco, and Lincoln graciously refused to cast any upon him, but it was evident that rebuilding and reinvigorating the army around Washington called for someone with much greater organizational and inspirational skills. There was only one man for the job. George B. McClellan was Lincoln's only successful general to date. A West Point graduate, he had been widely regarded as one of the most promising young officers in the army before he resigned to go into railroading. When the war came, he was given command of troops and operations in Ohio,

Indiana, and Illinois—a large responsibility for anyone, but McClellan was equal to the task. Before long, he led his small ninety-day regiments into western Virginia, to the relief of its strongly Unionist population. On July 11, forces under his command—though he was not present personally—won a minor engagement at Rich Mountain, and in the next few days he drove small Confederate forces out of much of the region. Though the work and responsibility were largely borne by others, he reaped the credit. After the humiliation of Bull Run, Northerners felt anxious for any hero to cling to, and McClellan was the only one they could find. The day after the defeat of McDowell, Lincoln ordered McClellan to come to Washington, and five days later, now a major general, he received command of the Division of the Potomac, including all the soldiers now in or on their way to Washington. It was a big task—the biggest there was—but he felt equal to it. Thanks to his diminutive stature, his men nicknamed him "Little Mac," but there was nothing small about his self-confidence. In this crisis, that may have been his most valuable asset of all.

Immediately upon assuming command, McClellan began the work of rebuilding the army, both physically and spiritually. He understood, as did Lincoln, the importance of being seen by the men, and soon scheduled a series of reviews and inspections, even while the work of drilling that Lincoln directed got under way. Wisely, Little Mac invited the president to be with him on the first great review of the army en masse, over three days in August, and Lincoln—who would likely have come with or without an invitation—accepted. The president had reviewed scores of regiments already, of course, but nothing to date on a scale like that August event. "Truly that was a sight that none will ever forget," said a Michigan volunteer, and he was right.[34]

The first review came on August 21, with eight regiments of infantry and several companies of cavalry and artillery, what a Pennsylvania soldier that evening described as "the finest sight I believe I ever seen." McClellan reviewed them first, riding along in front of and behind each line of the soldiers at attention. Then, to their surprise, they saw a carriage approach. As the vehicle passed the lines, Lincoln stood up and acknowledged their salute while the soldiers gave him three cheers. He joined McClellan as the men marched past in review, each taking the opportunity to have a quick look at the president. "I got a full view of Old Abe as I passed close by him," Private John McQuaide wrote home that evening. "The pictures I have seen of him has verry little resemblance of him." Another private never forgot how he and his comrades felt at that moment, "each one feeling proud of his Chief."[35] Three days later, Lincoln came to the army again to review General Israel Richardson's brigade, and this time announcements of his coming went out in advance. After that, he was seen by the troops regularly, and to all of the soldiers he gave the same modest yet kindly and reassuring presence that a lieutenant of the 65th New York encountered on the last day of the month. He saluted "Old Abe" with his sword as the regiment passed by the president, and strained his eyes to catch Lincoln's response. He caught a polite nod, "but at a casual glance could not see anything more." Nevertheless, this one man, like so many others, came away with the feeling that he had experienced a personal moment with the president.[36]

Little Mac's soldiers saw a lot of Lincoln on and off the parade ground that fall. When the 3rd New Hampshire band gave a performance one evening in the congressional cemetery, not far from the Capitol, the president unexpectedly visited, and they suited the music to the guest. "At no time during our term of service was 'Hail to the Chief' played with more feeling and spirit than this visit from our commander-in-chief," recalled one of the musicians. Soldiers passed Lincoln's windows at the White House daily, and often he spontaneously stepped out on the portico to welcome them. In September, he paid $335.50 out of the executive mansion's household funds to erect a tent on the grounds for the use of the volunteers. Whenever he could escape his office, he took his carriage to the camps ringing Washington. "Old Abe was on hand but he was in a carriage," became a frequent refrain in soldier letters home after a parade or review. On into October the army visits continued, and for a fortunate few there was that same personal moment with the president. He visited the camp of a Maine brigade on October 20, and after the review with McClellan found himself surrounded by soldiers with hands extended, hoping to clasp briefly his own. "I was lucky enough to shake hands with the President and Gen McClellan," Amos Downing of the 6th Maine boasted that evening. Whereas Little Mac promised that in the next campaign there would be no more retreating, then perhaps unwisely reminded them of how McDowell's army had been ill-used and many lives wasted, Lincoln simply said that he hoped and trusted that "all you sons of Maine will return soon. God bless you all." Downing found that "the President is smart and young looking and appears to take it quite cool." Better yet, he said, Lincoln "aint proud," and as if it were the greatest possible compliment concluded that Lincoln was "a downeaster in every way."[37]

What Lincoln managed to keep most of the soldiers from seeing was another side, the one that the weight of the war gradually bore down upon harder and harder. By late October, McClellan had been in command nearly three months but gave no sign of starting a campaign. Until Little Mac did move, any bright military news for the Union would have to come from somewhere else. There were hopes for a small movement up the Potomac, where a small Union command was to be ferried across the river to make a reconnaissance into the Virginia interior. Lincoln knew and loved one of the subordinate commanders, Colonel Edward D. Baker, an old friend from Illinois for whom the Lincolns had named their now dead son, Eddie.

On October 21, the day set for the operation, the president went to McClellan's headquarters in a brick house in the city to follow any news coming in by telegraph. At his arrival a staff officer announced him to the general, and then left Lincoln waiting in the antechamber with the journalist Charles Carleton Coffin. Already Little Mac's ego fed on keeping the president waiting, but Lincoln did not seem to mind. He sat resting his head on his hand, no doubt anxious and concerned, while they heard the telegraph clicking in another room. Finally the officer ushered Lincoln into McClellan's room. After a few minutes the president re-emerged, a changed man. He bowed his head, either unconsciously or else to hide tears, and held his hands clasped to his chest as if having a heart attack. Several long, deliberate strides got him to the door, but then he tottered momentarily, almost reeling, and stumbled on the outer steps, without falling. He had just gotten the news that Confederates had attacked the reconnaissance just after it crossed, driven the Federals back to Ball's Bluff, above the Potomac, and killed fifty or more; hundreds of others had drowned attempting to get across the river, and Edward Baker himself was killed.[38]

There had been three incursions into northern Virginia, and all led to disaster, two with the loss of close personal friends. Lincoln was distraught. Even as he led the mourning for Baker, just as he had for Ellsworth, the president longed all the more for something to happen to reverse the series of humiliations. Much as they admired the magnificent army that McClellan was building, critics began to snipe at his seeming lack of urgency about doing something with it. Lincoln, whatever impatience he felt, kept it to himself. "You must not fight until you are ready," he told the general five days after Ball's Bluff. Then, almost as if he hoped to relieve himself of his cares regardless of the outcome, Lincoln added, "I have a notion to go out with you and stand or fall with the battle." Sending other young men off to their deaths was beginning to tell on him.[39]

But until McClellan finally moved, there would only be more reviews. On November 20, he drove to a plain above the Potomac, to Munson's Hill and Bailey's Crossroads, and on a cloudy and frosty day saw the growing army once more. It was seventy-thousand strong now, well drilled, increasingly better uniformed and equipped, a living testimony to the joint efforts of Old Abe and Little Mac. "The display was grand and imposing in the extreme," said a private in the 36th Pennsylvania. A man in the 44th New York remarked on "a perfect sea of heads as far as the eye could reach." Lincoln, McClellan, all the ranking generals, and many of the Cabinet were present, and it was apparent that this was more than the usual past reviews. It was a ceremony of validation. At last, this was *the army.* Certainly there would be more regiments to come, but all the months of effort and sacrifice and training had sculpted a finished work that in future would only be enhanced. Already some called it "Mr. Lincoln's army."[40]

The soldiers spent all of the day before getting ready for the event, though some felt it was more like preparing for battle. Now, in their endless ranks, they covered more than two hundred acres. About 1 P.M., Lincoln, McClellan, and the rest appeared and started to ride along the lines. In the background a battery fired a round of salutes, almost muffled by the regiments' cheering, each in its turn, as the president and their general passed, a band all the while playing "Hail to the Chief." Little Mac, ever the showman, rode at a gallop, erect, bowing and waving, but not Lincoln. "Old Abe," wrote a Keystone State soldier soon afterward, "is a most miserable rider." Even at a hard gallop, the president's horse could not keep up with McClellan's, as Lincoln clung with one hand to the bridle and with the other clutched the animal's mane to keep his seat. With his long legs almost wrapped around the horse's underbelly, his hair and coattails flapping briskly behind him, and his hand only occasionally leaving the mane to hold his tall stovepipe hat or press it more firmly on his head, he presented an altogether comical sight. "He looked as though he was determined to go through if it killed him," thought a Michigan private, "but would be most almighty glad when it was over. I would gladly have given $10 to have been loose so that I could have seen the whole spectacle."[41]

And yet, though they laughed inside and told stories for days afterward, the volunteers thought no less of Lincoln for his ungainly show. If anything, it endeared him to them, evidence that he was truly one of them, a man of no airs or pretensions—no distant marble man, like the statues that were as close as most Americans ever came to seeing a president. Lincoln was a crafty and canny man, as most who underestimated him discovered to their cost, but he was not quite calculating enough to make such an undignified spectacle of himself on purpose. In fact, he coveted being regarded as a gentleman, and worked at making his manners less of the country court and more of the drawing room. But he could not help being himself all the same, and that is what the soldiers perceived. "It was the grandest sight I ever saw and I never expect to see the like again," one Pennsylvanian wrote home that night. Somehow the incongruity of the grandeur of the review, and the earnest but sadly comical appearance of the president, only made the day the more memorable. It bound the men closer to a man whom they regarded with sufficient familiarity to refer to him by the affectionate nickname "Old Abe" (none of them knew how much he disliked it). In spite of the cheering all along the lines, when Lincoln passed the brigade of Indiana and Wisconsin regiments there came not a sound. Some might have thought it disapproval or a want of enthusiasm. A soldier from those ranks knew better when he spoke for all by explaining that their "profound silence evinced the respect of the Western legions."[42]

Soon, perhaps very soon, he must send them off to another battle, one inevitably greater and more costly than Bull Run or perhaps anything yet seen on the continent. Until then, despite all the other calls on his time and attention, these men and this army—as well as the other, smaller burgeoning armies in the West—remained at the forefront of his concern. As soon as he had reports of men behaving with extraordinary bravery in the skirmishes and minor battles occurring now with frequency west of the Mississippi, he asked the War Department to devise some means of bestowing honors or awards, and sought to give one brave boy an appointment to the Military Academy. In addition to the routine of visiting the camps to show the volunteers the "rather tall pleasant faced man" from the White House, he sometimes took a hand at target practice with them, impressing a sharpshooter regiment with his handling of a target rifle. "Boys, this reminds me of old-time shooting," he said as they cheered and waved their hats, yet none of them could know what he himself rarely confessed: after killing a fowl once as a boy, he had never again aimed a gun at any living thing.[43]

"Much, very much, goes undone," Lincoln lamented to a friend shortly before the grand review, "but it is because we have not the power to do it faster than we do." Regiments sat waiting for delayed arms and materiel. "The plain matter-of-fact is, our good people have rushed to the rescue of the Government, faster than the government can find arms to put into their hands." He said virtually the same thing on December 3 in his message to Congress on the convening of its first regular session. "It is gratifying to know that the patriotism of the people has proved equal to the occasion," he wrote, "and that the number of troops tendered greatly exceeds the forces which Congress authorized me to call into the field." Better yet, Maryland, Missouri, and Kentucky, all of which had refused to send a single soldier at his April 15 call, now had among them over forty thousand men in the national service, Kentucky having abandoned its neutrality in September and sided uneasily with the Union.[44]

Much if not all of that success in raising the armies Congress owed to him. Now it remained to be seen what those armies could achieve, but it was already evident that the president would himself do almost anything that might advance their chances. When he visited the sharpshooters' camp that winter, one of the men averred that "his visit aroused their slumbering patriotism." That is what he meant it to do, but a private in the 62nd Pennsylvania put it much better. "The President was over to see us day before yesterday," Samuel Alexander wrote on November 23, adding that Lincoln "looks well and hearty but not very Pritty." The soldier went on: "He says if [we] do our duty we will all be home by Christmas."

"Well," said this one volunteer, "I will try and do mine."[45]

3

THE YEAR OF McCLELLAN

And Abram journeyed,
going on still toward the south.
[Genesis 12:9]

L INCOLN COULD NOT STEP OUT OF HIS OFFICE WITHOUT encountering a soldier in the White House. "Every person has a right to go through these rooms," a New York soldier wrote home in December. Like some others, he thought the house rather too grand: "No wonder it costs us so much to keep a President," he mused. Yet none held that against the man living there. Indeed, by the end of the year, the developing personal loyalty to Lincoln was such that the soldiers begrudged him little, even when he threatened to infringe on the very sense of personal liberty and independence that made every private think himself a guest by right in the executive mansion.[1]

Just a month before that private's visit, Lincoln responded to the mounting problem of presumed disloyalty and treason behind his lines with yet another in a series of suspensions of the privilege of the writ of habeas corpus. Amid fears of sabotage, and some outright acts of espionage by Northern citizens opposed to the prosecution of a war to restore the Union, the president saw no other recourse. Men were arrested and held on suspicion of disloyalty without being charged with specific treasonous acts. In the main, time proved his suspensions to be unnecessary, but in the temper of the moment they made sense. The suspension on November 11, 1861, however, did not apply to civilians, but to soldiers and sailors, officers and enlisted men alike. It should have outraged the volunteers; instead it passed with scarcely a comment. In fact, not a few in and out of the army regarded West Point itself as a "nursery of treason," given that a third of its serving graduates in the army had resigned their commissions and taken arms with the Confederacy. Very quickly it became apparent that the men who rushed to defend the Union felt no patience at all for those who stayed at home to carp and bite at Lincoln's heels, or for those in uniform who felt any reluctance to give their all for the cause. One of the loyal men from western Virginia who enlisted during the summer of 1861 cared nothing for the arrests that followed the suspensions. The rebels of the South were at least manfully facing the Union army, he thought, "but what of *Northern Traitors.* Will *Uncle Abe* not allso have to seal *their mouths* and stop their *wind.* If there is any thing on Gods green earth I could *love to hate* it would be a Northern *Rebble & Traitor.*" The volunteers were more than ready to give the president all benefit of doubt for any actions that advanced the greater cause. Indeed, whenever Lincoln clashed with either his Cabinet or Congress, the soldiers had already chosen their side. "I think the President is a good man and means to do the fair thing if they will let him alone," a New Hampshire private concluded.[2]

Not everyone expressed such admiration. In fact, within Mr. Lincoln's army there had been a slowly growing division for some time when 1862 dawned, the single source of it being the commander of that army, General George B. McClellan. His reception in Washington, and the adulation heaped upon him from all sides—and even by Lincoln at first—went rapidly to a head that was in any case always ready for expansion. When people told him he was the savior of the army, of the capital, and even of the nation, he felt no inclination to disagree. Certainly he did work a wonder with the raw material that Lincoln and the patriotic outpouring of the North gave him. The command that on August 17, 1861, the War Department dubbed the Army of the Potomac was now the finest yet seen in the hemisphere. It seemed only fitting when, on November 1, Lincoln made him general-in-chief, replacing the retiring General Scott; the country at large would not know of the shameful way McClellan had systematically undercut the old hero to force him out.

One problem was that, believing what the press and an admiring circle of sycophants on his staff and high command said about him, Little Mac bristled at being subordinate to the civil authority, and especially to Lincoln, of whom he almost instantly developed a condescending and patronizing opinion. He not only regarded the president as his intellectual and social inferior, but also passed on that attitude to those around him—or even fostered it. Whereas the common soldiers and their company officers almost universally spoke respectfully, or affectionately, of Lincoln, poking only good-humored fun at his quaint looks, McClellan's set adopted an aggressively sneering stance. When the 1st New York Artillery's Charles S. Wainwright, one of Little Mac's most devoted admirers, encountered Lincoln at the theater on January 10, 1862, he professed disgust at the president's ugliness. When Lincoln gave the audience the smile that the soldiers always found warm and open, Wainwright thought he "grinned like a great baboon."[3]

The tension remained beneath the surface; or when Lincoln did notice it, or took offense at some studied rudeness like being kept waiting outside Little Mac's office, he let it bounce off him. More open, however, was the increasing impatience of the president and the nation as the spring approached and still McClellan made no signs of taking action. The general gave away to the enemy the time in the late fall of 1861 that would have been good campaigning weather; then winter made the roads too impassable for active operations, as they would remain until March at least. Those months allowed the Confederates in Virginia to grow stronger, to build forts and earthworks, to raise more volunteers of their own.

Finally Lincoln tried to force McClellan into action with his General War Order No. 1 on January 27. Taking the commander-in-chief clause of the Constitution almost literally, he ordered that all of the land and naval forces of the Union advance against the Confederates on February 22, not uncoincidentally Washington's birthday. Though the order specifically mentioned six different forces that were to take the field, with the Army of the Potomac second on the list, it was hard not to see the directive as being aimed chiefly at McClellan, especially when, four days later, Lincoln followed it with a special order directly for the Army of the Potomac to move on the railroad near Manassas. Lincoln's goal may not have been a specific campaign of his own devising—though he had strong opinions with which, of course, McClellan disagreed—but, rather, to goad Little Mac into doing something, anything. The situation became all the more frustrating two weeks later, in mid-February, when a much smaller army out in the West, led by the virtually unknown Brigadier General U. S. Grant, achieved a strategically stunning victory with the capture of Forts Henry and Donelson, forcing the Confederates to abandon most of central and western Tennessee. If Grant could do that with fewer than thirty thousand men and a few gunboats, and in the heart of the winter, why could McClellan not do something with more than twice that number? Certainly the problem did not lie with the volunteers, who were anxious for action; Lincoln warned that, "if the Southerners think that man for man they are better than our . . . men generally, they will discover themselves in a grievous mistake."[4]

Personal tragedy only added to Lincoln's frustration: his son Willie contracted typhoid, and for two weeks lay under his father's gaze, until he died on February 20. It shattered the president and his wife. "My boy is gone," he said to one of his secretaries minutes after the child died; "he is actually gone." Lincoln vacillated between depression and vain attempts to transact some business, but spent most of his time in black despair. When he could think of the army and the war, in which nothing seemed to be happening, his frustration only deepened. On the day when his armies were supposed to advance, or at least make some show of getting started, Washington eschewed the customary illumination of its public buildings in respect for the president's grief.[5]

Lincoln's mourning gave Little Mac more time, but by now the grumblings about his delays became more public, even among the soldiers, who by and large felt devoted to the man who had given them pride in themselves and their army. Some even hinted that the general, a Democrat, might not want the South to come back into the Union, and thus procrastinated in order to avoid interfering with Confederate destiny. "I consider the talk about McClellan being a traitor is very foolish if not something a good deal worse," Private Charles Crockett of New York wrote in March. "I think he is full as much a patriot as those that talk about him." But other volunteers felt less sure when they saw his ceaseless protests that he could not move until he had even more regiments. In the 1st Minnesota, by April some of the men had taken to calling McClellan "Oliver Twist II" because he was always asking for "more." Yet, in the main, the army still regarded both leaders as heroes, however different they might be. When Lincoln relieved

McClellan as general-in-chief on March 11, leaving him just the Potomac command, there was no suggestion of reprimand or disapproval,
but only an intent to remove faraway distractions to allow him to con-
centrate all his energies on his own front.[6]

Finally McClellan moved. His design was to put most of his army
on transports and steam down the Potomac to the Chesapeake, then
down to Fort Monroe, at the tip of the Virginia Peninsula. From there
he would march northwest toward Richmond, take the Confederate
capital, and end the war. It was not a plan Lincoln preferred, yet it
would be sound if promptly executed, and the president was relieved to
have Little Mac making any campaign. On March 17, the army began
to embark, and Lincoln and his new secretary of war, Edwin M. Stanton, came to watch. They went aboard a government vessel; Lincoln
sat on the lower deck, pulled a pocket knife from his coat, and absently
whittled away at a stick while watching and waving at the boatloads of
soldiers starting downstream. The significance of the moment was not
lost on the men, who felt pleased that "our great President," as one
Michigander put it, had come to see them off and wish them well. Already many of them had found room in their knapsacks for a special
writing paper they would use for letters home from the front. At its
head sat a crude woodcut of Lincoln and McClellan on horseback, reviewing uncounted thousands as they marched past, with a preprinted
heading that said "Review of the ___ Regt, ___ Vol.," so that a soldier
need fill in merely the number and state of his outfit. So deeply had
those reviews impressed the volunteers that they gladly memorialized
them. More important, while the soldiers marched in faceless masses
in the background of the illustration, Lincoln and Little Mac were its
centerpieces. It conveyed a powerful message. This may have been a
people's army, but when the time came to give it a face and a personality, this was represented in the two men. It did not yet occur to the soldiers on those transports heading toward their first campaign that one
day they might have to choose between the two.[7]

McClellan did not move quickly, and all the strategic advantages of
his innovative plan he gave away by landing on the peninsula and then
taking root. Even with nearly a hundred thousand soldiers at his command by the end of the month, it took a peremptory order from Lincoln to make him start to advance in early April. When he did, he
immediately allowed what started as only fifteen thousand Confederates to stop him in his tracks for a full month at Yorktown. Not until
May 5, at Williamsburg, did he bring on a genuine battle. By this time

Lincoln, whose musing about coming to share the risk of battle may not have been entirely idle, decided that he would have to go in person to get McClellan to move.

The president, Stanton, and Treasury Secretary Salmon P. Chase boarded a steamer and followed the route taken by the army, stepping off at Fort Monroe on the evening after the fight at Williamsburg. Mc-Clellan could not see him right away, claiming pressing business in pursuing the Confederates after the fight. As a result, Lincoln spent May 7 visiting the soldiers in General John Wool's garrison, and then paid a special visit to the USS *Monitor,* the new ironclad that had electrified the country in its dramatic battle with the Confederate behemoth ironclad CSS *Virginia* just two months before. The president inspected every nook of the ship, talked with the officers, and then asked that all the seamen be mustered on the deck. Holding in his hand a hat that still showed mourning crepe for Willie, he walked slowly past the line of sailors, looking at each man. When he had finished and was leaving the vessel, they gave him three cheers.[8]

It may have been in part his discussions on the *Monitor* that decided Lincoln to embark on a little campaign of his own, to the absolute delight of the soldiers and sailors in and about Fort Monroe. More than a year before, Norfolk and its naval yard had fallen to the Confederates, and now it harbored the *Virginia,* better known as the *Merrimack.* It was effectively bottled up at Norfolk now, but could still be dangerous. Wool had a substantial garrison, and there were several formidable warships available. With these, Lincoln proposed that they land soldiers somewhere close to Norfolk and march overland to take the scantily defended city. Cut off as it was from the main Confederate army facing McClellan above Williamsburg, Norfolk should be easy prey. Officers of the navy protested that shallow water would not allow them to get within a mile of the shore near Norfolk, but Lincoln believed he saw a place on the map where the water might be deep enough. By moonlight on May 9, the president and his two Cabinet secretaries quietly steamed their little vessel *Miami* to the spot on the map, and got close enough that Lincoln could step ashore and indulge himself in a little walk on enemy territory. Having shown that it could be done, Lincoln reported his findings, and the next day Wool's troops went ashore to find the Confederates evacuated. A day later, the *Virginia's* own crew destroyed her, having no base now and nowhere to go.

The episode had rather little military significance at the moment, but it made a considerable impression on the men at Fort Monroe.

One of Wool's soldiers watched Lincoln's activity on May 10 as he helped orchestrate the amphibious operation. "Abe was rushing about hollering to someone on the wharf—dressed in a black suit with a very seedy crepe on his hat, and hanging over the railing," wrote the volunteer. "He looked like some hoosier just starting for home from California, with store clothes and a biled shirt on." Another wrote casually of seeing "Mr. Lincoln driving past to take possession of Norfolk." It did not matter that Lincoln himself did not participate in the actual occupation. The operation was *his*, and that was how the soldiers saw the matter. "It is extremely fortunate that the President came down as he did," wrote an officer of the *Monitor* that day; "he seems to have infused new life into everything." In what had been a scene of inactivity, he saw Lincoln "stirring up the dry bones." The day after the destruction of the *Virginia*, unable to see McClellan, Lincoln boarded the *Miami* and left for Washington. As the steamer made way toward the Chesapeake, the president stood on the deck with his hat off, bowing to the sailors on the *Monitor* and other vessels as he passed. He was one of them now, passing in review after a job well done.[9]

One reason he went back to Washington so quickly was that there were still fears for the safety of the capital. McClellan had willfully disobeyed direct instructions from Lincoln to leave Washington adequately defended when he embarked for the Peninsula, but after he departed Lincoln learned that the city was in fact quite vulnerable. Worse, the Confederate chieftain Thomas J. "Stonewall" Jackson seemed to be moving at will past small Union armies in the Shenandoah Valley, and there was very real, if unfounded, fear that he might move against the capital. McDowell commanded a small army that had been moving overland toward Richmond as a diversion to aid McClellan's campaign, and by late in May it was near Fredericksburg, halfway to the goal. Shortly after returning, Lincoln went to visit the command, again in company with Stanton, and again there were reviews. "The fact that Mr. Lincoln is a very awkward horseman did not lessen the Soldiers admiration for him as a man and as president," one Indiana soldier wrote in his diary. Lincoln even bantered with some of the men. There were no more than two or three Illinois regiments serving in the eastern theater, and when he rode past the familiar flag of his home state, he slowed his horse and asked, "What regiment is that?" Hearing that it was the 39th Illinois, he shouted back, "Well! You boys are a good ways from home, ain't you?" He later came to their camp and shook hands with the men, delighted to see an outfit from home.

Beneath all the cordiality, however, the men began to sense something. Lincoln had reviewed McDowell's men before they left for Bull Run. There were innumerable reviews before McClellan finally moved. When the president appeared at Fort Monroe, there was a move to take Norfolk. A Wisconsin volunteer found at the end of this review that "we look upon the presence of Abraham Lincoln as the forerunner of something to happen."[10]

What was to happen was that Lincoln would halt McDowell's progress toward Richmond and order him to help try to stop Jackson instead. At the same time, he issued an appeal for more soldiers. "For what purpose do you think Abe calls out 50,000 more soldiers," a western-Virginia volunteer wondered. It seemed that there were more than enough men in the ranks now to do the job. Indeed, if more men were to take up arms, many soldiers preferred to see them occupied in quelling disloyalty in the North rather than being sent to McClellan or McDowell. The Virginian believed that, even if the Confederates laid down their arms right now, there still would not be peace unless the dissenters in the North, already called Copperheads, ceased their howling, and that they would never do, "not while Abe Lincoln is at the helm of State." Still, the soldiers supported Lincoln's call for more men, as they always would. "In Abe Lincoln this army put its trust," wrote Private James Abraham; "what he orders they will accomplish."[11]

Unfortunately, Little Mac did not share that trust. In early June, when, after two months, he had fought only one real battle, then sat for another month within a few miles of Richmond before engaging the Confederates, he accused Lincoln of not sustaining his army. On June 26, when he finally met the enemy in the opening contest of what became the Seven Days' Battles, the result almost unnerved the general. For the first time he came face to face with the reality that many of the soldiers he had worked so hard to train and parade were also going to die. Lincoln ignored the accusations and feverishly worked to reinforce Little Mac. On June 30, he drafted another call for volunteers, thinking at first to ask for 150,000, but by July 1, when he issued the proclamation, he had expanded the request to 300,000. Meanwhile, the Confederates had driven McClellan back more than ten miles from Richmond in a series of aggressive battles; the Army of the Potomac still performed well, but Little Mac's dispatches indicated a man close to panic. "Save the army at all events," Lincoln wired him. "We still have strength enough in the country and will bring it out."[12]

Lincoln faced the problem that, even if all those 300,000 men appeared in a heartbeat, he could not do anything effective with them overnight. If he had a million men, he could not get them to McClellan in time to save the Army of the Potomac from the disaster Little Mac feared. Time, rather than men, posed the problem. On July 3, he wired to the Northern governors his belief that if he had 50,000 fresh soldiers in Washington at that moment he could end the rebellion, "but *time* is *everything.*" If it took a month to get the men, McClellan might have lost another 20,000 in casualties by then, meaning a net gain of only 30,000, and those untrained and inexperienced men compared with the veterans lost. Time now meant lives. But in the end, he could only wait. On July 4, there were no parades of soldiers, no reviews. Instead the president met briefly with the Association of the Surviving Soldiers of the War of 1812. "I have no pretty speech, or any other sort of speech, prepared," he told them. In accepting their good will and approbation, he merely expressed the hope that, "although far advanced in life as many of you are, you will, gentlemen, yet live to see better days than those which it is now our misfortune to behold."[13]

The next day, the panic subsided somewhat as McClellan wired the president that he had retreated to Harrison's Landing, on the James River, unpursued by an equally battered Confederate army, and already beginning to persuade himself that his withdrawal had been a masterpiece of military art constituting a victory in everything but name. Little Mac's self-confidence always soared when there was no enemy in his front, and Lincoln, for all his growing misgivings, knew enough to feed that confidence with compliments. "A thousand thanks," he wired on July 5. "Be assured the heroism and skill of yourself, officers, and men, are, and forever will be appreciated." But others, in lower stations, felt increasing doubts. "Who is to blame for the prolongation of this strife?" a western-Virginia soldier in the Shenandoah asked that same day. "I cannot believe it rests with the rank and file of the army. . . . Is McClellan the great chief that we had hoped for?"[14]

Two years later, Lincoln would look on this time and reflect on the irony that "I who am not a specially brave man have had to sustain the sinking courage of these professional fighters in critical times."[15] This was such a time. Shortly after sending his reassurances to McClellan, Lincoln boarded the steamer *Ariel* and made the voyage south, arriving at Fort Monroe on July 8. He moved on to Harrison's Landing to review the army, but first ran aground on the way, and took a soothing swim while waiting for the *Ariel* to be gotten off the mud. As a result of the delay, it was well after dark when he reached the Army of the Po-

tomac. Yet it all worked for the better; they held the review by moonlight, a scene that none present ever forgot.[16]

At 9 P.M., Lincoln and Little Mac began their gallop past the seemingly endless lines of the army. The soldiers were disappointed that
they could not see the president's face, but all knew him right away
from his stovepipe hat and the way he still refused to ignore their
cheers stoically, instead waving and lifting his hat as he passed. A soldier in the 5th Wisconsin found that "Lincoln was an excellent rider,
but upon this occasion he seemed utterly to disregard his horse, looking intently, kindly at the men, waving his hat as he rode along." Oliver
Norton of the 83rd Pennsylvania averred, "His riding I can compare
to nothing else than a pair of tongs on a chair back, but notwithstand-
ing his grotesque appearance, he has the respect of the army." Pennsylvanian Joseph Baker, from a different regiment, found that "he is just
what I had pictured him to be so much so indeed that I knew him at
first sight. The ugliest picture which I ever saw of him with the exception of some comic ones is none too ugly!!" Then Baker felt compelled
to remark on Lincoln's nose: "He has a monstrous handle to his
face."[17]

"Long and hearty was the applause and welcome which greeted
him," a company officer wrote home. Those who could see the president's face thought he looked "first rate and seemed to feel well." Mc-
Clellan, however, saw only a weak man of inferior character and
intellect—"an old stick," he called him privately, "and of pretty poor
timber at that." Such was Little Mac's mood that he either shut out the
cheers for the president, or else lied when, a week later, he wrote his
wife that "the army did *not* give him an enthusiastic reception—I *had to
order* the men to cheer & they did it very feebly."[18] His own soldiers
would have told him something different. "Talk of McClellan's popularity among the soldiers," said a New Yorker a few days later. "It will
never measure $\frac{1}{100}$th part of Honest Abe's. Such cheers as greeted him
never tickled the ears of Napoleon in his palmiest days." Almost every
soldier who wrote of the event in a letter or diary spoke of the enthusiastic cheering. "Whatever may have been the moving cause, the president was with us that day," said a man of the 61st New York, "and we
cheered his presence to the echo."[19]

Occasionally, in passing a regiment he remembered from earlier reviews, Lincoln paused and showed amazement and dismay at how
much the campaign had depleted its ranks. Indeed, when the cheering
stopped, the overwhelming feeling that the volunteers had after the re-

view was of the president's concern for the army. "What a depth of devotion, sympathy, and reassurance were conveyed through his smile," recalled a Wisconsin soldier. "How our hearts went out to him. We knew that 'Old Abe'—as he was called by the people who loved him, trusted him—was true." A very few actually believed that he had come to save it from *McClellan*, for there were ugly rumors starting that the general really was a traitor and had intended to hand over his army to the Confederates, but for Lincoln's arrival.[20]

Even though that was utter nonsense, there was no question that they felt the president was there for *them*. "His presence after the late disaster," said one, "seemed to infuse new ardor into the disspirited army." An officer on the *Monitor* commented a few days afterward, "His visit here has been a good thing, serving to give more confidence to the army by his presence among them." Surely this was what Lincoln intended to do—perhaps yet again harking back to Weems, who described Washington appearing before *his* volunteers while "his looks and voice rekindled all their fire, and drove them undaunted to the charge." Lincoln was acting the role of Washington, the role that even the adored McClellan seemed unable to play. In their general they saw the older brother, looked up to, emulated, idolized perhaps. But in Lincoln they saw—or sought—something more—caring, nurturing, wisdom, leadership of a different kind. "Abraham Lincoln has acted the part of a Wise Man," wrote a Massachusetts soldier a few days after the review. "No *one* man in this Country has so many supporters as Old Abe. . . . Let Abraham Lincoln say the *Word*, then let *every man*, wither Abolishonists, Proslaverites, Fanatics, Radicals, Moderates or Conservatives of whatever Party or Distinction, hold up both hands and with one unanimous voice say *Amen*."[21]

Unfortunately, Lincoln did not have time fully to read the mood of the army. When he left Harrison's Landing soon thereafter, he came away convinced, as he sardonically put it, that "McClellan . . . had so skillfully handled his troops in not getting to Richmond as to retain their confidence." Already, though, he felt a nagging sense that McClellan had wasted not only time but lives. As he sat on the *Ariel* and met with Little Mac, Lincoln occasionally looked through a telescope at the military hospitals lining the bank, waving his handkerchief at the wounded soldiers in their tents who waved at him. McClellan officiously presumed to hand Lincoln a letter advising him on domestic policy and war aims—which the president ignored—and quietly fostered in his high command his own delusion that Lincoln had purposely withheld reinforcements from him during the campaign in order to prolong the war until the abolition element in the Union was strong enough to force emancipation on the people. Little Mac's closest lieutenant, Major General Fitz John Porter, believed that Lincoln was thoroughly controlled by an incompetent Stanton, and indiscreetly asked rhetorical questions about Lincoln's causing defeat on the Peninsula to lengthen the conflict. Porter thought the president a dupe, and McClellan seemed to feel the same, regarding him with mere contempt while reserving the greater ire for the "villains" in Washington who controlled him.[22]

Lincoln could look at soldier numbers, too, but they told him a different story. The week after his Harrison's Landing visit he calculated that to date 160,000 men had gone into the Army of the Potomac. Yet McClellan told him to his face that he had only 86,500. Allowing for reports of almost 30,000 casualties in the campaign, that still left a staggering 45,000 unaccounted for, more men than in any of the other Union armies. It was evident that Little Mac and his generals had been extremely lax in managing their men, allowing flagrant absenteeism, granting wholesale furloughs at a critical time, frittering away strength on less-than-necessary outpost-and-garrison duty. If all those men could be gotten to Harrison's Landing now, he might overwhelm the Confederates, and Lincoln asked the general how this could be accomplished. The predictable response accepted no responsibility, dodged the question in the main, offered some explanation, and only reasserted that it was up to Lincoln to send more regiments.[23]

Two days before asking McClellan about the absentees, Lincoln sent the general another sign of his disapproval when he filled the vacant office of general-in-chief by appointing Major General Henry W. Halleck. This was as close as Lincoln ever came to answering Little Mac's letter suggesting policy. Lincoln would be the master of his own policy, and the appointment of Halleck was a signal that he intended to assert more influence rather than less in military matters by having his own man in place as McClellan's superior. At the same time, the president pressed on with the seemingly endless task of raising more men. On July 17, Congress passed a militia act giving the president the power to call out state militia for up to nine months' service, and by conscription if necessary. This was the Union's first flirtation with a draft, and it set an important precedent.[24]

At first it looked as though Lincoln might have to use that draft, for the response to the July call for three hundred thousand proved slow.

In fact, though, Lincoln complained to Stanton that they did not really need all of the three hundred thousand anyhow. Rather than raise new regiments, he preferred to fill the gaps in the old ones, realizing that a new recruit in a unit of veterans was worth two men in a fresh regiment. He was willing to use the mandated draft if it would achieve that effect, but otherwise preferred not to. Events would change his mind, however. Some of the governors persisted in offering regiments enlisted for less than the required three years, and when Curtin of Pennsylvania proffered sixteen regiments of nine- and twelve-month men, the president concluded, "If we do not take them after what has happened, we shall fail perhaps to get any on other terms."[25]

Lincoln wrestled now with a problem inherent in the Union's inevitable dependency on volunteers. Asked about the challenge by a French observer, he replied, "With us every soldier is a man of character and must be treated with more consideration than is customary in Europe." He ignored that at his peril. The independent American spirit explained in part why the army dwindled as it did, for men who would volunteer wanted, naturally, to go to the front in new regiments composed of their friends and neighbors, rather than be sent into existing regiments to plug holes. That was why, the same day Lincoln answered the Frenchman, he also authorized Stanton to go ahead with a draft of up to three hundred thousand men to complete any unfilled state quotas out of the July call. Lincoln had concluded that drafted men could be sent to any regiment, at the War Department's choosing. There was a system in place allowing men who did not want to fight to hire substitutes to go for them, but those too poor to do so clamored that if they had to go everyone should be so liable, another argument for a universal conscription. "In this free country of ours," Lincoln told his friend Lamon, "when it comes to rights and duties, especially in time of war, the gentleman and the vagrant stand on exactly the same plane; their rights are equal, their duties the same." The draft was a social leveler, imposing the obligation of service or substitution on everyone alike.[26]

To soldiers already in the ranks, the slow response to Lincoln's July call for volunteers was puzzling, and irritating, and using a draft to fill the quota was fine with them. "If the call of the President be promptly responded to," mused Private James Abraham of the new 2nd West Virginia Infantry, "and all our power brot to bear against *treason*, irrespective of state or personal interests, then will we have peace and not till then." Private James Burrill of the 2nd New Hampshire felt just as emphatic. "What ails the young men around there?" he wrote home. "Are they afraid of being shot in battle, or don't they want to leave home and its comforts?" All around him he saw veterans who averred that if they were at home now they would either shame the hesitant into enlisting, or else beat them. Many of those reluctant civilians had carried torchlights in enthusiastic parades promoting Lincoln's election. "I should suppose that a man who had patriotism enough to carry a torchlight and blow for Old Abe," wrote Burrill, "would have man enough about him to shoulder a musket and come in the field in response to a call from him."[27]

Lincoln got some help from an unexpected source, and yet it fit somehow into the picture in the public mind—partly by accident and part by design—that Lincoln and the cause of the Union were inextricably linked. The president maintained a higher degree of public visibility than any chief executive before him, especially with the soldiers. The repeated reviews implicitly hammered on the theme that Lincoln's cause was their cause. By contrast, in the other American nation, President Jefferson Davis rarely appeared before his soldiers. It was not in his nature either to seek or to acknowledge acclamation. Confederate volunteers never came to love and venerate Davis as they did General Robert E. Lee, yet Union soldiers in the East gave clear evidence that they loved both their general and their president. Moreover, if Lincoln gave no sign of actively seeking publicity or the spread of public adulation, he made little effort to discourage it, either. Already the popular press, especially the illustrated weeklies like *Frank Leslie's* and *Harper's*, repeatedly ran woodcuts showing Lincoln, and usually with soldiers or the armies. Lithographs for framing began to see wide distribution, placing the president in many a home in the North. On the other side of the lines, a great many Confederate citizens had no idea what *their* president looked like, nor would they three years hence.

Of perhaps greatest significance, this decade saw the birth of the mass production of photographs in a small visiting card or *carte de visite* size. Hundreds of thousands of Northern homes had albums with *cartes* not only of their family and friends, but especially of their loved ones in the army. The one photograph in most albums that was not of someone personally known to the family was of Abraham Lincoln. Jefferson Davis sat for no more than one photograph during his entire presidency, and even though *cartes* were popular and available in the South as well as the North, his image went into very few homes. Lincoln, on the other hand, almost never refused a photographer's request for a sitting. During the course of the war, cameras captured his changing visage at least seventy times, and many of those photographs found their way into public hands in large quantities, chiefly as *cartes* mass-produced by the Anthony Brothers of New York, or on stereopticon cards for the equally popular new three-dimensional viewers. More important still, many of the soldiers themselves carried small photos of their president with them in their knapsacks. Lincoln, on short, could be everywhere—in the home, in the field—and never far from view. Ironically, the camera made this homeliest of men the world's first photographic celebrity, with an enormous hidden impact on the attitude of his people and his armies toward him.[28]

There was another medium that could work for Lincoln. Within days after the issuing of the July 1 call for three hundred thousand men, James S. Gibbons wrote a poem, and on July 16 it appeared in the New York *Evening Post:*

> *We are coming Father Abraham, three hundred thousand more,*
> *From Mississippi's winding stream and from New England's shore,*
> *We leave our plows and workshops, our wives and children dear,*
> *With hearts too full for utterance, with but a silent tear;*
> *We dare not look behind us, but steadfastly before,*
> *We are coming, Father Abraham, three hundred thousand more.*

Instantly the verse caught on, for it spoke not only of the experience of the hundreds of thousands who had already gone to war, but to those who must leave their homes now to fight for the Union.

> *If you look across the hilltops that meet the northern sky,*
> *Long moving lines of rising dust your vision may descry,*
> *And now the wind, an instant, tears the cloudy veil aside,*
> *And floats aloft our spangled flag in glory and in pride;*
> *And bayonets in the sunlight gleam, and bands brave music pour,*
> *We are coming, Father Abraham, three hundred thousand more.*

By the time Lincoln authorized the three-hundred-thousand draft call on August 4, a publisher had set the poem to music, and in the next five months it went through more than twenty editions, eventually selling as many as two million copies. With the exception of Julia Ward Howe's "Battle Hymn of the Republic" and "Home Sweet Home," it may have been the most popular song of the war in the North. Author Gibbons himself was reputed to have called on Lincoln, wanting to sing it for the president. To everyone who bought or sang or heard the song, it reinforced the belief that these were *Lincoln's* soldiers.[29]

It would be too much to suggest that a song actually impelled men to enlist, but certainly renewed public attention was called to those who did not as their friends and family sang the song. Adding to the subtle pressure were variants that soldiers in the field penned to express their contempt for those too fearful or too selfish to answer the call. James Montgomery of the Signal Corps framed one of the best:

> *The clouds of war were brightening fast*
> *As through the land a message passed;*
> *It came from good old Uncle Sam—*
> *Dated Washington—Signed Abraham.*
>
> *Its purport was, as you must know,*
> *That the boys at home should a soldiering go,*
> *And it made them shiver as they read it o'er*
> *And stared at the three hundred thousand more.[30]*

Fortunately, response to the July 1 call for three hundred thousand did pick up, and Lincoln was not forced to resort to drafting. Still, he and Stanton worked feverishly with the governors to get new regiments as well as replacements on the road to the army, and again he bent his own rules in the interest of time. The regulations stated that all men enlisting before the quotas were filled would be used to form new regiments, and any beyond the quotas would go into existing units as replacements. However, Illinois actually had some counties fielding whole regiments by themselves, and was clearly going way over its quota, and the new enlistees felt concern about being separated from their comrades by being dispersed as replacements. "I think we had better take while we can get," Lincoln concluded, and told the secretary of war to go ahead and accept complete regiments even beyond the quotas up to a deadline of August 15. Meanwhile, when other factors threatened to cause delays, dampening the ardor that finally started bringing men forward, the president turned abrupt, even threatening. Federal officers went to each of the states to muster in the regiments formally and issue their bounties and pay, but those in Massachusetts dragged their feet. "Please say to these gentlemen," Lincoln wrote Governor John Andrew, "that if they do not work quickly I will make quick work with them. In the name of all that is reasonable, how long does it take to pay a couple of Regts?" Certainly the president's chief concern was getting soldiers to the front as quickly as possible, and yet, at the same time, there was always a secondary motive, fair play—especially over pay—and a desire to make the volunteers happy if he could.[31]

Events on the battlefield made speed even more vital, for he soon had yet another disaster to swallow. In June, he had brought one of his successful generals from the western theater, John Pope, east to take command of McDowell's forces and others in northern Virginia. Pope's newly designated Army of Virginia was first to make Washington more secure, and then to advance toward Richmond late in the month and take some pressure off McClellan while he battled in the Seven Days fighting. Once Little Mac settled his Army of the Potomac into what proved to be several weeks of idleness at Harrison's Landing, Pope was simply to hold his position in northern Virginia, but the vigilant Confederates, seeing McClellan undisposed to do anything, risked shifting most of Lee's army north to strike at Pope. Detecting the campaign about to start, Lincoln ordered McClellan to send substantial reinforcements to Pope, but the resentful Little Mac intentionally delayed, and some of the units and officers he did send, like Porter, proved less than cooperative. The result was that Lee gave Pope a severe beating on the old Bull Run battleground in late August.

McClellan's protestations to the contrary, almost everyone from Lincoln to the lowliest private saw that Little Mac had all but sacrificed Pope to his own vanity. "I have no more confidence in McClellan than I have in the devil himself," wrote a corporal in the 11th New York Artillery. It appeared to him that Little Mac had intentionally let Pope be overwhelmed instead of reinforcing him, so that Washington would be forced to turn once more to McClellan to bring order out of the chaos. Behind that design the corporal saw something even more sinister. "Our government is fast coming under a Prussian rule," he complained, "and unless something is done to break its control we shall soon be ruled by a despotism too powerful to overthrow." The despot he feared was Little Mac; already in some quarters he heard rumblings from the pro-McClellan forces that the army should rise and demand Lincoln's removal and replacement by a military dictator. There was no question who that should be.[32]

The corporal grossly overestimated the situation, yet at root he was correct, and so was Lincoln when he told Secretary of the Navy Gideon Welles that he perceived McClellan's design in bringing Pope down. "The country should not have been made to suffer nor our brave men been cut down and butchered," he anguished. He heard reports that some of Pope's men actually let themselves be captured so as not to be squandered in such an army. Yet Lincoln had nowhere else to turn. Pope was discredited, his army badly mauled, and the Union in an uproar at yet one more in the string of embarrassing defeats. "I must have McClellan to reorganize the army and bring it out of chaos," he lamented. "McClellan has the army with him."[33]

Like the corporal from New York, Lincoln was right, yet overestimated the situation. In fact, McClellan was starting to lose important support among the common soldiers, and had been since the Seven Days. It was hardly a flood of disaffection, and never would be, but a rivulet of discontent ran there. When Lincoln restored Little Mac to command of all forces in Virginia on September 2, a soldier way out west in Arkansas thought it wonderful. "Gen. McClellan is again at the head and were he declared Dictator to the army it would be all for the best," he wrote—but he had never served under the general. Another soldier out west felt otherwise. "There is Mclellan at the Potomac with a forse sufficient if ever he will have and still nothing done." The government's patience with the general could actually undermine a soldier's confidence in Lincoln. "Old Abe has got no back bone in him I begin to believe," complained Private John Boucher. William Dunn of the 85th New York had served under Little Mac on the Peninsula, and his response was gloom: "McClellan must get ready though the country is ruined by his slothfulness."[34]

While the general began the work of rebuilding the combined forces into a new Army of the Potomac, Lee's Confederates showed signs of moving northward, continuing the momentum of the offensive that had discomfited Pope. For his part, Lincoln was dealing with some important and far-reaching domestic and diplomatic matters, and left the volunteers largely to McClellan's care, yet he still found time to visit the soldiers occasionally, sometimes going as far as Centreville. Early in September, he came to see off a regiment on its way to the army. As usual, the men thronged his carriage, shaking him with their cheers and demanding a speech. The president almost always declined to make any substantial remarks, thinking it inappropriate, and usually responded with five or ten minutes of general thoughts and good wishes. Now he stood up in the carriage and told them that they took a heavy responsibility off to the front with them. The Confederates were moving, might even cross the Potomac and invade Maryland, and only their efforts would save the country. The soldiers kept him for some time afterward, shaking his hand, touching him, making some memory to keep for posterity. Most saw how thin and worn he looked. "One could see that he was troubled and anxious," wrote a New York man in his diary.[35]

Indeed, Lincoln did look haggard and worn, and almost everyone noticed it now. He was surrounded by soldiers wherever he went, and they saw it best. During the summer, he spent much of his time at the Soldiers' Home on the fringes of Washington to escape the heat, with a company of the 115th Pennsylvania assigned as a bodyguard. Lincoln liked the soldiers and found that having them with him was "very agreeable to me," though he often got in his carriage and left without telling them, in order to be alone. "The good President," wrote Private Harry Kieffer of the guard, "although he loved his soldiers as his own children, did not like being guarded." More alarming, however, Kieffer added, "I could not but notice how pale and haggard the President looked as he entered his carriage in the morning." Inevitably passing crowds of soldiers as he drove to the White House, Lincoln always lifted his hat or waved, especially when he passed the soldiers in the hospitals of sick and wounded that had sprouted all over the city. An ambulance driver passed the president on September 5 and had time for a good look at him. "I assure you he looks sad and care worn and he looked at the wounded in the ambulances sad enough," he wrote his sweetheart that evening. These were the very words that from now until the end of the war hundreds of soldiers, in a startling unanimity, would use to describe their first sight of Lincoln—"care worn." The lost battles, the squandered time, the growing number of full hospital cots, and worst of all the empty chairs at home all across the Union were starting to take a terrible toll on him.[36]

Finally there came some relief. On September 17, after Lee had in fact crossed the Potomac and headed north, McClellan met him near Sharpsburg, and beside Antietam Creek fought a day-long battle. In fact, Little Mac fortuitously came into possession of a set of Lee's plans, then met him when Lee had only half his army on the field, but squandered those advantages with a poorly conducted battle over which he exerted almost no control himself. Though it ended in a tactical draw, Lee had no choice except to withdraw to Virginia; yet, instead of pursuing a badly wounded foe, McClellan allowed him to get away. The general's capacious ego became all the more crowded with self-congratulation, fed hugely by Porter and others in his inner circle, but Lincoln saw only too well what should have been achieved, and especially the tragedy of letting Lee get away. Still, even a qualified victory was better than anything heretofore, and it gave Lincoln the opportunity to strike a blow at slavery that he could not have undertaken without the moral authority of a victory. But then came the inevitable disappointment. McClellan did not move, and showed every sign of doing nothing to follow up his advantage. Worse, one of his officers, Major John Key, was brought before a court-martial for expressing a remarkable sentiment. Asked why McClellan did not go after Lee and crush him, Key replied, "That is not the game." Instead, he said, the intent in the army was merely "that neither army shall get much advantage of the other; that both shall be kept in the field till they are exhausted, when we will make a compromise and save slavery." Lincoln himself interrogated Key; satisfied that such a sentiment had been expressed, he allowed the major to be dismissed from the service.

More worrying was the possibility that such sentiments were not confined to Key. Indeed, Lincoln knew well that much of the officer corps under McClellan were disaffected. Porter had been intemperately vocal, and several others only slightly less so. This, combined with the undeniable sloth of McClellan, created a potentially disastrous situation. If McClellan was confusing his duty to the government, as a servant of the constitutional democracy, with his own private political views—and, worse, if he was spreading that confusion in the army at large—then he would have to go, and for good. "If there was a 'game' ever among Union men, to have our army not take an advantage of the enemy when it could," Lincoln determined, he was going "to break up that game." It was time for him to go once more to the army in person.[37]

The president left Washington on October I and reached Harpers Ferry first; the next morning he reviewed General John White Geary's division, then moved on to Sharpsburg at noon. "Abraham looks quite care-worn and not nearly so well as he did when I last saw him," thought Geary. That evening Lincoln reached the main body of the army near Sharpsburg, and it did not take him long to sense the atmosphere at headquarters. McClellan was no traitor, and Key's statement was no doubt hyperbolic, but the difference of opinion between Lincoln and Little Mac over how to conduct the war became plainly evident, as did the general's long-demonstrated disinclination to regard himself as subordinate to the commander-in-chief. That McClellan allowed others to feed from, and pander to, his own disdain only made it the worse. Just as bad, Lincoln counted those present for duty at over eighty-eight thousand, even after the losses in the recent bloody battle, yet there they sat. In a bitter mood that evening, he stood with his friend Ozias Hatch on a hill overlooking the endless camps, and asked Hatch what he saw. "The Army of the Potomac," he replied, but Lincoln shot back in sour mood, "So it is called, but that is a mistake; it is only McClellan's bodyguard."[38]

McClellan staged a grand review for October 3, some of the men arrayed on the ground where they had fought Lee just two weeks before. It was a hot day with unremitting sun, and some of the regiments stood drawn up in line for hours as Lincoln and McClellan went past them, corps by corps. He started on horseback, and once more those who saw him could not help commenting on his ungainly appearance. "Ain't [he] the old bugger," said one of General Ambrose Burnside's men as the president passed, his legs dangling down over a horse much too small for him. "He wouldn't pay for skinnin'." A Maine soldier thought Lincoln a decidedly odd figure mounted, all the odder for wearing the stovepipe hat that only made an abnormally tall man seem taller, "yet he bore himself with a dignity that somehow made McClellan's urbane distinction less important." Others found a profound contrast between Lincoln's lanky appearance and McClellan's compact form. "Lincoln is not *very* handsome and not so *very* homely," thought a soldier of the 20th Maine, adding, "I thought Mc looked a little cross." Well might he have been cross: he had to know that the president, in surveying his army, was also carefully assessing him as well.[39]

Inevitably Lincoln saw the reduced numbers in some of the regiments, the worn look of the men, their tattered flags. Repeatedly he offered his sympathy for the awful casualties of the Battle of Antietam. "Mr Lincoln was manifestly touched," observed an officer in the 6th Wisconsin, "and he, himself, looked serious and careworn." Lincoln kept bowing low in response to salutes from the ragged banners, yet some of the volunteers found their hearts going out to him instead. "He looks the same as his pictures," thought one, "though much more care worn; one of his feet is in the grave." "How long and gaunt he looked," said another. "How the smile from a care-worn and anxious face touched the hearts of those bronzed, rough-looking men." Of course there were cheers, despite the grumbling at having been kept standing in the sun so long.[40]

The exposure told on Lincoln, too, and he showed a fair sunburn by the time he finished with Burnside's corps. He changed his horse for a covered ambulance and moved on to Fitz John Porter's corps, along the way revealing his melancholy at seeing the damage to the army by asking his companion Lamon to sing a favorite sad song. To change the mood, Lincoln had Lamon sing two or three happier tunes, and then they reviewed Porter. It did not entirely jar the president out of his mood, for he seemed distracted and less responsive as he passed Porter's soldiers, sometimes not acknowledging their salutes, his usual smile often absent. The men themselves may have been less responsive—quite possibly a mood coming down from Porter and his officers, for some of the officers here almost loathed the president. Tired, with the cavalry corps and William B. Franklin's corps yet to see, Lincoln cut his inspection of Porter short and did not stay for the customary march in review. Charles Wainwright, one of the most disaffected of Porter's officers, felt "utterly disgusted, a feeling which I think was pretty general throughout the command."[41]

Lincoln toured the battlefield briefly with McClellan, but seemed little interested, and soon left to finish the reviews. He had seen enough, perhaps; he had seen a lot. When he dined at headquarters that night, he even told a few amusing stories, suggesting that he may have shaken his mood of the afternoon. That night he slept in a tent next to McClellan's, then, the next day, made visits to the hospitals to see and speak with the wounded, before he departed to return to Washington. He had seen and learned what he came to see and learn, but behind him he left an army and a high command seriously divided about what *they* had seen, and what they felt. Little Mac himself thought that the president might feel more kindly toward him than he had believed in the past. It was perhaps only the last of the delusions and false perceptions that had dogged him from the moment he took command. In fact, he and Lincoln would never see each other again.[42]

Certainly there were a few soldiers who felt no enthusiasm about Lincoln's visit. One of Burnside's surgeons observed that, though the soldiers cheered the president, they did so "by no means so enthusiastically as [they did] General McClellan." Wainwright, of course, was virulently critical. When he saw Lincoln in the ambulance reviewing Porter, "with his long legs doubled up so that his knees almost struck his chin, and grinning out of the windows like a baboon," he felt outrage. "Mr Lincoln not only is the ugliest man I ever saw, but the most uncouth and gawky in his manners and appearance." Wainwright would repeatedly describe Lincoln as an "ape" or a "baboon," but that is hardly surprising: around headquarters in Porter's V Corps, such simian references were common, all deriving from sycophantic emulation of McClellan himself, whose favorite epithet for Lincoln was "the original gorilla."[43]

Yet there was a discordance between the officers and the rank and file. The farther up the chain of command one went in the Army of the Potomac, the more critical the officers were of the president, this growing out of the snobbery of some, especially the New Englanders, and the increasing loyalty toward McClellan, who was after all responsible for most of them being in command. At the level of the enlisted men, however, Lincoln's support soared, and so did the sense that they had pleased him, and a pride in that pleasure. The likes of Porter and Wainwright in the V Corps headquarters may have felt miffed, but when the men in the ranks saw Lincoln leave, they believed that he was entirely satisfied with them—as indeed he was.[44]

Almost every literate volunteer who kept a diary or wrote a letter home after the review made some mention of his own sight of the president, however brief. Some commented only on his sunburn or his clothing; his beard needed trimming and gave him a "rough camp look." Another thought that, for all his homeliness, "he ought to be wise and good and honest." Many more found something inspiring in his visit. "Mr. Lincoln seemed to tower as a giant," wrote a Wisconsin officer. Another would remember, years later, "We marched proudly away, for we all felt proud to know that we had been permitted to see and salute him." "I could easily perceive why and how he was called 'Honest Abe,'" a Massachusetts sergeant recalled. "He looked careworn and troubled, and I thought I could detect a look of pity as he scanned our line. I think his coming down, or up, to see us done us all good." One soldier of the newly dubbed Iron Brigade caught the prevailing mood better than the rest. "Altogether," he said after the president left, "he is the man to suit the soldiers." And now, for the first time, in their letters and their diaries the soldiers began to refer to Lincoln as *"Father Abraham."* [45]

Lincoln had always used his visits to the army as barometers, of the resolution and intent of the high command as well as of the spirit of the volunteers, and this visit proved no exception. Rather, it would be the single most important army visit he was to make, for it told him what he needed to know at a vital time, and that message was only emphasized on his way back to Washington. At Frederick, Maryland, successive crowds of soldiers swarmed around him as he waited to board the train east, each one wanting a speech, a chance to shake hands. To all he had time only to offer his thanks for their hardships and sufferings, "and for the blood they have so nobly shed for this dear old Union of ours." Once on the train, he stood on the rear platform of his car as it rolled through the Monocacy Valley; soldiers stood gathered along the route, some waiting hours when they heard the president would pass that way. To their ovations he responded with a smile and removed his hat. Their cheers were more eloquent than they could ever know.[46]

What Lincoln saw only added to his discomfiture over the waste of time and lives that characterized McClellan's leadership. Callers found him tired and depressed, confessing that he could not sleep at night and sometimes simply paced his room "as he thought upon the boys at the front." One visitor remembered, "Never have I witnessed such an impressive exhibition of elevated love of country blent with tenderness for human suffering—stimulating to action, yet deprecating its terrible necessity—contemplating new campaigns, while shuddering at human anguish and sorrowing for blood."[47] Lincoln may indeed have been pondering new campaigns—he always did—and the awful cost of the war remained a perpetual torment. He also felt oppressed by the figures he saw from the army. He now calculated as many as a hundred thousand men absent on furlough, virtually a full army in themselves. "It would astonish you to know the extent of the evil of 'absenteeism,'" he complained. "We scarcely have more than half the men we are paying on the spot for service anywhere," he grumbled. "The Army is constantly depleted by company officers who give their men leave of absence in the very face of the enemy, and on the eve of an engagement, which is almost as bad as desertion." This, too, he laid at McClellan's feet, for, however brilliant Little Mac was at building an army, he showed far too much indulgence for the good of the service.[48]

Just days after Lincoln returned from his visit to Sharpsburg, Brigadier General John Cochrane arrived as an emissary from McClellan to plead Little Mac's case that he should once more be restored to the position of general-in-chief—evidence of just how utterly the general failed to appreciate his position with the president. Far from any thought of promoting McClellan, the problem with which Lincoln was now wrestling was how to rid himself of the turbulent officer. It all depended on two things. One was the midterm congressional election in four states due in just a week, on October 14. In all four of them the fight would be hard, with a strong Democratic opposition. Relieving the popular Democrat McClellan before the polls would be suicidal, yet when the returns came in the result—though bad—was not so bad as he feared. All but two states still had Republican governors, and six-teen retained friendly majorities in their legislatures. That was essential for a good response to the inevitable future calls for volunteers. In Congress, Lincoln actually picked up five seats in the Senate, and held on to a House majority of twenty-five—hardly impressive, but, added to the number of so-called War Democrats who supported his policy, it was enough.[49] With his hold on Congress secure, he could safely dis-pose of McClellan.

The other question, though, was how the soldiers would respond: if Little Mac's support in the ranks proved strong enough, that alone could force the president to retain him somehow, even make him gen-eral-in-chief as a means of getting him away from a field command. By now Lincoln surely had some idea of the disaffection that Little Mac himself had sown in the command. He offended some regiments, like the 85th New York, by implying—so they believed—that their con-duct at Antietam had been cowardly. When McClellan reported unfa-vorably on the division commanded by Brigadier General Silas Casey on the Peninsula, and Casey was subsequently relieved, the division blamed Little Mac. Others suspected him because he had supported one of Lincoln's Democratic opponents in the 1860 election, and some simply distrusted him because of the general antipathy toward West Point and its clique.[50]

If Lincoln wanted more reassurance of the soldiers' view, he got it in the next three weeks. He scheduled another review at Centreville, and on October 22 crossed to Alexandria to visit several regiments there. They all gave him the reception he had come to expect. "As 'Old Abe' rode up and down the lines," a man of the 34th Massachusetts wrote the next day, "cheer after cheer rose up from the troops." He looked better to these men than he had appeared a few weeks before—"well and hearty," some said. The renewed indications of the support of the army boosted his spirits, and helped him make a difficult decision. The determination showed on his face. "'Abe' appeared comical enough when he put his 'stove pipe' hat on his head, it coming over his eyes," said the Bay Stater, but "in his countenance an earnest, steadfast, and honest look might be noticed, and the determination to carry out all his designs to the very letter, was plainly visible."[51]

It was enough. Sometime in late October, he finally came to the conclusion that "I am stronger with the Army of the Potomac than McClellan." His visit to the army convinced him that he had the good will and support of the volunteers, and that, though most of them regarded Little Mac with admiration, even devotion, replacing him would not seriously endanger the morale of the army. He must also have encountered at least some hints that soldiers who would be angered by McClellan's removal would not necessarily blame it on Lincoln, for even in the army high command there was a feeling, expressed by Porter, McClellan himself, and others, that Lincoln was largely just the tool of Stanton and others. Thus the blame, if any, might not even stick to the president, and that was crucial. Also, there was a bit of human nature working for him that Lincoln understood too well from his own experience. Enlisted men always resented their officers. He could not forget the first time he gave an order when he was Captain Lincoln, and one of his men told him to "go to the devil, sir!" Since the dissatisfaction in the army was almost all at the officer level, the common soldiers might side with Lincoln just to spite their superiors.[52]

He must have reached his resolution before the day in late October when two Pennsylvania soldiers saw him leaning against a tree beside one of the White House gates, absent-mindedly swatting at the grass with his walking stick. Curious, they stopped at some distance just to have what one called "a good, quiet look at the great man." Lincoln raised his head and saw them, broke out into a smile, and took off his hat to them. "Good evening boys," he said. "What regiment?" They called back, "116th Pennsylvania." "God bless you," answered Lincoln. He might have been saying it to the entire army.[53]

The Army of the Potomac did not move again until October 26, more than a month after Antietam. On November 5, some soldiers of the 133rd Pennsylvania sat talking at their campfire near Warrenton, Virginia. "Some of us do not like Gen McClelland," one wrote home that night. "He is not half the man the artists represent him." Furthermore, "many of us do not think he acted rightly in staying so long at Sharpsburg. We have our own opinion of matters. We want something done." That same day, Lincoln did it.[54]

"The army, like the nation, has become demoralized by the idea that the war is to be ended, the nation united, and peace restored, by *strategy*, and not by hard desperate fighting," Lincoln wrote in defense of his relief of McClellan. He knew that he would have to offer some explanation, even if the army stood behind him, and the reaction commenced immediately upon McClellan's replacement by Burnside on November 7. The news got out the next day, and his defenders were quick to speak out. "I think the President will find out that he has done him injustice in removing him," wrote the son-in-law of the man who actually delivered Lincoln's removal order. "I believe that if any other man but McClellan had had command of the army we would [have] been w[h]ipped any how," a Pennsylvania private wrote home. "I tell the[e] Mcclellan is slow but sure," he said; "now mark it, my firm belief is that Mcclellan is *the* man." A Minnesota soldier found his comrades and officers "stunned and exasperated almost to the point of mutiny." Some of the officers tried to resign, only to be persuaded to reconsider. "The estimate of an army of the character and capacity of its commander, who had led it in many battles, is always accurate; and the confidence of this army, from its oldest corps commander to the men in the ranks, in McClellan was unbounded." Another man in the same regiment confessed, "I hardly feel any interest in this war since General McClellans removed it was a grand mistake." Many were anxious to see the result of the action.[55]

A Maine private felt "a great current of dissatisfaction in this army," especially among the older veterans. "It is quite plain that until this feeling is allayed, no commander will be likely to succeed with this army. . . . We think 'Little Mac' the smartest and most ill-used person on earth." Worse, he found that "no stone is left unturned to keep alive this feeling of distrust among the privates and lower-grade officers." Indeed, McClellan's friends, like Wainwright, were quite vocal in expressing their opinions on the removal, and there were suspicions that some of them actually hoped to foment a mutiny against the administration, but their outspokenness exaggerated their numbers. Most of the aggrieved volunteers took the attitude of Elisha Rhodes: "This change produces much bitter feeling and some indignation. Like loyal soldiers we submit."[56]

Significantly, many of those outraged followed the Porter line that others had forced the president to the action. "Politics is believed to be at the bottom of it," wrote James Elliott of the 71st Pennsylvania, who also noted that "murmurings loud and deep are heard in every camp." "I am so mad that I can hardly write," fumed a man in the I Corps. "The God-d—— abolitionists of the North have succeeded in their hellish work of removing little Mac." Others blamed the more ardent Republicans in Congress and the Cabinet, especially Stanton, who was known to detest McClellan, and castigated the administration generally. A private in the 20th Maine spoke of "a great deal of Bitter Feeling towards the *Crowd in Washington* as we termed them." "I confess he did not accomplish anything but was *he* to blame?" asked another

Pennsylvania private. "I say, and *history* will one day say, no, . . . and what shall I say of the authorities at Washington tampering with Mac and his army? O pshaw! the fact is Mac is *the* man."[57]

The soldiers refused to blame Lincoln. "We know that President Lincoln did not do it," said a Minnesota private, "but we do not blame him when there was so many that wanted him removed and they had such a great influence that he complied with their request. And in reality we can say that he did not do it." One Pennsylvanian did not hold Lincoln accountable, thinking it a move necessary to spur enlistments and raise morale in the nation at large; others actually wrote that the move was entirely justified. A chaplain declared that Little Mac had been too easy on Rebel civilians. "I shall leave criticism to others better able to do justice to the cause and the men," he said, "but shall venture the assertion that fine rebel mansions, and property in general, are too closely guarded, too carefully watched." A Massachusetts soldier confessed to being "disheartened, disgusted and discouraged, not because McClellan has been supplanted," he said, but because of the reaction he saw among some of his fellow volunteers, especially the "unreasonable complaint of our officers." McClellan may have been almost worshipped by the soldiery generally, "but that does not necessarily denote that he is the ablest General in the field by any means." Some of the officers were even trying to resign, protesting they felt greater respect for Confederate leaders than their own, and this same Bay Stater thought what they really needed was a good kick in the pants. "I would like to purchase a pair of boots for a special purpose," he mused, "and I would have them greatly fortified at the toe."[58]

And for every soldier who expressed outrage at the removal, there was at least one who felt hearty approval, especially among the newer regiments that felt no longtime attachment to Little Mac. "We wanted some one to lead us on to victory as soon as possible, and we didn't care who it was," said a man of the 141st Pennsylvania, "only so that [we] got there at the earliest practicable moment." A boy of the 14th Indiana cited "his losing campaigns, his fruitless victories, his 'masterly inaction' after the battle of Antietam," and concluded that "the general imbecility shown in all his subsequent movements, convinced me that something was wrong and a change of commander necessary." Little Mac had more than a year in command, said another Hoosier, "& I think he should have given some evidence of military genius in that time." A Michigan soldier succinctly captured the widespread feeling that "no one seems to have any heart for the war except Lincoln, some of the lower officers & the privates." It was simple, said an officer of the 3rd Massachusetts Cavalry. "The President and General Halleck made up their mind he must go."[59]

He went on November 10, in an emotional scene that saw many soldiers weeping as he rode past them for the last time. "Boys felt bad," wrote a Vermont soldier in his diary. There were cheers along most of the line, but some felt that these were less spontaneous than contrived by some of Little Mac's adherents. In Burnside's corps there was little expression of feeling, for they still resented McClellan's failure to send them support during a brutally costly series of attacks at Antietam. Besides, they liked the idea of their commander taking over the army. Already all of the campfire talk of going home, or marching on Washington to oust Lincoln and make a dictator of McClellan, had ceased; it had always been confined to a very few officers in any case, and never more than what Brigadier General Carl Schurz of the XI Corps called "headquarters bluster."[60]

Some of the grumbling continued, and would for months to come, but there were other sentiments as the general who had built this army saw it for the last time. "I think President Lincoln has initiated a very wise idea, and I only hope that he may speedily follow it," wrote a man of the 34th Massachusetts. McClellan had been too slow, and the men were already growing easier about the idea of his replacement. Lincoln wanted action, and that suited him. "I am willing he should go," said a sergeant major of the 93rd New York a few days later. "Hee is too slow to suit me." "Praps it is for the best," said another Massachusetts private. "I hope i[t] is." "All right with me," echoed another boy from the Bay State, and a man in the 61st New York confessed, "I was glad of any change—it seemed to me that no one could be more inefficient than McClellan." Scarcely was Little Mac out of sight that day when one Michigan private told his diary, "Farewell McClellan, I am afraid you are about played out." Two days later, when Porter, too, was relieved and left the army, the cheers seemed so feeble that some thought they sounded more like groans.[61]

The year of McClellan was over, and Lincoln had won the first of two great battles for the loyalty of his soldiers. The other was already under way even before the final crisis with Little Mac, but its outcome lay in the future, and would go a long way to determining whether Old Abe would truly become Father Abraham.

4

THE PRICE OF FREEDOM

And God said unto Abraham, Let it not be grievous in thy sight
because of the lad, and because of thy bondwoman;
in all that Sarah hath said unto thee, hearken unto her voice;
for in Isaac shall thy seed be called.
And also of the son of the bondwoman will I make a nation,
because he is thy seed.

[Genesis 21: 12–13]

THE CONTEST WITH McCLELLAN EXCITED ALMOST NO comment among the soldiers of the other armies of the Union. In their diaries and their letters home, they scarcely even mentioned the matter, and almost all of those few who did sided with Lincoln. After all, they fought with armies that had been winning victories almost from the first—Forts Henry and Donelson, Shiloh, the fall of New Orleans, Corinth, Iuka, Pea Ridge, and more. They claimed half of Tennessee, northern Mississippi, Missouri, much of Arkansas, and eastern Louisiana, and stood poised for the drive to take control of the great river. They felt no affection for McClellan, from their vantage only a general who did not move and did not fight. Under their own generals, and especially the rising star Grant, they stayed happily removed from the internal politics and troubled heart of the Army of the Potomac.

Yet a question divided them, too, one that haunted the entire

Union, military and civilian alike, and it had the potential to do Lincoln and the Union war effort immeasurably greater harm than the relatively parochial matter of Little Mac. It was the other battle Lincoln had to fight, the domestic issue, the inevitable tug over slavery and freedom. When he ran for the presidency, and immediately after taking office, he said repeatedly that he would not touch slavery where it already existed by sanction of the Constitution. Privately he may have wished to strike a blow for emancipation or even abolition, but politically it was too explosive. Kentucky, Maryland, Missouri, and Delaware were slave states that did not secede. To move against slavery might drive them into the enemy camp. Moreover, however firmly most of the huge Democratic voting bloc in the North stood behind restoring the Union, Democrats were in the main opposed to any tampering with slavery. Democrat and Republican alike, an equally sizable chunk of the electorate stood against any attempt to turn the war from a battle for the Union to a struggle for black freedom. What was true of the people at home, echoed in the sentiments of the armies.

Almost from the first, Lincoln kept tight rein on some of his more enthusiastic generals. Benjamin Butler, headquartered at Fort Monroe in Virginia, refused to return runaway slaves to their Confederate owners in his command in the spring and summer of 1861. Arguing that they were "contraband" of war, since their owners would otherwise use their labor to further enemy defenses, he maintained that they should be declared free. On August 30, 1861, Major General John C. Frémont went much further by decreeing martial law in his Missouri command, and dictated the confiscation of real property of disloyal citizens. Slaves being property in the eyes of the law, he declared them emancipated as a military measure. Logical as it might have seemed to strike at the rebellion by making all objects of enemy ownership subject to seizure, any attempt to tamper with slaves struck at issues and attitudes that ran too deep even in the North for Lincoln to allow Frémont's order to go unrescinded. Eight months later, another general, the president's friend David Hunter, issued a similar proclamation covering his command on coastal Georgia, and again Lincoln revoked the order. Precipitate action such as this could be disastrous, especially prior to the important fall-1862 elections. If Lincoln lost his majority in Congress—a majority that depended for much of its strength on Democrats committed to the war but opposed to emancipation—he could lose the whole game. As time went on, he came more and more to see that emancipation could be used as a military weapon, a threat perhaps to coerce the South into laying down its arms, or, more practically, a crippling drain on the Confederate labor force, by wooing slaves to run to freedom in the North. But it could only be approached safely on those grounds, and not on the higher moral plane of social justice, for that carried with it the explosive notion of black equality, and even the prospect of free blacks' being allowed to take arms and serve in the armies. Making a Negro a soldier was tantamount to saying that he was the equal of a white man, an idea that few in the North enthusiastically embraced and fewer still were willing to fight for, or so it seemed.

Some in the ranks thought from the first they could not dodge the question. When Lincoln issued an order on August 6, 1861, seizing certain kinds of property of enemy citizens, and declaring free any slaves specifically used by the Confederate military in their war effort, one Missouri volunteer heartily approved, and said he would go farther by confiscating slaves generally. "The Government is beginning to take the proper stand in the Slave question," William Dunham of the 36th Ohio argued in November. "I have always said the country would be driven to take this position, the Ruler of the Earth will not allow this to stop till Slavery is blotted from this land." He prophesied that, however reluctant the government might be to address emancipation, there would be no end to the rebellion until it did. "It is the *cause of the war*," he told his wife a month later, "and why not deal with it *practically*." An Illinois soldier expressed outrage when Lincoln rescinded Frémont's emancipation order, and found that others in his regiment "were fierce in their denunciation of the President." By late spring 1862, soldier Wilbur Fisk of the 2nd Vermont suggested that, in failing to strike at slavery, the government asked its soldiers tacitly to fight for its preservation. When Congress did not move quickly enough on confiscation acts seizing slaves from those in rebellion, he even complained that Lincoln's government did more to protect enemy property rights than Jefferson Davis. When Lincoln presented a special message to Congress on March 6 asking it to cooperate with any state that adopted voluntarily a gradual policy of emancipation, and including government compensation to the slaveowner, some of the men and officers around Fairfax Courthouse, Virginia, received it well.[1]

Lincoln advanced slowly and cautiously toward emancipation, wisely allowing himself to appear to be led rather than leading. Following his March 6 confiscation order, he gladly signed an April act abolishing slavery in the District of Columbia, and then appealed again, on May 19, for the slave states of Maryland, Missouri, Kentucky, and Delaware to try some form of gradual compensated emancipation. He confessed to Senator Charles Sumner of Massachusetts that he would issue a general emancipation proclamation on the Fourth of July "if I were not afraid that half the officers would fling down their arms and three more states would rise."[2] Unfortunately, at that stage Lincoln was not yet accurately reading the army—at least the Army of the Potomac—mistaking the attitude of the officer class for that of the rank and file, where the real power lay, and where support, or tolerance, for emancipation was more widespread than he thought. In his July 14 message to Congress, he asked for appropriations to compensate states that abolished slavery on their own, still trying to make emancipation a local issue rather than trample on presumed state rights by imposing a national edict. Three days later, he signed another, much stronger confiscation act, declaring that not just the slaves actively employed by the Confederate military, but those belonging to anyone who supported the rebellion, should be free upon their arrival behind Union lines. It was only a short step from there to an act of full emancipation, at least in the states in uprising.

Still, the soldiers stayed with him in the main. Out in Arkansas one volunteer groused, "When I came into it I thought we were to fight for the Union and the Constitution and Laws," and a New Yorker with McClellan cursed the North and said he wished he had never voted for Lincoln.[3] Yet for every such expression there were ten in support of the act. A western-Virginia loyalist with McClellan asserted in August that, if "the policy of the government changed to the interest of Freemen & Freedom," they would triumph. Many soldiers actually approved of Hunter's emancipation order and felt disappointment at the president's cancellation. "But the President said *No* and *all were* satisfied," said Private James Abraham, "believing that in Abes judgment the thing was *yet* Premature." As soon as Lincoln did decide the time to be right, however, "500,000 Patriots will double quick to enforce his demands." When it came to the acts of the president, he said, "*we of the army* look upon Abe as Thomas Jefferson did Roger Sherman when he said 'The man that never does a foolish thing.'" Another of McClellan's privates from Massachusetts, while still at Harrison's Landing, said it plainly enough for all. "If he says all Slaves are hereafter Forever Free—Amen. And on the other hand if he says not one Slave shall be Freed. Amen."[4]

Lincoln knew that he wanted to issue some form of general proclamation as early as June 1862, but then the problem became one of timing. By August, Northern governors were turning the tables and putting pressure on *him* to move against slavery, in part no doubt to relieve them of the political liability, but also because their reading of public sentiment suggested that it would help rather than harm in filling their volunteer quotas. Then, too, he seems to have come to a better understanding of the sentiment of the men in the ranks, which was vitally important. Wisely, he determined to exclude the loyal slave states from the proclamation, and also any parts of the Confederacy already occupied by Union arms and thus no longer in rebellion. That would make it strictly a *war* measure, and not on the face of it a social one. But he needed something else first: a battlefield victory, and not one out in the West. It must be in the East, where the rival governments lay, where most of the press covered events, and where public attention focused disproportionately. Only the authority of a battlefield triumph there could back his proclamation with the moral authority it needed.

Ironically, McClellan gave it to him at Antietam, equivocal though the victory might have been. Two days later came another win, in the West, at Iuka, Mississippi, and together they were more than enough. On September 22, Lincoln issued a Preliminary Emancipation Proclamation. At the very first, he tried to deflect some criticism by re-emphasizing, "Hereafter, as heretofore, the war will be prosecuted for the object of practically restoring the constitutional relation between the United States, and each of the states." There was not a word about any humanitarian crusade, no moral judgment about slavery. He did reiterate his intention to ask Congress again to take measures to offer financial help to the loyal slave states if they would voluntarily abolish slavery, but then quickly went back to his exigencies-of-war posture when he promised that on the coming January 1 he would issue a final proclamation. At that time he would define those portions of the Confederate states still deemed to be in rebellion, and as of and from that date all slaves kept by whomever and for whatever purpose in those areas would be held to be free, and the military forces of the Union would make all efforts to protect and honor that freedom as soon as the slaves presented themselves to federal authorities.[5]

The document was well conceived, and carefully balanced to suit the moment. The promise that Lincoln would define the areas involved on January 1 gave notice of more than three months, in case— an unlikely event—any portions of the Confederacy should decide to lay down their arms in the interim to protect their property in slaves. More significant, however, the paper lacked any echo of the timeless eloquence that Lincoln seemed to conjure at will in his speeches and other public documents. Rather, of all his public papers, it would be by far the most mundane, legalistic, utterly lacking in emotive force or literary power. The omission can hardly have been accidental. Lincoln knew how closely he was sailing against the wind. That was why he emphasized that the war was for the restoration of the Union. Any suggestion of moral crusade, social justice, equal rights, and the like would only have served to inflame the conservative elements in the country and the army. To calm them further, he also reiterated his often stated wish that means might be found to colonize former slaves elsewhere, in either Africa or the Caribbean, thus suggesting that newly freed blacks might not be around to pose a social threat or economic competition.

Even then, the document stirred up some elements in the army. When Lincoln visited McClellan at Sharpsburg in October, some of the regiments gave noticeably less enthusiastic cheers for him. "His proclamation, issued last month, has caused considerable discontent among the regiments of Maryland, Virginia, Pennsylvania, New York, and the West," said an army surgeon. McClellan's officers, of course, ridiculed the proclamation, evidencing unbridled disgust, and some indulged in more of the "headquarters bluster," suggesting that perhaps the army ought to march on Washington and force the president to recall the order.[6]

Some men of the 1st Minnesota went on a rampage when they heard of the proclamation. They looted an army sutler of $4,000 worth of goods, though they probably merely seized on the event as a pretext for what they felt inclined to do anyhow. A private in the 2nd New Hampshire wrote home to his parents that he was a good Democrat and "don't believe in niggerism"; a man attached to headquarters of the XII Corps freely confessed, "I am very glad not to have the responsibility of voting." Lincoln had forfeited his claim to the respect of the people, he thought. "The more I think of it the more angry I am with the government for placing in such a dilemna good citizens like myself who desire the complete subjugation of the rebels." He compared Lincoln's regime to Robespierre's, and predicted its fall after the proclamation. "The support of the war is a very distinct thing from the support of the President in theory," he concluded.[7]

Yet far, far more of the men in the ranks saw the Emancipation Proclamation more temperately, and in the main they were sophisticated enough to divorce its usefulness as a weapon of war from what-ever disturbing social implications it portended. "Of the results and effects of this Proclamation it is impossible for me to conjecture," an Ohio soldier mused two weeks after the announcement. "There is at present, a great deal of oppisition to it from some men, yet I think the oppisition will be only temporary and only met on Partisan grounds." The 37th Illinois, out in the western theater, rose almost in unison in support of the measure, one man averring, "All acquiesce in it as a mil-itary necessity, and think a policy has now been reached that must soon end the war." Samuel Nichols of the 37th Massachusetts concluded on October 17, "I think all true men of all parties see the necessity and patriotism from which this state paper emanated," even if not all felt ready for it just yet.[8]

A private in another Massachusetts outfit said on October 4, "I am glad more than ever that I enlisted sence I have read the President's Proclamation because I think the fight is freedom or slavery." A volun-teer in the 83rd Pennsylvania echoed the sentiment when he said that the document "meets my views exactly. It is broad and deep, but yet so simple a child can understand it." Undoubtedly it would help win the war, he thought. That was the essential truth that so many soldiers saw while so many like McClellan could not. "Lincoln['s] motto appears to be 'Save the Union. If slavery aids the rebellion it will have to go by the board, but the Union must be preserved,'" concluded Corporal John Strathern of the 8th Pennsylvania. "This is what I call getting at the root of the matter. It is power that they are fighting for, and this is what has given them power in times past. It is slave labor that feeds their Army." An Illinois soldier, having recently despaired of the course of the war, exclaimed one week after the announcement, "My hopes are somewhat revived since Old Abe has come out with his proclama-tion." Now he thought the war might be over in six months. "The curse of slavery has got to go by the board and no mistake," he felt. "Emancipation is becoming popular through out the whole Union every boddy knows that slavery was the cause of this war and slavery stands in the way of putting down this rebellion and now let us put it out of the way."[9]

Two days after issuing the proclamation, Lincoln responded to a ser-enade in its honor, and very carefully redirected any compliment away from himself toward the men in the ranks. His difficulties were many, he confessed, but "scarcely so great as the difficulties of those who, upon the battle field, are endeavoring to purchase with their blood and their lives the future happiness and prosperity of this country." Instead of taking applause for himself, he asked for three cheers for the men and officers of the army, especially those who so recently had turned back the Confederate invasion at Antietam. "Let us never forget them," he pleaded. The unspoken subtext was that support for emancipation was support for the soldiers, a way to bring more of them home, and sooner. No one got that message better than the broad mass of the soldiery itself. "The President's Proclamation," said a Massachusetts boy, "is just the thing." There were increasing signs that the volunteers saw Lincoln as one of their own, as somehow spiritually attached to them. When John Fordyce went off to war in the 138th New York early in 1862, he left behind a son named George Washington Fordyce. John died in uniform this November, but before he did he told his wife that he had concluded that the president was a great man, and asked her to change their son's name to Lincoln. The soldiers even began to make the president's birthplace a point of note. Union soldiers passing through Hodgenville, Kentucky, turned aside to look at the patch where the log house had stood. It had been moved or torn down since 1809, when the infant Lincoln appeared, and now nothing remained to tell its story but a well and a pile of rubbish. Perhaps it was fitting, for with the proclamation Lincoln escaped the bonds of time and place. One day there would be no more vestiges of the centuries-old institutions he was overturning than there were of his place of birth. Lincoln himself said it best, as usual, the eloquence missing from the proclamation returning with full force in his December 1 message to Congress. "Our strife pertains to ourselves—to the passing generations of men," he said, "and it can, without convulsion, be hushed forever with the passing of one generation." He was leaving history behind, and the soldiers made it clear that they were coming with him.[10]

There was still a lot of ground to travel first. The Antietam victory gave Lincoln enough momentum to push the Preliminary Proclamation safely through even before the fall elections, and once he passed the polling without too much damage, he could safely solve the McClellan problem, but the war and the future of emancipation both depended upon the battlefield ultimately. Good as things were in the western theater, he needed a winning general or two in the East as well. Some of the men in the Army of the Potomac seemed hopeful of Burnside. A man of the 40th Massachusetts wrote at the end of November, "They think out here he is smarter than Mac. he is doing the right thing now."[11]

So it seemed, but then, through mischance, lack of cooperation from the War Department, and his own desperation, Burnside all but shattered his army in fruitless attacks when he crossed the Rappahannock River at Fredericksburg in December. And so there was another humiliating defeat, more thousands killed and maimed, the Army of the Potomac no closer to Richmond, and Lincoln no closer to victory. The unknown faces of the slain haunted Lincoln. "Oh, if there is a man out of hell that suffers more than I do, I pity him!" he cried as the casualty reports arrived. "Would that I had one of their places. There is not a man in the army with whom I would not willingly change places to-night." Some wondered if he meant the living or the dead. Dark rumors went through the camps that the president was at the edge of madness in his frustration. "I don't wonder at it," thought Robert Shaw. The renewed wave of criticism was inevitable, and when Lincoln's anguished comment about trading places with a private hit the public press, Shaw found in the army that "perhaps a good many people would rather have him in that position too."[12]

He had to try to put the best face on it, but a disaster, even in Lincoln's prose, still came out a disaster. "Although you were not successful," he said in a congratulatory order to the army, "the courage with which you, in an open field, maintained the contest against an entrenched foe, and the consummate skill with which you crossed and recrossed the river, in face of the enemy, show that you possess all the qualities of a great army." It was his first published congratulatory statement to the army, ironically for a defeat, yet it showed he understood the need to convince the men that the loss was not their fault—as indeed it was not—and also that the criticism of his failure to issue a similar order after Antietam had taught him a lesson.[13]

It was hardly enough to quell discontent, of course. For a brief time some soldiers spoke openly of losing confidence in the president for putting Burnside in charge. There had already been spurious charges that Lincoln told jokes and sang rude songs while passing the graves of the dead at Antietam during his ambulance review, and now, in January 1863, *Harper's Weekly Illustrated Newspaper* ran a bitterly satirical cartoon depicting a mourning Columbia asking Lincoln, "Where are my fifteen thousand sons murdered at Fredericksburg?" It showed him responding by saying, "This reminds me of a little joke." A Massachusetts soldier quite friendly to Lincoln found confusion in the army, and worried even more about what was happening in Washington, as rumors flew of a shake-up in the Cabinet and a struggle for power within the Republican Party. "I should not be at all surprised to see Lincoln kicked out, and a dictator put in command," he speculated glumly.[14]

Lincoln himself spoke of the "awful arithmetic" of war, of how he had the force of numbers on his side if only he could find a general who knew how to use them. The Union could fight another Fredericksburg every day and absorb horrific losses for a week, and still at the end of it would have a strong army, while Lee's Confederates would be reduced to nothing. Of course that was entirely unacceptable; still, it illustrated that the problem lay not with the soldiers but with the commanders, and the men in the ranks agreed. "If we had experienced generals like the rebels, we might crush this unhappy rebellion pretty soon," thought a private in the 55th Ohio, "but somehow we either have traitors to lead us or generals that 'know nothing.'" He found the volunteers in the Army of the Potomac disheartened, but still willing to keep trying. The trouble was, Fredericksburg seriously impaired their confidence in their commander, and an abortive campaign in a sea of mud in January only made it the worse. Burnside must go. But whom to put in his place? One of his generals, Joseph Hooker, began campaigning actively in his own behalf; meanwhile, much of the army high command, loyal to their old companion Little Mac, clamored for his return.[15]

This plea did not want for substantial echoes among the rank and file. "There is but one man that will ever get much fighting out of this army, and that is McClellan," a soldier wrote to his father in February. A man of the 5th United States Cavalry asserted, "I trust the spirit of this army is not wholly crushed and believe that with their *favorite commander* once more at the head . . . the army may yet be saved." Rumors soon swept the camps that Little Mac would be returned to them, else they could never win, because the Confederacy's generals were every bit as good as their own, as one private put it, "except *our* Gen. McClellan who I think is the best man in either army." When the rumor passed from tent to tent, a Michigan soldier told his family, "I was rejoist and so are all the boyes. . . . If it is better to go safe and sure well prepared and calculated with science and disipline then let us have the long head of our little Mac." A Pennsylvania volunteer wrote home after hearing the story, "I wish he would if he dose I will enlist for three years." A man in the commissary department of the XII Corps claimed, "There's not a soldier I know of but what turns toward McClellan as a last hope, the only refuge left where the army and the Union can find succor. I do not exaggerate the strength of this feeling when I say that were he to say the word the army would turn upon Washington itself and not leave a house untouched or a government official unhung." He waited anxiously for the return of his general. "'No one but McClellan' is the watchword," he said, "and will be until he and the army he has created are again joined."16

Burnside's neglect of the welfare and comfort of the army only made it worse. Pay came slowly, hospital conditions worsened deplorably, and hope for improvement dwindled. "Gradually the army is becoming wasted away—depleted and dissatisfied all to please the people who take away from the soldier not only the comfort necessary to life for himself, but the very pay he has earned to feed his wife and little ones at home," complained an admitted McClellan adherent. "The hope that he will be restored to them, the soldiers, alone keeps them in existence as a military organization. . . . The army has ceased to make voluntary sacrifices." Those were the words of a chronic grumbler, and a man also disgruntled at being denied higher rank, but even discounting for his personal viewpoint, the army was in a precarious state. McClellan's appearance in the camps on New Year's Eve 1862 to dine with a few officers and be serenaded only enhanced the desire for his return, and the expectation that Lincoln would have no choice.17

Those reporting the cries for McClellan, and even some of those making them, did not represent entirely the sort of devotion to Little Mac himself that some thought. After all, the army had not seemed *that* sad to see him go in November. But defeat, a setback in the mud in January, and a bitter winter all exacted a heavy toll on morale, allowing the McClellan faction in the officer corps to campaign vigorously for their favorite. Mostly the men in the ranks simply wanted someone who would lead them to victory, restore their confidence in themselves as an army, and end the war the sooner so they could go home. Burnside had shown that he could not do it. Hooker was an aggressive, confident general with some following, inspirationally closer to being another Little Mac than any other major commander, but he had Burnside actively opposed to him. By default, that left the field to those campaigning for McClellan, and for some time after Fredericksburg, Lincoln felt serious pressure applied both from within and without the Army of the Potomac to return to it the one man he least wanted to see in any command.

This could not have come at a worse time. Some elements among the volunteers started to complain about his administration in other areas. Some thought him too soft on the dissenters in the North, the Copperheads, who called for peace without reunion. He should "pray less and guide more," thought an Illinois soldier, "and garnish the halls more with secesh and traitors." Yet others protested just as much about the arbitrary arrests of civilians who too strongly criticized the administration.[18] Worst of all, right in the middle of the mess came January 1, 1863, and the promised final Emancipation Proclamation. What Lincoln had started on the crest of the Antietam wave, now seemed almost a mockery in the face of humiliating defeat. Shortly after the announcement of the final proclamation, a Connecticut soldier accosted his regimental chaplain in winter camp. "Chaplain, do you think President Lincoln had any right to issue that proclamation?" he asked. "I suppose *he* thought he had," replied the cleric. "Well, I suppose a soldier's got a right to hold his own opinions, Chaplain—hasn't he?" "Oh, yes!" replied the other. "If he'll take care and *hold* 'em, and not always be slinging them around carelessly before others."[19]

But the soldiers could not *"hold* 'em." There were those like Robert Shaw who fully approved of the act but decried that it could do no practical good since it only applied to slaves in areas not then under Union control. One soldier referred to the proclamation as "that *Rebel Back Bone Braker* of Old Abe's, one of the harmlessest things Ever written on paper." On top of that, and remembering the brutal 1831 Nat Turner slave revolt in Virginia, some feared that, in encouraging slaves to rise up and escape, it might promote a servile insurrection, which could quickly get out of control and descend into barbarism. The McClellan element in the army jeered. "What is to become of us with such a weak man at the head of the government?" asked Wainwright, "one who tries to be all things to all men, and turns off things of the most vital interest with a joke." A soldier of the Iron Brigade wrote home, "The soldiers dont like the proclamation freeing the damed negroes," and a man in the 7th Wisconsin reported even more outspoken sentiments: "Ask any soldier what he thinks of the war. He will answer, 'I don't like to fight for the damned nigger.' It's nothing but an abolition war, and I wish I was out of it." When escaped "contrabands" passed some of the camps, soldiers sometimes yelled "you black devils" at them, calling them "some more of the Presidents proclamation."[20]

A few soldiers satirized the proclamation viciously. One private complained to his hometown Indiana newspaper, "Old Abe's 'free papers' to all, including Africans and the rest of mankind, also the apes, orangoutangs and monkeys in South America caused me an hour's hearty laugh, two hours tender cry, four hours big with mad, and I am swearing in all the languages known to Americans and Europeans." Another Hoosier lamented, "I think the Union is about played out. I use to think that we were fighting for the union and constitution but we are not. We are fighting to free those colored gentlemen. if I had my way about things I would shoot ever niggar I come across." The strong sentiment, especially among Indiana, Ohio, and Pennsylvania soldiers, even promoted defeatism. "I dont think old Abe and the rest of his niggar lovers can free the slaves because the south has a little to say about that," one remarked. "Old Abe has got to whip the south first and that is a thing he will not do very soon." A New Jersey soldier declared, "The Army of the Potomac is no more an army. . . . Ever since the removal of McClellan and the issuance of the proclamation things have taken a downward course."[21]

It got worse. In the 109th Illinois, 125 men passed a resolution condemning the proclamation; in the 47th Illinois, one private believed that every single man opposed the act except a handful of "crazy Irishmen." A sergeant of the 28th New York wrote an open letter to his hometown newspaper opposing emancipation and discouraging further enlistments. Whereas opposition to the Preliminary Proclamation had been restrained in the bloom of the Antietam victory, now, in the aftermath of Fredericksburg, the open expressions in the camps became more and more intemperate. Privates denounced the act, and their company officers were even more vocal. "The negro question is very repugnant to me," complained a lieutenant in the 133rd New York who would be court-martialed for his offensive language about Lincoln. A captain in the 122nd Ohio went much further, calling Lincoln's a "Black republican abolition administration," and the conflict a "nigger war," asserting that they were under a military despotism, and then circulated in his company antiadministration documents and copies of the notorious Copperhead newspaper, the Columbus, Ohio, *Crisis*. Eventually some officers called for soldiers to lay down their arms in protest.[22]

Courts-martial were inevitable, and the only real way that commanders had of combating the more outspoken malcontents. Shouting "I would sooner vote for Jeff Davis," sent Private Jacob Crook before a court. He, like the sergeant who encouraged men at home not to enlist, was drummed out of the service. Officers found themselves sentenced to dismissal as well. "This is a negro war," complained an Ohio lieutenant. "If I had known, I would never have joined. The Emancipation Proclamation is unconstitutional." He lost his commission, as did the Pennsylvania lieutenant who proclaimed his sympathy for the South and slavery and argued, "I do not feel disposed to immolate myself for the gratification of others." "I wish to resign," said an Illinois lieutenant. "I am dissatisfied with the Emancipation Proclamation." Instead a court discharged him dishonorably, as it did the drunken Pennsylvania lieutenant who said he would sooner shoot Lincoln than Jefferson Davis and hoped that all soldiers would desert. Captain John Gibson of the 114th Illinois may have been the most vituperative of all. "I did not [enlist to] fight for Emancipation or to fight for the god damned negroes," he said. "Old Abe Lincoln is a god damned shit and if I had to choose between him and Jeff Davis, I don't know who I'd vote for. I hope to sink in hell if I ever draw my sword to fight for the negroes."[23]

Inevitably there were desertions, though none could say that their act came solely because of the proclamation, or that the men may not have been disposed to do so anyhow, especially in the morale slump after Fredericksburg. In part they were encouraged by disaffected friends and family at home, who actually wrote to soldiers telling them not to fight for emancipation but to leave the army instead; generally, army morale and attitude on the question felt considerable influence from what was being said at home. Early in March, Sergeant James Stradling met with Lincoln and told him that some soldiers were going absent without leave, blaming it on the proclamation; the president confessed that he expected it would propel a few men into deserting. "I expected many soldiers would desert when the proclamation was issued," he told the sergeant, "and I expected many who care nothing for the colored man would seize upon the proclamation as an excuse for deserting. I did not believe the number of deserters would materially affect the army." Yet he thought that the number of men committed to abolition and emancipation who would be inspired to volunteer as a result of his act would offset those who left. Lincoln asked Stradling to go back to his regiment and tell his fellow soldiers that their president had but two motives. One was justice to several million enslaved people. The other was that emancipation "would be a club in our hands with which he could whack the rebels."[24]

Though the grumbling continued for some time, it dwindled, and Lincoln in the end was proved right: desertions did not damage the army, nor was disaffection because of the proclamation anywhere near so widespread as the general approval, once the soldiers got used to the idea. In the 103rd Illinois, the first word of the final proclamation produced a stir, officers talking of resigning and some of the men of deserting. But by January 22, Private Charles Wills boasted, "We were too strong for the d——d compromising lick-spittles, and to-day you can't hear a whimper against it." Many in the 109th Illinois threw down their arms, but most laid the blame at the feet of their colonel, whom others regarded as a "traitor," and expected a rash of courts-martial to settle the malcontents. The same soldiers of the 1st Minnesota who rioted on first learning of the act, came to accept it as they learned more of Lincoln's intent. The same Hoosier private who initially reacted to the proclamation by saying, "I choked with wrath," and wrote satirically of Lincoln freeing all the simians in creation, soon thereafter calmed and maturely decided, "I have been trying to dispense with politics and do my duty." In the Iron Brigade, which took it badly at first, a few months' time saw opinion evenly divided, and the longer the war went on, the more the soldiers tended to come to Lincoln's way of thinking. Though the higher-ranking officers' discontent lasted longer, the men in the ranks largely agreed with the private from the 55th Ohio who told his diary, "I am no abolitionist—in fact despise the word—yet I can't see any other remedy for our agonized nation, than the removal of the cause." Wisely he concluded, "It is better that slavery perish than that freedom perish."[25]

Helping to persuade them was the example of the considerable majority of volunteers who were with the president from the first. On December 31, 1862, a soldier of the 3rd Wisconsin noted that this was the last day for rebels to lay down their arms or forfeit their slaves. "The theme of reflection now is, with those who even reflect on anything, the President's 'Emancipation Proclamation'. Will he carry it out or will he revoke it?" Some said they thought Lincoln would back away from it at the last minute. "I cannot think so," said this soldier. "I have too much faith in him to think so." Among the Illinois troops out west, where the disaffection ran stronger, a private of the 99th admitted that he did not favor freeing blacks, with all the risks of social upheaval that entailed, but "nether is sutch the intention of old Abe." Lincoln's talk of colonizing the freed slaves mitigated those social fears considerably, and when these men attended a speech by noted abolitionist Owen Lovejoy, one noted that "every mention of old Abes name in connection with his late proclamation drew forth tremendous applause. I think the President has struck the blow in the right time."[26]

Tens of thousands in uniform agreed. "Thank the Lord for this!" said an Ohio private in the West, and a Minnesotan wrote home, "I now feel that we are upon the right road at last." In a Missouri regiment where there had been fears of Lincoln's backing down before January 1, the appearance of the final proclamation met resounding cheers. "You should just have seen the soldiers, and heard their cute sayings," wrote a man of the 21st Missouri, "such as 'Bully for Old Abe and his pet lambs', and 'Hurrah for freedom in Missouri.'" They hailed the action as "the wisest measure of the war," and in February the regiment all but unanimously drafted a resolution approving any actions the president should take to end the war. Neighbors from Iowa felt the same. "If some of those infernal growlers of the North were in the same fix I was in last summer, I think they would soon learn to keep still and let the Emancipation Proclamation alone," a man of the 6th Iowa wrote to his father. "Dad, I will tell you what I want you to do. Stick to the administration."[27]

The soldiers in overwhelming numbers saw emancipation as perhaps their strongest weapon to date. "Not only do I endorse the proclamation," wrote James Abraham, "but endorse every other proposition looking to the overthrow of this Giant and Hell born plot of traitors." A New Hampshire volunteer wrote home on the day the proclamation took effect, "The question of negro slavery is a hard one. Every one has a mind of their own about it." His own mind was that "I believe in putting away any institution if by so doing it will help put down the rebellion, for I hold that nothing should stand in the way of the Union— niggers nor anything else." Soldiers expressed profound relief when January 1 came and Lincoln did not retreat. On January 2, before news of the final proclamation reached him, a Missouri soldier confessed, "I am awaiting with great anxiety to here weather Old Abe sticks up to his sept. proclamation if he shrinks back in the least from that the thing is done and my hopes are gone." He felt no doubt that a powerful weapon lay within their grasp. "If they don't let us fight them in evry way that will tend to weaken them in evry way this war will go on and on."

Not a few soldiers shared outright anger at civilian criticism of the proclamation. "All of that excitement at home is working on the army," wrote an Illinois private in late January, "and even if it requires bayonets, the good of the army demands that the agitation cease." Soldiers saw all of the Copperhead outcry as the real source of desertions, because it encouraged the wavering to abandon their duty. "The soldiers of Illinois and Indiana are boiling over with rage and indignation," one Illinoisian with the western armies grumbled in February. "I freely confess that in times of peace there existed no power to issue a Proclamation to free the slaves." Secession had changed that. "The seceding states have forfeited all right to the protection of their slaves," he felt, and "now the necessity of Emancipation is forced upon us by the inevitable events of the war, and is made constitutional by the acts of the rebels themselves." A Pennsylvania private condemned his home-state press for its abuse of "a measure the greatest on which President Lincoln has put his great foot."[28]

Many private soldiers, regardless of their level of education or intellect, possessed the insight to reduce the issue to the simplest and most fundamental truths. "The proclamation issued by the President is either the best or worst thing which could be done," a New Jersey soldier wrote the day after the Preliminary Proclamation appeared on September 22. Months later, after the final version, most volunteers thought they knew which it was. "I would rather live in peace with the niger than in strife with traitors," said Jacob Behm of the 48th Illinois. "I am sure of one thing. that when Slavery is removed this Rebellion will die out and not before." Emancipation, even when unpopular, posed far the lesser evil facing America. Private A. Caldwell of the 46th Pennsylvania perceived that "this is a contest not between North & South, but a contest between human rights and human liberty on the one side and eternal bondage upon the other," and theirs was a terrible responsibility to posterity. "The down trodden and oppressed of the earth are watching us with fearful anxiety," he said on January 11. "With the fall of the Union the fate of all Republics is sealed. With our success Man's charter will be fully restored." Private Van Willard of Wisconsin made it clear just after Fredericksburg that he knew the choice lay with the people and soldiers of the North. "They hold their destiny under their own controle; the knife that is to sever the sacred bonds of union, if they are to be severed, is in their own hand. Greece and Rome are no more, and if we allow this Union to be dissolved, their fate will be our own." He, like so many others, now saw emancipation as one keen edge of that knife that the soldiers could turn against the foe. On December 31, 1862, just hours before the final proclamation was to be issued, he walked past the White House, thought about Lincoln's determination to follow through with it, and wrote in his diary, "God bless you Abraham!"[29]

"The proclamation has been issued," Lincoln told one of his generals two weeks after the deed. "We were not succeeding—at best, were progressing too slowly—without it." One thing that the soldier response allowed him to do was to bypass the outcry for reinstating McClellan. In desperation, and under heavy pressure, the president considered turning once more to Little Mac, despite his utter lack of confidence in him and the public embarrassment he would suffer after having dismissed the man. Worse, to bring McClellan back would almost make him invincible within the Army of the Potomac, an admission that his support there was greater than Lincoln's. McClellan may have been a bit of a megalomaniac, but he was no traitor, and the talk of a dictatorship never gave him serious temptation. Besides, he already had his eyes on another means to ultimate power in the 1864 elections. But if Lincoln brought him back now, it would be nearly impossible to dismiss him in future. If the outcry at the proclamation had been substantial enough, not at home but in the army at all levels, the president just might have had no choice. As it was, by January 25, 1863, Lincoln gauged the reaction to be sufficiently limited that he did not have to buy the army's loyalty by turning to Little Mac. Instead he gave the command to Hooker, a commander of somewhat lesser conceit than McClellan but of immeasurably greater aggressiveness.[30]

During this terrible winter of 1862–63, Lincoln seemed to leap from risk to risk, and even before he could fully measure the response to the proclamation he took another, when he began to address the efficacy of enlisting black soldiers. This new kind of volunteer was the inevitable concomitant of emancipation. Indeed, it was one that many had feared, and yet others prayed for. Opinion in the ranks divided on the subject along the same lines as attitudes toward emancipation itself, with even those giving the latter only lukewarm support still willing to try enlistment of freed slave men. "Now that the negro is to be free," wrote one Missouri foot soldier, "we want them armed, so that they may fight for freedom." Some, in fact, advocated using black troops as far back as the beginning of the war. Others took the pragmatic view that, the more blacks who served in the army, the fewer whites would be needed, and some of them might even be able to go home. A Michigan soldier noted, "After the emancipation proclamation, the idea that a black man could stop a bullet as well as a white man grew." Another frankly opined, "When Uncle Abraham gets his Niggers armed and in the field he can get along without us." Soldiers in all armies of all times are inveterate complainers, however, and when the volunteers turned to grousing over the issue of Negro soldiers, others discounted much of it simply because the issue was new, a novelty, something to replace their older, worn-out complaints. In early 1862, when the subject arose, some men felt like the soldier of the 103rd Illinois who said he would get out of the army if blacks were armed, and after the proclamation many had not changed their views. "I am by no means an enthusiast over the negro soldiers yet," wrote Charles Wills. "I would rather fight the war out without arming them. Would rather be a private in a regiment of whites than an officer of negroes." Yet the vitally important point, in the end, when it came to this issue, was his decision that "I don't pretent to set up my voice against what our President says or does."[31]

Something Lincoln may not have anticipated actually helped him retain the support of the volunteers through the proclamation controversy, and that was the reaction among the conservative element in the North. The soldiers were already disposed to take an increasingly dim view of the opposition to the war, natural enough since they saw themselves out risking their lives on the front lines while some safe at home sniped at the administration. The renewed outpourings stimulated by the Emancipation Proclamation may well have diverted some of the soldiers' unease over the act by redirecting their ire homeward. "The cowardly rotton hearted pups," one man grumbled. "I hate these northern traitors worse and worse. I would rather this day take up my gun and blow one of their brains out than to kill two of those who like men are in arms against us." Some perceived the intent of the Copperheads and others as being to discourage future enlistments, which meant to a soldier in the field that he might be left without succor to meet the enemy. Hearing that his hometown had voted in a spring election for an outspoken opponent of the administration, Henry Hoyt of the 19th Connecticut fumed. "I had supposed there was more *loyalty* there." He wished he could see the Copperheads in Confederate gray attacking his line, or in Richmond actively helping the enemy government. "They would not do half the harm as now. But instead of that they will stay there *under the protection of the best government ever was, and we down here trying to uphold that government, sacrifising our all & suffering the hardships of a soldiers life.*" It made him so indignant that he concluded, "I believe I *hate* them worse than the *rebels* themselves."[32]

"Confining a lot of these traitors would have an excellent effect on the soldiers," said an Illinois volunteer. "If the President will only suppress the paper [Chicago *Times*] and several others of the same stripe, and hang about 200 prominent copperhead scoundrels in the North, we may then hope that the army will once more be something like its former self." Another commented, "We respect the meanest gray back in the south that has the boldness to come out like men and meet us in open field," but they felt the lowest contempt for the Copperheads. When Lincoln signed a new conscription act on March 3, instituting the first real draft to fill unmet quotas and making all white males of a certain age eligible, the Copperheads screamed, and the soldiers cheered. "All men in the Army believe in the Draft," said a New York captain. "I think that some of them do not believe in much else beside the President and Drafting." A Minnesota soldier responded to the news by saying, "I suppose 'Old Abe' will give it the finishing touch & then, Mr. Copperhead, you can have a chance to fight for your country." In fact, the draft actually began to boost enlistments, since many otherwise reluctant men did not want the stigma of being a draftee. And after the initial shock of the proclamation, enlistment picked up again anyhow. Way out in Arkansas, a Union cavalryman saw that it continued at a fair enough pace, and observed that "the old frontiersman, sitting musingly in his chimney corner, on the slope of a mountain spur, could not see wherein the election of Abraham Lincoln had injured him. The fear of negro equality had never disturbed him." Even among the loyal Southerners that Lincoln hoped to enlist, emancipation seemed not to diminish volunteering, for it continued at the same pace after the proclamation as before. Immediately after the president announced the final edict, the enlistments in the 1st North Carolina Infantry, U.S.A., went up to over five hundred, and recruiters had to start the rolls for a second regiment.[33]

Of course the soldiers still grumbled, and about everything, as was their wont. Yet, through a season of heavy challenges to a host of ideas and ideals, from individual and state rights to the love of McClellan and the dislike or fear of freed blacks, the soldiers remained firm. Some felt their confidence in the president shaken thanks to all the challenges he had presented to them. "If people expect me to come home less a Republican than I went out they will be disappointed," Private Jonas Elliott of Ohio wrote to his wife in early March. "I may not then support Abraham Lincoln as ardently as I did but Republicanism does not consist in the support of Abraham Lincoln." Their greatest discontent remained what it had always been, that they were not beating the enemy. "We enlisted to fight," one complained in late January, "but the[y] keep us blacking our boots and brushing our close." He wanted to fight. A few days later, a Pennsylvania soldier who had stayed loyal to Lincoln through it all told his mother that his enlistment was about to expire but he would not be coming home. Though he did not like soldiering or the war, he was determined to see it through. "I have made up my mind that a country that is worth living in in time of peace is worth fighting for in time of war so I am yet willing to put up with the hardships of a soldiers life."[34]

5

THE FRIEND OF FRIENDS

And Abraham gave all that he had
unto Isaac.
[Genesis 25:5]

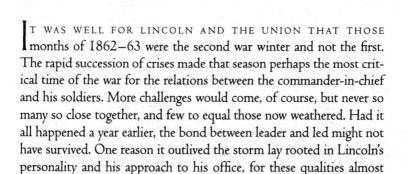

IT WAS WELL FOR LINCOLN AND THE UNION THAT THOSE months of 1862–63 were the second war winter and not the first. The rapid succession of crises made that season perhaps the most critical time of the war for the relations between the commander-in-chief and his soldiers. More challenges would come, of course, but never so many so close together, and few to equal those now weathered. Had it all happened a year earlier, the bond between leader and led might not have survived. One reason it outlived the storm lay rooted in Lincoln's personality and his approach to his office, for these qualities almost perfectly suited the character of the America of his time.

There was never a more accessible president. In those very first reviews in 1861, Lincoln told the soldiers that, if they ever had a problem, ever felt themselves ill-used, they might look to him *personally* for remedy. It may have seemed a statement to be taken symbolically rather than literally, but the common folk of that era were a literal people.

When Lincoln told them to bring their problems to him, he no doubt meant exactly what he said, and the volunteers took him at his word. As a result, after eighteen months of war, when the internal crises began erupting, Lincoln's personal involvement with the soldiers had amassed such a store of personal good will with the volunteers that it repaid his time and effort with their forbearance and patience.

The entreaties came to him from every direction cast in every mold, but most of them were simple, unaffected, and earnest. "I sit down to write to you (a Soldiers Friend!)," a Pennsylvania private began. "I am but a poor farmer Boy. I have lost my health in this Nobel Cause of ours." His mother was a widow, he needed to be at home to support her, and he was too ill to serve longer. "My kind Friend of Friends you have the power to help me a grate deal," he went on. "I did not no [w]ho to turn to fore Redress and some of my friends told me to write to the President that there I would get my right." It was a refrain he heard time and time again. "I have a grate Confidence in our Good President hoe has dun a grate deal fore us poor Soldiers."[1]

Indeed he had. Sick men wrote to him or appeared personally at the White House appealing for furloughs home, and he granted them. If he did not see a soldier in person, the president often ordered a medical examination to see if a discharge for disability was in order. He sent scores of men to hospitals, and occasionally did not wait for the results but relied on his own eyes to tell him a man was no longer fit for duty. Many cases came to him from sick men complaining that their surgeons and regimental hospitals ill-treated them, and in those he demanded speedy action. A soldier suffering from typhoid brought his mistreatment to Lincoln's attention, and the president immediately ordered, "If this boy is sick in this case he must be dealt with as other sick men are dealt with by the rules." Soldiers of unusual youth especially attracted his concern, for quite a number of boys under the lawful age managed to enlist, and some suffered terribly in battle. Even cases of presumed insanity came to his desk. At every appeal, if he did not intervene personally, he referred the matter to the appropriate office of the War Department, and usually with the injunction that he be informed of the result. Rheumatism, typhoid, scurvy all passed across his desk thanks to soldiers who felt the president would take an interest in their cases, and each got its few moments of his attention.[2]

Then there were the pleas from parents, fathers and widowed mothers alike, especially for minor sons who had enlisted without consent. To all Lincoln responded by checking on the validity of the claim; and if it was true, he ordered the release of the boy as long as any bounty money given him was repaid. "Of course I can not discharge a soldier merely because a mother asks it," he reminded some, however. "There would soon be no army." But every appeal got its hearing. It helped if the minors were sons of old friends or political associates, for Lincoln was no more above a little cronyism or doing favors for special friends than any other president. Occasionally he almost chided the patriotic lads who could not wait for legal age and defied parental wishes to enlist. "The United States don't need the services of boys who disobey their parents," he told Welles in discharging two underage fellows.[3]

In fact, some parents asked the president to act as a surrogate in handing down fatherly or avuncular advice to their troubled young sons, and when he could Lincoln obliged. It was not hard for him to remember, after February 1862 and the death of Willie, that he had already lost two sons of his own, whom he would never see as teenagers. Of his other sons, Thomas—"Tad"—was yet too young for this kind of advice, and the eldest, Robert Todd, was away at college; when they were together, they had little to say. Thus these sons of other parents helped fill a need in Lincoln. He was only fifty-three in the summer of 1862, when Ann Campbell—a cousin of Mary Lincoln's—appealed to him to persuade her son not to give up his appointment as a cadet at West Point because he felt unhappy there. Yet Lincoln spoke of himself constantly as an "old man." Robert was the age of most of the volunteers in the army, so, even if he could not act very fatherly to his own grown son, he could see himself as a father *figure* to the men at large. Perhaps that is why he so often spoke of them not as his soldiers but as "my boys." Even while gripped by anxiety over the fate of the Army of the Potomac, then locked in mortal combat on the Peninsula, Lincoln found a few moments to be fatherly to young Quintin Campbell:

> Your good mother tells me you are feeling very badly in your new situation. Allow me to assure you it is a perfect certainty that you will, very soon, feel better—quite happy—if you only stick to the resolution you have taken to procure a military education. I am older than you, have felt badly myself, and *know*, what I tell you is true. Adhere to your purpose and you will soon feel as well as you ever did. On the contrary, if you falter, and give up, you will lose the power of keeping any resolution, and will regret it all your life. Take the advice of a friend, who, though he never saw you, deeply sympathizes with you, and stick to your purpose.[4]

The boy stayed, and graduated in 1866. For all Lincoln knew when he wrote, he might well have to call on the young man one day to meet the enemy.

Hard to refuse were the appeals that came from widowed mothers, pleading that they depended on a son in the army for their livelihood. "Discharge this boy," or "Let this woman have her boy," Lincoln wrote time after time on such appeals, frequently overruling Stanton. Harder still to resist were the pleas that came from women whose husbands had been killed in the war, and who may have lost one or two sons as well, now begging for a last one to be sent home to them. "Let it be done," the president would order. Indeed, by 1863, something of a myth had already grown up about widowed mothers' requests and how the president responded to them; in the later years of the war, it is quite probable that some of the widows' pleas were from women whose husbands were very much alive. Fathers, too, appealed to Lincoln, but the basis changed subtly. To get an underage son out of the army, the father might have to hire a substitute instead. One man had paid for two substitutes for himself and had three other sons eligible for the draft, and a fourth a prisoner of war, and when he called in person to ask that his only married son be discharged to return to his family, Lincoln could not deny him. "Let it be done," he said, and so it was.[5]

The president also made efforts to procure something to assuage the grief of those left behind after a soldier's death. The widow of a soldier killed in late 1863 appealed to him, "I haint got no pay as was cummin toe him and none of his bounty munney." She asked Lincoln to help her find a job in Washington, adding, "I no yu du what is rite and yu will see to me a pore widder wumman." And so he did. To one widow he gave an appointment as postmaster; for another, whom he called "the best woman I ever knew," he strained a point to give her only surviving son a commission as a lieutenant in the 3rd United States Infantry after he had already served a year in the volunteers.[6] The suspicion is inevitable that sometimes Lincoln was taken advantage of, especially by those able to see him personally and plead their cases face to face. Yet he may not have been entirely credulous, either. It made him feel good to do kindnesses for people, a tiny moment of relief amid the seemingly endless burden and gloom of the war. He may well have chosen to err on the side of generosity now and then simply because it relieved him, and he needed that.

When Lincoln visited the forts and camps ringing Washington, he had no choice but to go through an inspection and review whether he wished it or not, but his real interest often lay in other areas. He looked at the soldiers' quarters, their hospitals, ate their food. At one fort he told the colonel of a new Regiment, "You seem to have a fine body of well-drilled soldiers, so far as I understand it, but I am especially pleased to see that they are well taken care of."[7] When soldiers brought their complaints of scarcity of supplies directly to him, he took action, for he never forgot those days in the Black Hawk War when his government had not fed him well enough. Late in 1863, when a Federal garrison found itself besieged in Knoxville, Tennessee, the scarce rations severely damaged morale. "The spirit of the troops declined with the rations," wrote an Ohio soldier hungry as the rest, "and curses were lavished by many hungry wretches upon generals, president, government, rebels, selfs, etc." Lincoln knew what hunger did to a soldier's patriotism, and could not afford to let bureaucratic inefficiency starve his volunteers. Most of them seemed to understand that if rations were delayed it was not his fault. *"The government isn't to blame, neither is our worthy chief, 'Abraham' (although misled, ignorant soldiers swear at 'Abe' for it),"* said one man in the ranks in the fall of 1862. When soldiers saw officers eating well while the enlisted ranks went hungry, they knew where to place the blame: *"It is all owing to miserable, petty officers."*[8]

Lincoln's interest in the weapons of war was well publicized, especially his occasional trials at marksmanship with a new version of rifle or carbine. Yet he also turned his attention to more mundane items that could make the volunteer's life less uncomfortable. When a woman already known to him for her tireless ministrations to soldiers came to him with an invention to protect the men's ears, he recommended it to the quartermaster general: "I certainly would prefer having it over my ears in cold weather." Naturally he took an even greater interest in the infantryman's most vital asset, his feet. With men expected to march hundreds of miles in campaigns, sore or worn feet were as good as an enemy bullet in putting a man out of action. Lincoln submitted his own feet to an operation by chiropodist Dr. Isachar Zacharie, and was so pleased with the result that he recommended the doctor to generals in the field for treatment of corns, bunions, and other problems in their men, even though some officers felt considerable intolerance toward the doctor, "the lowest and vulgarest of Jew Pedlars," and declared, "It is enough to condemn Mr. Lincoln that he can make a friend of such an odious creature." Lincoln gave a fair hearing to the manufacturer who promised he could deliver a million pairs of "military sandals" to prevent and cure sore feet, referring him to the surgeon general, and even took an interest in soldier stockings. He wore one pair of "Sandal Socks" given him by a manufacturer and recommended them to military authorities, and when he learned of an eighty-four-year-old woman who had herself knitted three hundred pairs of socks to give to soldiers, he took the time to offer her his personal thanks.[9]

The president's interest in the *things* of a soldier's life was sincere and directed toward improving his condition, but in the main he left that to the appropriate offices in the War Department. His personal interventions were not many, in the main limited to suggestions and what some officers no doubt thought meddling, and perhaps chiefly intended to give the impression that he was aware of their work, the hope being that they would do their jobs better knowing that he was in fact watching. Yet in one area he did actively interfere more than in any other, and that was army pay. He knew from his Black Hawk days that pay was a powerful inducement to the out-of-work to enlist, and vitally important to a man or family with no other source of income. A private soldier's $13 a month was not a lot, but it could support a poor family, and when it came late, or not at all, it worked an unacceptable hardship.

From the beginning of the war to the very last, he remained especially sensitive to pay issues. Appropriations did not meet demands, and the supply of hard specie and government scrip constantly lagged behind. Repeatedly soldiers experiencing pay shortages brought them directly to his attention. In January 1863, the problems were such that Lincoln signed a congressional joint resolution providing an immediate issue of pay to the army and the navy, allowing the Treasury to print up to $100 million in new notes if necessary. He did it, he said, to "give every possible facility" for the "prompt discharge of all arrears in pay due to our soldiers and our sailors." At the news of the special bill, soldiers like the men of the 4th Iowa at Tuscumbia, Alabama, now two months behind in their pay, were greatly encouraged. "We are daily looking for Mr. Lincoln's paymasters," one soldier wrote in February. "When they do come they will make many a poor soldier's face glow with purer patriotism."[10]

At the same time, there were many men and officers, and sometimes whole regiments, that for reasons of irregularities in enlistment were not formally mustered into the volunteer service. They did full duty, fought and died, yet could not be paid on technicality. In every case brought to him, Lincoln insisted on a quick resolution. "I have said a great many times," he argued, "that all whose service we receive, should be paid." Consistently he struck a distinction in qualifications for pay between being mustered into service and actually having served, and came down in behalf of the latter. "It is happening in many cases that persons do military service for the government without having entered regularly, and gotten upon the pay-rolls," he observed. "But the service we actually receive we should pay for." A case arose with an entire regiment, Colonel Hiram Berdan's celebrated sharpshooters, whom he raised privately, without authorization by state or federal government. As a result, they served through more than a year's service, including hard action and many casualties, yet still were unpaid even after Antietam, until Lincoln gave Stanton orders to consult with the proper authorities and disregard regulations if need be, in order to get them paid and properly organized on the payrolls so there would be no further injustice in the future.[11]

The soldiers may not have known much firsthand of their president's efforts in their behalf behind the scenes, but there were other, much more visible evidences of his concern that they could not miss, and that once seen were quickly passed through the ranks by word of mouth, where even embellishment and exaggeration worked in favor of their regard for him. Lincoln often visited the sick and wounded in the military hospitals, chiefly those in and around Washington, but also those in the field when he came to the army. His wife, Mary, raised $1,000 herself for relief of the convalescent, and Lincoln personally spent part of it buying lemons and oranges for the hospitals. Unannounced, he might simply appear in a ward to talk with the men in their cots. "I can't stay, boys," he said in one hospital where he rapidly went from ward to ward. "I hope you are all comfortable and getting along nicely here." When time allowed, he went to each bed, shaking hands with every soldier in turn. What he saw often left him shocked and horrified. His friend and companion Lamon sometimes saw the president disturbed "almost beyond his capacity to control either his judgment or his feelings." On visiting a hospital with the Army of the Potomac in the field, Lincoln saw a desperately wounded man who had lost his leg, an all-too-common sight. The president gently kissed him on the cheek, spoke with him a few moments, and asked to see the actual wound; when he did he could only say, "You must live! You must!" On those rare occasions when he actually knew the wounded, or the family back home, he became even more emotional. Informed by Lamon that two sons of a widow Lincoln had known in Illinois were both wounded, perhaps mortally, the president almost broke down. "Here, now, are these dear, brave boys killed in this cursed war!" he exclaimed. "My God, my God! It is too bad!" Most common of all, however, were the tears when the president passed through the wards. An officer's wife spoke of seeing the "tall gaunt figure of Abraham Lincoln . . . his moistened eyes even more eloquent than the lips, which had a kindly word of cheer for every sufferer."[12]

Lincoln gave at least a tacit blessing to almost any enterprise that promised to offer some aid or comfort to soldiers, both those in the hospitals and those in the field. Repeatedly he offered his written and spoken thanks to the legion of women who turned out to feed regiments as they passed through a city, often at special establishments like Philadelphia's Union Volunteer Refreshment Saloon and the Cooper Shop. There any soldier passing through could find a meal, and the president endorsed them, "as I have frequently heard, and believe, they are indeed worthy of all praise." Civic groups throughout the North held Soldiers' Fairs at which anything and everything was sold to raise money to send to the hospitals, or to buy both necessities and treats for the men in the field. Often invited to attend, the president rarely did prior to 1864, yet his protestations of desire to aid in their good cause were sincere enough. Moreover, they became well publicized, and when he actually did appear, as at the Union League Club in Philadelphia in June 1864, anything he said spread through the whole Union in the press, and reached the soldiers in their camps. "I have been more than delighted in witnessing the extraordinary efforts of your patriotic men and lovely ladies in behalf of the suffering soldiers and sailors of our country," he said. Indeed, he made a point of repeatedly complimenting the volunteer work of the women, "good mothers, wives, sisters, and daughters," who did "all you and they can, to relieve and comfort the gallant soldiers." He seemed to understand that he needed to help sustain their morale as well as the soldiers', and missed no opportunity to recognize that the great services "they have rendered to the defenders of our country in this perilous time" were such as "can never be estimated as they ought to be."[13]

Interestingly enough, in the early days of the war Lincoln seemed more interested in individual volunteer work for soldier welfare than in organizations created for the purpose, though this may have been as much a result of the opposition of the well-entrenched military hierarchy in the several bureaux of the War Department. During his first months in office, Lincoln rarely challenged an old bureaucracy that regarded civilian organizations, and most attempts to effect change, as little more than well-intentioned meddling.

No more than a few weeks after the very first volunteers reached Washington in April, some in the Union realized that these men would need more care than the government could—or would—provide. For the first time in their lives, these volunteers were away from home. They were going to get childhood diseases to which they had never been exposed. They would be homesick. Few had ever cooked a meal, yet the military provided neither trained cooks nor even manuals on how to prepare food, leaving the soldiers to their own often dreadful devices. Army rations might not be bad in garrison and around Washington, but in the field and on the march the nourishment of a soldier's diet could be greatly reduced, and that was before he cooked whatever he had in a ubiquitous sea of grease. The United States military forces went suddenly from barely sixteen thousand Regulars to more than seventy-five thousand after Lincoln's first call, and then even higher with each subsequent call, so that by the end of 1861 more than five hundred thousand stood under arms. Yet at the commencement of the war the army had less than a dozen thermometers, and the octogenarian Surgeon General Thomas Lawson declined to buy medical texts because he thought the expense unwarranted. Clement Finley, who replaced him in May 1861, proved no more progressive in his thinking. Recognizing this woeful unpreparedness in the face of an unprecedented demand, citizens began to look for means to care for their own in uniform.[14]

The most effective and influential of all would be the United States Sanitary Commission. It grew out of the Women's Central Association of Relief, started in New York in April 1861 and headed, despite its name, by a man, Dr. Henry Bellows. The association sought to improve the hygienic conditions in camp and the diet, and promote effective care in the hospitals, as well as sponsoring soldiers' "homes" for the long-term disabled and relief "saloons" for traveling volunteers. Unspoken in its aims, but implicit, was its desire to act as a watchdog on War Department care of the soldiers, especially once Washington's unpreparedness for managing a huge army became evident. The military establishment from the outset resented such efforts, and when Bellows and his supporters first broached the subject of a nationwide organization to promote these ends, Lincoln probably reflected War Department prejudices more than his own in reportedly likening the idea to a "fifth wheel to the coach."[15]

Nevertheless, even though the president's initial reaction may have seemed restrained, he gave his full approval in the end, when Bellows and others formed the Sanitary Commission. On June 9, Lincoln signed the order establishing the commission, authorizing them— without government compensation—to act in an advisory capacity to the government on matters of sanitation, "to the means of preserving and restoring the health, and of securing the general comfort and efficiency of the troops; to the proper provision of cooks, nurses, and hospitals." Some thought that his involvement with the commission thereafter was "shadowy," and even that Lincoln only tolerated voluntary humanitarian organizations in general thanks to the pressure of public opinion, but they were surely in error.[16]

Within three months of its formation, the Sanitary Commission won Lincoln's compliments for its "work of great humanity, and of direct practical value to the nation, in this time of trial." He advised General-in-Chief Scott on September 30, 1861, that the nation owed the commission gratitude and confidence, and personally endorsed its efforts by adding, "There is no agency through which voluntary offerings of patriotism can be more effectively made."[17]

Saying, in essence, that the commission should take precedence over the several other volunteer relief agencies then in operation hardly constituted lukewarm support. But then Lincoln allowed Bellows and his followers to make an even greater intrusion into government business. In December, he met with Bellows, McClellan, and others, for half an hour or more, to discuss the inefficient and antiquated management of the medical department under the all-but-fossilized surgeon general. Already Finley and his functionaries had dismissed Bellows and others as nuisance do-gooders when they offered their services and their privately raised funds for soldier relief, and so they called on Lincoln as a last resort. Stories later emerged that, after hearing their complaints, Lincoln sent for Finley and asked him why the military would turn down such philanthropy, and the old man had nothing to reply. Such a scenario is certainly possible, but it is just as likely that less confrontational means persuaded Lincoln to exert the sort of influence he used with Scott, to encourage McClellan and others to foster the Sanitary Commission's efforts.[18]

Certainly Lincoln could quickly learn for himself that Finley was past being effective at his post, and that the medical bureau in general was woefully inadequate for the demands being made upon it. McClellan would certainly have alerted him to this from an early date, and probably Scott before him. If not, the denunciations of Bellows and his assistants Dorothea Dix and Frederick Law Olmsted came loud enough that no one could ignore them. Olmsted called Finley "a self-satisfied, supercilious, bigoted blockhead . . . the oldest of the old mess-room doctors." Bellows told Lincoln that he believed nine of ten soldier deaths in 1861 could have been prevented simply by better sanitation; though somewhat hyperbolic, he was largely correct. Between investigation, and the insistent complaints of the commission, the War Department finally gave way and replaced him with the much younger Surgeon General William Hammond, who immediately began reforming the department under the Act to Reorganize and Increase the Efficiency of the Medical Department of the Army, signed by Lincoln on April 16, 1862. For the first time in American history, it provided for the appointment of the surgeon general and his assistants on the basis of merit instead of seniority, and brought in train some rather sweeping reforms in hospital administration, patient handling, and inspection and monitoring of performance.[19]

The Sanitary Commission made enemies in pressing so hard for Finley's ouster and the institution of reform, especially Secretary of War Stanton, who resented their interference; apparently he never forgave Hammond for being their favorite candidate for replacement. The thirty-four-year-old Hammond's own management style did not help him in the days ahead, and despite the manifold improvements he achieved in treatment of the wounded and sick, he lasted only until August 1864, when he was court-martialed and dismissed on largely erroneous charges. Lincoln distanced himself from the Hammond trial, presumably because by then the War Department was so well organized in all its departments, and Stanton so firmly in control, that the loss of Hammond would not impair the continuing progress of medicine for the soldiers.[20]

For a man who supposedly felt an uncertain interest in the affairs of the Sanitary Commission, Lincoln certainly gave their leaders and staff plenty of access to himself. He met several times with Bellows, and listened patiently to member Cordelia Harvey, who insistently told him that sick and wounded soldiers on the lower Mississippi suffered from the climate and its fevers and should be brought north. He objected to that on the basis that many of them would probably desert if moved closer to their homes, though why he should think that, he—or she— did not say. If her 1865 account of their conversations is to be believed, she and Lincoln met on several successive days to wrestle with the question, until he suggested in frustration that he should just discharge them. To that she protested that the men were loyal and would not desert, and promised him he would be glad if he let her have her way. Finally he agreed, she said, but added sadly that, thanks to the oppressive burden of the war, "I shall never be glad any more."[21]

By 1864, with increasingly unprecedented numbers of men in the armies, and concomitantly staggering numbers in the hospitals, the commission began to emulate other relief organizations by organizing a series of Sanitary Fairs in the major cities of the North, to raise funds for soldier welfare. They invited Lincoln to every one of them, from New York to Missouri, yet most he had to decline. He made the trip to Baltimore on April 18, however, offering compliments to the "fair women" who constituted the backbone of the organization. Unable to attend the St. Louis fair in May, he sent an open letter urging on their work, saying, "Our soldiers are doing well, and must, and will be well done by." After first turning down the invitation to the Philadelphia fair in June, Lincoln changed his mind and went after all, to compliment the organizers on what they were doing for the soldiers. In all of his public statements to Sanitary Commission volunteers, he reminded them—and, through press coverage, the nation—that, "say what you will, after all the most is due to the soldier, who takes his life in his hands and goes to fight the battles of country." Having said that, however, he gave unrestrained praise and thanks for "what is contributed to his comfort when he passes to and fro, and in what is contributed to him when he is sick and wounded, in whatever shape it comes." On the same visit, he made a brief address at the Union League Club, stating as his purpose, "I came among you thinking that my presence might do some good towards swelling the contributions of the great Fair in aid of the Sanitary Commission, who intend it for the soldiers in the field."[22]

The president freely gave something else of real tangible value in the efforts of the commission and some other relief groups. Time and again he donated personal letters and autographs, and important public documents, to be auctioned to raise money at the fairs. In October 1863, he gave the original draft of the Emancipation Proclamation, even though it meant enough to him that he had planned on keeping it himself. "I had some desire to retain the paper," he said, "but if it shall contribute to the relief or comfort of the soldiers that will be better." It brought $3,000 that went to the Chicago Soldiers' Home, and then was reproduced in thousands of lithographs that produced substantially more in ensuing years. As a result, Lincoln received a gold watch from the fair, the premium for the donor whose gift raised the largest sum. He contributed a letter to go into a bound volume of distinguished holographs, and repeatedly gave his autograph. "Though much pressed for time," he told one applicant, "some portion spent in efforts to relieve and comfort our brave soldiers can not but be well spent." His autograph could raise $100 or more for "our gallant and suffering soldiers," and he happily turned over gifts given to him to the commission that they might be auctioned instead.[23]

Lincoln understood that what he could do best for relief organizations was to lend the weight of his executive prestige, and in the public forum of open letters in the press and the occasional speech. To do anything more would be inappropriate in a president, especially given the sometimes zealous rivalry between relief agencies. Executive decorum—not to mention the pressure of official duties—did not allow him wisely to take a more active role, and prudence suggested that if he did so for one he must do it for all, or else be drawn himself into their bickering and in-fighting. Given the nongovernmental nature of such organizations, Lincoln did as much as an official could by public endorsement and encouragement, and the contribution of some of his time, as circumstances allowed. With no official capacity, and with no mandated oversight, there was little more that he could do. Besides, the Sanitary Commission especially made itself such a nuisance to the War Department—in a good and needed cause—that it forced the president sometimes to take sides between it and an arm of his own administration. If anything, it is surprising that he did not distance himself farther from this group of well-intentioned people who sometimes put him in an embarrassing position. That he did not suggests that he genuinely appreciated their work and the good they did, because they shared his overriding concern for the welfare of the Union volunteer.[24]

The president gave the same kind of assistance, though on a lesser scale, to other worthy causes for soldier benefit. When Boston presented him with a huge ox named General Grant late in 1864, he turned it over to a Sailors' Fair the next day, where it raised $3,200, and when the Metropolitan Fair in New York was held in early 1864, one of the items for auction was a handwritten copy of the address he had given at Gettysburg, Pennsylvania, just a few months before, and which, he said, "you are at liberty to use for the benefit of our soldiers."[25]

Lincoln actually intervened personally in hospital matters outside the Sanitary Commission far more than within it, presumably because he could do so as chief executive. Barely had the war started when he met with an army surgeon, prior to Bull Run. "You are getting up a hospital for those who may fall sick or be wounded in the defense of the Union," he said. "I want to aid you in your preparations for taking care of the poor fellows who will need all that we can do for them. When you need anything don't let there be any red tape. Come to me at once without hesitation, and you shall have anything you want if I can get it for you." This was in spirit the same thing he told the young volunteers, and it is apparent that he meant it.[26] In June 1862, when army doctors in the Peninsular Campaign asked to take over the extensive shaded grounds of a home belonging to the wife of General Robert E. Lee at White House Landing on the Pamunkey River, thinking it the healthiest spot for the sick and wounded to recuperate, Little Mac at first overruled them. He was protecting it under guard because, so he believed, the property had once belonged to George Washington, and it would look amiss for Union troops to occupy such a place forcibly. When the surgeons brought their plea to Lincoln, however, the president was under the misapprehension that Little Mac had actually made a promise to Mrs. Lee to protect the property. A doctor complained to him, asking, "Are our brave soldiers to die off like rotten sheep there because General McClellan chooses to protect the grounds of a rebel?" The president may have taken a secret bit of glee in overruling Little Mac. "McClellan has made this promise, but I think it is wrong," he told the physician. "He does not want to break the promise he has made, and *I will break it for him.* . . . This business must be settled now, done up at once!"[27]

Lincoln also frequently intervened to facilitate the work of army nurses, chiefly women, who were a new feature in the wards. In March 1862, he introduced Dorothea Dix to the director of the military hospital at Winchester, Virginia, and thereafter occasionally dealt with the crusty humanitarian who, in time, would become superintendent of all female nurses in the Union. She could be hard on her staff, especially if they were too attractive or too friendly with the patients, and Lincoln actually helped get one of her disgruntled nurses reassigned. Sometimes ladies presented themselves, either in person or by letter, wanting to offer their services to go south and minister to the soldiers, and he helped them with passes and transportation, as he did the lady who had a special system for Diet Kitchens for soldier hospitals. When the Sisters of Mercy appealed to him for help in establishing military hospitals in Washington and Chicago, he ordered that they be given every requirement. And to anyone who contributed to the welfare of the sick, like the citizens of five Massachusetts communities who bought and donated a considerable store of hospital goods, he offered his thanks and "my grateful appreciation of their efforts for the health and comfort of those brave men, to whom we are all so deeply indebted."[28]

There was a special category of soldier for whom the president felt an extra concern, and yet for whom he could perhaps do the least, because, for once, the higher dictates of military policy tied his hands. To any discerning eye, the aftermath of the first battle along Bull Run revealed that neither side was prepared to deal with the issue of prisoners of war. The Confederates had no prisons in operation at the start of the war, and thereafter struggled to provide facilities that would keep pace with the burgeoning population of captured Union soldiers. Lincoln showed a concern for prisoners immediately after Bull Run. "I don't like to think of our men suffering in the southern prisons," he said. "Neither do I like to think that the southern men are suffering in our prisons." Yet at first he saw an exchange cartel as a form of recognition of the existence of the Confederacy, something he studiously guarded against. To treat with them formally over prisoners might be interpreted as according them status as belligerents, rather than insurrectionists, and that could have serious diplomatic repercussions.[29]

Nevertheless, authorities found a way around that obstacle. Prison populations gradually swelled until July 1862, when the antagonists agreed on a policy calling for the exchange of prisoners of war. The system carried with it numerous inconsistencies and pitfalls, but in the main it worked to keep soldiers on either side from staying an inordinate amount of time in a prison camp before being returned home. The problem by early 1864, however, was that the number of releases got out of balance. In April, Union authorities halted it, because the Confederates were not freeing as many prisoners as the Union, and also because the South refused to treat on an equal basis the captured black soldiers who were serving by then. The result was a sudden and dramatic swelling of the prison camps on both sides, but in the South, where so much was in shortage, the captured men were bound to suffer more.

By the summer of 1864, the stories of hunger and suffering coming out of the Confederacy inflamed and outraged the North, and many gave in to the misconception that the ill-treatment was intentional.

"Would to God this dinner or provisions like it were with our poor prisoners in Andersonville," the president lamented after a meal that summer, as stories of thousands dying from malnutrition and disease captured headlines. He tried to find some rational reason for what appeared to be intentional cruelty. Confederates were still Americans, people of the same race as those in the Union, and he found it hard to believe they could inflict such suffering purposefully. Indeed they did not, though generations would pass before the myth of Confederate cruelty was laid to rest.[30]

Men released or escaped from the prison camps often met with the president; particularly after the collapse of the exchange system, Lincoln found their stories of life in the camps intolerable. He heard how the prisoners were depressed, thinking themselves abandoned by their government. Many said it especially rankled them when the subject of black soldiers helped lead to the breakdown of the cartel. "The Everlasting *Nigger* must be protected and the soldier may take care of himself," grumbled an inmate in Camp Sumter, at Andersonville, Georgia. Whereas soldiers aggrieved over other issues, like the dismissal of McClellan, seemed content to blame others in the administration, prisoners of war—perhaps coached by Confederate authorities—held the president to account. "We must stay here because they can't agree on some nigger question," said a Vermont sergeant at Andersonville. "Father Abraham I wish you had my ration of wood to boil coffee for your family," said another. "I think you would soon bring on an exchange."

When the death rate reached 125 in a single day, a bitter soldier wrote in his diary, "What do you think of that, father Abraham? Could you enlist that many in a day?" As the 1864 election approached in the North, one prisoner grumbled, "If the government don't get us out they may go to the Devil with Abraham Lincoln. I will not vote for him again." When he met with the prisoners, Lincoln sometimes tried to deflect the conversation from the horrors—perhaps because hard but necessary policy forced him to leave thousands to suffer, for the benefit of hundreds of thousands. In 1864, he spoke with one of a number of men who successfully tunneled out of a prison in Richmond and made their way through the lines to safety. "I congratulate you on your escape," said the president, and then with a twinkle added, "What did you do with the dirt?" But he could not escape the realities of the situation. After talking with one man not long out of the prison at Salisbury, North Carolina, Lincoln exclaimed,

"This is terrible," and urged Stanton to liberalize the exchange policy in order to get at least some more men out. The secretary of war pointed out that the Union would be exchanging healthy Confederate prisoners for sometimes skeletal Yankees—a poor trade, since the fit Southerners would go right back into their armies. Supposedly Lincoln remained adamant and insisted, "The boys are coming home," but in fact he left the matter to Stanton, who had the stomach to maintain a necessary policy. Not until January 1865 did the exchange system begin to work substantially again, by which time Union military authorities saw the end in view. By then, tens of thousands had died, and more would follow. It was the one danger faced by the soldiers that the president could not alleviate, and it pained him immeasurably. "Nothing has occurred in the war which causes me to suffer like this," he said in 1864. Some, however, could only see that their leader had abandoned them. When one Vermont boy died in a prison in the fall of 1864, his parents erected a headstone in his hometown with a bitter inscription saying that he had died in an enemy land, "entirely and wholly neglected by President Lincoln."[31]

"There was no flabby philanthropy about Abraham Lincoln," said Assistant Secretary of War Charles Dana. "He was all solid, hard, keen." Cordelia Harvey of the Sanitary Commission saw the same qualities, finding in him "the most yielding flexibility with the most unflinching firmness, childlike simplicity and statesmanlike wisdom and masterly strength." Lincoln encouraged the practical, either that which reasonably could be achieved, or that which he sincerely believed would do good though the results might not be measurable. Thus, perhaps his helplessness in alleviating the situation for his prisoners made him the more receptive to attempts to reinforce the spiritual well-being of the soldiers. In the fall of 1863, for instance, he gave his personal assurance of support for the efforts of the Sons of Temperance when they suggested establishing branches of their order in every army camp, with the officers instructed to encourage and hold evening meetings. "I am not sure that consistently with the public service, more can be done than has been done," he told them. Having seen more than enough courts-martial for offenses committed by inebriated soldiers to know that it was a serious problem, he could give their efforts his blessing, but little more.[32]

He involved himself far more in the matter of chaplains for the armies. In the hospitals, for instance, there were none at all at first, and no provision in army legislation for them. Thus, when concerned citizens and physicians approached him in the matter, he could only offer to appoint chaplains to the wards with the proviso that there was no money to pay them. As early as June 1861, Lincoln began appointing hospital chaplains, or authorizing his generals in the field to do so themselves; that fall, he actively solicited suggestions for appointees, Protestant and Catholic, asserting, "The services of chaplains are more needed, perhaps, in the hospitals, than with the healthy soldiers in the field." Though asking his appointees to serve without pay for the time being, he promised to try to persuade Congress to make an appropriation that would do right by them, and in his annual message in December he was as good as his word. Even after the hospital chaplains became a regular fixture in the military, he tried to protect them from bureaucratic cost-cutting that would have reduced their number and increased their work burden; he also initiated a review of legislation requiring chaplains to be Christian, in order to allow the appointment of Jewish chaplains as well.[33]

As for the healthy soldiers in the field who already had chaplains by regulation, Lincoln gave approval to the plan of the American Tract Society to distribute religious books to them. As far back as his very first public political expression in March 1832, he made his concern that people read and be informed very plain; now, in this crisis, the benefits accruing from having some of that reading be of an uplifting and sustaining spiritual nature was obvious.[34] It made him the more receptive to Charles Demond and six others when they called at the White House in December 1861. The month before, the Young Men's Christian Association had organized a special wartime body called the United States Christian Commission, its mission distributing Bibles and religious readings, furnishing yet more nurses, and whatever else might come under the scope of spiritual matters not already tended by the chaplains. Now they sought Lincoln's support, and immediately he gave it. "Your christian and benevolent undertaking for the benefit of the soldiers, is too obviously proper, and praiseworthy, to admit any difference of opinion," he told them. "I sincerely hope your plan may be as successful in execution, as it is just and generous in conception." They gave the very first copy of one of their tracts to the president, and he promised to read it carefully.[35]

Lincoln certainly welcomed the work of the commission, for his opinion of the chaplaincy in the Union army was not high at the start of the war. Like every branch of the military, it was paralyzed by seniority and parsimony. "I do believe that our army chaplains, take them as a class, are the very worst men we have in the service," one of his clerks recalled him saying. By the summer of 1861, he had hundreds of regiments in service, and a total of thirty chaplains. Regarding ministers as essential to the moral and spiritual health of the volunteers, he issued two general orders in May requiring every colonel commanding a regiment to appoint an ordained Christian minister as chaplain, to maintain "the social happiness and moral improvement of the troops." That December he expanded his reach to encompass Jewish chaplains, and three years later was even willing to accept women as chaplains, though Stanton blocked any such move and Lincoln did not pursue it further.[36]

"If there were more praying and less swearing," Lincoln said, "it would be better for our country; and we all need to be prayed for, officers as well as privates." However undefined and sometimes controversial Lincoln's own religion may have been—he never affiliated with any denomination, but came to believe firmly in divine predetermination of human events—he accepted completely the existence of a higher being, and the necessity for all men to seek its shelter and guidance. "The importance for man and beast of the prescribed weekly rest, the sacred rights of Christian soldiers and sailors, a becoming deference to the best sentiment of a Christian people, and a due regard for the Divine will, demand that Sunday labor in the Army and Navy be reduced to the measure of strict necessity," he declared in a November 1862 order to his armies. The following year, he began a national tradition by setting aside the last Thursday in November as a day of thanksgiving—not for any particular victories in the field, as with former thanksgiving proclamations, but for the people of the Union, and for "all those who have become widows, orphans, mourners or sufferers in the lamentable strife in which we are unavoidably engaged." A president could not *order* his soldiers and civilians to pray, but he could try to *lead* them to prayer, and that is what Lincoln was doing.[37]

What little active participation Lincoln was able to give to religious efforts, he devoted chiefly to the Christian Commission, though, as with the Sanitary Commission, his involvement could never properly be more than public encouragement and approval and an occasional speech or open letter. He had to decline presiding at a commission meeting held on Washington's birthday in the hall of the House of Representatives in 1863, but offered an endorsement for publication, saying, "Whatever shall be sincerely, and in God's name, devised for the good of the soldier and seaman, in their spheres of duty, can scarcely fail to be blest." A year later, on February 2, and again in the House, this time Lincoln came in person, just as that same year he also for the first time attended a few of the Sanitary Commission fairs. By 1864, with war-weariness draining morale at home and in the field, and with a contest for re-election ahead that could determine the fate of the Union and not just this one president, he needed to be seen more publicly. There was nothing of hypocrisy about it, for he had openly supported them all along. Now, in the interests of the soldiers and their cause, he needed some of that support to rebound to him if they were all going to reach their goal of peace. Commission members were deeply touched by the president's presence, and even allowing for the hyperbole and flattery that no one could resist when complimenting the chief executive, director George H. Stuart captured the gratitude of many at Lincoln's giving them some of his time. "By this means, the people at home have been cheered and strengthened to give their sons, brothers and husbands to the War, many thousands have been rescued from the grave, and restored to the service; our forces have been steadied and strengthened for battle, and nerved to fight it out to the end, and an untold amount of suffering has been saved, and good done our brave defenders." Lincoln would not have said that about his involvement with the commission, but he might well have said it about the organization itself.[38]

When commission managers called at the White House that summer, Lincoln complimented them on a record of which they could be proud, and in January 1865—after the election—he attended their anniversary meeting. Two days before, the leaders of the group called on him at the executive mansion, more than a hundred men in all. Gathering in the East Room, they formed a large semiellipse beside one wall; when Lincoln came in from the Green Room, they saw him looking worn and tired, his hat in his hand. "The care itself was furrowing his features and deepening their pensiveness," thought one. Chairman Stuart greeted the president and made a short speech thanking him for his contribution to their efforts. All the while, Lincoln bowed his head, apparently not listening, or else lost in thought, "with an abstracted air that left his eyes lustreless," noted one of the visitors, "as though his thoughts were among the imperilled and suffering men for whose comforts he was ever ready to yield his own." Perhaps so, and perhaps not, for by this time the president had heard so many testimonial speeches that maintaining interest and attention must have been a strain. When Stuart finished, however, Lincoln showed he had been listening by raising his head and denying the credit they had just given him. Moreover, he denied credit to them, too.

We have only been doing our duty my friends, whatever we have been able to do together. You owe me no thanks for what I have done for the country, whatever that may be,—and I owe none, to you. We cannot repay the soldiers. . . . We have all been laboring for a common end. You feel grateful for what I have done that is right; and I certainly feel grateful for what you have done that is right; and yet, in the fact that we have been laboring for the same end—the preservation of our country and the welfare of its defenders,—has been our motive and joy and reward.[39]

Stuart suggested a prayer and Lincoln assented. Two days later, at the anniversary ceremony in the House, with Vice-President Hamlin, several of the Cabinet, and other dignitaries present, Lincoln joined in the singing of the "Battle Hymn of the Republic," whose lines about the "watch fires of a hundred circling camps" called to every mind the men in the field. Some attendees saw tears in the president's eyes, and toward the close he scribbled a request on his program and sent it to the chairman, asking for a reading of one of his favorite poems, "Your Mission":

If you cannot in the conflict
Prove yourself a soldier true,
If, where fire and smoke are thickest,
There's no work for you to do;
When the battle-field is silent,
You can go with careful tread,
You can bear away the wounded,
You can cover up the dead.[40]

Everything Lincoln did with the public organizations like the Sanitary and Christian Commissions, the Tract Society, the Temperance Association, and more, found its way into the Northern press sooner rather than later, and once it was in the papers it inevitably went into the camps of the armies. Every soldier knew that the president supported the nurses and the hospitals, that he often visited the sick. Every soldier knew of the efforts to unravel tangles in pay and supplies. If every soldier did not have personal experience of the chief executive's intervening directly to help him with his own problem, the knowledge that Lincoln *would* have done so is shown to have been universal by the simple fact that so many soldiers actually did approach him personally. They knew that they were never far from his mind—

the wounded, the dead, the troubled, or just those wanting a few minutes from their president to consider a personal problem, or only a shake of the hand. Inevitably it was the face-to-face contact that Lincoln had with so many that cemented the bond, the understanding among these, his children, that "Father Abraham" would take care of them. Every day that he held open office hours, the line of callers and petitioners coursed through the hallways of the White House, sometimes down to the front door itself, and in every line there were soldiers, officers and enlisted men alike. Though neither he nor his secretaries ever had time or inclination to prepare a tally, it is certain that Lincoln must have given brief private interviews to at least two thousand soldiers during the war, and probably substantially more.[41] Lincoln himself explained his policy of maintaining an open door to all to a British journalist in 1864. "This ready means of access is, I may say, under our form of government, the only link or cord which connects the people with the governing power." In short, the volunteers had a right as citizens to a private audience, and by making himself as accessible as possible, he was twining extra strands into that binding cord between citizen and administration. "However unprofitable much of it is," he said of the inevitable time wasted on petty matters, "it must be kept up."[42] What Lincoln did not say was that every soldier who called, whether he left entirely satisfied or not, went away with an experience he would relive and retell for the rest of his life. More immediately, every soldier who felt that at least he had been given a fair hearing went back to his regiment a living ambassador for Lincoln.

The soldier's experience with Lincoln began with courtesy. The president's secretaries and household staff, including military attachés, sometimes tried to insulate him. Commission holders especially were likely to assume that a private soldier's business was less important than that of any officers waiting, and insist that the poor soldier go to the end of the line. On one occasion when Lincoln saw this in action, he upbraided the officer responsible and told him, "Hereafter, whether the caller is an officer or private, Major, be a gentleman."[43]

They came to him with every sort of plea, and he met them with everything from tears to rude jokes to fatherly understanding, as seemed to befit the case. When a soldier who had lost a limb in the war called to ask for a job in the capital, Lincoln asked to see his discharge papers and, told there were none, teased the fellow: "What, no papers, no credentials, nothing to show how you lost your leg? How am I to know that you lost it in battle, or did not lose it by a trap after getting into somebody's orchard?" After a mutual chuckle, though, he added, "I will see what can be done for you." In fact, he often sought to help disabled-veteran callers secure employment in one of the government departments, adding in his recommendation to the appropriate department head, "I shall be glad if he can get it."[44]

He seemed to take special interest in the appeals of the younger volunteers who came into his office. Perhaps he thought of the dead Ellsworth as he looked on these other boyish faces. Indeed, one of them belonged to a cousin of Ellsworth's, whom Lincoln helped with his campaign to obtain a commission. When an eighteen-year-old boy of the 41st Illinois came all the way east to seek Lincoln's help in getting an appointment to West Point, the president heard him politely and passed along his application. When another boy, only a year older but already a twice-wounded combat veteran of thirty months' service, came on the same mission, the president wrote an endorsement, saying, "I want this 'soldier boy' to have a chance." Young drummer boy Robert Hendershot of the 8th Michigan especially impressed Lincoln. At the mere age of twelve he was in action at Fredericksburg, and discharged on disability soon afterward. The boy came with his drum to the White House, seeking an appointment to the Military Academy. Of course he was several years too young for that, but Lincoln found him "very brave, manly and worthy," and took a special interest. "I know something of this boy," he told Stanton. "He must have a chance, and if you can find any situation suitable to him, I shall be obliged." He could not satisfy all of them, or even very many, but to each there was some kind word. When one young soldier wanting to be an officer called in the spring of 1862, the president told him, "My son, go back to the army, continue to do your duty as you find it to do, and, with the zeal you have hitherto shown, you will not have to ask for promotion. It will seek you." There was always a compliment for the man's good service thus far, and the expressed wish that he had more like this particular soldier in his armies. "Shake hands with me," he would conclude the interview, "and go back the little man and brave soldier that you are." Sometimes the young faces had no great favor to ask other than to go home. When a lad of the 140th Pennsylvania who was obviously not recovering well from a battle wound called, the president observed to Stanton, "He is nothing but a boy . . . but I believe he is made of the right kind of stuff," and suggested letting him go home to recuperate.[45]

Almost as numerous as the soldiers who called were their parents, especially the mothers. Any kindness done for the family of a soldier was the same as helping the man himself, as when the president assisted the wife of a New York volunteer in getting back home when she was stranded without funds in Washington. The widow pleading before Lincoln was so commonplace as to become a literary cliché in later years, yet it had its foundation in fact. Lincoln himself used the mother as a prime example of the kinds of request he received when explaining his callers to the British writer. "For instance," he said, "a mother in a distant part, who has a son in the army who is regularly enlisted, has not served out his time, but has been as long as she thinks he ought to stay, will collect together all the little means she can to bring her here to entreat me to grant him his discharge. Of course, I cannot interfere and can only see her and speak kindly to her." A caller in January 1865 heard the president talking to one such woman seeking to get her husband out of the army because the family were impoverished. "I cannot grant your request. I can disband all the Union armies, but I cannot send a single soldier home," said Lincoln. "I sympathize in your disappointment, but consider that all of us in every part of the country are today suffering what we have never suffered." Of course, as commander-in-chief, Lincoln could send a soldier home, or certainly had the influence to make it happen; no sooner did he deny the woman than he apparently had a change of heart and gave her what she asked.[46]

In fact, Lincoln discharged numerous soldiers on the personal appeals of mothers and wives. When a woman with a husband and two sons in the army called and asked for the release of her younger boy, who had already been wounded and served time as a prisoner, Lincoln granted her plea. A widow with one son killed in action and the other, an eighteen-year-old, suffering feeble health, asked for his discharge, and Lincoln agreed. One day in November 1863, at the end of a long spell of incessant callers, Lincoln thought he had seen everyone, then heard a weeping woman outside in the corridor. One of his secretaries told him that she had been coming every day but the lines were always too long for her to get in before office hours closed. Lincoln asked her to come in and heard her story of a husband and two sons in the army, the boys too distant to help her, and her husband for some reason no longer sending home the pay that supported the household. Lincoln stood by the fireplace, his hands behind his back, his head bent low in the attitude he usually assumed when listening to someone's case. When she finished by asking him to discharge one of her sons to come home and take care of her, the president said almost to himself, "I have two, and you have none." He meant, of course, that his two surviving sons, Robert and Tad, were safe and either at home with him or close enough. He wrote an order for the discharge of one of her boys on a card and handed it to her. A few days later she returned, having gone to the Army of the Potomac to get her son only to discover that he had just been killed in action. A shocked Lincoln sat at his table to write for her a discharge for the other son. His old friend James Speed, soon to be attorney general, was in the office at the time, and later remembered how the bereaved mother tenderly stroked and smoothed the president's hair as he wrote the order.[47]

Not all of the soldiers who gained an audience were impressed with the president, nor were they suitably grateful to him for giving them some of his time. One young officer, Francis Donaldson of the 118th Pennsylvania, had been court-martialed for insubordination and impertinence to his superiors, of which he was substantially guilty since he regarded few as his equal, let alone superior. On March 3, 1864, backed by influential newspaperman John Forney, he gained an interview with Lincoln hoping to have his finding set aside, and that night wrote an account that is just as revealing of Lincoln's manner in treating his soldier callers, rank and file, alike, as it is of Donaldson's petulant and undeserving nature. He had been forewarned not to use notes in stating his case, but simply to present it freely and openly, "because no one was more susceptible to downright honest unstudied, innocent candor than the President, and none more ready to detect dissimulation than he." But Donaldson was not ready for the man who greeted him. "The size of the President nearly overcame me," he said.

He was, apparently, the tallest man I ever saw, and so thin too and so ugly. He had a long black double breasted frock coat which hung like a wrapper on his lean frame, and it was positively the dirtiest coat I ever beheld for a man having any pretensions to gentility. . . . When this homely, dirty, shabby, lean, lanky man appeared I lost all sense of the dignity of the surroundings and found myself filled with amazement that this was indeed Abraham Lincoln, President of the United States. . . . How can foreign nations, or indeed our own people, have respect for institutions when such a slovenly car[e]less man is the *first gentleman of the land*. . . . I was the worst disappointed man conceivable.

As Donaldson wrestled with his stunned first impression, Lincoln walked up to him and grabbed his hand and shook it in one single up-

and-down "pump-handle" fashion, putting his other on the officer's shoulder, then led him by the hand to a chair and pulled up one of his own to sit directly in front of him. Donaldson felt a slight blush, he confessed, "from a recognition of his kindly act of encouragement," and then his companions started to state his case for him, but Lincoln interrupted and told the lieutenant to speak for himself. "Just tell me as briefly as possible your trouble—from the beginning," said the president. As Donaldson spoke, Lincoln looked straight at him, resting his hand on his chin. "Whether his thoughts were following my words or were far away I cannot say," the officer wrote that night. "He was apparently giving close attention to my speech." When the man finished, Lincoln asked for his court-martial papers, took a pencil from his pocket, and wrote a favorable endorsement.

"Now young man," said the president, "inasmuch as I have done you a service, I want you to promise me one thing. Mr. Forney says you are engaged to be married. Now I want you to go right home, marry the young lady, and have lots of children, all boys, because the war bids fair to be prolonged indeffinitely and we will need all the men we can get." The witticism seemed almost lost on Donaldson. He had gotten what he wanted, yet "I came away disappointed at the appearance of the President but nevertheless entertaining kindly feelings towards him. I think he belongs to the common people, has a sympathetic heart and is probably not bull dog enough to master the knobby problems thrust upon him." In his snobbish conceit, he concluded that, though he had gained his object, it came "at the expense of my loyalty to a *Republican Form of Government*" that could elevate such a commoner to the highest office.[48]

Most callers were more deserving, yet Lincoln could lose his patience, as much from a greater frustration weighing upon him as from the case at hand. To one soldier who insistently demanded that Lincoln take action on his complaint, the president finally exclaimed: "Now, my man, go away, *go away!* I cannot meddle in your case. I could as easily bail out the Potomac River with a teaspoon as attend to all the details of the army."[49] His secretaries and bodyguard often expressed their amazement at his patience, and that he could get any work done with the steady stream of callers with petitions and favors to ask. Lincoln insisted that he must see everyone. "I feel—though the tax on my time is heavy—that no hours of my day are better employed than those which thus bring me again within direct contact and atmosphere of the average of our whole people," he replied, and then added, "They do not want much, and they get very little." Some soldiers called just to be able to say that they had seen their president, as did a volunteer with the 1st Minnesota on his way back to his regiment in December 1862 after a furlough for a wound. He came through Washington and decided to stop at the White House. A guard halted him at the door, and on a whim he asked to see Lincoln on some invented errand. At that instant Lincoln himself stepped outside. "Well here I am, my man, what can I do for you?" the president asked, at the same time giving the soldier's hand a shake and squeeze that left it sore. "Oh: nothing in particular," replied the stunned volunteer. "Only that I was on my way to my regiment at the front [and] I would like to be able to tell the boys that I had had the pleasure of shaking hands with Abraham Lincoln." "Well, now you can do that," said the president, then raised the bandage covering the soldier's wounded eye and peered at his injury. He told the boy to take care and grasped his hand once more. "Good bye," said Lincoln, "God bless you."[50]

If one thing above all others characterized the special spiritual relationship that developed between Lincoln and the soldiers of the Union, it was this unprecedented accessibility. The volunteers knew they could approach him because he was, as one of his aides said, "what we term a natural man." Whether in the chair of the president or sitting on the porch of a country store telling stories, "he appeared to his neighbors essentially the same Abraham Lincoln."[51] It was no wonder that the nicknames seemed to stick to him like the pencil smudges on his worn frock coat. "Old Abe," "Honest Abe," "Uncle Abe," and more, all spoke to the affectionate regard that the men in the ranks felt for him. Indeed, it was a feature of this war that, the more the soldiers either loved or despised a leader, the more sobriquets they invented for him. In Lincoln's case, the nicknames revealed a familiarity that showed the soldiers' sense of identification with him as essentially one of them, only a generation older—and that made him all the more "Father Abraham."

There was never a doubt that he returned the feeling. Early in the war, John P. Nourse of Pennsylvania called on Lincoln hoping to secure an appointment to the Naval Academy at Annapolis. Ahead of him in line was a large delegation of dignitaries, including Chase, Sumner, and others, and when they went into Lincoln's office Nourse could just glimpse through the open door the president's tall figure. Lincoln saw him peering in and asked, "Young man did you want to see me?" Scarcely waiting for a reply, he took Nourse's hand, led him into the room, seated him on a sofa, and sat down beside him. While he kept the others waiting, Lincoln asked Nourse questions about his age, his home and family, even the kinds of games he liked to play as a boy, and then hit him with the most direct question of all, "What are you going to do with yourself?" Nourse was disarmed, as was Donaldson. "All his conversation was in such a fatherly manner," the Pennsylvanian recalled. Consequently he felt no nervousness at all in mentioning his desire to enter the Naval Academy and serve in the Union fleet.

"Thank God for my boys," exclaimed Lincoln. "They are the ones I must rely upon to crush this Rebellion." As they talked, for perhaps half an hour, Lincoln stretched his legs seemingly halfway across the room and alternately clasped his hands behind his head, or let one fall on Nourse's knee as he smiled and asked yet another question. When the interview ended, Lincoln showed the boy to the door and repeated, "God bless! my boys." In the aftermath of that few minutes with Lincoln, this one young man gave up his ambition for an appointment and decided instead to enlist in the 13th Pennsylvania Infantry, to become truly one of Father Abraham's "boys."[52]

6

PROMISES KEPT

And Abraham stood up from before his dead,
and spake . . . saying. . . , give me possession
of a buryingplace with you,
that I may bury my dead out of my sight.
[Genesis 23:3–4]

WEATHERING THE McCLELLAN DISMISSAL, THE FRED-
ericksburg debacle, and the Emancipation Proclamation hardly
left the president feeling invincible. Though he survived every crisis,
each exacted its price, both in personal toll on him and at some cost to
his standing with segments of the soldiery. The mass stood by him,
but he felt concern over a rise in desertions and disaffections that, even
if they did not endanger either the overall morale of the army or the
cause, still became something of a public embarrassment.

On March 6, 1863, several weeks after replacing Burnside with
Hooker, Lincoln met with his new commander of the Army of the Potomac and with influential Republican Senator Benjamin Wade, chairman of the powerful Joint Committee on the Conduct of the War. As
they concluded their meeting and Hooker left, the president saw Wade
to the door and noticed Sergeant James Stradling waiting next in line.
He came seeking help getting transportation back to his regiment, but,

seeing him now, Lincoln said, "Senator, we have had the head of the army here a few minutes ago, and learned from him all he cared to tell. Now we have here the tail of the army, so let us get from him how the rank and file feel about matters." After apologizing to Stradling for referring to him as the "tail" of his army, Lincoln mentioned the high rate of desertion. He said he could spare generals easily enough—there were some he wished would desert—but not the men in the ranks. He wanted to know why the men abandoned their service, asking if the army was against him, or the proclamation, or their generals. Stradling's answer is lost to history, yet in the possible reasons that the president suggested Lincoln showed that he had a fair grasp on much of the cause.[1]

Lincoln saw a lot of soldiers in March, and probably asked the same question of several. At the same time, he derived comfort from them in the face of his concern, for overwhelmingly they displayed the kind of determination that saw them through momentary setbacks or disenchantments. Like Lincoln, they recognized the greater issues at stake, and swallowed matters that they might have found temporarily unsatisfying. This month a few survivors of the daring April 1862 railroad raid in Georgia (later called the Great Locomotive Chase) stopped at the White House. Lincoln was meeting with journalist Noah Brooks when the men arrived, and Brooks watched the president as he spoke with them. "Mr. Lincoln's manner toward enlisted men, with whom he occasionally met and talked, was always delightful in its bonhomie and its absolute freedom from anything like condescension," he recalled. "Then, at least, the 'common soldier' was the equal of the chief magistrate of the nation."

As each man introduced himself, Lincoln took his hand, and then, as they told more about their adventures, of what they had suffered as prisoners of war, and of their escape, he listened intently, occasionally asking questions that showed he already knew much of their story. Brooks saw that, regardless of where Lincoln's mind actually may have been, he gave those six men the impression that in those moments nothing in the world mattered more than meeting with them. And perhaps nothing did, for when they left he obviously felt relieved. With considerable feeling, he told Brooks that the bearing of those soldiers, the way they had taken their lives in their hands knowing that they might meet death—as several of their comrades did—"presented an example of the apparent disregard of the tremendous issues of life and death which was so strong a characteristic of the American soldier."[2] He got the same message from his visits to the wounded. At St. Elizabeth's Hospital in Washington, the chaplain introduced the president to the men, but he declined to give any sort of speech. None was necessary, he said, for these men with their crutches and their empty sleeves were orators in themselves, their battered bodies mute testimony to their sacrifice. "Their very appearance spoke louder than tongues," said Lincoln. He learned something else important, too, from the healthy and the convalescent alike. The soldiers never lost their rude wit. Men whose will or determination to continue abandoned them, almost always first lost their sense of humor. He knew himself how vital was that lubricant of the soul in facing troubled times, and seeing it in the men gave him to understand that they were yet ready to go on. He never tired of recounting humorous stories he had picked up in the army, telling Brooks, "It seems as if neither death nor danger could quench the grim humor of the American soldier."[3]

The visits with the soldiers may have helped reinforce Lincoln's own morale and determination, yet they also showed him that it was time to go to the Army of the Potomac once more, as spring and the inevitable campaign approached. They were two years into the war now. He could no longer count entirely on that initial motivation that had brought volunteers in their hundreds of thousands to the army. When the novelty of soldiering wore off, when the drudgery and boredom and the realities of camp sickness and sudden and violent death in battle dominated daily life, then a man needed something more to be willing to continue. It took victories—of which there had been but one, at Antietam, for the Army of the Potomac—it took support from home, pride in their regiments and their army, and a source of inspiration.[4] They could get that last from some of their commanders, yet by now Lincoln seemed to understand that they got it from him, too.

Not once during the entire course of the war did the president visit one of his armies in the western theater. Indeed, the only army he ever reviewed or spent any time with personally was the Army of the Potomac and its subunits or adjuncts, like Pope's command and Butler's later Army of the James. Of course, the western armies served at some remove from Washington, though rail transportation might put Lincoln in their theater in no unreasonable time. Yet that did not really matter, for they had been winning an almost unbroken chain of victories from the start, and now camped deep in Mississippi and Tennessee and Louisiana. The very distance Lincoln would have had to go to get to them was evidence of the successes they had enjoyed. In short, much as it would have pleased him to see them, when it came to the issue of inspiring the men by his personal presence, the western soldiers did not need him.

It was another matter for the noble, ill-starred Army of the Potomac. After Fredericksburg they needed every encouragement, and so, in March, Lincoln and Hooker arranged for yet another series of reviews, on April 6–10, the grandest and most extensive yet, with more than a hundred thousand soldiers under his view and at the same time seeing him. Lincoln advised Hooker of his arrival a few days earlier, and before long the news that the president was coming to see them swept through the army camped in and around Falmouth, Virginia.[5] Lincoln left Washington April 4 in company with Mary, his son Tad, Attorney General Edward Bates, and a few other friends, and arrived the next morning at Falmouth. Hooker sent an officer with an ambulance to convey Lincoln to his headquarters, but on meeting him the soldier asked if he would prefer to make the short trip on a horse. "Well, Captain," said Lincoln in a moment of characteristic deference, "*you* be boss."[6]

The first day, April 6, Lincoln reviewed the Cavalry Corps commanded by General George Stoneman, some ten-thousand strong. The mounted men thought they had made a good impression on the president, as certainly they had, yet his mind was elsewhere for a time, even as the endless lines of horsemen rode past him. He was doing the numbers again, as he had with McClellan. Hooker had reported to him that there were 136,724 actually present for duty, the mightiest host ever seen on the continent. Yet Lincoln could not help noting another 33,188 absent on other duty and, worse, 44,855 who were sick, under arrest, or absent without leave. In short, though the army in sum appeared to number 214,767 by his calculations, Hooker actually had just less than two-thirds of them with him for the coming campaign. It ought still to be more than enough, but Lincoln could not help worrying about all those who were absent, and what the weight of their numbers might have added in the coming days.[7]

Rain forced a postponement of the infantry review scheduled for April 7, disappointing the men of the 83rd Pennsylvania, who had gotten out the tattered remnants of their regimental flag left from the Peninsular Campaign, like children anxious that "Abraham," as they called him, might see it next to their new banner. The following day, with winter snow still on the ground in heavy drifts, Lincoln mounted a horse and went out onto the muddy field, accompanied by a surgeon from New Jersey who later confessed that they had a "gay ride" and "a fine sight." Before them through most of the day stood arrayed the III, V, and VI Corps, and from every one of them Lincoln received an enthusiastic reception. As he rode past they presented arms, the drum corps played, and the soldiers cheered lustily. Once more the incongruous apparition of an overly tall man, elongated by a stovepipe hat and mounted on a horse too small for him, touched the sense of fun in the volunteers. "The President's legs looked longer than ever, and his toes seemed almost to touch the ground," one soldier wrote home. Another believed the only way to keep those legs from dragging the ground would be to tie them in a knot beneath the animal's belly. Everyone thought the stovepipe looked "a little the worse for wear," and the president had even forgotten to tie down his trouser legs. As he jogged along at a trot, swaying loosely in the saddle but riding well, his pants slowly began to creep upward, until they rose above his boot tops, exposing his long white underdrawers. At the same time, the wet ground meant that his horse spattered mud all over him as they rode, and the ride settled his hat far back on his head, until it rested on his ears and threatened to topple off. With his stovepipe towering above Hooker, who rode beside him, and his legs dangling almost to the ground, he looked like a character sketched by "Boz" in a Dickens novel, and none present missed the fun. "Altogether he presented a very comical picture, calculated to provoke laughter along the entire length of the lines," said a volunteer. Yet they did not laugh, even when he rode down the street of log huts of the 12th New Hampshire's winter quarters and had his hat knocked to the ground by an overhanging branch. They smiled at that, but they did not laugh.[8]

What stopped them was his face. One company officer commented on "the sweet and comely face of the President," but most saw far more. They would have laughed, said a soldier, "had it not been for that sad, anxious face, so full of melancholy foreboding, that peered forth from his shaggy eyebrows." In front of the V Corps he impressed some as "care-worn and anxious, and we thought there must be a 'heap of trouble on the old man's mind.'" The men stood in a cold and biting wind for more than an hour as he passed. "Abraham looks poorly," thought one, "thin and in bad health. . . . He is to all outward appearances much careworn, and anxiety is fast wearing him out, poor man; I could but pity as I looked at him, and remembered the weight of responsibility resting upon his burdened mind; what an ordeal he has passed through, and *what is yet before him!* All I can say is, *Poor Abe!* with faith still good in the honest man."9

There was that same adjective again time after time—"careworn." Two out of three soldiers in the review that day who wrote of it in their diaries and letters home mentioned the sad look of the president. "Perhaps my imagination added the unusual paleness to his cheek, and the expression of care that his countenance wore," said a man in the 2nd Vermont, but he did not think so. "President looks care worn," noted a Massachusetts man. "I assure you that Abraham Lincoln looks like a man almost weighed down by cares and responsibilities," said an Indiana soldier. A staff officer thought Lincoln thin and pale, and heard several remark that they feared Hamlin might soon be president by Lincoln's death. "He looks care worn," wrote a chaplain from Pennsylvania. "His labors must be arduous. He certainly is sinking under the load of care." The cleric confided to his diary that night, "I could not help uttering the prayer God bless Abraham Lincoln."10

As he passed, Lincoln apparently felt so preoccupied that often he stared fixedly at the ground, lost in deep thought. Repeatedly, when met by three cheers, he looked up and doffed the awkward stovepipe. A soldier in the V Corps who saw Lincoln remove his hat as he passed later wondered if the president might actually have taken off his hat to him personally. Despite orders to keep their eyes fixed immovably to the front, countless soldiers cocked their heads slightly, to shift their eyes for a better look. Very quickly word spread through the ranks that, as he passed some gaudily uniformed Zouave units, Lincoln had asked Hooker if they did not run an additional danger by being such noticeable targets, but the general responded that the men derived a special pride and élan from their uniforms. It was another evidence of the president's concern for the men, that some of them might be made into easy marks. Such an understanding could only enhance the cheers they gave him. When it came time to review the III Corps, the soldiers lined both sides of the road as Lincoln passed between them, the men thundering out their cheers for "Father Abraham." A New York soldier commented that the cheering was not at all military and ordered. "The men could not be restrained from so honoring him," said Private Rice Bull. "He really was the ideal of the Army."11

All these scenes repeated themselves in the next day's review, on April 9, this time with the old I Corps. Again men's imaginations seized on that same word, "careworn." Glad as they were to see the president, they could not miss the sadness in his visage, especially when he passed some unit he recognized, only to see once again its depleted ranks. Antietam and its earlier fights had badly reduced the old Iron Brigade, and when it passed before him, Lincoln turned to Hooker and said something about his admiration for those men. In the ranks, one of those looking back noticed that, though he had seen Lincoln several times now, "every time I noticed that the lines of care upon his kindly face grew deeper." When the president rode past one New England regiment, a volunteer studied him intently and saw tears in his eyes. "Why he wept I know not," wrote a Maine soldier that same day, "whether he was thinking how many had fallen, or how many will soon fall. It might be neither. But this I know: under that homely exterior is as tender a heart as ever throbbed, one that is easily moved toward the side of the poor and downtrodden." Standing with the officers of the 121st New York, surgeon Daniel M. Holt later wrote home, "Father Abraham, wife and son condescended to look lovingly upon his children." When Holt smiled at Lincoln, he got a grin in return. "Poor man, I pity him, and almost wonder at his being alive," mused the doctor. "The gigantic work upon his hands, and the task upon his physical frame must be very great."[12]

April 10 saw the last of it; as Lincoln reviewed the XI and XII Corps, the dawn turned much warmer and more pleasant. Many of these soldiers were German immigrants, some with only rudimentary English, yet they, too, hurried to their diaries and letters to describe the moment afterward. They, too, found him "careworn." The president held his hat in his hand much of the day, rather than taking it off and putting it back on as the men cheered him. "He looks as if he had all he could attend to," said one New Yorker. "I think by the time his time is up he will be ten years older than when he took his seat." A Pennsylvanian wrote to his sister that night: "Well to day we were reviewed by Father Abraham. . . . This is the first time ever I saw uncle Abe to have a fare sight of him. He looked very care worn." A musician from the 55th Ohio felt disappointed that the breaking of his horn that morning "deprived me of the pleasure of playing for Father Abraham," but he did get a very fine view of the president. "Father Abraham resembles his pictures or rather his pictures resemble him, remarkably," he said. "He looks very pale, though, not fine and healthy." Another Pennsylvanian recalled that as Lincoln rode past him "I regarded him with profound veneration and sympathy, knowing full well what a crushing weight of responsibility and suspense and anxiety was at that time oppressing him."[13]

Certainly that sadness, the look of the burden that showed so visibly on Lincoln's face, was no pose, yet even if it had been it could not have been calculated to better effect. For, in seeing Lincoln so visibly carrying the weight of responsibility for the war, the soldiers saw that in his way he suffered as they did, and though he did not face death in battle or disease and discomfort in the camps, still that landscape of cares in his face let them know that he, too, was a casualty. It bound them to him in a way they never experienced with any commander of their army. Moreover, something in his manner drew them. It was not just the apparent clumsiness, the comicality, and the absence of pretense in his appearance, though what shocked the generals the soldiers found endearing. There was a familiarity in his manner that won them. Brooks, who was along, noticed that when Lincoln rode past officers, or they marched past him, he touched his hat in salute and acknowledgment. But when enlisted ranks passed in review, he took off the battered old topper and stood bareheaded. When the party left the army to return to Washington, thousands of the men spontaneously lined the road he took and cheered him off. The visit exhausted Lincoln, his weariness evident to most of the men, but he insisted on concluding the several days of reviews with a visit to the army hospitals at Falmouth, where he shook hands and spoke with almost every man. Several of them wept when the president came to them, and Brooks saw that "they were made happy by looking into Lincoln's sympathetic countenance, touching his hand, and hearing his gentle voice."[14]

"It is a great relief to get away from Washington and the politicians," Lincoln told Brooks after the visit to the army. Yet, though he relaxed when visiting with the soldiers, he confessed that "nothing touches the tired spot," that spot that so many saw in his face. Like the others before it, this biggest of all of his reviews of the Army of the Potomac had been a success. He came not to wrestle for power with its commander this time, but to test the spirit of the men themselves, to see if their mettle was still strong enough after a season of discontents and challenges, and he saw what he had hoped to find. Many of the soldiers knew what he had come to see. Even as they stood about in groups cheering him when he left to return to Washington, some, like one man from Maine, believed that the tears they had seen in his eyes were for those about to die, that Lincoln's coming portended a battle soon. "And so, as I wended my way to camp," he wrote in his journal, "a feeling of uneasiness and horrible uncertainty possessed me."[15]

Yet Lincoln found something else as well. A week after the visit, Private Wilbur Fisk of the 2nd Vermont spoke of the great change he had seen in the ranks since the terrible winter. Before, men had spoken freely of intending to desert, of their disillusionment with what had become an "abolition war." "It is very materially changed now," he said. "Confidence in the Government, and respect for it, is reestablished." The soldiers gradually came to grasp the full depths of the principle at stake in the contest, and Lincoln's wisdom in his course. He was leading them and the Union "to an issue that God must forever approve," and since they understood that, said Fisk, "the more determined and anxious are they to carry out the war successfully."[16]

Unfortunately, they would have to wait yet awhile. Immediately after leaving the army, Lincoln sent Hooker some advice on the coming campaign, and then, a week afterward, returned quietly to confer with the general, but this time did not visit with the men in the ranks. A few days later, Hooker launched an audacious offensive that at first took the Confederates by surprise and caught them at a severe disadvantage. But Lee in danger was Lee at his most dangerous, and in early May he delivered the most brilliant stroke of his career, shattering a couple of those corps Lincoln had so recently reviewed, and sending the Army of the Potomac in retreat once again. More than once during the Battle of Chancellorsville Charles Woolsey of Hooker's staff received anxious inquiries from "Father Abraham," as he called him, asking the progress of the battle. When he got the word that Hooker had suffered a humiliating defeat, Lincoln was distraught. "We are ruined; and such a fearful loss of life!" he wailed to Stanton. "My God! This is more than I can endure. . . . Defeated again, and so many of our noble countrymen killed! What will the people say?"[17]

In fact, the country and the soldiers said what Lincoln might have hoped they would say. "God bless you, and all with you," Lincoln telegraphed to Hooker on May 6, two days after the close of a battle that cost over seventeen thousand casualties. The next day the president went to the army in person and remained all day, assessing the situation and, more important, assessing Hooker, who seemed to have lost none of his self-confidence. As for the men, less than half the army was seriously engaged in the fight, and thus the rest stood fresh and ready to strike back. "We are laying here in a state of glorious inactivity," John McCowan, a Pennsylvania artilleryman, wrote to his wife a few weeks later. "It is time that the Army of the Potomac won a victory for they have been so often defeated that the men have got disheartened and the opinion is freely expressed that it cannot do any thing but keep Lee and his troops from going north while the armies of the South West crush the rebellion." Hooker might have been beaten, but they were not, and they wanted another try at the Army of Northern Virginia.[18]

In fact, they were not even able to keep Lee from going north, but that is what gave them their chance for revenge. Five days after Mc-Cowan wrote to his wife, the Confederates set in motion an audacious full-scale raid across the Potomac and through Maryland that by June 24 saw elements of the Army of Northern Virginia entering Pennsylvania. While Hooker pursued, keeping his own army between the enemy and Washington, Lincoln called out a hundred thousand militia for six months' service on June 15 to meet the crisis. At the very same time, the enlistments of some of those nine-month regiments he had accepted in spite of regulations calling for three-year men began to expire, and the president had to plead with some to stay in service. In the case of the 27th Maine, he even offered the newly created Medal of Honor to those who volunteered to remain through the emergency. All this angered many in the three-year outfits. "Why can't he learn wisdom from experience," complained a Massachusetts soldier. It aggrieved the full-term men to see others get away with shorter terms of service, the more so when the expiration of such enlistments came at this perilous moment. "This war may be, and I think it will be, a long one," said Lieutenant Stephen Weld, "and President Lincoln had better open his eyes to the fact." They wanted him to resort to and fully enforce the draft to ensure that the Union had all the men it needed, and that every man served his full share of time in uniform. Ironically, even in their frustration at Lincoln, men like Weld revealed just how well the president had achieved one of his purposes: now they saw the defense of the Union by bearing arms not as a matter of choice but as the duty of every able-bodied man.[19]

In late June, even while Lincoln scrambled to marshal every available resource, he decided when Hooker resigned, in a difference of opinion with Halleck, that he would not attempt to retain him. Once more, and only fleetingly, there was talk of recalling Little Mac. "All the soldiers and officers are still strong McClellanites," Weld said on June 28, but it would not be so, for that was the very day that Lincoln decided to gamble on someone else, Major General George G. Meade. Just a few days later, Meade justified Lincoln's confidence by stopping Lee's invasion at Gettysburg and handing him a terribly costly defeat that almost shattered the Army of Northern Virginia. Meade's army held the field and was no less battered itself, but at last the Army of the Potomac had a real and unequivocal victory. The day after the fight ended, July 4, Lincoln sent Meade congratulations and announced that the army had covered itself with the highest honor, asking the nation to extend its condolences for "the many gallant fallen." That same day, he got word that Vicksburg, on the Mississippi, had fallen to Grant after a forty-seven-day siege. Truly the back of the rebellion seemed broken at last.[20]

Three days later, citizens in Washington came to the White House grounds to serenade Lincoln, and he stepped out and spoke to them briefly of Vicksburg and Gettysburg. But then, as always, he quickly turned from the overall picture of the war to the personal level of the individual men who fought and won the battles. "I would like to speak in terms of praise due to the many brave officers and soldiers who have fought in the cause of the Union and liberties of the country from the beginning of the war," he said. A week later, he did so even more emphatically, by issuing a proclamation of thanksgiving for the victories, and recognition of the "sacrifices of life, limb, health and liberty." He set aside August 6 as a day to "visit with tender care and consolation throughout the length and breadth of our land all those who, through the vicissitudes of marches, voyages, battles and sieges, have been brought to suffer in mind, body or estate."[21]

Now that he had a victory in the East at last, the theme of sympathy and solicitude for the dead and wounded was one that he returned to over and over, and used to mark the victories in the West as well, and even the successes on the waters. Indeed, everything that Lincoln said and did with regard to the men in the ranks applied to the enlisted seamen of the Union navy. Their numbers were vastly smaller, and their scenes of service more limited, yet they must be remembered, too. "Nor must Uncle Sam's Web-feet be forgotten," he wrote in an open letter in August.

At all the watery margins they have been present. Not only on the deep sea, the broad bay, and the rapid river, but also up the narrow muddy bayou, and wherever the ground was a little damp, they have been, and made their tracks. Thanks to all. For the great republic—for the principle it lives by, and keeps alive—for man's vast future—thanks to all.[22]

In the immediate aftermath of Gettysburg, those who wanted Lincoln to start enforcing the draft got their wish, for, with volunteer quotas still not filled, and very heavy losses in Meade's ranks, the government had to have more men and soon. Until now conscription had only been a threat, but in mid-July it became reality, and almost at once fear and resentment, especially among the poor and the immigrant classes, welled over. The act authorizing conscription allowed drafted men to hire substitutes to go in their place, or else to pay a $300 commutation fee. When the first names were drawn in the New York draft on July 11, those able to afford neither felt penalized for their poverty. Already a parody came bitterly from some lips:

> *We're coming, Father Abraham, three hundred thousand more.*
> *We leave our homes and firesides with bleeding hearts and sore.*
> *Since poverty has been our crime, we bow to the decree;*
> *We are the poor who have no wealth to purchase liberty.*[23]

Two days after the drawing of the first names, bitter rioting erupted, not only fueled by resentment at the draft, but also directed at free blacks in the city who competed for jobs with the Irish immigrants. At once Lincoln ordered troops to maintain order, sending regiments from western states like Wisconsin rather than locally raised outfits that might have friends among the rioters or quail at using force if necessary. After a few days, and over one hundred deaths, the disturbance simmered down, controlled by volunteers who wanted the draft to go on and had no hesitation about enforcing it if need be. In the process, though they may not have realized it, the volunteers helped Lincoln change the relationship between the citizen and the national government: now the enforcement of the draft bypassed the state and made the individual directly accountable to Washington. Heretofore a male citizen's duty was only to his state, to enroll in and perhaps actually serve in the militia. Now one of the definitions of citizenship had changed, and it was Father Abraham and his "children" who, for their own reasons, made it happen.[24]

The chief effect of the draft was to encourage more men to enlist, which suited Lincoln's and the soldiers' purpose perfectly. Governors even asked him to postpone enforcement in order to give them a little more time to raise volunteers for their quotas under the latest call, so that their sons could avoid the stigma of being conscripted. But Lincoln refused to suspend or delay, fearing that the system of relying on volunteers was by August "so far exhausted, as to be inadequate." He identified a number of motives to impel a man to volunteer, all of which had come into play since the outset of the war. Patriotism, political feeling, ambition, courage, spirit of adventure, peer pressure, and more, all sent men to the armies. But now he believed that those forces had moved all the men who would be subject to them, "and yet we must somehow obtain more, or relinquish the original object of the contest, together with all the blood and treasure already expended in the effort." He did not ask or expect drafted men to like it, nor did he impugn them for being unpatriotic.

Every man had his own reasons for not volunteering. Yet always Lincoln returned to the driving imperative for more. "There can be no army without men," he said. "Men can only be had voluntarily, or involuntarily." In the increasing dearth of the former, he must turn to the latter. To those who argued that there were still enough men willing to volunteer without resorting to conscription, he said, Fine, volunteer yourselves and prove me wrong, and I will abandon conscription. A million or more men had volunteered before this, to sweat and suffer, and many to die. "Their toil and blood have been given as much for you as for themselves. Shall it all be lost rather than you too, will bear your part?" As for the substitute and commutation clauses, the hiring of substitutes was not objected to, yet a man willing to enlist for another might hire himself out for any amount he could get, $1,000 or more. At least the $300 commutation available to all put escape within reach of many who would not be able to afford a substitute. It was imperfect, he confessed, but better than no opportunity for escape at all.[25]

During the course of the war, not more than a quarter-million would be drafted, and of them, all but forty-six thousand managed either to hire substitutes or pay the $300 commutation, with the result that all the agitation over the issue greatly outweighed its real direct impact in raising manpower. Yet there is no question the soldiers stood with him. "I believe the draft is right and just and the President has a good policy and that is—putting down the war at any and whatever cost," said a New Hampshire volunteer in September. "Would you be willing to have it stop now and all the blood that has been spilled, spent for nothing?" he asked his parents in virtually an echo of Lincoln's own sentiment. Moreover, men in the ranks saw conscription as a way finally to shut up the Copperheads—by drafting them, too. If anything, they objected to the substitute and $300 commutation loopholes. And when the president issued another three-hundred-thousand call in October, the men in the army in Virginia all but cheered. "When lincolns three hundred thousand more comes thay will begin to make tracks," a Rhode Island artillerist wrote home. Private Charles Stevens of the 77th New York told his wavering friends in October that he expected to be home within a year, when his three-year enlistment expired, but sarcastically added that he did not expect to see many of them when he arrived, "for of *course* you will all answer Uncle Abraham's call for 300,000 more." He would be so lonesome that he would have to re-enlist himself, he feared. "We shall all be looking for you fellows about next January or Feb for then you wont say we are coming father Abraham *300* dollars more, for we are going to have that struck out of the *book*."[26]

Even in the admittedly inequitable operation of the draft, Lincoln tried to ensure a measure of fairness. Some men worried that, if they paid their commutation or hired a substitute, they might still be drafted at some future call, until the president directed that all such men should be exempt from conscription for three years, just as if they had been serving in uniform.[27] Then he held out another opportunity to men to escape the draft by volunteering with his call for three hundred thousand more on October 17. Looking ahead, the president knew that the enlistments of those first three-year regiments that had come forward in such great numbers in 1861 would be expiring within a few months. Many would re-enlist, he hoped, but to replace those who did not, this new call offered bounties, premiums, and even advance pay. Furthermore, to encourage the governors to work hard to get the men out, all volunteers would be deducted from the draft quotas assigned to the states.[28]

Somehow it worked. Volunteering proceeded well after the October call, yet the demands for manpower, and the imminent discharge of hundreds of thousands of the first three-year men, forced Lincoln to yet another draft call, in February 1864, this time for half a million, and then, two months later, another two hundred thousand for the army, navy, and marine services. The men who actually came into uniform through the draft were hardly the best, proved less motivated as soldiers than the volunteers, and seemed more likely to misbehave and desert. The veterans did not like them much, either. "The blood which is to nourish the nations heart in coming time is not so generous and free as it once was when nothing was seen of the conscripts despairing dulness," complained a private in the 2nd United States Artillery. Yet the old soldiers knew they had to have the men, however gained. "The soldier's greatest hope is that old Uncle Abe will enforce the draft right up to the handle, and if he can't do it any other way, let about twenty thousand men go home and do it for him," grumbled a Wisconsin soldier later that year. "We would like to go back and fight northern cowards and traitors than to fight rebels."[29]

Actually, Lincoln had a greater hope than that, and it lay with the veterans. It is an axiom of warfare that the first men to rush to arms are the best, the most spirited and motivated. Progressively after 1862, the quality of the new men coming into the armies gradually declined, with the exception of the young who were just passing the lawful age for enlistment. Men who had to be motivated by bounties, or who were hired to go in place of others, or who were drafted risked less, put up with less, and in the main gave less. Thus Lincoln's very considerable concern over losing that first huge wave of three-year men. It did not help that Congress passed a joint resolution prohibiting the payment of a $300 bounty to those veterans who might choose to re-enlist, a slap in the face to an old soldier who saw raw men of apparently lesser patriotism being paid to enlist while the government would not pay the same to keep an experienced man of proven worth. Lincoln asked Congress to change its mind, and it did. Better yet, when the three-year regiments started preparing to muster out, more than half of them chose to "veteranize" by re-enlisting, giving Father Abraham a whole army of seasoned men worth twice their numbers in new recruits. Far more of them than perhaps he expected shared his sense of their mission. Edward Everett Hale's inspirational new short novel *The Man Without a Country* had just appeared in the *Atlantic Monthly*, and many a soldier read it, including one twice-wounded veteran of Gettysburg. "It made a deep impression on my mind," said Charles Fuller of the 61st New York, "and it confirmed the sentiment I had cherished that it was well worth hardship, wounds, loss of limbs, or life even, to have a hand in preserving in its integrity such a country as ours."[30]

If only his generals in the East would use those men properly. Out in the West, by now Grant dominated the war, and the string of Union victories went on unchecked until September when an embarrassing defeat at Chickamauga, followed by the Confederates' siege of the defeated army in Chattanooga, stopped the Yankees for a while. Lincoln soon moved Grant to the command in that area, and by November he was preparing to break out and continue the delayed advance toward victory. In the East, however, nothing seemed to happen. Meade had allowed Lee to escape back to Virginia after Gettysburg, being too battered himself to offer an effective pursuit. Lincoln usually understood the limits of his own grasp of military science, but he was never able to fathom that a victorious army could be just as disorganized and exhausted by an encounter as the vanquished, and thus unable to follow up its triumph. He nearly lost Meade in his chagrin after Lee got away, but managed to keep him, though Lincoln was not quite satisfied. By September, when the general had still not advanced to bring on another campaign, Lincoln fretted to Welles, "It is the same old story of this Army of the Potomac. Oh, it is terrible, terrible, this weakness, this indifference of our Potomac generals, with such armies of good and brave men." The president's frustration became general knowledge, even among the soldiers. In a New Jersey artillery battery, from a state heavily Democrat and never overly fond of Lincoln, some of the soldiers that fall marched and sang a variant of the old "John Brown's Body" tune, to the words "Old Abe Lincoln stands shaking in his boots."[31]

Fortunately such critical comments were increasingly rare by the fall of 1863. Far more common was the New York soldier's simple statement, at this same time, that Lincoln "had got the good will of the soldiers by his zeal & patriotism." The volunteer might have added that Lincoln had earned it by his now widely known concern and empathy, and his near-constant association with the enlisted men. Though he did not like the pomp or the nuisance of having that military guard of Pennsylvania cavalry with him whenever he traveled from the White House, he yielded to necessity, and actually enjoyed the men's company, even though often he and Mary could not hear each other speak in their carriage, for the jingling and clanking of sabers and spurs. If anything, the president felt more concerned for the soldiers than they were for him. Seeing several of them to be awkward new recruits, he worried that they might hurt themselves accidentally with their unfamiliar weapons. One evening, in a heavy rain as he left the War Department, he saw the resigned look on one of the guards who would have to get soaked to accompany him and said, "Don't come out in this storm with me tonight, boys. I have my umbrella and can get home safely without you."[32]

Yet he rarely went abroad without a man in uniform. "I hardly feel respectable these days if I haven't a soldier for a companion," he told a congressman this fall. "Citizen's dress doesn't amount to much nowadays." He spoke with New York volunteer John Cunningham that fall at a photographer's studio, while waiting for his sitting, and told the man, "I count you and every soldier a friend." Nor did he mind that there was a soldier ahead of him for the artist's camera, and he declined any suggestion that he should go first. "Soldiers come first everywhere, these days," Lincoln explained. Pointing to his own civilian broadcloth, he said, "Black-coats are at a discount in the presence of the blue, and I recognize the merit of the discount."[33]

Lincoln's conversation with Private Cunningham may have taken place during his November 8, 1863, visit to the studio of noted photographer Alexander Gardner. If so, the president saw a soldier not only in the flesh, but also in the numerous photographs Gardner had taken at the front and in the camps during the past year. There were whole regiments on parade, and individual volunteers in moments of repose, a field hospital, scenes from Fredericksburg and Antietam, and images of his own visit to McClellan and the army the year before. Then there were the photos of Gettysburg, more than a dozen of them, and most poignant of all the dead, lying singly and in piles, Union and Confederate alike. There he saw the reality of what men like Cunningham might find for their future.

No more than a day or two earlier, Lincoln had received a note from David Wills of Gettysburg. In the aftermath of the terrible battle, Wills led a movement to create a soldier cemetery on the battlefield to hold some of the three thousand dead whose bodies had not been removed for burial by family. The date of November 19 had been set for formal dedication of the plot, and invitations were sent to dignitaries at every state and federal level. Lincoln received one sometime in October, and let it be known that he would come. That created a dilemma for Wills, since the principal orator of the occasion was to be Edward Everett of Massachusetts. Wills probably did not expect Lincoln actually to attend, since he so rarely left Washington, but now that he was coming it would be impolitic not to ask him to say something. Yet it would have to be brief. Thus Wills wrote asking for only a few "appropriate" sentences, adding, "It will be a source of gratification to the many widows and orphans that have been made almost friendless by the Great Battle here, to have you here personally! and it will kindle anew in the breasts of the comrades of these brave dead, who are now in the tended field or nobly meeting the foe in the front, a confidence that they who sleep in death on the Battle Field are not forgotten." So it would.[34]

Mary Lincoln did not want her husband to go. Their son Tad lay ill, and the memories of their boys Eddie and Willie lost to sickness were heartbreakingly strong. But Lincoln, though not feeling well himself, denied his wife for once. He felt he had to go to Gettysburg, for this was a call to be a father to ease the grieving of a nation, a greater duty even than that to his own little boy. Stanton made some of the arrangements for the trip, but when the president found that he was scheduled to leave by train the morning of November 19, tour the battlefield immediately on arrival, then attend the ceremonies and make his remarks and come home that night, he balked. "I do not like this arrangement," he told the war secretary. "I do not wish to so go that by the slightest accident we fail entirely." He was determined to attend, to say what he wanted to say to the soldiers and their families, and the nation, and he would not allow the risk of a train delay, or even his own advancing symptoms of variola to stand in the way.[35]

He left the day before, just to make certain. When he arrived, shortly before suppertime that evening, one of his first sights on stepping onto the station platform was the stacks of new caskets waiting to remove some soldier bodies to cemeteries near their homes. The town teemed with people who had come for the event on the morrow, and the people milled around Lincoln as he made his way to the Wills home on the town square for dinner and to spend the night. After a pleasant meal in good company, he went upstairs to a second-floor bedroom, accompanied by a single soldier, Sergeant H. Paxton Bingham of the 21st Pennsylvania Cavalry, assigned as bodyguard. Then, at 11 P.M., Governor Curtin finally arrived and came to Lincoln, who joined him in stepping out to visit Seward, staying at a nearby house. Still the crowds filled the streets, and as they walked Lincoln could hear the people singing "We are Coming, Father Abraham." Even after the president returned to his bedroom, the singing went on until well after 1 A.M., that same refrain echoing to his ears from the street.[36]

The next day he rode to the cemetery on a horse that was, as usual, too small for him, yet, as always, no one laughed. He gave up the idea of touring the battlefield. Perhaps he did not want to see it. He had seen death from battle. He could still remember those five men on the Illinois prairie that he had found when scouting in the Black

Hawk War, recalling the little round red spots on their heads where their scalps were missing, remembered even that one of the men had been wearing buckskin breeches. He had seen enough of death to know its face, and enough of battlefields, at least for now. Besides, as he rode with the procession into the cemetery itself, he could see the battle's by-product in the rough grounds, with eleven hundred earth mounds telling of their contents, and twenty-two hundred more to go.[37]

Everett spoke first, and for almost two hours. Then came a brief dirge, with words about "our Country's braves, who fell in Freedom's holy cause."[38] Then it was time for the president. He spoke for two minutes. He reminded them of what the Founding Fathers had created, and of how that creation now stood threatened by internecine war, a conflict whose rushing tides had washed up on the hills surrounding Gettysburg and left behind these dead for them to mourn. Even in burying them and marking their resting place as a spot for men to venerate for all time, he reminded the audience of the task they had died to advance, and that their work remained incomplete. Something more than death must come from their sacrifice, something not just for their generation but for all generations, and not just for the Union but for those everywhere who treasured freedom.[39]

Lincoln never met Private Wilbur Fisk of the 2nd Vermont Infantry. If he had, he might have gleaned from the young man something of the inspiration for his two minutes of immortal words. "I believe if there is anybody in the world that fulfills the Apostle's injunction, 'beareth all things,' and 'endureth all things,'" said Fisk, "it is the soldier."[40] The president agreed. Again and again he spoke of the "suffering" of the soldiers, and tried to find in the hardships they endured and the sacrifices they made a means of inspiring the rest of the Union to match its courage and determination to that of its men in uniform. Never did he come so close to distilling it all to an essence as he did at Gettysburg. Surely the mood of the moment was still with him when he reached Washington again the next day, full of emotion for his now healing son Tad, and his extended children in the armies. That very day, after a plea from the man's distraught wife, he suspended the sentence of a lieutenant convicted of desertion to save him from execution; and on finding that a number of Iroquois men, some no more than sixteen, had been enlisted by unscrupulous brokers who never paid them their bounties, the president discharged them from the service. He had done justice to the memory of the dead at Gettysburg. The task of seeing justice done to the living was never-ending.[41]

Even as young Tad got better, Lincoln's health deteriorated seriously in the days following his visit to Gettysburg. When word came that Grant had ended the siege of Chattanooga and driven the Confederates from his front back into northern Georgia, the president was too unwell to attend a victory celebration designed to help encourage volunteering. "Nothing would be more grateful to my feelings," said Lincoln in declining. "Freed from apprehension of wounding the just sensibilities of brave soldiers fighting elsewhere, it would be exceedingly agreeable to me to join in a suitable acknowledgment to those of the Great West, with whom I was born, and have passed my life." It was one of the few times he specifically paid tribute to those western soldiers—not that he valued their triumphs the less. They simply had not needed the nurturing required by their counterparts in the East. That, and the fact of his being in Washington, naturally drew most of Lincoln's—and the world's—attention to the Virginia theater and its army. Now, in some measure, he redressed the imbalance. "Honor to the Soldier, and Sailor everywhere, who bravely bears his country's cause," said Lincoln. "Honor also to the citizen who cares for his brother in the field, and serves as best he can, the same cause—honor to him, only less than to him, who braves, for the common good, the storms of heaven and the storms of battle."[42]

By the time he spoke at Gettysburg and paid his tribute to the soldiers of the West as well as the East, Lincoln had more than geographical boundaries to differentiate his children. He could sort them now by color, too. The issue of enlisting black soldiers arose almost from the moment the war started, especially propelled by the unauthorized emancipation orders of ardent abolitionist generals like Frémont. Free Negroes in the North tried repeatedly to offer themselves as soldiers, including two regiments offered from Indiana in August 1862. In declining the offer, Lincoln said that at that moment he was "not prepared to go the length of enlisting negroes as soldiers."[43] In fact, the July 1862 confiscation act contained a provision for the enlistment of blacks, but had not been pressed because of Lincoln's fears of the result in the border states. At that very moment, he had already done a draft of his Preliminary Emancipation Proclamation, but he knew that any suggestion in it of arming blacks might still send tens of thousands of wavering but loyal border-state men into the Confederacy. Moreover, as yet he was enlisting volunteers through the several states, officially as state militia called for the emergency. The 1792 militia act under which he operated called for the enrollment of all "free, able-bodied, white male" citizens. Opinion divided on whether that language required whites to enroll and left it voluntary for blacks to do so—since the word "free" could only have meaning when applied to blacks, all whites being free at birth—or if the failure to mention Negroes specifically constituted a tacit prohibition of their enrollment. In the end, however, most states enacted their own specific prohibitions, which seemed to settle the issue.[44]

Yet, by the end of 1862, when it was evident that he could weather the emancipation issue, Lincoln was ready to start looking at its inevitable result, pressed from many sides by whites and blacks alike. On Christmas Day 1862, Lincoln told Sumner of Massachusetts that he intended to raise colored regiments and use them to hold the Mississippi and other important points in the Deep South, thus freeing white troops for active operations in climates more suited to them. "The colored population is the great *available* and yet *unavailed* of, force for restoring the Union," he told Andrew Johnson of Tennessee. "The bare sight of fifty thousand armed, and drilled black soldiers on the banks of the Mississippi, would end the rebellion at once. And who doubts that we can present that sight, if we but take hold in earnest."[45]

When the final proclamation appeared, it contained a clear statement that blacks would be accepted into the Union army, and immediately it sent a surge through the black population, free and slave, North and South. In occupied areas of the Confederacy, Union officers read it aloud to assemblages of free "contrabands" and runaway slaves. At Beaufort, South Carolina, listening blacks began to sing spontaneously "My Country, 'Tis of Thee." In Virginia, officers in the XI Corps read it at battalion drill on the morning of January 3, 1863, to see it heard "with great jubilation" by Negroes from the vicinity. The very next day, slaves on a nearby plantation owned by a Confederate sympathizer put down their tools and stopped working. It was only the shortest of steps to picking up rifles instead. Indeed, conditioned by centuries of obeying the white man's word as law, many slaves regarded the proclamation of Father Abraham as tantamount to a requirement that they enlist. "The hour demands of us . . . action, immediate pressing action!" said editor Thomas Hamilton in the New York *Anglo-African.* "It is a fight for freedom and we are bound to go in." White armies had tried to end the rebellion and failed. "Our tried and trusted ruler calls upon the negro 'to come to the rescue!'" Black leader Henry Garnet added that black men must step forward and volunteer in order to create a legacy for their posterity, "an heirloom in which their children and children's children would remember with pride that their fathers were not cowards when the country called them to its defense."[46]

"Give us fair play," said the great black leader Frederick Douglass, "and open here your recruiting offices, and their doors shall be crowded with black recruits to fight the battles of the country." And so they were. Lincoln took an immediate interest in raising these new soldiers, and especially in enlisting them in occupied portions of the South from among runaway slaves. He authorized Northern governors to send recruiting agents south to enroll blacks, allowing them to count for unfilled portions of the quotas assigned to their states, and argued that such an enlistee actually counted twice as weapons in the cause: once as a soldier in the ranks, and again as a man whose labor was now denied to the Confederacy. Within days after issuing the final proclamation, Lincoln began encouraging white officers who wanted to command black troops to go south to start organizing their regiments. "It is a great day for the black man when you tell him he shall carry a gun," said Lincoln. "The time has come when I am for everybody fighting the rebels. Let Indians fight them; let the Negroes fight them; and if you have got any strong-legged jackasses in Iowa that can kick rebels to death, they have my hearty consent."[47]

At first Lincoln did not feel entirely certain how to employ these new weapons. He considered putting them in different uniforms from those of white troops, but in the end equipped them exactly the same in every respect. He had a notion to put all of the new Negro regiments into a single corps, perhaps assigning it to General Benjamin F. Butler and attaching it to the Army of the Potomac, which would be the most visible of assignments and do the most for encouraging further enlistments, but Butler objected. Called upon by friends of Frémont's who promised that he could rally ten thousand blacks if promised their command, Lincoln was willing to put aside his considerable dislike for the troublesome man, and said he would gladly give Frémont the command if the ten thousand came forward. Indeed, he told a group of the general's friends that he would "gladly receive into the service not ten thousand but ten times ten thousand colored troops," for he expected them to perform "essential service in finishing the war."[48]

Naturally there was opposition. A little of it came from blacks themselves, who attacked Lincoln for only freeing those slaves who technically, as of January 1, 1863, were not under his power to free, and more for leaving those under his rule enslaved. Unable at the moment to see that the proclamation was only a first step on the inevitable road to full emancipation, some, like George Stephens, argued bitterly that "United States Emancipation is a symbol of national selfishness, an indice of a blind infatuation, and a fulmination of Executive folly and indecision." Accustomed to generations of white indifference, Stevens and others simply failed to see the necessity of such a halfway policy.[49]

Much more of the opposition, of course, came from whites, who objected both to the war's being turned into a crusade for freedom, and to being asked to fight alongside blacks. Lincoln's response to one such complaint could have been sent to many. "You say you will not fight to free negroes," he began. "Some of them seem willing to fight for you." To the extent that blacks ceased lending their labor to the foe, they thus helped the cause of the Union. "Whatever negroes can be got to do as soldiers, leaves just so much less for white soldiers to do." Yet blacks were just like other people. "Why should they do anything for us, if we will do nothing for them? If they stake their lives for us, they must be prompted by the strongest motive—even to the promise of freedom. And the promise being made, must be kept." The president even tried to shame his opponents on this question. Peace would come, he said, and when it did "there will be some black men who can remember that, with silent tongue, and clenched teeth, and steady eye, and well-poised bayonet, they have helped mankind on to this great consummation; while, I fear, there will be some white ones, unable to forget that, with malignant heart, and deceitful speech, they have strove to hinder it."[50]

Among the rank and file, opinions followed much the same line as reactions to the proclamation, except that once men swallowed emancipation it was much easier for them to digest black enlistments as well, for every sable soldier in the field was one step more toward sending all soldiers home with their job complete. In the camps, like those of the 59th Illinois, the volunteers often debated "about Old Abes black foot pads." In the end, said one Illinois private, "we have come to the conclusion to let him do as he pleases as we can't hinder him." If not absolutely enthusiastic, the soldier response was to cooperate and make the best of it, and that was all Lincoln needed.[51]

Once the enlisting began, Lincoln appeared to show the same concern for the black volunteers as for the whites. He saw that they got the same equipment, lent his support to black clergymen going off to war with them as chaplains, and rather quickly shifted from his original intent to use the new regiments in garrison and guard duty and decided that they could be front-line soldiers.[52] Yet the new regiments, to be commanded by white officers and eventually designated United States Colored Troops for the most part, presented some special demands to the president, and special responsibilities. Confederate authorities reacted instantly, and angrily, to the proclamation and the announcement of Negro enlistments. They almost immediately responded with an edict that any captured blacks would be regarded as runaway slaves and returned to their masters or sold back into slavery, while their white officers would be treated as men inciting servile insurrection, punishable by death under state laws. Just as troubling was the prospect that many Confederate soldiers would find fighting Negroes so inflaming that they might not grant them the normal usages of civilized warfare, perhaps even executing prisoners on the spot.

"I know it is right that a colored man should go and fight for his country," the wife of a Negro soldier wrote to Lincoln, but she implored that he not let any Confederate acts of barbarity go unpunished. Indeed he would not. Lincoln immediately responded to the Confederate threat with one of his own, in his Order of Retaliation on July 30, 1863. For every black soldier executed, he would shoot a captured white Confederate soldier. For every man returned to slavery, a Southern prisoner of war would be put to hard labor. For once, the erroneous but pervasive image of Lincoln as a monstrous tyrant so prevalent throughout the Confederacy worked to his benefit. In fact, the president had not the heart for avenging one innocent victim by retaliating against another. He never ordered the executions or hard labor that he threatened, and it is extraordinarily unlikely that he ever would have. But Confederates did not know that, and since they chose to believe the worst of him, their false beliefs may actually have helped control their own behavior.[53]

Yet there were exceptions. Black soldiers fought well in a few engagements in 1863, most notably in the siege of Port Hudson, Louisiana, that summer, and in assaults near Charleston, South Carolina, in July. When captured, they were not put to death but sent on as prisoners of war to the same compounds as white prisoners, though often not accorded quite the same treatment. Worse, of course, the refusal of Southern authorities to include blacks and their white officers in prisoner exchange led to the virtual breakdown of the system, dooming tens of thousands to remain in festering prison camps. Though Lincoln allowed some exchanges to continue at first, he vowed to hold back some Confederates as hostages for the good treatment of his black soldiers, and again promised retaliation for any mistreatment.[54]

There were no outrages until the Confederate attack on the mixed white and black garrison of Fort Pillow, Tennessee, on the Mississippi River, on April 12, 1864. The Federals were overrun, and in the aftermath a host of influences conspired to produce an atrocity. Many of the white Yankees were Tennesseeans, despised for their disloyalty to the Confederacy by the Tennessee soldiers in the victorious army. Moreover, those Union soldiers were hardly the best to take the field, some of them believed to be guilty of mistreating the families of Confederates under their command. There were even old prewar feuds still in effect between men on the two sides. Tossing several hundred black soldiers into the mix only made it more volatile. Despite attempts to surrender, many white and black soldiers alike were cut down, often after laying down their arms, and the Fort Pillow "Massacre" was born.

First reports were unclear as to what had happened, and when Lincoln spoke at the Sanitary Fair in Baltimore six days later he knew few details but promised that his government would demand the same treatment for all its men in enemy hands. "Upon a clear conviction of duty I resolved to turn that element of strength to account," he said of Negro enlistments, "and I am responsible for it to the American people, to the christian world, to history, and on my final account to God." Within another two weeks, the president was certain that a massacre had indeed taken place, and sought advice from the Cabinet on what should be done. On May 17, he drafted a response, to be sent through Stanton, to Confederate authorities. He would not retaliate for those already killed, but he would set aside a certain number of Confederate officers and enlisted men who were prisoners as hostages against any future atrocity. Furthermore, since the foe continued to refuse to exchange black soldiers, he would set aside an equal number of white Confederate prisoners as a continuing guarantee, whom he would stand ready to exchange for the Negroes at any time. Most menacing of all, however, if he did not receive a satisfactory answer within a reasonable time, he would assume that captured blacks had been murdered or enslaved, and would himself take "such action as may then appear expedient and just."⁵⁵

In the end, Lincoln thought better of sending even that, at least until the Committee on the Conduct of the War had conducted an investigation into the affair. Perhaps the most important message was not the one he did not send to Jefferson Davis, but the one that his public announcements sent to his black soldiers and their leaders in the Union. He would give them every protection he could, without distinction as to color. It was an important message, especially since at the same time he was in the middle of another controversy, this one over equitable treatment of Negro soldiers by their own government. Lincoln repeatedly had to intervene to prevent abuses. Reports came to him that an officer in Kentucky was physically forcing some former slaves to enlist. "The like must not be done by you," the president warned him. "You must not force negroes any more than white men." Meanwhile, he ordered Stanton to investigate the charge. Some recruiters were indeed heavy-handed. When a wife tried to stop recruiter James Ayers from pressuring her husband, he told her, "Father Abraham dont want women and haint sent me after them. . . . I want your man."⁵⁶

The issue that caused the greatest trouble was pay. "When a man leaves home, family, and security, to risk his limbs and life in the field of battle," said Douglass, "for God's sake let him have all the honor which he may achieve, let his color be what it may." Part of that honor was equal earnings for equal risks. Initially the War Department promised black volunteers the same $13 a month that was paid to whites, but then it decided that these new soldiers were actually enrolled under the authority of the July 1862 Militia Act, which provided only $10, regardless of color, and $3 of that was to be charged to the soldier for clothing. Thus the new United States Colored Troops found themselves receiving a net of just $7 a month. "Are we *Soldiers*, or are we *Labourers?*" an infuriated man in the black 54th Massachusetts wrote to Lincoln in September 1863. "We have done a Soldier's Duty. Why Can't we have a Soldier's pay?" In a stinging rebuke, he pointed out that, if the Union was going to demand equal treatment for its soldiers from the enemy, "would it not be well and consistent to set the example herself by paying all her *Soldiers* alike?"⁵⁷

The protests were strong and immediate. "Lincoln despotism," charged one black. In the 21st United States Colored Troops, a sergeant ordered his men to stack their arms on November 19—the same day that Lincoln spoke in Gettysburg—and was charged with mutiny and eventually shot. In the black 55th Massachusetts, seventy-five enlisted men sent a letter to Lincoln threatening "stringent measures" if they were not given equal pay. By June 1864, more soldiers were being charged and shot for mutiny. The 54th Massachusetts refused to accept its pay entirely for eighteen months, and desertions among black troops escalated above the rate for white soldiers, and stayed there. "Do you think that we will tamely submit like spaniels to every indignity?" said one soldier attacking the administration. Governor John Andrew of Massachusetts appealed to Lincoln to redress the inequity, and the Negro soldiers themselves repeatedly applied to him for justice. "If you, as Chief Magistrate of the Nation, will assure us of our whole pay, we are content," wrote one.[58]

Lincoln took less of a direct role in the controversy, perhaps because he felt his hands tied by the attorney general's ruling on the 1862 Militia Act. But by June 1864, the problem threatened to undermine morale seriously, and he asked Bates for another opinion. Bates responded that he had found a way to justify not applying the 1862 act to blacks. Thus they were entitled to the same pay as white soldiers, without distinction. With that, and action by Congress, at last the controversy was laid to rest, and the Negro troops were raised to their full proper pay and reimbursed retroactively for what they had been denied. In settling the controversy, the president appeared more to be led than to lead, and yet he may have chosen to have it appear that way. Certainly his very pointed request to Bates to rethink his earlier ruling carried with it the unspoken message that Lincoln *wanted* a new opinion that would solve the problem.[59]

It was a difficult struggle for everyone, Father Abraham and his black children, and progress came slowly, yet it came. By the close of the war, Lincoln was recommending commissioning black officers in the regiments, and one actually rose to become a major before it was over. At the end of 1863, more than a hundred thousand had enlisted in the United States Colored Troops, and in his message to Congress the president reported, "So far as tested, it is difficult to say they are not as good soldiers as any." When some suggested in August 1864 that the Union ought to offer to help return runaway slaves to their masters as a condition for the South's laying down its arms, Lincoln refused even to consider the question. "Why should they give their lives for us, with full notice of our purpose to betray them?" he retorted. "Drive back to the support of the rebellion the physical force which the colored people now give, and promise us, and neither the present, nor any coming administration, *can* save the Union." To others he said it even more emphatically. "This is not a question of sentiment or taste, but one of physical force which may be measured and estimated as horse-power and Steam-power are measured and estimated. Keep it and you can save the Union. Throw it away, and the Union goes with it." The suggestion that blacks should be asked to fight on the condition that they might be re-enslaved in the future was ridiculous. "It *can* not be; and it *ought* not to be."[60]

More than that, however, as 1865 approached, Lincoln was ready to look beyond the enlistment of Negro soldiers. As early as January 1864, he discussed what should be done at the close of the war, especially with regard to the former Confederates. He envisioned, as did most men of reason, a universal amnesty as the best and fastest way to start healing. But he added that he could not see any way to allow universal forgiveness to the foe without at the same time granting universal suffrage, "or, at least, suffrage on the basis of intelligence and military service." In short, that meant that a black man who fought for his country had a right to a vote in it as well. The Negro regiments had fought and bled and died toe to toe with their white counterparts in saving the nation. He saw it as his moral obligation to recognize that "they have demonstrated in blood their right to the ballot, which is but the humane protection of the flag they have so fearlessly defended." Restoration of the Union, in sum, would have to bring with it civil and political equality. "When you give the Negro these rights," he said, "when you put a gun in his hands, it prophesies something more: it foretells that he is to have the full enjoyment of his liberty and manhood." Just how far Lincoln would have pressed enfranchisement for his black soldiers would have to remain a mystery.[61]

For the newly freed and the newly enlisted black men who served in the Union army—in the end more than 179,000 of them—perhaps the greatest moment was when they, too, shared that experience of paying their respects, of marching past their president in their new uniforms, looking as smart and martial as any. On April 23, 1864, and again two days later, newly mustered black regiments in a division attached to the IX Corps passed through Washington on their way to the Virginia front. They marched proudly down Pennsylvania Avenue, past Willard's Hotel, where Lincoln and their commander, Burnside, stood on a balcony watching. When the six black regiments came in sight of the president they went wild, singing, cheering, dancing in the street while marching. As each unit passed they saluted, and he took off his hat in return, the same modest yet meaningful acknowledgment that he gave his white soldiers. He looked old and worn to the men on the street, but they could not see the cheer in his breast as he witnessed the culmination of their long journey from slavery, and pondered, perhaps, what it had cost him to be a part of it. Even when rain began to fall and Burnside suggested they step inside while the parade continued, Lincoln decided to stay outdoors. "If *they* can stand it," he said, "I guess I can."[62]

7

THE QUALITY OF MERCY

For I know him, that he will command his children
and his household after him, and they shall keep the way of the Lord,
to do justice and judgment;
that the Lord may bring upon Abraham that which
he hath spoken of him.

[Genesis 18:19]

FATHER ABRAHAM OFTEN SPENT HIS EVENINGS AND NIGHTS at the Soldiers' Home in suburban Washington, especially in the warm months. Sometimes he even ate with the men in the huge dining room, whose long tables seated up to two thousand at once. Now and then, like soldiers everywhere, the volunteers managed to get liquor onto the premises, and when that happened a drunken fight or two was sooner or later inevitable. In the president's presence, the men would be on their best behavior, and likely he saw nothing of this sort with his own eyes, but he may well have heard the rumpus from his room. Often as not the result would be a court-martial.

Soldier misbehavior was nothing new to Lincoln. He had seen his own men get drunk and disorderly in the Black Hawk War. He had found two of them missing when they deserted, and knew firsthand the temptation to step outside the rules when he broke them himself and wore the wooden sword in punishment. More than that, he possessed a keen understanding of the average American of his time, and of the impossibility of making that free-spirited, independent creature conform to a strange new set of rigid disciplines in the military. In the abstract a volunteer could admit the need for subordination and rules, but in actual practice his naturally independent instincts would get him in trouble time after time. Lincoln may not have expected it when he took office, but the nature of the clash between those volunteers and the military-justice system, combined with his own accessibility and acknowledged concern for the common soldiers, made it inevitable that the president himself would be drawn into the tug between spirit and subordination.[1]

The scope of the problem is evident in the fact that, during the whole course of the war, about two million men served in Lincoln's armies and more than a hundred thousand went before courts-martial: one of every twenty soldiers, or 5 percent of the army, a surprisingly high proportion unless one takes into account the considerable number of infractions, many of them quite minor, that could result in charges. Moreover, there was in the very nature of the armies an inbuilt dynamic that guaranteed frequent clashes over discipline. Elected officers in the volunteer regiments came largely from the professional classes, especially at the higher ranks of regimental command. Such officers, not having been trained or experienced in handling large numbers of men, could easily rely on excessive discipline for control. Many of the higher-ranking generals came from the old prewar Regular Army, and felt a disdain for the jumped-up new volunteer colonels who had gotten their rank overnight. Add that many of those volunteer officers had been lawyers and politicians, unused to taking orders from anyone, and the situation begged for clashes of ego that found settlement in court. On top of it all, wartime loosened the bonds on everyone's behavior, providing an arena in which those already disposed to stretch the law as civilians felt tempted to stretch it even further in uniform.

Fortunately, not all of those hundred thousand cases ended up on Lincoln's desk, but hundreds of them did, most on appeal from either the convicted soldier, his family, or his friends, and capital cases by the president's own explicit instruction. To all of them Lincoln applied a maxim that he expressed early in the war, when he reinstated an army captain unfairly dismissed on the accusation that he had been a disunionist. "Fair play is a jewell," said the president. "Give him a chance if you can."[2]

All of the petty and ordinary crimes came to Lincoln at times—robbery, theft of rations and liquor, and the like, even a soldier caught selling obscene photographs. If he could find any mitigating circumstances, he overturned convictions with pardons and returned the soldiers to duty. Being a lawyer himself, he examined the trial proceedings to determine if the accused had been fairly tried, and more than once rejected a conviction because the charged had been denied his rights in defense. He also showed concern about the consequences of the punishments meted out. Officers unfairly dismissed from the service he wanted fully exonerated, so they could be appointed again if their men or their governors chose. Meanwhile, at the most common of punishments for minor infractions, forfeiture of pay, Lincoln repeatedly balked. "I do not like this punishment of withholding pay," he told Stanton, "it falls so very hard upon poor families." To get around it, he repeatedly either set aside the punishment or in some cases allowed the convicted soldier to re-enlist in a new regiment, to qualify for the enlistment bounty. In one instance, when two Illinois regiments were charged with poor behavior leading to their capture, he ordered that the soldiers suffer no loss of pay after their release.[3]

A few cases came to him of men convicted of preparing and selling to other soldiers false and forged discharges. In one instance Lincoln pardoned the offender from a sentence of hard labor for the balance of his enlistment, and in another showed that he was always prepared to mitigate a sentence for a man with a good previous record. A private in the 71st Pennsylvania was sentenced to serve out the rest of his enlistment without pay and then receive a dishonorable discharge. But Lincoln noted that he had been a hero at Ball's Bluff, fought at Gettysburg, and captured three enemy battle flags, and even had the plea of a United States attorney in Philadelphia on his behalf. In the end, he invoked executive clemency to allow the man to finish his service honorably, and with pay. He also granted forgiveness in cases of false documents signed by men who could not read, and in general extended extra understanding to the illiterate, who were often the dupes of others.[4]

From time to time, other sorts of cases begged his attention: an officer dismissed for selling captured Confederate cotton, another dishonorably discharged for unbecoming conduct, an unjust conviction for fraud. In a large proportion of the cases the president granted pardon, or else a pardon with some condition, most often the stipulation that the offender either serve out his term honorably, or enlist in a new regiment, or even the navy, if dismissed from an old command. Occasionally a more serious case came to him that grew out of the unique circumstances of the raising of this volunteer army. A Pennsylvania cavalryman in hospital was induced by a broker, who made his living on commissions paid by men for whom he found substitutes, to go to Philadelphia and enlist as a substitute in the I I Ith Pennsylvania. Such an act presented an extremely serious issue for the military, just as did enlisting for a bounty, then "jumping"—deserting—to enlist again, for another bounty. A few unscrupulous men made a fair income through bounty jumping and multiple enlistments, and to discourage the practice the War Department made these crimes punishable by death. When the case of the gullible Pennsylvanian ended with a sentence of death and it came to Lincoln, however, he saw that the man had voluntarily confessed and wanted to atone. An admission of guilt and expression of contrition almost always seemed to touch Lincoln, who regarded such things as the first steps to redemption. His order was that the offender serve out his new three-year enlistment honorably, and in return he would grant a pardon, thinking that "it was better to have this young man for three years, than to shoot him."[5]

Inevitably, more serious matters came to him, crimes of the sort he had seen in civil practice years before. Murders accounted for 6 percent of all courts-martial. Occasionally these were cases of soldiers killing civilians, but most often the victims were fellow enlisted men. Perhaps the first Lincoln saw came in May 1861, the accused a man in the famed 69th New York. On appeal from the men of the regiment, the president commuted the death sentence to imprisonment, but usually he looked on his own for anything that could justify a lesser sentence. When the offender was drunk, or a mere youth like a fifteen-year-old cavalryman, or if unusual provocation had led to the act, he extended commutation or even pardon. In several cases he took insanity into account, even ordering medical examinations himself and giving precise instructions as to how the accused was to be tested. Lincoln sometimes initially commuted a death sentence to life imprisonment, or periods like ten years or eighteen years at hard labor, and then later extended a full pardon if he could justify clemency. Nevertheless, in some cases, when he examined fully the facts of the case, he let harsh prison sentences stand; in a few cases, he purposely withheld a stay of execution until the last minute, to allow the guilty men to suffer and perhaps learn a lesson.[6]

Far more numerous were the specific military infractions that came to the White House on appeal. One of these, a charge of sleeping on guard duty, would have more influence on the spread of Lincoln's reputation for magnanimity and mercy than any other single case, yet, ironically, he may have had little or nothing to do with it. Private William Scott of the 3rd Vermont Infantry was with his regiment in the defenses surrounding Washington and northern Virginia in the summer of 1861. One night, when he took his turn at sentry on the Chain Bridge over the Potomac, he fell asleep; an officer caught him, and charges were filed. On September 4, a court found him guilty, and since his was the first case of this kind brought to trial, it sentenced him to be shot as an example to all. No record exists of any appeal made to Lincoln, or of any order for a pardon coming from the White House. It does appear, however, that Lincoln learned of the case; on the morning of September 8, he even called on McClellan and asked him to pardon the boy, suggesting that the general could say Mrs. Lincoln had asked for the reprieve if he feared the public would think him too soft for doing it on his own. The general agreed. Since this was the first case of its kind, they preferred to make an example of leniency rather than harshness. That same day, McClellan announced that Scott would be pardoned and returned to the ranks. Seven months later, on the Peninsula, Scott fell mortally wounded in the action at Lee's Mill, and apparently remained unconscious from the moment he was hit until he died.[7]

Rapidly the story changed somehow, partly no doubt by word of mouth and campfire gossip, but mainly through the agency of Francis De Haas Janvier, a Washington clerk who heard the Scott story—or an exaggerated version—and commemorated it in a narrative poem that he called *The Sleeping Sentinel*. On January 19, 1863, the actor James E. Murdoch gave the poem its first public reading, at the White House with Lincoln present, and then again, later that day, in the Senate, with the president and first lady again in attendance. Murdoch opened, appropriately enough, with Portia's "quality of mercy" speech from *The Merchant of Venice*, and then launched into the poem. In it, Scott was the only son of a widow, and had been kept at his sentry post longer than his normal watch. Then, after his trial and conviction, the word of the injustice went abroad as far as Lincoln in the White House:

> *And yet, amid the din of war, he heard the plaintive cry*
> *Of that poor soldier, as he lay in prison doomed to die!*

The news only reached the president on the day Scott was to die. Frantically he called for his carriage and raced to the scene, arriving to find the soldier standing in front of the firing squad, the order to shoot almost on the provost's lips. Soldiers filled the air with cheers as Lincoln reprieved him on the spot and exacted in return a pledge that Scott would redeem himself thereafter. And so he did: at Lee's Mill, Scott led a charge and went down with six bullets in his body, but before he died he expressed thanks to Lincoln for giving him the chance to die like a soldier, praying that "God, with His unfailing grace, would bless our President!"[8]

It was almost all a fiction, which Lincoln knew as well as any, yet he seemed to enjoy the performance, unaware that he was seeing the inauguration of one of his most enduring myths. Several times he actually did pardon men sentenced to death for sleeping on sentry duty, one of them because the volunteer was known to have a lethargic condition that made him fall asleep even during conversation, and another because the "man" was just sixteen.[9] Certainly it would be out of character with the rest of the president's record of leniency to allow a man to die merely for falling asleep. "I am wondering whether I have used the pardoning power as much as I ought," he told one caller. "I feel that the picket who sleeps at his post is imperiling, it may be, the entire army, and I know how serious that is. But the officers only see the force of military discipline; perhaps it is right, but I see other things. I feel how the man may have been exposed to long watches with no opportunity for proper rest, and so sleep steals upon him unawares. I would not relax the discipline of the army, but I do want to be considerate of every case."[10] Why he did not choose to correct the misstatements in Janvier's poem poses a puzzling question. Perhaps Lincoln simply took it for what it was, a work of literature, and thus not bound by rules of fact. Or quite possibly he saw that the poem might work to his advantage, for in its popularity it could boost soldier morale by promulgating through fiction the *fact* that soldiers should expect mercy and justice from their Father Abraham.

Of far greater concern were those genuinely overt transgressions of military law, one of the most common—and least surprising—being insubordination, sometimes even classed as mutiny. The very word "subordination" rankled the Enlightenment values of young Americans, running counter to all their instincts and even much of their national mythology, all the way back to the militia myth itself. The volunteer army depended upon the cheerful acquiescence of men willingly taking orders from others who, in a different context, were their social and civic equals. Some men, some situations, and some elected or appointed superiors simply made that subordination too irksome to bear. Men convicted of the crime of refusing to obey orders or promoting insubordination could be, and were, sentenced to be shot, yet Lincoln understood well enough that, if insubordination was a crime against military discipline, subordination was a crime against American nature, and he showed leniency. "When he is shot you do not know that you approve the shooting of as true a man as lives," a friend wrote to Lincoln in pleading for one convicted mutineer. Often petitioners also reminded Lincoln that the condemned had voted for him in 1860; they may or may not have, but the transparent appeal for gratitude was hardly necessary. "This offence is not so common as to require so severe an example," he said in relieving one soldier's death sentence; during the course of the war, he invariably commuted all such sentences for mutiny to imprisonment, or merely reprimand.[11]

Moreover, Lincoln knew that insubordination, like a number of the less heinous offenses, often had alcohol as a driving impulse. Though almost totally abstemious himself, and supporting of the Temperance Union's efforts, the president knew that men and liquor were inseparable, especially in the tedium of the camp and field. Some convicted men told him openly the story of their infractions, perhaps adding a bit of embellishment in the hope of winning his favor. "i went out and got Drunk and while i was eating my breakfast i cheared for the President and damed Mcleland," Joshua Painter of the 21st Veteran Reserve told him. When his corporal arrested Painter and called Lincoln "a dam nigger," Painter kicked the man and choked him. "If you will releas me i will keep sober and be a good man," begged the repentant soldier. Lincoln was willing to see officers cashiered for drunkenness, for they were supposed to be leading by example, but the common soldiers more often got his forbearance when their cases went to him. If a soldier struck his officer or was insubordinate while intoxicated, the president generally pardoned him on condition of future good behavior, especially if the man had a favorable record in combat. Even manslaughter could be mitigated by inebriation and win a pardon for a man with an otherwise good record. When one soldier was to be executed for wounding another while in his cups, Lincoln sent a telegram to the officer in charge: "If you have not shot Barney D. yet—don't."[12]

Striking a corporal was one thing. When an enlisted man struck or attacked a commissioned officer he entered an altogether different degree of crime, and the prescribed punishment was often death. Yet striking a superior officer was the second-most-common offense committed in the army, and one of the more frequent sources of appeals to Lincoln. "I would beg you to touch the hem of your garment as did one of old," pleaded the wife of a New York private who had drunkenly hit his officer and gotten a stiff sentence in return. Again the president looked for mitigating circumstances, as he did in concluding that passion and not some other motive caused a German immigrant volunteer to strike his officer while drunk, allowing him to reduce the sentence from death to one year in prison. Indeed, hard labor, frequently with a twenty-five-pound ball and chain attached to one leg, seemed to be a preferred alternative to execution, though in some cases, especially when one of the governors asked it as a favor, Lincoln simply discharged the soldier and annulled the sentence. Perhaps remembering his own army days, both as an officer whose men occasionally talked back to him, and as an enlisted man himself who may have felt the pent-up resentments against the brass endemic with all soldiers, he inclined almost to sympathy with some offenders. When a Pennsylvania congressman asked clemency for a boy convicted and sentenced to be shot for hitting an officer, Lincoln responded that Congress should provide the remedy to the problem for this whole class of offenders. Asked how, Lincoln answered, "Pass a law that a private shall have a right to knock down his captain."[13]

Lincoln seemed especially compassionate about cowardice in the face of the enemy, for which a man could be branded, drummed out of the service, or even executed. He had never faced a hostile foe, never known the kind of fear of imminent death that every soldier confronted on the eve of battle. He told Brooks that he would not like to face the prospect of sudden death. He thought himself physically rather a coward, not at all good material for a soldier, certain that, unless caught up in the excitement of a battle, he would surely drop his rifle and run. "I have not fully made up my mind how I should behave when minie balls were whistling and these great oblong shells shrieking in my ear," he told a Connecticut congressman shortly after Gettysburg. "I might run away." When cases of convictions for cowardice came before him, he remembered, and liked to recite, an old story about an Irish soldier who ran in battle and explained, "Well, Captain, it was not me fault. I've a heart in me breast as brave as Julius Caesar; but when the battle begins, somehow or other those cowardly legs of mine will run away wid me."[14]

"I have no doubt that is true of many a man who honestly meant to do his duty but who was overcome by a physical fear greater than his will," Lincoln told Judge Advocate General Joseph Holt. As a result, he called them his "leg cases," and it seemed fearfully unjust to penalize or shoot a man simply for being afraid. "No one need ever expect me to sanction the shooting of a man for running away in battle," he told Representative Daniel Voorhees of Indiana. "I won't do it. A man can't help being a coward any more than he can help being a humpback. . . . In any contest or controversy which arises between the head and the heels, I never knew the heels to get anything but the best of it." In frustration, he told Voorhees, "No, sir, they needn't send any leg cases to me at all. I'll never order a man shot for any such offense." Nor did he. Over and over Lincoln pardoned or commuted sentences. The worst he would do to a cowardly officer was approve his dishonorable discharge, and with an enlisted man he usually countenanced nothing more than a period of hard labor; both sentences could be reduced or even erased entirely if the condemned was willing to re-enlist in a new regiment or continue to serve with a good record.[15]

Even in cases of treason, Lincoln preferred to err on the side of leniency, though most of those that arose were charged against civilians, and relatively few came to him from the armies. The loyalty of officers from the old Regular Army became a controversial issue in the early months of the war, first with the resignation of almost a third of them to go over to the Confederacy, and then because a substantial proportion of the remainder were Democrats evidencing some degree of opposition to the war, and rather too much loyalty to McClellan. Still, as in the case in which the president enunciated his "fair play is a jewell" policy, he refused to punish an officer for treason without giving him every opportunity to refute the allegation. In November 1861, he instructed then Secretary of War Cameron that any officer dismissed for disloyalty who did not subsequently go over to the other side was still entitled to a hearing if he maintained his loyalty.[16]

The single most numerous category of all the cases that came to Lincoln's personal attention were those of men who left the ranks without permission, either absent without leave or by outright desertion. Indeed, of all his wartime correspondence, these make up the largest single body of his papers, and it was here, perhaps more than in any other capacity, that he came in direct personal contact with soldiers in trouble. Scores of men who, through carelessness, confusion, wavering commitment, or a host of other causes, found themselves absent from their commands and liable to arrest and prosecution if caught, came to Washington and approached Lincoln himself. They saw him during his regular visiting hours at the White House, or even cornered him on the streets of the city. One afternoon in December 1864, a newspaper correspondent walked across the White House grounds and saw there, in a little grove between the mansion and the War Department, Lincoln and a soldier sitting beneath a tree in conversation. Obviously the volunteer was stating a case and presenting his petition for some kind of action. Lincoln took the ever-present pencil from his pocket, scribbled something on the man's papers, and sent him on his way with some encouraging words.[17]

Throughout the war, men afraid of being arrested called on Lincoln first to seek his protection, and more often than not he obliged. Their numbers were especially large after 1863, when the draft and sometimes unscrupulous enlistment practices brought into the service men who were too unfamiliar with English, too unintelligent, or simply too confused to understand their obligations fully. He gave them his safe conduct back to their regiments, and with it a pardon for any supposed absence without leave or desertion, on condition that they serve faithfully thereafter.[18] For men who were caught and convicted of being absent without leave, sentences varied from forfeiture of pay for the time absent, to forfeiture of $12 a month for anywhere from two or three months up to the entire balance of their enlistment. There could be prison time at hard labor, too, but there would be no executions if Lincoln could help it.

Desertion presented the far greater concern, and by far the greatest tax on Lincoln's clemency. Like so many other military crimes, it was punishable by death, and was the one most likely in most cases to bring the maximum sentence. There were relatively few in the early months of the war, but gradually they grew, especially after the string of defeats in the East; like the absences without leave, they mushroomed in 1864 with the influx of newer and less motivated men into the ranks. Lincoln's approach often seemed idiosyncratic, for no pattern can be discerned in the alternate punishments he prescribed, his only consistency being clemency from death sentences. When a man gave himself up, the president seemed especially inclined to leniency. "Treat him with mercy as he makes the disclosure himself," was his advice on almost any such case. When a soldier had fought well in the past, Lincoln pardoned him for a desertion that might just have been a case of uncooperative legs. Among the increasing numbers of foreign-born volunteers, he often waived severe punishment in cases where the offender might simply not have understood his duty.[19]

Lincoln set his own measurements for determining a deserving candidate for clemency, and they seemed almost all-inclusive. If the offender was very young, he always commuted or pardoned the sentence—for any infraction, including desertion. In one case he simply ordered the boy to re-enlist in the navy instead—it was harder to desert from a ship—and in another actually ordered a rebuke of the mustering officer who had enrolled an underage offender.[20] When the officers of a man's regiment vouched for his good character and asked to have him back, Lincoln invariably complied, and then he turned his policy somewhat to stays of executions and pardons *if* the officers would accept a man back into the ranks.[21] Lincoln often made re-enlistment for two or three years a condition of pardon—sometimes in the navy, as with the young boys, and more often simply in a different regiment from the one the man had deserted, so that the only real punishment was the additional time a man had to serve beyond the term of his original service.[22] The great bulk of these came in 1865, when Lincoln could feel the end of the war was in sight and there was little if anything to gain from imprisonment or any sterner sentence. Lincoln revealed the idea underlying his approach in 1863, when he told a soldier, "I trust you will survive the war and see a reunited country and be happy in the fact that you did your part to make it so." Looking ahead, he foresaw how important it would be in the new Union for the war generation of young men to have something to look back upon with pride, a stimulus to better citizenship in the days ahead. Men who could feel that they had helped save their country would take care of it in the future, and even a man who had deserted might be redeemed by an act of charity that allowed him to stand shoulder to shoulder with other honored veterans, without the stigma of a conviction to weigh him down. Nothing revealed his philosophy more than the simple docket he scribbled on one pardon: "Let him fight instead of being shot."[23]

The scale of the desertion cases that came to Lincoln was the direct result of his own insistence that no soldier should be executed for any crime without his having a chance to review the record. On the one day April 14, 1864, he went over sixty-seven cases, issuing pardons, commutations, remissions, and a few approvals of sentences.[24] Judge Advocate General Holt often had to sit with him for hours as he pored over the documents in the capital offenses. "He was always very loth to act on these," Holt said a few years later, "and sometimes kept them a long while before disposing of them, which was generally by commuting the sentence to imprisonment at hard labor." Generals sometimes became impatient at the delay in meting out justice, but Lincoln would respond that the matters were, as he put it, "still in soak," and he would not be rushed with men's lives at stake.

The most difficult cases went into a separate pile for harder study, but in February 1864 he finally gave up handling them on a case-by-case basis and simply issued a blanket order that all standing capital convictions for desertion be suspended and commuted to imprisonment. In vain Holt argued that stern punishment was necessary as an example; Lincoln would not listen. "I don't think I can do it," he said. "I don't believe it will make a man any better to shoot him, while if we keep him alive, we may at least get some work out of him." Whenever a case arrived, Lincoln first telegraphed to suspend execution while he studied the matter. A pigeonhole in his desk bulged with the court-martial papers stuffed into it, and frequently he kept Holt with him interminably as they considered each one, Lincoln all the while looking for any excuse to pardon or commute. "He shrank with evident pain from even the idea of shedding human blood," said Holt, and often referred to the depressing number of capital sentences as nothing but "wholesale butchery." "In every case he always leaned to the side of mercy. His constant desire was to save life." John Hay actually looked on with some amusement "at the eagerness with which the President caught at any fact which would justify him in saving the life of a condemned soldier." He was the tenderest of men, thought his secretary, and yet he sent tens of thousands to their deaths. Still, though he could stand back and view the war as a large picture, and the carnage as necessary, Hay found that it "could not make him unmindful of the intimate details of that vast sum of human misery." Lincoln himself once mused to Voorhees, "doesn't it seem strange that I should be here—I, a man who couldn't cut a chicken's head off—with blood running all around me?"[25]

From time to time on a Friday, Lincoln stood in his White House office and mused to whoever might be with him, "This is the day when they shoot deserters." Occasionally he could hear the discharge of rifles in one of the forts or camps in the distance, and went to his window to stare pensively toward the Potomac. "You do not know how hard it is to have a human being die when you know that a stroke of your pen may save him," Lincoln told a petitioner in 1862. When a man pleading for commutation of a death sentence for a New York deserter suggested to the president, "Perhaps you could contrive [a] way consonant with duty and honor, to the service, to forgive, or commute his sentence," he did not know that this was exactly what Lincoln did in *every* case. "I have been trying to avoid the butchering business lately," he said again and again as he passed along his pardons and commutations.

At first his secretaries did not even show him all of the applications for pardons and stays, but soon the president insisted on seeing every one, and keeping them readily at hand for consideration right up to the last minute. Lincoln's private secretary William Stoddard said that in the end the president "was downright sure to pardon any case" if he could find "a fair case for pardoning." The comic writer David Ross Locke called several times at the White House, and saw Lincoln at his work, grasping "eagerly upon any excuse to pardon a man when the charge could possibly justify it." Speaker of the House Schuyler Colfax thought that "no man holding in his hands the key of life and death ever pardoned so many offenders, and so easily." Herndon, who knew Lincoln so well, realized that when the president studied the stacks of capital cases on his desk he was not thinking of crime and punishment: "He was purposely in search of occasions to evade the law, in favor of life." On one Saturday morning in July 1863, Lincoln and Hay pored over a hundred cases for six hours. Lincoln knew it occupied too much of his time, but he would not be deterred, especially as Fridays approached. "Get out of the way," he told a friend one Thursday. "Tomorrow is butcher day, and I must go through these papers and see if I cannot find some excuse to let these poor fellows off."[26]

There was a lot of butchery to avoid as the desertion rate mounted. The first actual trials came in May 1861, a mere seven in number. They gradually increased through the balance of the year, but were never more than sixty-one in a single month. They went up in 1862, but not until October did they exceed a hundred per month and stay there, with the rate almost doubling after December and Fredericksburg. In 1863, actual desertions ran at more than forty-five hundred a month. In March alone, six hundred cases went to court-martial; throughout that year they averaged more than three hundred per month, and rose to nearly four hundred per month in 1864, as the actual monthly desertion rate peaked at seventy-three hundred.[27] By January 1863, General Halleck estimated that almost 290,000 soldiers were absent from one cause or another, at least seventy-five thousand of them deserters. When caught and brought to trial, they accounted for exactly one-third of all courts-martial, and a daunting number of them prompted pleading, flattering, and often heart-wrenching letters from family and friends that tugged at the president's already vulnerable sympathy.[28]

"Oh! President you are a Husband and a father and cannot but feel for him!" pleaded the friend of a poor man who could not afford a substitute and enlisted to get a bounty. When he was never paid either that or his soldier pay for three months, and was denied a furlough, he deserted to go back to care for his wife and three children. Private Henry Snyder of the 8th Pennsylvania Cavalry got thirty days with a ball and chain and forfeiture of $12 of his $13 pay for five months for his desertion. "Knowing that you take a great interest in the welfare of the Union Soldiers, and that you are always ready to see that Justice is done to them," he said to Lincoln, he argued his aged and helpless mother as his reason for deserting: "It is very hard when I know she is suffering." The mother of Frederick Hopkins of the 116th New York, who was fined $10 a month for fifteen months, wrote the president because of his widespread reputation for clemency, and because of "a knowledge of the marked kindness & consideration which has ever characterized the conduct of your Excellency, in regard to those engaged in the 'service of their Country.'" Private Martin Zurman of the 5th Veteran Reserve complained that he was old and in frail health, with not long to live, yet had a wife and family who needed him. He confessed leaving camp without leave to go on a drunken spree, "not an uncommon occurence amongst 'Soldiers,'" but had no intent to desert permanently. He appealed to Lincoln, "trusting to the kindness which 'You' have always shown towards 'Soldiers.'"[29]

Lincoln found such appeals hard to resist, and scarcely tried if he saw any spark of hope in the offender. His leniency caused considerable chagrin among a few of his army commanders. "Some of my generals complain that I impair discipline and subordination in the army by my pardons and respites," Lincoln told Colfax, "but it makes me rested, after a day's hard work if I can find some good excuse for saving a man's life, and I go to bed happy as I think how joyous the signing of my name will make him and his family and friends." McClellan, though he seems not to have protested, certainly fostered among his coterie the impression that Lincoln's leniency was detrimental to discipline. After one visit to Little Mac's headquarters early in the war, Lincoln told General George Stoneman, "Tomorrow night I shall have a terrible headache. Tomorrow is hangman's day and I shall have to act upon death sentences."[30]

General Benjamin Butler complained more than most. Early in

1862, he called on the president to point out the attrition from desertion in the Army of the Potomac and argue for harsh retribution. "How can I have a butcher's day every Friday?" Lincoln protested. Butler replied, "Better have that than have the Army of the Potomac so depleted by desertion that good men will be butchered on other days than Friday." In the late fall of 1863, when Butler took command of Federal forces on the Virginia Peninsula, he raised the issue again. "I believe in you," Lincoln replied, "but not in shooting deserters." Butler, seeing the sorrowful look Lincoln always got on his face when he discussed this subject, suggested that the president could shift the responsibility to Halleck and not torment himself with the problem. "But I can't do that," Lincoln protested. "The responsibility would be mine, all the same." He told Butler that, since he now commanded a small army of his own, "you can shoot them for yourself." But then, Lincoln later ordered an immediate suspension of all executions in Butler's command, and the general complied grudgingly, though not without pointing out that a raid on Richmond on February 6, 1864 ordered to attempt to free prisoners of war, had failed in part because a deserter had given away the plan to the foe. "You may see how your clemency has been misplaced," chided the general, but Lincoln remained unmoved. When another army commander came to him claiming that mercy to the few was cruelty to the many, Lincoln remained adamant. "General, there are too many weeping widows in the United States now," he said. "For God's sake don't ask me to add to the number; for, I tell you plainly, *I won't do it!*" Perhaps one of the reasons that he retained Meade in command of the Army of the Potomac for the balance of the war was that the general felt some sympathy with the condemned, and himself occasionally asked the president for leniency.[31]

Another category of critic was not so open or direct as the generals. As with every other aspect of the war, politics had its role in the business of pardons and commutations. A large proportion of the cases in which Lincoln acted were brought to his attention by governors and congressmen trying to protect constituents. Naturally, the most populous states had the most soldiers in the field, and therefore the greater number of men going to court-martial. New York led them all, followed by Pennsylvania, Illinois, Ohio, and Indiana, with only Missouri furnishing a greater percentage of cases than its proportionate population would have suggested. And the cases in which Lincoln personally intervened followed the same population lines: the most interventions for New Yorkers, followed by the others, with again Missouri, and also Kentucky and Maryland, presenting a disproportionate share of cases.

He had to keep the leaders of the larger states happy by acceding to their requests for personal action, even if he had not been so inclined anyhow, for he was buying loyalty in Congress and cooperation in the statehouses. With states like Maryland, Kentucky, and Missouri, it was politic to make extra efforts to show mercy, to help bind those sometimes uncertain slave states to the cause. Lincoln showed even more disproportionate mercy in dealing with miscreants from among the loyalists of the Confederate states who enlisted in Union forces. He intervened in more cases involving Tennesseeans than he did for Indianians, more for Virginians than for men from Connecticut. He was using clemency as a political tool, rewarding friends and converting foes, and using it well, yet at the root of it he was always saving lives.[32]

Unfortunately, the politicians who individually begged his reprieves for their own constituents often turned around on the floor of Congress and collectively condemned his notorious leniency, and it rankled. He complained to Senator Henry Wilson of Massachusetts, when he came to ask a pardon for a soldier, "My officers tell me the good of the service demands the enforcement of the law, but it will make my heart ache to have the poor boys shot. I will pardon him, and then you will all join in blaming me for it. You all censure me for granting pardons, and yet you all ask me to do so." When Senator Lafayette Foster of Connecticut asked for a stay of execution for one of his constituents, the president bristled. "Why don't you men up there in Congress repeal the law requiring men to be shot when they desert, instead of coming here to me, and asking me to override the law and practically make it a dead letter?" Foster protested that he wanted only a stay, not a pardon, but Lincoln saw through that. "You know that when I have once suspended the sentence of that man I can't afterwards order him to be shot." He told another congressman, who brought the condemned's weeping wife with him, "These cases kill me! I wish I didn't have to hear about them! What shall I do? You make the laws, and then you come with heartbroken women and ask me to set them aside. . . . Then if I leave the laws to be executed, one of these distressing scenes occurs, which almost kill me." When a general tried to relieve Lincoln's mind by saying that Congress had taken the responsibility for executions upon itself with legislation and he could leave the matter to them, the president replied bitterly. "Yes, Congress has taken the responsibility," he said, "and left the women to howl about me."[33]

"Must I shoot a simple-minded soldier boy who deserts," he protested, "while I must not touch a hair of a wily agitator who induced him to desert?" The longer the war lasted, the more entrenched became his resolution against capital punishment. He told friends that, if the world had no "butchers" but him, he expected there would be no bloodshed anywhere, for he could not learn to love killing his fellow men. It was always safe to be lenient, even though he confessed, "I am to-day in bad odor all over the country because I don't have as many persons put to death as the laws condemn." He could even joke occasionally about his reputation for clemency. He told one applicant for pardon that he would have to refer the matter to Bates, "but I guess it will be all right, for me and the Attorney General's very chicken-hearted!" In lighter moments he even explained his policy in jest. He simply could not execute deserters, he told John Hay in July 1863. "It would frighten the poor devils too terribly to shoot them."34

It was to buy time to keep from "frightening" too many of those volunteers in trouble that Lincoln resorted to wholesale suspensions and amnesties. There was some precedent, for in the early days of the American military the army had offered general pardons for deserters no fewer than three times, in 1792, 1807, and again in 1810, in a period when more than half of all courts-martial were for desertion.35 Lincoln first did so on March 10, 1863 with a proclamation that all men absent without leave, for whatever reason, who returned to their units by April 1 would be received with no other punishment than forfeiture of pay for the time they had been gone. Those not back by the deadline would be treated like deserters if caught. His move had a happy effect. One officer with the Army of the Potomac believed that he saw thousands of absentees returning to the field that month. Whereas at least 30 percent of all absentees from Hooker's command had been deserters in January, by the end of March they made up only 4 percent instead.36

That did not, however, solve the problem that, as late as August 1863, men were being convicted, sentenced, and sometimes shot whose cases never came before Lincoln. Realizing that he could not rely on the condemned or their friends to seek his help in every instance, in January 1864 he ordered a suspension of execution in all capital cases, and followed that in February with a general order directing that the sentences of all deserters were to be commuted to imprisonment during the remainder of the war. At the same time, he authorized commanding officers to return certain of the condemned to duty if mitigating circumstances allowed. Of course, that did not affect the new cases that continually came to trial, and so the stream of capital offenses continued to wash up on his White House desk. "All this proceeds from one thing," complained an officer at Meade's headquarters. "The uncertainty of the death penalty through the false merciful policy of the President. It came to be a notorious thing that no one could be executed but poor friendless wretches, who had none to intercede for them; so that the blood of deserters that was shed was all in vain—there was no certainty in punishment, and certainty is the essence of all punishment." One of McClellan's old followers simply exclaimed condescendingly, "Poor, weak, well-meaning Lincoln!"[37]

Significantly, as Lincoln well realized, only the officers clamored for use of the firing squad, something they knew they would never risk facing themselves, since officers exclusively composed courts-martial, and virtually never meted out capital sentences to one of their own, regardless of his crimes. Thus it was rather easy, and hypocritical, for them to argue about the good of the service and maintaining an example. That left the president much easier in his conscience about seeking the excuses he needed for setting aside death verdicts. When two brothers in the 14th Kansas Cavalry deserted and received death sentences, he regarded it as simply too great a burden for one family, and suspended the executions. When a soldier absent without leave was captured, released on parole, but convicted of desertion, the president gave him a suspension.[38]

As with other crimes, he took special care over deserters who were ignorant and illiterate, unwilling to shoot a man simply because he was stupid, and showed even greater concern for those adjudged to be mentally incompetent. He showed mercy with the foreign-born, who often simply did not understand their orders, and at least some of whom had been enrolled by unscrupulous brokers who never told them what they were undertaking. He also showed mercy to men who were promised a bounty they never received and therefore made the logical assumption that they were not bound by their enlistment. One such appealed to Lincoln that not only did he not receive his bounty, but also he never actually signed his enlistment papers: a lieutenant had signed for him, making the legality of his being held to service even more questionable. He was the sole support of his wife and widowed mother—the most common plea of all—and pleaded that "it will kill them both wife & mother if I am shot." Making matters worse, he was a Republican and had worked hard for Lincoln's election in 1860—

again, a commonplace in many appeals for clemency—and exclaimed, "Now it is hard that I have got to be shot at the hands of the party which I helped plase in power."[39]

Just as in the cases of insubordination, where Lincoln could see the basic independence of the American spirit clashing with military discipline, so in some desertions the president took into account the inevitable clash between independent private and sometimes officious officer. "I had to desert on account of my tyrannical captain's treatment towards me," complained one condemned man, and another went to a conviction for telling his sergeant, "If you arrest me I will rip your god damned guts out and scatter them on the parade ground." Such cases no doubt reminded the president of his suggestion that Congress make it lawful for a private to strike his superior. Lincoln also had to make allowances for another kind of soldier, who, until this very moment, had never experienced free will of his own and had no experience of the discretion and voluntary restraints imposed by being a free man in the military. Desertions among the new black regiments were not just over the pay issue, but came, not infrequently, from pure ignorance and inexperience. "I am hear in prison in fort Jefferson and was cort marshell as a desirter," implored Corporal John Johnson of the 15th Corps de l'Afrique, a black regiment raised in Louisiana. "It was sumthing [I] knowd nothing about that it for to leave the Regt for good." He was sick, and simply went home until recovered, then tried to return to his unit. "I never knowd it was any harm for a man to leave the army to get well when he was sick," he argued. "I like to be a soulder very well becouse when I listed for I did not [enlist for] any money I listed for to trie to be a servist to the united states. . . . It was veary well that they put me in prison for it made me know sumthing about souldering that I never would have knowd." In the end, the patriotic Corporal Johnson got his pardon. In general, black soldiers received tougher sentences than whites accused of the same offenses, especially in racially sensitive crimes like rape. A number of Negro soldiers would be executed during the war, but most of them after April 1865, when Lincoln could no longer intercede in their behalf.[40]

In the years ahead, a cliché emerged placing a destitute and pleading mother or wife at the root of every appeal to Lincoln to suspend a death sentence. In fact, half or more came from politicians, a few generals, friends, the condemned themselves, and Lincoln's own spontaneous intervention. Yet wives and mothers did lie at the heart of a great number of the appeals he received, as arguments used by others if not as supplicants themselves. Lincoln told a friend from Springfield, "I can put off war governors and secretaries and senators and all that, but there's the women." He rarely refused appeals that described the women as "almost crazy" with worry. Wives wrote that their children were hungry and crying for their fathers. "Pardon my beloved husband, the father of my poor little children, and make a parted family once more happy," implored a New York wife. They appealed to Lincoln, "knowing that you are a generous and kind hearted man," pleading their destitution, and offering excuses in behalf of their husbands, such as drunkenness; one said her man had been lured to a bordello and there drugged to make him desert.[41]

Most poignant of all were the cases that included letters from wives that had induced their men to leave their regiments. "You have rote a number of times that you was agoin to draw your pay but that aint agoin to cloth the children," the wife of a convicted deserter from the 11th United States Veteran Reserve had written to him. "If you cant support them thare I wish that you would come home then and support them here. . . . It is pretty cold wether here and the children are all barefoot." Just as touching were the direct appeals. The wife of a man convicted for desertion, who had already spent thirty-one months in prison and lost an arm in combat, protested, "I think the Nation have to suffer anough in a Sivell Warr at the best with out inflicting Punishment where it is not necary." She was living on $2.75 a week and taking in sewing in order to send a little money to her crippled husband. "If you only could know how you make me suffer and all for nothing atoll," she pleaded. "If you have one sparkl of humanity or feeling left in your body you must help me." The wife of a man who deserted to go home and get married begged, "I aske you in the name of my heavenly Farther oh do release him." Some even appealed to Mary Lincoln, as one wife to another, to use her influence with her husband. Most touching of all was the simple trust they seemed to place in their president. "Nowing that you are A friend to those that is in trouble," wrote a mother of fifteen with several sons in the army, setting aside the pride that so distinguished the poor, ". . . This is the first time that I ever had to beg and I think that you will be A farther to me [so] as to . . . reprive my son . . . if you have any pitty on the poor." If it was his own son awaiting execution, he would know how to sympathize with her, she said. "I do belive that you will be A farther to me."[42]

Pleas based on the youth of some offenders always impelled Lincoln to act like "A farther" to the condemned. He sometimes told friends about the occasion when he had been resting upstairs at the White House and a mother called to plead for her son's life. She refused to leave, and Mary Lincoln would not let her husband be disturbed. Finally, however, Lincoln went downstairs. "That woman was a mother, and her boy eighteen years old was to be shot next morning at six o'clock for neglect of duty. Would you have gone down?" The relation of sons to mothers especially seemed to touch him, no doubt because he had seen firsthand the devastation the loss of Willie and Eddie wreaked on Mary Lincoln. When the case of one boy accused of desertion for going home to see his mother came before the president, he immediately pardoned the lad. "I don't think that I can allow a boy to be shot who tried to go home to see his mother," he explained. "I guess I don't want to read any more of this." Lincoln supposedly assured one mother that he never allowed the shooting of anyone under the age of twenty, and that he never would. A Massachusetts congressman saw the president console the father of another condemned boy, "My dear man, if your son lives until I order him shot, he will live longer than ever Methuselah did."[43]

The pleas were even more touching, if possible, than those for husbands. "It is nothing to you, but think of sparing a man's life," said the brother of one condemned youngster, adding that he had been "hearing and often reading of your kind heartedness." Of course, the president thought of nothing but sparing their lives. He remitted the sentence of one boy who had fought well at Fredericksburg only to see his own father killed beside him, a trauma that left him so shocked that he deserted.[44] In a host of other cases he simply suspended the executions of youngsters, and in the cases of some as young as fifteen discharged them from the army with no penalty for desertion other than the refunding of their bounty money for enlistment.[45] As for the young men who stayed in the service after he had commuted their sentences, he remained reluctant to penalize them financially. "He should have his pay for duty actually performed," Lincoln ruled in one case. "Loss of pay falls so hard upon poor families."[46]

Interestingly, many parents of minor deserters felt the same concern for their sons' future as veterans as did Lincoln. One mother implored that the prison where her sixteen-year-old boy was serving his commuted sentence subjected him to associations that "will in all probability have a banefull effect on his future life." Another, the mother of a drummer who had enlisted illegally when only sixteen, wrote that the boy now languished in prison for desertion. "I ask you in the name of humanity to take that sentence from him," she said. "Dont discourage him that he will not try to do the best he can." One act of charity now, they argued, could prevent a boy from taking the wrong road in life. "I know viry well our Beloved President interests himself in behalf of the oppressed," wrote one woman. "Let a Mother's anguish plead for her."[47]

And so he did, especially in 1864 and later, when it became evident that numbers of impoverished young boys, too immature to cope with army discipline or being away from home, were enlisting to get bounty money and pay to support their families. Over and over Lincoln commuted and pardoned, docketing on the case papers that one was "an old soldier though only a boy," or that another should be pardoned "and given to his parents." Occasionally the youths were the sons of people known to him. "I must not let him be executed," the president decided of the son of one old acquaintance; in pardoning another, he said, "What possible injury can this lad work upon the cause of this great Union? I say let him go." Now and then he did allow a youngster to be convicted and even sentenced before issuing the stay or pardon, just to teach the boy a lesson. And he could even indulge himself in a little jest occasionally. One boy deserted to go home to marry his fiancée after hearing that she had another hot suitor. "I want to punish the young man," Lincoln said with a grin. "Probably in less than a year he will wish I had withheld the pardon. We can't tell, though. I suppose when I was a young man, I should have done the same fool thing."[48]

As with men guilty of being absent without leave, Lincoln often pardoned deserters on condition that they serve honorably the balance of their enlistment. Not only did he suspend executions for desertion, but he also pardoned or remitted the balance of prison terms. Yet, at the same time, he frequently imposed a prison sentence himself in exchange for sparing a man's life, and he rarely gave any reason for his decisions, or for the varying degrees of the punishments he imposed. Generally he was harder on men whose records revealed repeat offenses, and easier on first-time deserters, or those who had deserted but later re-enlisted and fought well. Contrary to what some of his critics believed, he was not naïve. He recognized that not every deserter was really the deserving son of a poor widowed mother. He freely admitted that in some cases he commuted the death sentence of an offender who was "really a very bad one," and that his only motive was his aversion to "the butchering business." Sometimes he simply found the man's story so interesting that he overlooked a desperate character and searched for an excuse. "If a man had more than one life, I think a little hanging would not hurt one," he told Lamon of one hardened offender, "but after he is once dead we cannot bring him back, no matter how sorry we may be; so the boy shall be pardoned."[49]

In the end, Lincoln did not remain content for the cases and appeals to come to him. Even though he eventually issued instructions that no capital sentence was to be carried out before he had had a chance to review the case, from late 1863 onward he actually made inquiries on his own to locate cases that might have slipped through his net. He sent out orders to locate some men who had been convicted in order to suspend their sentences, and then made follow-up inquiries to be certain that his suspensions were carried out. Often his first action on hearing of a conviction was an order not to execute the man until further notice from the White House. Sometimes he only got news of a sentence the day before it was to be carried out, and immediately he issued telegraphic orders to halt further proceedings. In at least one case the president actually issued his stay of execution even before the court-martial decided on a conviction.[50]

The Sleeping Sentinel had already made the image of a condemned man standing in front of a firing squad only to receive clemency at the last instant something of a cliché. Yet it happened. In October 1863, a private of the 122nd New York, condemned for desertion, rode out to the parade ground sitting on his coffin, and stood before a squad of his fellow soldiers waiting for the word to fire. A plea for mercy had gone to Lincoln that morning, but the messenger had not yet returned. "I thought the poor fellows chances of a pardon were very slim," wrote a friend. But just as the rifles were about to bring down the condemned, the president's reprieve arrived. The colonel of the regiment admonished his men not to draw from this the lesson that desertion was not a serious crime; rather, they should see in the man's narrow escape an example of what might happen to any of them if leniency were denied the next time. At that the New Yorkers gave three cheers for Lincoln "which were given with a right will"—most especially, no doubt, by one man with a very new lease on life. Lincoln's anxiety was prompted, in part, by the fact that more than once the president discovered that a man had been shot before he had a chance to impose executive clemency.[51]

Lincoln told his old friend Joshua Speed—brother of attorney general James Speed—that he found a special pleasure in pardoning men condemned to death, for in the act he relieved two people, the soldier and the person who was pleading for him. "Well, I have made one family happy," he said to a congressman after one pardon, "but I don't know about the discipline of the army."[52] Yet in his personally granted pardons, reprieves, and stays of executions—hundreds of them during the war—and in his general amnesties and blanket suspensions of executions, he was redressing one of the greatest inequities in army discipline, for capital sentences fell only on the enlisted men. During the entire course of the war, not one officer would be executed for any crime, and as far as is known, only one, Lieutenant Edward King of the 66th New York, ever received a death sentence from a court-martial, in his case for desertion—a sentence that Lincoln commuted. In fact, the highest-ranking soldier known to meet his death before a firing squad was a sergeant.[53]

The inequities of sentences offered a flagrant example of the artificial class gulf created in the military. Drunkenness in a private could bring imprisonment, loss of pay, or worse, whereas in an officer it resulted in a reprimand, or at worst dismissal from the service. Overstaying a furlough, which constituted being absent without leave, could cost a volunteer his pay for months or imprisonment, and might even make him liable to be tried as a deserter. An officer could lose one month's pay. Commissioned ranks could be found guilty of mutiny and officially, under the 7th Article of War, be sentenced to death, yet not one officer so convicted faced worse than loss of rank or pay. An enlisted man's standard punishment was death. And for murder, desertion, rape, and a number of other capital crimes for which soldiers were routinely condemned to death, and many actually executed, officers received anything from a fine to dismissal from the service. The worst sentence on record for an officer was that he be "disgracefully dismissed," with the record of his offense and conviction being sent to his hometown newspaper for publication. Moreover, courts-martial showed a frequent reluctance to convict, even in the most flagrant cases. One lieutenant colonel reportedly raped a woman in front of several witnesses, and still walked away with an acquittal.[54] No wonder Lincoln excused his intercessions. "I know it is a small thing, as some would look at it, as it only relates to a private soldier," he said of one of his pardons. "But the way to have good soldiers is to treat them rightly." He was acting as a social leveler, asserting, "A private soldier has as much right to justice as a major general."[55]

That did not stop the officers from carping. "As to shooting deserters and cowards, whether men or officers, by court martial," complained Colonel Charles Wainwright, "that is out of the question, as all such cases have to go to Washington and Mr. Lincoln always pardons them." Young Robert Shaw, a lieutenant in the 2nd Massachusetts by November 1862, complained then that Lincoln's pardons greatly blunted the force of military discipline. And yet Lincoln did let men die. Deserters who went over to the enemy and were then captured hanged for want of his forgiveness. A deserter who set up as a bounty broker to find substitutes went to his death; to bounty jumpers in general he offered no solace, advising officers of the courts to "please let them know at once that their appeal is denied." In spite of a father's pleas, Lincoln allowed the execution of a boy who deserted three separate times. In August 1863, five deserters appealed together for mercy, pleading their families' need, and asking for commutation to hard labor. When Meade gave the president the details of their offense, however, Lincoln declined to intervene. He seems invariably to have shown little mercy to rapists; Hay observed that in general Lincoln had no sympathy for crimes involving meanness or cruelty. Sometimes he gave a man a stay of execution for a few days so that he might compose himself for death. Never did he actually pass a death sentence himself; that power lay only with the court-martial. But he acquiesced in the doom of more than 350 men, at least 141 of them for desertion, simply by saying to the officers in charge, "The subject is a very painful one, but the case is settled," or "I do not interfere."[56]

Interestingly enough, the clemency that Lincoln granted to his own soldiers, he seemed inclined to extend to the foe as well. He often suspended the execution sentences of partisans and guerrillas when they were very young, and allowed the discharge of youthful prisoners of war without waiting for exchange if they took an oath of allegiance. If a prisoner released on his parole not to fight again until properly exchanged broke that parole and was captured as a combatant, he was liable to be shot, yet Lincoln would not sanction the executions. He rationalized that such men had no doubt been told by their superiors, mistakenly, that they were free to fight again, "and it would be hard to put them to death under such circumstances." He also refused to hold former disloyal sentiments against any man who took the oath of allegiance and conducted himself as a good citizen, though he often came under heavy pressure to arrest or penalize such converts. "I dislike an oath which requires a man to swear he *has* not done wrong," said Lincoln. "It rejects the Christian principle of forgiveness on terms of repentance. I think it is enough if the man does no wrong *hereafter.*" He seemed to harden his heart only when there was no sign of repentance. A Maryland mother pleaded with him to release her Confederate son, held a prisoner of war, yet Lincoln responded by saying, "Now that he is taken prisoner, it is the first time, probably, that you have ever shed tears over what your boy has done. Good morning, Madam, I can do nothing for your boy today." Therein, in fact, lay the president's philosophy on all military justice: forgiveness of the past and the promise of redemption for the future. "When a man is sincerely penitent for his misdeeds and gives satisfactory evidence of the same," he told Elizabeth Cady Stanton, "he can safely be pardoned, and there is no exception to the rule."[57]

It was a rule well known early in the war, publicized by the stories and letters published in the newspapers, by the caricature of reality in the popular poem *The Sleeping Sentinel,* and so spread by word of mouth in the armies that the officers grumbled knowledgeably, and the soldiers universally understood that there was someone to turn to for justice, or at least for hope. As children looked to their fathers for both discipline and forgiveness, so the children of Father Abraham knew that in him they had one sure friend to offer help in extremity. "On the whole," Lincoln told a visitor during the war, "my impression is that mercy bears richer fruits than any other attribute." The fruit it bore him was the love and respect of a generation of American volunteers.[58]

8

VOX MILITUM

*After these things
the word of the Lord came unto Abram in a vision,
saying, Fear not, Abram; I am thy shield,
and thy exceeding great reward.*

[Genesis 15:1]

As the spring of 1864 approached, a war-weary Union faced its fourth year of war, still with no resolution. In the western theater the advances had continued almost unabated. All of Tennessee was lost to the Confederates, and a major army group commanded by General William T. Sherman stood poised to invade northern Georgia, heading for Atlanta. The Mississippi flowed under the firm control of the Union, and most of Alabama, Mississippi, and eastern Louisiana were open to Lincoln's forces at will. The blockade grew ever tighter along the Confederate coastline. Only in Virginia was the story different, but unfortunately that was the most visible theater of all, the one that all the world looked to in order to gauge the progress of the war, and there advances came not in states or counties but seemingly in inches. The Army of the Potomac stood no closer either to Richmond or to eradicating Lee's command than it had been since Fredericksburg.

That interminable status quo was wearing down the Northern people, who, like so many in the world, often saw the war only in terms of what was happening in Virginia. In part to break this stagnation, and also to give active coordination to all his armies' efforts, Lincoln the preceding winter took his premier general from the West, Grant, and put him in command of all armies everywhere. Grant wisely chose to place himself personally in the East with Meade, where they faced their greatest adversary. If Grant could not shift Lee, perhaps no one could, and in that case the war might drag on indefinitely. Therein lay the potential catastrophe, for if the people became too weary of war or too tired of waiting for victory, or if the men in the ranks lost heart in the cause, then Lincoln might no longer be able to sustain the effort and would have to give up. The Confederacy would have won simply by not losing. Lincoln knew that could happen when a larger antagonist lost the will to keep fighting an underdog. Weems had told him all about it, for that was how Washington and his generation won the Revolution, by wearing out Britain's resolve to continue.

Events off the battlefield could decide the Union's future this year. For the first time in its history, the nation would conduct a popular election for the presidency in wartime, and Lincoln was determined that the election take place, despite suggestions from some quarters that he use the wartime emergency as a pretext for setting aside the election, just as he temporarily set aside other constitutional provisions like habeas corpus.[1] He simply found that unthinkable. Prosecuting a terrible war in order to preserve the rule of law and the will of the majority, as he saw it, he could hardly take a step that denied the constitutional right of that majority to choose its leaders. To attempt to stay one day longer in office than his mandated term would be usurpation, justifying the accusations of tyranny and dictatorship that Copperheads at home and Confederates across the lines threw at him. There would have to be an election.

Nor was there ever any likelihood that Lincoln would not seek renomination. The unanswered question was whether his party and thereafter the people, would stand by him. Equally important was what the soldiers would do, for, again for the first time in history, most of them would be able to vote, and their ballots at home might be even more decisive than their bullets had been in the field. How they voted, in turn, depended upon their feelings on a variety of issues that he and they had passed through together—the dismissal of Little Mac, the Emancipation Proclamation, the draft, the string of unsuccessful generals in the East, the costly defeats like Fredericksburg, and more. So far he seemed to come through them with the soldiers' support substantially intact, if not unanimous, and other matters—like his well-known concern for their comfort and welfare, and most of all his storied magnanimity—worked in his behalf. But would it be enough, and, most of all, did the men in the ranks have the stomach to continue the fight for another year, perhaps even another term?

In fact, long before the nominating conventions were to meet that summer, most soldiers expected Lincoln to be renominated, and just as many expected him to win. "I believe that in taking everything into consideration, President Lincoln has done as well as could be expected," a New Hampshire Democrat soldier said at the end of 1863. There were other men he would have preferred to see in the White House, but he would vote for Lincoln if nominated. An Ohio volunteer serving in the West wrote, in March 1864, "I think most of the soldiers are in favour of Lincoln again for president." An Illinoisian found wide speculation that "Old Honest Abe will be a candidate as sure as he lives." Another Illinois volunteer in Tennessee was sure the president would be re-elected. "I know he will be if they let the soldiers vote which I think they will I am going to vote for old Abe if I get a chance." The Army of the Potomac seemed more divided. A soldier of the Iron Brigade predicted, "If left to the soldiers of our Army, Little Mac would be the next President"; a Pennsylvanian thought that "the expression in the army is nearly universal for Lincoln"; and a New Yorker wrote home, "What we ask yo of the North is two elect Honest old Abe for 4 years more and this Army will dwo the rest."[2]

Lincoln, as usual, had been taking several opportunities to pay his thanks publicly to the soldiers for what he usually termed their "sufferings," and increased his, until now, infrequent public remarks, no doubt realizing that he needed both to expose himself more to the people in the election year, and to underscore his regard for the volunteers if he hoped to have their votes. He spoke at a Sanitary Fair in March, complimenting the men in uniform. "While all contribute of their substance the soldier puts his life at stake, and often yields it up in his country's cause," said the president. "The highest merit, then, is due to the soldier." On May 9, days after Grant and Meade launched their spring offensive against Lee, Lincoln again spoke out. "I am, indeed, very grateful to the brave men who have been struggling with the enemy in the field," he said. On into June he continued his frequent appearances before civilians and soldiers alike. "I propose that you constantly bear in mind the support you owe to the brave officers and soldiers in the field," he told a group of citizens, then, two days later, addressed the 130th Ohio on its way to the front, offering his thanks and assuring them that their services had never been more needed. "I know you will do your best," he said.[3]

He needed their best, for Grant and Lee were engaged in a brutal slugging match in northern Virginia. At heavy cost, the Army of the Potomac finally pushed the Confederates back, slowly but steadily, throughout May; by early June, the armies stood barely ten miles from Richmond. Unable to push farther on that line, Grant executed a brilliant maneuver that shifted the army completely around Lee by surprise and put him on the outskirts of Petersburg, the back door to Richmond. At the last moment, Lee caught up and managed to hold the Yankees in place, Grant's men by this time simply too exhausted and cut up from a month of continual fighting to make the heavy push that might have brought victory. Observing it all from a distance, Lincoln continued to praise the "soldiers in the field, who are bearing the harder part of this great national struggle." At the Philadelphia Sanitary Fair on June 16, he reiterated, "Say what you will, after all the most is due to the soldier, who takes his life in his hands and goes to fight the battles of his country."[4] Sincere and consistent as his sentiments were, Lincoln had to know that his increased public exposure worked to his advantage with the men in the field, since his public comments invariably got reported in the press and spread through the armies. By eschewing personal credit and passing it all on to the men in the ranks, he could both bolster their morale and pride, and at the same time win their gratitude and admiration. It seemed to be working. "My vote is for Abe if I live," said one Potomac soldier in early June. Another punched a Confederate during a truce for collecting the dead and wounded when the Johnny Reb called Lincoln "a damned Abolitionist!" Meanwhile, with Sherman now advancing toward Atlanta, soldiers continued to express their confidence and optimism. "I want Abraham Lincoln for President, and I think he will be," said one. Even in faraway Arkansas, an Iowa volunteer observed now, "Old Abe is bound to be our next President." No other candidate even stood a chance in his part of the western army, he told friends at home. "Uncle Abe is the Soldiers Choice. If you do your part at home, we will reelect Lincoln."[5]

The nominating convention of what was now called the National Union Party did its part on June 8, when it nominated Lincoln for a second term and chose Andrew Johnson of Tennessee, a Democrat, as his running mate. There had never been any very serious opposition, though moves had been made for Frémont, and even earlier suggestions of Grant, which the general instantly laid to rest. The platform included commitment to a constitutional amendment ending slavery everywhere, and a determination to prosecute the war to total victory with no room for compromise with the insurrectionists. In the armies the news met with widespread approval. "The best news is the nominations of Abe Lincoln and Andy Johnson," said an Illinois soldier in the West. "It gives unbounded satisfaction to the soldiers." Lincoln himself felt satisfaction that the nominating convention had paid high tribute to the men in the ranks—whose votes would be needed—and in his published acceptance letter he, too, offered again his gratitude to the volunteers, "as they forever must and will be remembered by the grateful country for whose salvation they devote their lives."[6]

A week after the nomination, when several days of assaults failed to penetrate Lee's rapidly strengthening position in the fortifications around Petersburg, Grant and Meade had to settle for commencing a siege on June 18. It was not what Lincoln had hoped for. Worse, though at first the people at home did not grasp the scale of the losses incurred by Grant in his overland campaign, gradually these began to sink in, and the North was stunned. Unfortunately, they could not see what had been achieved for that cost. In the three previous years, successive commanders of the Army of the Potomac had racked up more than a hundred thousand casualties simply in maintaining a static situation. In six weeks, the Army of the Potomac had sustained more than sixty thousand casualties, but it had driven Lee out of northern Virginia and bottled him up in the defenses of Richmond and Petersburg. As an open-field commander, he was effectively out of the war, and every day that the cordon around him grew longer and stronger brought Grant closer to bagging either Richmond, or the Army of Northern Virginia, or both.

The president himself saw the long lines of ambulances bringing the wounded back to Washington's hospitals. "Look yonder at those poor fellows," he told a friend. "I cannot bear it. This suffering, this loss of life is dreadful." Quickly Grant came under heavy fire, and Lincoln himself may have been disappointed, having come to expect so much from his finest commander. He had to wonder about the state of the army, and to worry about the impact of the stalled—though so far essentially successful—campaign. After three years of war, he feared that the people of the Union might not have the stamina or willpower left to last out a long siege.[7]

He decided to go to the army and see for himself. In fact, Lincoln had not reviewed the Army of the Potomac for over a year now, or even visited it in the field since the previous April. With other concerns on his mind, and with the army competently commanded by Meade, the president felt able to stay away except for a quick visit to Butler's command at Fort Monroe in December. Now, battered and exhausted as it was, the army might derive some good from a visit, even though this time there would be no grand reviews. A simpler format was more Grant's style, and it suited Lincoln. He simply got on a steamer on June 19 and arrived the next day without fanfare at Grant's headquarters at City Point. "I just thought I would jump aboard a boat and come down and see you," he explained, though of course Lincoln's army visits were never that simple. He rode abroad among the soldiers with Grant and Meade, borrowing Grant's charger Cincinnati for the ride, and making his usual impression on the men.[8]

On June 21, he asked to see the black regiments of the XVIII Corps. "I want to take a look at those boys," he explained. "I was opposed on every side when I first favored the raising of colored regiments, but they have proved their efficiency, and I am glad they have kept pace with the white regiments in the recent assaults." The blacks cheered him enthusiastically as he rode through their ranks, taking off his hat to them. "God bless Master Lincoln," they shouted. "Lord save Father Abraham!" The next day, he took a steamer to Fort Monroe to visit with Butler, and there rode through the lines of the newly designated Army of the James. At one point he actually came within range of Confederate rifles; though these were fortunately silent, officers advised him to take cover. "Oh, no," he said, "the commander in chief of the army must not show any cowardice in the presence of his soldiers, whatever he may feel." The volunteers saw that Lincoln seemed to look in good spirits, and he even offered a few "funny remarks" as he chatted with them. By now, out of habit, a growing number of them called him "Father Abraham." Lincoln saw what he needed to see, apparently. The men were bruised and tired, but they still met him with enthusiasm, and by his reckoning, if they still stood by him, they were ready to stand by the cause. In private conversation he also no doubt received further assurance that Grant, despite feelers put out to him, had no intention of trying for a presidential nomination from the Democrats, who had yet to choose their nominee.[9]

With his renomination just secured, and the Army of the Potomac apparently a long siege away from any dramatic success against the foe, the last thing Lincoln needed was what happened next. Late in June, Sherman received a bloody check at Kennesaw Mountain that stopped him momentarily, though he continued on his drive for Atlanta. Worse was what happened in Lincoln's own back yard. Dangerous even when besieged, Lee detached a corps from his army and sent it on a daring raid north in a move intended at once to draw Federals away from Petersburg and also to embarrass the Lincoln administration and possibly damage the president's electoral prospects. On July 5, the Second Corps, commanded by General Jubal Early, began crossing the Potomac, and a few days later advanced across Maryland toward Washington itself. Between them, Lincoln and Grant marshaled considerable reinforcements for the garrisons in the capital's defenses, but it promised to be a close issue. By July 10, Early's Confederates reached Rockville, no more than ten miles from the city, and the next day they advanced into the suburbs.

Everyone from the District militia to invalids from military hospitals, and even men in the prisons under sentence for desertion, were turned out to man the forts northwest of the city. On July 11, Lincoln himself went out to Fort Stevens, the position most threatened, and mounted the forward parapet to look at the threatening Confederates through a field glass. Officers more than once advised him to get down for fear he would be hit, and one soldier bluntly told Father Abraham that he would get his head knocked off. When it became apparent that no full attack was imminent, Lincoln did leave the parapet and took his carriage down to the 6th Street wharf, where two divisions of the VI Corps were arriving, sent by Grant. The soldiers saw a man in dust-covered clothing anxiously waiting. "Every lineament of his countenance indicated a mental strain which almost prostrated him," thought one volunteer. Still, Lincoln chatted freely with officers and men, and walked among them with his hat in his hand while they gave him their cheers. Occasionally he even gnawed at a bit of soldier hardtack in his other hand, no doubt the gift of one of the men. He urged them all to "hurry up and not lose a moment."[10]

The next morning, the president probably kept abreast of developments thanks to a flag-signal station atop the Soldiers' Home that communicated constantly with Fort Stevens. Finally he could stay away no longer, and Lincoln and Mary got in a carriage and followed the 121st New York on its march to the works. "*Father Abraham* wife and son followed us," the regimental surgeon wrote proudly. "We have learned to love him as well as he appears to love his boys in blue, and we all would be willing to sacrifice anything for such a man." When they arrived at the works on 7th Street, they found it crowded with spectators wanting to see the anticipated battle. Lincoln left his carriage and went to find General Horatio Wright, commanding the VI Corps and now senior officer in the fort. Soldiers on all sides saw the tall figure of their president, and most noticed the grave and, as always, "careworn" look on his face. Wright invited Lincoln to join him on the parapet, thinking he would decline, but to his chagrin the president accepted and came with him. Despite the heavy skirmishing fire now coming from the Confederates, he repeatedly exposed himself as he looked out toward the foe. As more regiments marched into the works, they could see him standing out, sometimes turning to watch them enter, then stepping back to face Early. Mary Lincoln repeatedly told him to get down, but he would not leave, even when a surgeon beside him went down wounded.

Wright now expressed his concern, for no general wanted to have the president killed on his watch, but Lincoln refused him, too. "The President evinced remarkable coolness and disregard of danger," the general admitted. After the surgeon fell, Wright ordered the parapet cleared entirely, and told Lincoln that he would remove him forcibly if necessary. Lincoln seemed to find the prospect of a president's being manhandled off at the order of his subordinate rather amusing, but finally yielded to the extent that he agreed to sit down behind the parapet. "He failed to understand why I should be exposed to the danger and he should not," said the general. Even then Lincoln still stood erect occasionally to take quick looks out over the ground in advance of the fort, each time exposing nearly half his body to enemy fire.

During the intermittent fire, Lincoln saw the wounded colonel of the 98th Pennsylvania carried off on a stretcher, and went to speak with him for a moment, asked about his wound, and then said, "You have saved the Capital. I shall not forget you." Meanwhile, Early realized that the fortifications were too strongly defended to make a major assault worthwhile, and so he began a slow withdrawal. Quite possibly under some pressure from Lincoln, Wright ordered a desultory counterattack, but it was poorly organized. The 98th Pennsylvania was ordered out even though it was out of ammunition, and Lincoln himself witnessed a fiery exchange between a captain and the brigade commander. Soon they had their ammunition, and then they went out, along with the 2nd Rhode Island and other regiments, and several soldiers attested that they made their charge with spirit, knowing that Lincoln was watching. "For a short time it was warm work," said one private, "but as the President and many ladies were looking at us every man tried to do his best." When the Confederates were evidently pulling back, Wright called off the fighting, and as the soldiers returned to Fort Stevens they saw that "the President's face was wreathed with smiles."[11]

Even though Early was thwarted, the embarrassing threat to Washington only added to Lincoln's concerns about his re-election. Then, at the end of July, Confederates took and burned Chambersburg, Pennsylvania, an event of military insignificance, but still another public-relations weapon in the hands of the Democratic opposition. Fortunately, Sherman continued to move after his check at Kennesaw, and by early August had his armies on the doorstep of Atlanta, threatening to lay siege. On August 5, Admiral David G. Farragut steamed into Mobile Bay, effectively closing it as a port of entry for the Confederacy, making the blockade ever tighter. Still, the press and the opposition fixed their gaze securely on the stalemate around Petersburg and Grant's inability to bring it to a speedy conclusion.

This was all grist for those seeing a McClellan resurrection in the offing. It was evident by now that he would never take a field command again under Lincoln, even though he was still officially "awaiting orders." But if events on the battlefield and war-weariness crippled Lincoln sufficiently, it was just possible that Little Mac might look to a higher office than army command. Rumors had circulated for months before this summer that the Democrats were flirting with the general, and McClellan made his availability no secret. Although their convention was not to meet in Chicago until the end of August, false stories hit the army weeks before that he already had the nod. "I think if the soldiers had a chance to vote he would be elected," said a New York private when he heard a bogus rumor that the nomination was an accomplished fact. "I don't believe that President Lincoln has committed as many unpopular acts in as short a time, during his whole administration, as he has since he has been renominated," a Wisconsin volunteer wrote home on August 9. "The fear is pretty generally expressed in the army that he will not be elected, if McClellan . . . is nominated at Chicago." A Rhode Island artillerist told his sister in mid-month that "little mac will be president if the soldiers can vote," and a New York cavalryman believed that "the soldiers are all unanimous in upholding peace."[12] Peace in that context meant peace without victory, either an acknowledgment of Confederate independence or at the very least some bargain to bring the South back into the Union, such as abrogating the Emancipation Proclamation and offering other guarantees on slavery protection.

> The soldiers are discontented and think the war has lasted long enough and if a peace man is nominated for the presidency he would have the strong support of the army.... I do not look upon Father Abraham in the same light as when home. My politics have undergone some changes and Abe and no more of his stripe get my vote this fall. The army are strongly in favor of a peace man and I hope to god he gets the chair and the war is stopped. If you underwent what I have you would say the same.[13]

The situation looked similar to some west of the Appalachians. "The democratic feeling is quite strong in the Western Army," wrote a soldier in Mobile, "and if we gain no great military success before November, I think McClellan will give Lincoln a close run; Abraham's popularity has gone up and down more than once before now." A soldier with Sherman outside Atlanta simply believed, "Mr. Lincoln is becoming almost daily more unpopular."[14]

Of course, most of these enlisted men, regardless of their sentiments, had a limited field of observation. When they spoke of the feeling in the army, they really meant the campfire opinions they heard in their own company among close friends, and perhaps at large within their regiment. None of them had true soundings of feeling in their armies as a whole, and thus their limited observations, filtered through their own personal bias, produced grossly exaggerated statements on both sides. Nevertheless, McClellan did seem to enjoy a considerable following, chiefly in his old Army of the Potomac, and among Democrats everywhere in the field, including many of those who adhered to the War Democrat faction. But then, on August 31, the Chicago convention, as predicted, actually gave its nomination to Little Mac. That in itself was no more than many soldiers—hardly a majority—expected and even wanted. What they did not expect was the rest of the convention's acts. For a start, Chicago nominated as his running mate George Pendleton, a man notoriously opposed to the war from the outset, who had tried to hinder the supply of the armies in the field and actually expressed public sympathy for the South. Both he and Little Mac stood on a platform that was tacitly committed to reinstating slavery where it had existed before the war, and worse, that condemned the entire war as a failure and supported an immediate end to hostilities and the opening of negotiations with the Confederacy. In short, peace—apparently at any price—was more important than the Union. Of course, the platform—and McClellan—explicitly maintained that peace should be on the basis of the restoration of the Union, and the general privately went even further to say that if the South would not negotiate a return to the Union the war would go on.

But the only message the Chicago platform sent to the soldiers in the field was that their efforts had been wasted, all for nothing, and that, after all their suffering and dying, the Democrats would give up and admit defeat. Many men in uniform thought that Jefferson Davis himself could not have written a better platform, and it immediately crushed a fair proportion of McClellan's support in the armies. A Federal prisoner of war in South Carolina said the platform "will kill him" when he learned of it. "The blood of our fallen comrades cries out against it," wrote a New Jersey soldier. "McClellan was once the idol of the army of the Potomac, but he is cast down with all others who support the 'copperhead.'" Over and over, men who otherwise liked Little Mac said they could not stomach Pendleton and the peace wing of the party. "A man must be judged by the company he keeps," said one private. "I cannot swallow McClellan, his platform is too shallow," said a volunteer in the trenches at Petersburg; another thought he saw that "McClellan is fast loosing what friends he had in the army and I have no doubt Lincoln will have a large majority of the army vote. The Chicago platform is more than our heroes can stand." A man in the 103rd Illinois, in the fortifications surrounding Atlanta, suggesting that he would be just as happy to shoot Northern traitors as Southern rebels, wrote home angrily that he wished the members of the Chicago convention could be forced to "charge us in these works."[15]

That single issue of stopping the war short of victory immediately started to erode Little Mac's support, and to bolster Lincoln's among those otherwise disposed to vote against him. A cartoon in the illustrated press showed a soldier saying "Good bye, 'little Mac'—if that's your company, Uncle Abe gets my vote." A private echoed the sentiments of thousands when he wrote home, "I do not see how any soldier can vote for such a man, nominated on a platform which acknowledges that we are whipped." Another also spoke for many: "I cannot afford to give three years of my life to maintaining this nation and then giving them Rebles all they want." A major with Sherman declared, "We must have the man who dares to say: the Nation must live.

We can trust ourselves to no other pilot." Others with Sherman who at first reacted favorably to news of Little Mac's nomination turned dramatically when they saw the platform, "whose principles no *Soldier* can uphold," said one. Another averred that "'Mac' has lost thousands of votes within three weeks."[16]

Every bit of that disillusionment redounded to Lincoln's credit with the soldiers. "Old abe is slow but sure," said a Michigander, but "he will accept nothing but an unconditional surrender." An Illinois soldier besieging Atlanta promised that "Good Old Abe will show them a trick yet," and a Rhode Islander with Grant echoed that "old abe is the best man to finish this thing up in good shape." Another man with Sherman put the soldier case for Lincoln most succinctly: "Every one that is against him is against the union." Outside Atlanta, a soldier of the 59th Illinois simply concluded, "I feel like trying Old Abe for another term. My faith in him is unshaken yet."[17]

The one suffering from uncertain faith at the moment was Lincoln. The reverses, the bogging down of Grant at Petersburg and Sherman before Atlanta, Early's raid, and more, all weighed upon him as the summer wore on. He, like so many of the volunteers, saw some elements of soldier sympathy for McClellan in the army, and even more on the homefront, and allowed it all to play on his mind to the point where he once again misread army sentiment in Little Mac's favor, just as he had prior to Antietam. Early in August, General Meade thought he detected in Lincoln a feeling that his election chances were waning, and suggested pressing for an advance at Petersburg in the hope that some sort of victory might brighten prospects. On August 19, the president told a visitor that he did not believe McClellan, as president, would have any chance of ending the war without disbanding the more than one hundred thousand black soldiers and returning them to slavery; this would mean having to fight the South and an army of betrayed colored soldiers as well. Four days later, he drafted a confidential Cabinet memo stating his fear that he might not be re-elected, and posing the problem that McClellan would only be elected on the basis of policies that precluded the maintenance of the Union and emancipation.[18]

It was for Lincoln perhaps the lowest point of the war. He knew he had all of the tools for winning marshaled, and yet faced the prospect that his people might no longer have the will to use them. Once again he turned to public speaking, and to soldiers more than any other audience. He now pleaded the case for the war perhaps more emphatically and eloquently than ever before, confessing, "Whenever I appear before a body of soldiers, I feel tempted to talk to them of the nature of the struggle in which we are engaged." If only it "might be more generally and universally understood what the country is now engaged in," he told the 164th Ohio. "There is more involved in this contest than is realized by every one," he said, begging them to "rise up to the height of a generation of men worthy of a free Government, and we will carry out the great work we have commenced." To the 166th Ohio a few days later he expanded the theme. "It is not merely for today, but for all time to come that we should perpetuate for our children's children this great and free government." He said that he was a living witness to the fact that any man, however poor and humble, could rise to the highest office in the land, and only because of their constitutional freedoms, and they were fighting for them "in order that each of you may have through this free government which we have enjoyed, an open field and a fair chance for your industry, enterprise and intelligence; that you may all have equal privileges in the race of life."[19]

The president, as usual, spent a lot of time at the Soldiers' Home that summer, often in the company of his bodyguard. Many of them wanted to be at the front rather than on this soft duty, but he joked with them, "I reckon it is pleasanter and safer here than there." They were a ragtag bunch, but he had grown fond of them and seemed to confide in them. Their concern for him was evident one August evening when an apparent would-be assassin took a shot at him and knocked off his hat. They knew he was troubled when they frequently found him alone in his room reading from the Bible.[20]

But then came glorious news. On September 2, a telegram from Sherman arrived at the War Department. He had taken Atlanta, breaking the logjam in Georgia, and even though Grant was still stymied by Lee in Virginia, Sherman's success made Northerners feel they had momentum again. Many a soldier had said that if there was one significant victory before November it might ensure Lincoln's election, and this seemed to be the one. Lincoln capitalized on it as he never had on a military victory before. On September 3, he issued two orders of thanks, an order for a celebration, and a proclamation of thanksgiving—for Sherman's victory, and for Farragut's the months before. Salutes of a hundred guns were to be fired at the Washington Arsenal and at every arsenal and navy yard in honor of Mobile Bay, and another hundred guns for Atlanta. He offered the thanks of the nation to the admiral, to the generals, "and to the sailors and soldiers." In thanksgiving he asked that on the following Sunday prayers be offered in every church "for the Divine protection to our brave soldiers and their leaders in the field." The sentiments were completely sincere, but the recognition could not hurt in November; by uniting the people in prayer for the soldiers who were fighting, he hoped to unite them to what he knew was the soldiers' cause, not just his own.[21]

Certainly the great mass of the soldiers had a very definite idea of that cause. The president spent more than enough time in conversation with soldiers over the years to know that they were much more than rude simpletons or military automatons. He took their measure well when he called them "thinking bayonets." "It is a very great mistake to suppose the soldier does not think," a New York captain wrote to his wife that spring. "Our soldiers are closer thinkers and reasoners than the people at home." More than that, he believed, "it is the soldiers who have educated the people at home to a true knowledge ... and to a just perperception [*sic*] of our great duties in this contest." A Kentucky infantryman in the West added, "The soldier had no better way of employing his time than to think, and his condition naturally led him to calculate as to who should be the next President."[22]

Even before the summer's nominations, the campfire discussions began to take heat, with men advocating the merits of their particular favorites—Lincoln, Frémont, McClellan, and more—and their arguments frequently turning intemperate. As the summer wore on, politics dominated conversation in the field. "We had some pretty warm discussions here on the coming election & which is the best candidate," a Connecticut private wrote home from faraway St. Augustine, Florida. "About two thirds are in favor of Lincoln—the rest for McClellan." A Pennsylvanian with a considerable interest in politics and the war confessed to his mother, "I get a little excited on the subject sometimes." As the campaign got under way, Republicans and Democrats alike flooded the armies with pamphlets advocating their candidates. "We get so much reading material we cant read one half," a volunteer with Sherman complained. "It is because the election is so near at hand."[23]

Soldiers held formal political meetings and rallies in their camps, just as they had at home in 1860 as civilians. Even prisoners of war in the camps like Andersonville managed to stage a public forum, with speakers and straw polls. Anyplace could become the arena for political discussion. In Virginia's Shenandoah Valley, soldiers from a Vermont brigade regularly gathered at a spring near Front Royal to exchange news and views. One day Lincoln had far the majority of defenders, though Little Mac found a few, most of them basing their opposition to the administration on emancipation and arming blacks. Some thought that McClellan was a great general and the president held him down out of jealousy, and they hoped to see the general elected to put the abolition crowd in its place. Others said they simply wanted peace, which Little Mac would bring; Lincoln supporters, however, argued that no soldier could hold his head high given the kind of peace the Democrats offered. A Vermont sergeant suggested that the Confederacy was all but whipped. "How deeply chagrined we soldiers would feel to surrender to the South now, and find that had we held out a little longer, the whole rebellion would have tottered to the ground," he said. There should be no armistices and no negotiations. "We have got to fight this thing out. A Government that couldn't vindicate itself, wasn't worth having."[24]

Those debates were repeated all across the continent. Yet most soldiers fought the real battle for their votes—if there was one—in private. Private Marcus Woodcock of the 9th Kentucky Infantry expected that he would vote for McClellan, and he took pen and paper and began writing an essay to support his decision. On several sheets he outlined the case for Little Mac, and then began to list the points that stood against Lincoln. He lifted his pen, thought, and realized, "I could make no point." He wrote page after page without being able to define a single major issue against the president. In the end, the worst he could write was, "I cannot assert that Lincoln has, as yet committed any very objectionable act toward the people, but we must not vote for him for fear he *may* do something wrong." He himself recognized that the point was so absurd he would be embarrassed for anyone to see it, and ripped the document to bits. He would vote for Lincoln.[25]

By October, the electioneering in the armies was inescapable. Soldiers raised "Lincoln liberty poles" in their company streets at Petersburg, and a rustic army chapel nearby, on the New Market road, displayed a picture of the president hanging on its central pillar. There were torchlight parades for Lincoln and for McClellan; even some regimental mascots seemed drawn into the fray, most notably the bald eagle kept by the 8th Wisconsin and named "Old Abe." Many regiments came into the army with nicknames like the Lincoln Cavalry, the Lincoln Light Guards, and the Lincoln Rifles, and more had adopted McClellan's name in the days when he commanded the Army of the Potomac. Now old regiments changed their sobriquets to express their position, the 34th Massachusetts going from the "Worcester County Regiment" to "Old Abe's Pet." Soldiers even quipped that the real "mass meetings," as political rallies were called, were those held at Mobile and Atlanta and Petersburg, where the debating was done with guns and the "speakers" were Grant and Sherman and Farragut. "With our generals and soldiers lays Lincoln's election," said an Illinois soldier after Atlanta.[26]

Perhaps the hottest issue for the Democrats in the camp debates was emancipation, what a private with Sherman called "the 'nigger question.'" "You must think that I am against the Union," one New York McClellan supporter explained. "I am far from that but I cannot go for a man that thinks more of the niger than a white man." Certainly old deep-seated racial notions lay at the bottom of much of Lincoln's soldier opposition. "Some of our rabid abolitionists are making it nothing but a nigger war, and that is not what I came for," grumbled a disillusioned Republican. "Let us restore the union to its former place then if necessary to free them to keep it do it." Another who would vote for Little Mac asked the more penetrating question that went beyond pure prejudice. "If the negroes are freed what are we to do with them?" He foresaw white unemployment, a possible rebellion among the Irish immigrant population that currently made up most of the low-paying labor for which blacks would compete, and perhaps at the end of this war another one, this time a social war. A Massachusetts soldier simply wished that he had another alternative to Lincoln, preferring "a man who was not bound personally, as it were, in honor by the emancipation proclamation." A major from what by now had become the state of West Virginia declared that "nothing will keep me any longer in the army" if the people re-elected Lincoln after emancipation.[27]

Yet, for every opponent, there were several who supported emancipation as a war aim, whatever their private feelings about blacks. In one Illinois regiment an officer observed that, though many of his men reacted badly to the proclamation in 1863, by the time of the presidential campaign they had come around, recognizing it as a valuable weapon in the war, and were going to support Lincoln. "Slavery is the sole cause of the rebellion," said a private in the 48th Illinois, "and it is the political, civil, moral and sacred duty of us to meat it." There could never be a permanent peace until they had destroyed the institution, and "no other than the present Administration will ever distroy the cause of this war."[28]

Ultimately it was in the conviction that the war had to be fought out to victory that the majority of the soldiers made their decision. "No

Soldier wants to give the Rebs a favor or an inch of ground," said a New York private with Sherman. Men throughout that command quickly reduced the election to a single issue of continuing the war and saving the Union, and Lincoln embodied that cause. He stood up to the crisis, unbending in the face of all adversity, and never yielded, and they would not, either. "Never in a war before did the rank and file feel a more resolute earnestness for a just cause," said a Vermont man with Grant, "and more invincible determination to succeed, than in this war; and what the rank and file are determined to do everybody knows will be done." Alfred Hough of the 17th Pennsylvania observed the campaign from garrison duty in Chattanooga, and asked the salient question faced by every volunteer: "And what are we poor soldiers to do in this case," he mused. "Can we who really feel what we are fighting for, and now have the additional incentive of pride to carry us on, quietly skulk away to our homes? No! we must fight on through our whole lives for principle." If Lincoln and a congressional majority to support him were elected that fall, the war would end. "If *any other* person with supporting Congress is elected I can see nothing but anarchy, a long war and eventually a dismembered country." It actually pained a man in the 37th Massachusetts to think of the humiliation of going home less than a victor, in "shame and disgrace, as would follow in the event of success of anybody on that sneaking Chicago platform, insulting alike to soldier and to common humanity." He hoped that the men in the ranks might end the war before the election, but if they did not, he cautioned his friends at home to think well before they voted against Lincoln, imploring that "they must not ignominiously sell their birthright." A New York surgeon knew that a vote for the president was a vote for more fighting before it would all end. "I want peace as much as any other man, but not a *dishonorable* one," he wrote on the eve of Atlanta's fall. "We had better fight a year or two longer than submit to disgraceful compromise."[29]

McClellan's supporters, and there were many, quickly found themselves on the defensive, thanks to the Chicago platform. When one man in the 144th New York declared, "Any man that supported the present administration and voted for Abe Lincoln this fall was a traitor to his country," his fellow privates spontaneously arrested him and confined him to the cook house. Still, Little Mac had some powerful friends in the army, especially in the Army of the Potomac, where the commanders of the II, V, and VI Corps were all on his side, and many on their staffs as well, some of them accusing the administration of forcibly mustering out of service officers friendly to Little Mac and replacing them with Lincoln appointees. In Butler's small army, now advanced to Bermuda Hundred, southeast of Richmond, the regiments supporting Little Mac cheered him every night, boosted by their regimental officers, and some felt that perhaps two-thirds of them would vote as they cheered. Officers favoring the general went through the camps "swearing" soldiers to vote the right way on election day, though there was a great discrepancy in the way observers read soldiers' intentions. Some thought that the old veterans would go for Little Mac and the newer men for Lincoln out of gratitude for their bounties, but others saw the older soldiers arguing for Lincoln and trying to persuade the new recruits, miffed at the draft, away from McClellan. "There is more votes for Mc than there is for Abe," wrote a New York private. "Soldiers do not like him at all He gives us very little to eat three hard tack and a pint of coffee for breakfast Three hard tack and a piece of Salt Horse for dinner. Hard tack and coffee for supper. Poor grub that." Obviously, perceptions of the winds of soldier sentiment depended heavily on the bias of the observer, yet, in general, men who announced themselves for Little Mac risked being branded as cowards or ignoramuses. One soldier, clearly defensive over his choice, wrote home begging a friend "not to think hard of me for voting for MC."[30]

The struggle between McClellan and the platform he ran on proved too great for many an enlisted man who otherwise might have voted against the president. "You think perhaps I am a McClellan man," an artillerist wrote home in October. "Yes I would rather follow him than any man of earth for I know him to posess the true principle of the Soldier and a man, but I could not vote for him it is the wrong partty that comes in power with him if he is elected." More and more Democrats in the regiments announced that they could not swallow the platform. "Not an officer in our regiment will support McClellan," found the chaplain of the 120th New York. "They can't, they say, as soldiers vote for him. Poor man! the loyal thousands of the army used to greet the mention of his name with a perfect enthusiasm. Now he is cheered for by traitors." A colonel from New York who arrived in the Army of the Potomac a Little Mac supporter, left soon thereafter, downcast at seeing the absence of any real support among the soldiers who once loved him. Moreover, the enthusiasm of Confederates for McClellan worked against him. Southern soldiers saw in a Little Mac victory perhaps their last chance of achieving independence, and thus often shouted across the lines at Petersburg their encouragement for Yankees to vote against Lincoln. "The rebs are holloing for McClellan all the time," a man with Grant wrote in October. When one Confederate prisoner was brought through the lines, several McClellan supporters heard him read a newspaper to other prisoners, all of whom cheered for Little Mac, and the effect was electric. "It was the shortest and most effective political address I ever heard," said an Illinois private. "A speech without words—simply three rebel yells—changed all the McClellan voters into Lincoln men." Deserters coming within Union lines told Yankees that if Lincoln were elected they would give up but if Little Mac prevailed they still saw hope for independence.[31]

"I cant fite for the Union and vote against it," concluded a New York artilleryman. Echoing Lincoln's famous words from the debates with Douglas in 1858, he concluded, "A house divided against it self can not stand." Another New Yorker decided in early October that "Lincoln must be Elected again and again untill this cruel war is over." A vote for Little Mac was a vote for a traitor. By the latter part of the month, visitors to the Army of the Potomac detected such momentum for the president that they doubted McClellan would get even a respectable vote; even some of the more conservative officers of the old Regular Army had turned away from him. A Rhode Island volunteer concluded more succinctly than most, "I dont think that there will be any more show for mclellan then there is fore me and that is but little." Another expressed himself more emphatically: "I would just as soon vote for Jeff Davis at once as to vote for McClen." A New York lieutenant captured earlier in the Atlanta campaign had been a Little Mac supporter when made prisoner, but came back "a Lincoln man to the backbone" after seeing the enthusiasm for McClellan behind enemy lines. As for the foreign-born in the ranks, especially the Germans, they were even more likely to favor Lincoln. "I goes for Fader Abraham," said one. "Fader Abraham, he likes the soldier-boy. Ven he serves tree years he gives him four hundred tollar, and reenlists him von veteran. Now Fader Abraham, he serve four years. We reenlist him four years more, and make *von veteran of him.*"[32]

Of course, some soldiers felt either undecided, or else disillusioned with both Lincoln's acts and McClellan's platform. "You wanted to no who I was going to vote for," one man wrote home. "Most any body!" he said. "So, I wont vote at all." In the end, however, he sided with Lincoln. Another man, from Ohio, simply refused to vote, "for I am sick of the miserable demagogism of our party leaders on both sides." A soldier in the 144th New York concluded, "I think I shall hardly take the trouble to vote this fall." He did not like Lincoln and could not abide the Chicago platform, "and therefore I am indifferent about voting." Old soldiers seemed bitter toward McClellan; one said he would like "to be where he could just give him one of his boots in his hinder."[33]

By margins of three to one or better, the soldiers were lining up behind Lincoln as the campaign approached its close. "i cant see little Mc in the white house for a few days," said a Pennsylvania cavalryman the week before the election, "not while old Abe is able to swing the maul." A Massachusetts boy at Petersburg declared simply that McClellan's election would be "the worst thing that was ever done for the country."[34] Yet all of their speculation during the months leading up to the election was based on the supposition that the soldiers actually would be able to vote, and that was by no means a given. Prior to the war, soldiers away from home at election time simply could not vote. Wisconsin and Minnesota first acted to correct the inequity in 1862, followed soon afterward by Ohio and Vermont. Connecticut and New Hampshire legislatures attempted to follow suit, but their state supreme courts overruled them. In all, by 1864 thirteen Union states allowed for soldiers to vote in the field and have their ballots tabulated independently and added to state totals; four other states provided for proxy voting, by which soldiers were to mark their ballots in advance of election day, and then somehow get them to their home states to be cast along with the civilian vote. Indiana, Illinois, Delaware, New Jersey, and Oregon, however, maintained that their soldiers could only vote by being present in person on polling day. Before 1864, the Democrats generally opposed soldier voting, simply because so many of the generals in the field were Republicans and it was assumed that they would assert undue influence on the men in their command. But Democrats changed their tune now, with McClellan as their candidate, for they believed that the soldiers were still besotted with Little Mac. Indeed, one of the leading Democrats, Manton Marble, publisher of the New York *World*, asserted of the soldier ballot, "We are as certain of two-thirds of that vote for General McClellan as that the sun shines."[35]

After the near disaster the administration sustained in the 1862 elections, Lincoln tried to take advantage of his support in the armies by allowing Ohio and Pennsylvania troops to be furloughed home in 1863 for the off-year election. This move helped elect Republican governors, showing the effect of the soldier vote. By 1864, fortunately, those two states had come into line in allowing soldier voting in the field, but the five holdouts, especially Illinois and Indiana, presented a problem and a potent threat. The states that prohibited absentee voting were all heavily Democratic anyhow. If Lincoln managed only a slim majority from the civilian vote, and if somehow he got their soldiers home to vote and they went for McClellan, then it could cost him those states, and conceivably the election. Nevertheless, there was never any question that the president wanted his volunteers to exercise their franchise. After all, the free expression of the will of the majority was largely what they were fighting for. "I would rather be defeated with the soldier vote behind me than to be elected without it," he told a friend that fall.[36]

Indiana held its internal election in October, and did not allow absentee voting. Immediately after the fall of Atlanta, Lincoln asked Sherman if he could safely furlough his Indiana soldiers briefly to go home to vote. He did not ask that they be allowed to stay for the November presidential election as well, though Sherman knew clearly enough what Lincoln hoped, and complied as best he could. Governor Oliver Morton himself asked Sherman to extend the leaves, too, and soon there was pressure to furlough Illinois's and other states' troops home in November. At the same time, the administration had to face some concerns from commanders in the field who might prove to be obstacles. When he heard rumors that William S. Rosecrans, now commanding in Missouri, would not let men in his department vote for fear they would get drunk and cause public disturbances at the polls, Lincoln quickly made it clear that nothing was to impede every lawful voter's right. When the October elections came in Indiana, Pennsylvania, and Ohio, Lincoln followed the voting from the telegraph office at the War Department, anxiously watching to see what influence the soldier vote would have. His faith was rewarded, for the results seemed to indicate that, where the soldier vote could be segregated for study, the volunteers from the western states went by margins of ten to one for the Union Party candidates, and by somewhat lesser proportions for those from the eastern states. One of the closest tallies came from right near Washington, a hospital contingent going only by two to one for the administration's candidates. "That's hard on us, Stanton!" Lincoln joked at the news. "They know us better than the others." But it was still a victory, and what the October result told Lincoln was that his fears of late August were unfounded, at least within the army. The soldiers were with him.[37]

In late October, when Pennsylvania editor Alexander K. McClure visited the White House, the president expressed his belief that now there was no real doubt of his re-election. But he knew that he must do more than win. When he came into office in 1861, it was with barely 40 percent of the popular vote, and only because all of his opposition had splintered. He must have a real mandate now as validation of his war policy, and of emancipation, which meant he could not afford to lose any of the big states that were close, especially New York and Pennsylvania. They only allowed proxy voting, which, given the added inconvenience of getting ballots from the field to the polls, meant that not all of the soldier vote might get counted. McClure suggested furloughing home thousands of soldiers from Virginia, calling them the "bayonet vote"; Lincoln eventually passed the suggestion on to Grant and Meade, who agreed. Meanwhile, Lincoln personally continued to do what little the constraints of the time allowed a candidate to do. Convention said that a man did not actively canvass for his own election. But as president, Lincoln received many invitations to speak, and he could always address regiments that called on him when they passed through Washington; and so he did.[38]

Lincoln spoke before groups of soldiers at least half a dozen times in the last ten days of October, always on the same themes of thanks to them for their services and their sufferings. "In this purpose to save the country and it's liberties, no classes of people seem so nearly unanimous as the soldiers in the field and the seamen afloat," he said on October 19. He called for cheers from civilian crowds for the men in uniform; before soldiers, he thanked them for the votes they had given in the October elections, and by implication for those they would give in a few days. "While others differ with the Administration, and, perhaps, honestly, the soldiers generally have sustained it," he told the 189th New York. "They have not only fought right, but, so far as could be judged from their actions, they have voted right." He acknowledged the vital role of the men who stayed at home to vote and sustain the armies in the field, but to the soldiers he gave all the praise for the victory he knew would come. The nation could get along without some voters if it had to, "but the soldiers we cannot get along without."[39]

Lincoln might have profited from making some well-publicized visits to the armies, especially Sherman's and others in the western theater whom he had never seen, but Sherman was on the move again, and too overt an appeal for army votes might have given the Democrats ammunition. As it was, a McClellan Legion had been formed by a number of officers, carefully politicking in an effort to separate Little Mac from the Chicago platform; well in advance of the election, they had already raised the chimerical issue of fraud in the civilian vote in places like Maryland, where military commanders could exert undue influence. "All loyal men may vote, and vote for whom they please," Lincoln replied. He did make a brief visit on October 25 to Butler's Army of the James, but it was unheralded and little-reported. Otherwise his chief personal contribution to soliciting the soldier vote was to issue a denial of a Democratic charge that, only a few days after Antietam, with soldier dead still on the ground, he had ridden across the battle-field in an ambulance, singing jolly songs and telling smutty stories, all to Little Mac's revulsion. Such a lie was naturally conceived to disillu-sion soldiers, who seemed scarcely inclined to believe it even without Lincoln's refutation.[40]

Yet Lincoln had taken active measures to collect soldier support, as he did with civilians, and much of it subtle—some perhaps even unin-tentional. The *cartes de visite* depicting him continued to issue forth from the photographic houses in ever-greater number, especially with the election coming. The illustrated news weeklies repeatedly showed him, sometimes on state occasions but just as often in kindly cartoons that played on the caricature of his penchant for rustic wit. Most of all, by his own efforts in the reviews over the years, the remarks before reg-iments calling at the White House, his simply being observed walking the streets of Washington or riding abroad in his carriage, Abraham Lincoln had been seen in the flesh by more people than any president up to his time. Of the soldiers alone, by now a quarter-million or more had had some glimpse of him of their own. The continuing acts of charity, from the highly publicized reprieves of executions, to the un-sung gifts of little delicacies from the Lincoln family to their body-guard of the 150th Pennsylvania, were all become common knowledge, and a part of what the volunteers knew, or believed they knew, of their president. Even his favorite song was reputed to be the "Soldiers' Chorus" from *Faust*. It was no wonder that the mail often brought Lincoln soldier gifts, like the pipe carved from a laurel root by an invalid German volunteer, or that a recruiter wrote a song for him two weeks before the election:

Lincoln is the man we need, Johnson too is handy
Yanky doodle Boys hurrah, for Uncle Abe and Andy

We've got a Grant from Abraham to beat the Rebels hollow
And when we have A man to Lead why we're the Boys to follow.

No wonder, too, that, when a New York regiment marched up Broadway that month, and a spectator yelled out to ask whom they were going to vote for, nine of ten of them shouted back, "Old Abe."[41]

"Lincoln is gaining ground every day," a soldier in Arkansas wrote early in October. "'Little Mac' cant be spoken of in the same day with Lincoln." Other men in uniform became increasingly convinced that "the Army is all right in reference to the coming election," and that only Lincoln could end the war in victory. "Let Old Abe settle it," said a soldier with Sherman, "and it stays settled"; a recruiter agreed, from his vantage, "If we elect Father Abraham and Johnson it will settle the question."[42] Many regiments felt unable to wait to see the outcome, and began holding mock elections of their own in September and October. On September 19, the 24th New York Cavalry went ten to one for Lincoln. A week later, the 6th Iowa did the same, with 105 for the president and a mere 5 for Little Mac. Illinois regiments, unable to vote either in the field or by proxy, held the most straw polls, and Lincoln won almost all of them: 241 to 11 in the 34th Infantry, 235 to 37 in the 59th Infantry, and so on. Many of the soldiers felt bitter that they could not vote in the real election; some regiments held protest meetings and drafted resolutions, one of them referring to McClellan as "the hero who had won no battle and captured no city except Tranton, New Jersey." "We Illinoisans in the army amount to no more than so many negroes, in the election, for we are disfranchised," complained a major. Most felt certain that, if the state's men could vote, they would go overwhelmingly for Father Abraham.[43]

All across the front, from Arkansas to Fort Monroe, soldiers expressed the determination of one Iowa soldier that "Old Abe will get my vote this time if [I] get a chance to poll it for any one." A Massachusetts boy wrote home, "I wish I could get a chance to vote." The results of the October elections in Pennsylvania and Indiana gave them an increased desire to have their voices heard, especially those like men of the 7th Pennsylvania who were actually in battle "whipping Rebels that day, so we had no time to vote." When the results became known, some men hailed it as a greater victory than recent successes on the field, and foretold that, when they cast their ballots for president, the administration triumph would be overwhelming. A general with Sherman predicted on the eve of the balloting that the western soldiers would go nine to one for the president. Some of the states whose soldiers were allowed to vote absentee held their ballots in mid-October, with election commissioners in the ranks to make certain that every eligible soldier who wished to vote got the opportunity. In some cases they voted while in the line of battle in Georgia, or in their dugout bomb-proofs around Petersburg as their guns shelled the Confederates. "I voted the way we was shooting," said one Pennsylvanian, "for Old Abe and the Stars and Stripes." Across the lines, Confederates knew the balloting was taking place, and between shell explosions shouted encouragements to vote for Little Mac.[44]

Soldiers who had to vote by proxy received tickets with Lincoln's or McClellan's name on them, and then mailed them home for filing. "I have made out my voting papers to send to Chandler to vote for me," a New York volunteer wrote on October 21. The vote could not actually be legally counted until it had been properly cast at home, and so many soldiers worried that their mailed ballots might go astray, or friends and family would neglect to get them to the polling stations on election day. In many regiments, the soldiers selected a man going home on furlough or discharge to cast all their ballots. "I have voted a strate Union ticket," one man boasted. "I thought I would give him my vote." Significantly, "him" properly referred to the Union, but to so many of them Lincoln and the Union were the same. Not forgetting the men at sea, Lincoln and Secretary of the Navy Welles made special efforts to send boats to the offshore and Mississippi squadrons to pick up the sailors' votes. A number of other soldiers found themselves away from the army on leave, and cast about for someplace where they would be allowed to vote in person, even if outside their states. Many thought they could do so in Washington, the capital of all the states. "If there should be any chance for me to vote in this city or in Washington with any Maine soldiers I shall go to the polls and vote for Lincoln," a Downeaster wrote home. Men languishing in hospitals lost their chance if they came from the wrong states, and the Illinois soldiers, of course, simply lamented to home folks, "I wish I could get there to vote for old Abe."[45]

At the same time that they sent their proxy votes home, the soldiers also urged their friends and families to vote, and for Lincoln. "I shall vote for the blue-blooded Abraham," wrote one officer, who believed that the men in the ranks universally identified the support of Lincoln with the cause of reunion. "I hope that all of my friends will think and vote as they please," Private George Richardson of the 6th Iowa wrote, "but there is only one way to be a true friend to the soldiers and that is to support Lincoln. . . . There are plenty of good Union men who will vote for McClellan but they are only killing their own interests. . . . The Army is for Old Abe." A New York volunteer advised his sister to "tell father to go the whole hog for old Abe and the Union"; an officer from a black regiment advised friends to "do all you can for the reelection of old Abe & you will do the best thing you can for the country's good." A lieutenant with Sherman urged his friends to make certain that a good supply of preprinted Lincoln ballots got sent to the army, vital for the illiterate men in the ranks who could not write their own. "Urge all loyal men not to forget their friends in the army," he said, "and not let it be said that the soldier had to write out his ticket to support the just and noble cause their hearts bleed to support."[46]

Meanwhile, as November 8 approached, the War Department hurriedly tried to find excuses to send home as many men as possible to Illinois, Indiana, and the other states that did not allow absentee voting, while also managing the balloting in the field. Assistant Secretary of War Charles Dana frankly confessed, "All the power and influence of the War Department was employed to secure the re-election of Mr. Lincoln." The president actually helped individual soldiers get transportation home to vote when necessary, and in some commands out of the combat zone, troops whose enlistments were nearly expired anyhow were rushed home. A surprising number of volunteers even deserted to go home to vote, or at least that was the excuse they offered. Some left with passes and overstayed their time, others were absent without leave, and a few simply decided not to return. One prisoner who had already deserted and been incarcerated to await sentencing, complained directly to Lincoln that his pro-McClellan captain refused to have him sentenced for fear he would be acquitted "& then Little Mack would loose a vote." Understandably, courts-martial showed extra leniency with men who deserted to vote, whether they believed them or not, and it was even suggested that sentences in all such cases should be remitted. "I went home to vote for Lincoln" became a popular refrain before the courts. The president himself got to watch a microcosm of the soldier vote late in October, when a Pennsylvania regiment temporarily bivouacked on the White House grounds held its balloting. Tad came running into his office and told him to go to the window to watch the volunteers.[47]

November 7, 1864, the day before the election at large, was a tense day both in Washington and in the army camps. "I presume that tomorrow Little McClellen will get defeated worse than he ever did before Richmond or any place else," a soldier in the 45th Ohio wrote from Tennessee. "Well, tomorrow is election day for us," said a boy in Marietta, Georgia. "Let the wild World wag as it will, vote for old Abe still," crowed a Pennsylvanian. "Old Abe is the man that fears no noise so far away from home, his head is level and his clothes fit him." From regiment after regiment the letters home poured out the same message. "Tomorrow the great fight for president takes place & old Abe will still be the man." Some men, especially the Pennsylvanians, exulted that they were for the first time to have the ballot in the field, and many reminded the wavering that it was a soldier's duty to vote. "All we want to close up the game is Abe for Presiden," wrote a Wisconsin volunteer, "and then the game is up, the Union saved." In far-off Atlanta, an engineer from Missouri spoke of "life or death to our republican form of government and free institutions." It was more than a contest between two men to these soldiers, he said. "The welfare of millions yet unborn is dependant upon us."[48]

Then came the day. "This is Election Day & we will see what it will bring fourth," wrote an Ohio soldier. "Good morning to all this election day," said a soldier with Grant. "I am going to do all I can for Abe." Lincoln and Stanton had feared that there would be attempts to disrupt the voting in New York, and actually had Grant ship a few regiments north to the city to provide security. In fact there was no outbreak, and the soldiers, being New York regiments, had to be kept on their barges all day on the New Jersey side of the Hudson so that they were not technically in their home state; otherwise the ballots they had cast in the field would have been nullified. In fact, the election passed off quietly everywhere, especially in the armies, where so many soldiers commented on the calmness of the affair that it is evident that they, too, had feared it might be otherwise.[49]

West of the Mississippi, the 178th New York was on the march across Missouri, but halted for the day to let the soldiers vote. The 14th Wisconsin went to the state capitol in Jefferson City to vote, had trouble finding enough ballots, and altered some intended for another district to make do. "I cast the first vote I have *ever* cast, for the Election of Lincoln," wrote a proud private. "In doing so I felt that I was doing my country as much service as I have ever done on the field of battle." His company of the 14th went unanimously for the president, and the regiment as a whole gave Lincoln a 140-to-32 majority. Several Iowa outfits voted at Brownsville, Arkansas, and every one went for the incumbent,

McClellan getting a mere 24 votes in the 20th Iowa. The majority in the 12th Michigan was three to one for Old Abe. In Little Rock, the majorities were much the same, the 33d Iowa going for Lincoln by more than ten to one, and the 40th Iowa fifteen to one. Of the 480 men in the 1st Iowa Cavalry, Little Mac got one vote.[50]

East of the great river, men with Sherman's army, now on the move toward Savannah, hoped they would be halted for the day so they could vote, "so as to fight treason with our votes as well as our guns," one said. Most agreed with the corporal who wrote in his diary that morning, "This Day will Decide weather the Union will be Saved or Distroyed." Many of the regiments from appropriate states had already sent off their ballots. Others were too actively engaged on the march to be halted, yet most that were eligible managed to cast votes. No one saw much evidence of Little Mac support. "If every body north votes the same as the army," wrote an Illinois private, "McClellan will scarcely believe he was ever a candidate." In one brigade Lincoln emerged on top by twelve to one. A Missouri brigade went 4,625 to 906 for the president, and in the 23rd Missouri Infantry the challenger did not receive a single vote. In one division every single Ohio regiment polled for Father Abraham. Even some of the Illinois and Indiana regiments that could not vote in the field still held straw ballots, the 11th Illinois going for its favorite son by a 116 majority and the 72nd Indiana going fourteen to one for Lincoln and then cheering wildly when the result was announced. "We almost imagined we were at home and really voting for President," said one. There were still pockets of strongly felt opposition. "Whether slavery be right or wrong, I dont believe in carrying on a bloody war for years for the sole object of abolishing slavery," complained a Minnesota artilleryman, and in some of the Kentucky regiments McClellan ran particularly well; he outpolled the president two to one in the 9th Kentucky Infantry, where Lincoln had especially infuriated the men by allowing the court-martial and trial of their colonel for attempting to discourage black enlistments. Still, the overwhelming majority stood with Private Jacob Early of the 99th Ohio, who proudly wrote home that evening, "I have bin to the election and give old Abe a lift." An Ohio chaplain in Atlanta was even more moved by his act. "Cast a vote for President," he told his diary that day. "My native land! 'My country! tis of thee I sing.'"[51]

Elsewhere on the peripheries of the war the story was the same. At Hilton Head, among the troops besieging Charleston, South Carolina, the 144th New York went 250 to 28 for the president, one of its privates declaring that "Old Abe must go in." Farther north, in Annapolis, Maryland, where the Union maintained a parole camp for released prisoners awaiting exchange, the men who could not for the moment fight could still vote, and many of them did. In Butler's Army of the James, the men heard rumors that the Confederates would launch an attack that day in the hope of disrupting the voting. Yet there was no attack, and the election passed quietly. McClellan did a little better here, but Lincoln still beat him, 153 to 76 in the 76th Pennsylvania and more than three to one in the 67th Ohio; after the voting one Ohio soldier found the Democrats in camp decidedly quiet. "They have nothing to say just now," he said, for "the[y] Dont want to hear any thing of the lick Majorities that *Lincoln* has." Out on the water, most of the sailors never got the chance to vote: the coordination proved too cumbersome, and the fact that a fair number of them were Irish—and largely Democrats—hardly encouraged the Navy Department to struggle too hard. Moreover, the recent abolition of the spirit ration had made the administration rather unpopular with the tars. "I had no opportunity to vote being at sea," wrote a man on the USS *Gettysburg.* "If I could I should have voted for Mr. Lincoln though I do not think he has a *single* qualification for the head of the nation—except that he is pledged to continue the war till a lasting peace is established."[52]

Even the men in the Confederate prison camps held elections, although their ballots were nothing more than expressions of sentiment that would never get included in the actual voting. In the compound at Danville, Virginia, Lincoln beat Little Mac 276 to 91, though one Massachusetts prisoner came away somehow thinking that this constituted "a large majority in favor of McClellan." The four thousand or more men held at Milen, Georgia, gave Lincoln a 934 majority; at Columbia, South Carolina, the officers voted 67 to 7 for the president, and the enlisted men gave Old Abe a majority of 9. At the now infamous Camp Sumter outside Andersonville, Georgia, the prisoners used red and white beans as ballots. Among Vermont prisoners, the president got a majority of 158; overall among prisoners he topped Little Mac by five to two in spite of widespread disillusionment with his administration for not restarting the exchange system to get them back home.[53]

Most eyes turned toward the voting in Virginia, to the Army of the Potomac and its satellite command, the Army of the Shenandoah, commanded by General Philip H. Sheridan. Election day dawned warm and foggy for Sheridan's men, with the expectation that Jubal Early's Confederates, facing them, would try an attack to interfere with the balloting. The Yankees were on their guard, for, as one Vermont soldier said, "they did not wish to be disturbed in their privilege of voting for Uncle Abraham." Private Wilbur Fisk, writing home that day, told of how "thousands of bits of paper are falling into ballot boxes today, all over the country. It is a little thing, and can be done very easily, but mighty consequences hang on the result." Quite possibly the Union men outmaneuvered the McClellan supporters a bit by impeding their printing of a sufficient quantity of Little Mac ballots, but the complaints of the Democrats went unheeded. "Soldiers don't generally believe in fighting to put down treason, and voting to let it live," said Fisk. His brigade went two to one for the president; one Rhode Island outfit boosted that to ten to one.[54]

In the end, however, the army around Petersburg grasped most of the attention, for here it was more than an election. This had been McClellan's army, whose soldiers loved their commander as did no men in any of the other armies of the Union. Yet they also loved their president, the man who had helped Little Mac build the army and stood by them through the years of defeat and disappointment. This vote today would be a referendum on their loyalty, showing who had won the spiritual struggle for the army's heart, as well as the moral battle to cement them to the cause of restoration of the Union. Grant and Meade took steps beforehand to ensure that both sides enjoyed fair and unhindered freedom to express their sentiments. Campaign literature circulated freely in the ranks, and officers were prohibited from exerting their influence to sway the votes of their men. "Good morning to all this election day," said a Pennsylvania private. "I am going to do all I can for Abe." There was some difficulty in getting out the proper number of preprinted ballots, but that did not materially affect the day's proceedings, and even the fact that some parts of the Petersburg line were under fire did not keep men from the polls. It helped to hear Confederates shouting from their earthworks with cheers and encouragements to vote for McClellan.[55]

"I dont think I shall ever forget my first voting," a Maine volunteer wrote that night. "I threw my votes with as good a will as I ever did any thing in my life." Lincoln triumphed everywhere. In the 24th Michigan he beat McClellan 177 to 49, and overall in the Iron Brigade by almost five to one in spite of its Indiana regiment's heavy opposition to emancipation. The 17th Connecticut went for the president by three to one, even though it had been raised in heavy Copperhead territory at home. Among the Pennsylvania regiments Father Abraham made nearly a clean sweep, beating Little Mac three to one in the 140th Infantry, five to one in the 48th Regiment, and a stunning forty to one in the 141st Infantry. In one Massachusetts cavalry unit he beat his opponent better than two to one; in the V Corps as a whole his majority was 3,097 of 7,255 votes cast. In the IX Corps Lincoln carried twenty-five of twenty-seven regiments, and lost only two regiments in the XVIII Corps as well. He carried the battered old II Corps, and in the entire command a majority of the soldiers from every state represented in the Army of the Potomac went for the president.[56]

"Every *soldier* wishes Abraham Lincoln's reelection," a Maine volunteer had said. His success would "do more to dishearten the Rebels and crush the Rebellion than many a victory." As the regiments learned the tallies, they met the news with cheers of joy. "McClellan's defeat is as good as a Union victory," said another Downeaster. Soon no small embarrassment could be seen in those few regiments that had returned majorities for Little Mac. The captain of a company in the 1st Michigan, which went against Lincoln by a slim twelve votes, confessed that he felt "mortified to think that the old Regt. after fighting the rebels for three years should vote for the northern friends of rebellion." Lincoln men accused their McClellan friends of fighting one way and voting another. "I think some of them are ashamed of it even now," wrote one private that same evening.[57]

Father Abraham started that day in his office, but found himself unable to work, and so went to the War Department, where he spent hours at Stanton's office with Dana and others, watching the telegrams of returns arrive. He did find time to issue a brief message of encouragement for yet another Sailors' Fair being planned: "To all, from Rear Admiral, to honest Jack I tender the Nation's admiration and gratitude." By that evening, more than enough results were in to tell him that he was going to win a substantial triumph; in the end, he captured 55 percent of the popular vote and an overwhelming electoral triumph. It took longer for the definitive word to get to the soldiers in the field, but by November 10 the major armies had the news. Generals ordered the firing of hundred-gun salutes; the soldiers lit tar barrels and bonfires. In Sheridan's command and elsewhere, the regimental bands played "The Star-Spangled Banner," and on the lines of trenches at Petersburg the cheering of the soldiers and their volleys in celebration aroused the curiosity of their foes. "What are you'uns all cheering for?" shouted one Confederate. When told that there was a big victory, the Southerner at first thought it meant a battle somewhere, until a Union volunteer shouted back, "Old Abe has cleaned all your fellers out up North. . . . Fact, gobbled the whole concern; there is not peace men enough left in the whole North to make a corporal's guard." So felt many more. In Lincoln's election they saw the doom of the Copperheads and what they took as treason in their rear. One man in the 15th United States Cavalry was inspired to predict that "the sky of our political horizon is growing brighter and lighter each day."[58]

If ever Father Abraham wondered whether his soldiers felt gratitude for his labors in their behalf and that of the Union, their vote gave him a glorious answer. In the armies he carried nearly eight votes out of ten, even though almost half of the soldiers had been Democrats before the war. In Sherman's armies, where Lincoln was especially popular, he took 86 percent of the vote, and only one regiment, the 17th Wisconsin, returned a Little Mac majority. In the Army of the Potomac, Lincoln wound up with seven out of ten votes. In the state of Pennsylvania alone, out of fifty-one regiments with Grant and Meade, just six went for McClellan. Overall, of 150,635 soldier votes cast, Lincoln received 116,887 and Little Mac 33,748, and this did not count the soldier vote from a few states that did not break down their vote totals between soldier and civilian.[59]

And yet, for all the administration's effort in the belief that the army vote might be decisive, in the end it was not. In those states where the soldier vote was isolated from the total—Iowa, Kansas, Kentucky, Maine, Maryland, New Hampshire, Ohio, Pennsylvania, Vermont, Wisconsin, and California—it became evident that, had the soldiers not voted at all, Lincoln still would have won the popular and electoral contest in each of them except Kentucky, the only state taken decisively by McClellan. That would have given the president 96 of the 117 votes in the Electoral College that he needed to win. Indeed, only in Pennsylvania, Kansas, New Hampshire, Ohio, and Wisconsin could the soldier vote have made a difference, if through some miracle McClellan had gotten considerably more than half of it rather than less than one-third, as he actually received. In Nevada and Oregon, the *difference* in the popular vote between Lincoln and McClellan was greater than the *total* number of soldiers in service from those states, again meaning that the absence of that vote could not possibly have meant the president would not get their five electoral ballots, which raised him to 101. In Missouri and West Virginia, too, the actual total of men in the service at the time was scarcely equal to Lincoln's majorities, so, unless McClellan had received every single vote cast by soldiers from those states, the army vote could not have affected the outcome, which added another 14 electoral votes and brought Lincoln to 115. Then there was Minnesota, whose soldier vote arrived too late to be counted, so the field balloting made no difference at all in its decision; Lincoln would have gotten its 4 electoral votes in any case. That brought him to 119, 2 more than necessary to win the election, and not one of those electoral ballots was decided by voting in the field.[60]

Certainly soldiers' votes may have decided some vital and otherwise close state contests, especially New York, Indiana, and Illinois, for the kinds of Lincoln majorities in the regiments that soldiers from those states recorded in their diaries revealed that they were voting overwhelmingly for Lincoln. Nevertheless, the loss even of such powerful states could not have dented Lincoln's sure electoral victory, but only reduced his majority and his mandate. Yet, in a way, that did not matter. Re-election was vital to Lincoln and to the Union, but that the nation had risked a popular election in wartime and come through it peacefully, and with a majority clearly committed to continuing the work of ending the war and restoring the country, counted for much more. Most important of all for the soldiers, they had been allowed their say in the matter in which, after all, they more than any others bore the greatest risk. In voting for Lincoln they voted to keep fighting—and dying, if need be. "Is it possible that a soldier, after serving in this victorious army for three years can cast his vote for men whose platform declares that we have fought and struggled in vain?" one of Sherman's veterans had asked. November 8 showed that it was not. Lincoln's thinking bayonets had shown that they were also thinking ballots.[61]

"We have talked of elections until there is nothing more to say about them," Lincoln said a month after the polling. He issued his warm thanks to the soldiers and sailors when the results were fully known, and happily agreed with a friend who suggested that the army vote showed that "the soldiers are quite as dangerous to Rebels in the rear as in the front." On December 6, in his annual message to Congress, the president once more paid tribute to the courage and determination of his men in the field, and the still-untapped resources at home. "We are not exhausted," he told the nation. It was the message that the soldiers had sent with their votes. They would see the cause through to the end.[62]

The day after the election, callers found Lincoln back at his desk, poring through the papers in the case of a soldier condemned to be shot for desertion. In spite of the elation of victory, the grueling grind must go on. He also looked into a few charges of fraud and tampering at the army polling places, with allegations evenly divided between Republicans and Democrats. Unfortunately, he could not be out in the field with the soldiers to let their jubilation sustain his own. "This is gratifying news," one of Sherman's officers said when he heard the election result. "A better and truer man was never entrusted with power," said a Maine soldier with Meade. "That friend of humanity and champion of human rights, Lincoln, is again at the helm of the ship of state." An Illinois soldier delighted that his state's vote had gone for the president, though he lamented not being able to lend his own. "Thank God Abraham was elected without our vote," he said. "I am rejoiced." Some quipped that McClellan seemed as harmless on the hustings as he had been to the enemy on the battlefield.[63]

Soldiers left no doubt that they saw in the outcome something greater than just an election result, and they shared this vision with Lincoln, who had helped them to see it. A New York sergeant called it "a grand moral victory gained over the combined forces of slavery, disunion, treason, tyranny." A cavalryman who had been deeply attached to McClellan two years before now suggested to his father that the results provided proof "overwhelmingly conclusive of the fact that this is a peoples war—I thank God that the result is as it is—it is the heaviest blow the rebels have received in a long time." The men saw in the president's triumph what a Pennsylvania artilleryman regarded as an assurance that "the sacrifices that the soldier has made, have not been in vain, and that the war will continue until the parties who brought our present National troubles upon us, will be compelled to submit to the law and the *cause* of our troubles removed forever." A boy in the 17th Connecticut told his mother that none rejoiced more than the soldiers over the events of November 8: "I begin to think now we can see the beginning of the end."[64]

Certainly some were disappointed. At City Point, Virginia, one lieutenant from the 50th New York used some harsh language about Lincoln the day after the election, and soon found himself before a court-martial and dismissed from the service. But such were even more a minority in the aftermath than they had been on election day. Instead soldiers wrote and spoke of "the coarse, honest, good-natured, tolerably able man" they had voted for, and, not for the first time, they compared him to another. "Future history will place Mr. Lincoln's name next to Washington," a Pennsylvania volunteer said two weeks after the election. "The first the founder the second the preserver of our country."[65]

And so, once again, Lincoln had come back to Washington, and in comparing the two the soldiers were setting him beside not the *historical* Virginian but the man that they all knew from Mason Locke Weems, the Father of His Country. For all Americans of the time, the family was the most stable institution they knew, but for most of the volunteers, the army had now been their family for three years or more. They were, as they called themselves, "the boys," their officers the men they alternately resented and looked up to, like older brothers. And their figurative and even spiritual father, as Washington had been to his soldiers in the Revolution, had become the man whom for three years they had seen taking their welfare to heart, showing them kindness and concern, revealing on his perpetually "careworn" face that he shared the burden of their sufferings, the man who never lost his faith in them, who gave them pride in themselves and hope for their cause.[66]

Though the affectionate sobriquet had appeared in the volunteers' letters and diaries from time to time ever since 1862, the election of 1864 saw an explosion in its use. Suddenly, everywhere, President Lincoln became Father Abraham. "The best we know of is the re-election of Father Abe," an Illinois soldier wrote on November 14. "Our three years soldiering has not been in vain." Out at sea aboard the USS *Gettysburg*, a seaman noted, "We hear that Father Abe is reelected, and I hope it is true." In the 61st Illinois, out in the West, Corporal Leander Stillwell reflected, "For the last two years of the war especially, the men had come to regard Mr. Lincoln with sentiments of veneration and love. To them he really was 'Father Abraham,' with all that the term implied." And in the regiments of the United States Colored Troops, to which he had literally given birth, there was no doubt that Lincoln sat at the head of their table. "Do you know Lydia," an officer of one wrote home, "I am getting to regard Old Abe almost as a *Father*—to almost venerate him—so earnestly do I believe in his earnestness, fidelity, honesty & Patriotism. I begin to look upon him some as the ancient Jews did upon Moses—as a chosen instrument of God for the deliverence of the Nation."[67]

Deliverance, indeed. And now that Lincoln was to stay in Washington, it seemed at hand. A soldier composed a new set of verses that November and concluded them with:

My story's told, rejoice our land, for Lincoln re-elected,
Our country and our President divinely be protected.

A few months later, on March 4, 1865, when Lincoln took his oath of office for the second term and spoke of a nation that preferred charity and hope to malice, a chaplain with an Illinois regiment expressed the hopes of the volunteers everywhere: "God bless him & spare his life to see the close of this war."[68]

9

"WHERE ARE YOU NOW, FATHER ABRAHAM?"

Then Abraham gave up the ghost,
and died in a good old age,
an old man, and full of years,
and was gathered to his people.
[Genesis 25:8]

THAT CHRISTMAS OF 1864, TIRED THOUGH THEY WERE, the men in blue felt a renewed resolve. "We can see the beginning of the end," a New Jersey soldier wrote to his sister on the holiday. "Soon we of the army of the Potomac expect to arrive at the acme of our hopes and march through the streets of Richmond with the stars and stripes flying. . . . Then will I say to Father Abraham, 'Mine eyes have seen my desire, let now thy servant depart in peace.'"[1]

With the end in sight, they thought more than ever of going home. Hundreds of thousands had come through years of perils, and most appeared destined to survive. Lincoln himself had looked ahead to the last months of the war and told a friend, "I cannot pretend to advise, but I do sincerely hope that all may be accomplished with as little bloodshed as possible." The last faint possibility of a negotiated peace came in February 1865, when Lincoln met with Confederate commissioners at Hampton Roads, Virginia, and there rejected all discussion

not founded on reunion and emancipation. When news of his firmness reached the armies in the field, a New York artilleryman declared,
"We shall come forth from the fire of trial and have proven to the
world that the American people can and will govern themselves and
that our country is indeed the land of the free and the home of the
brave." When volunteers passed through Washington now, they tried
more than ever to get a glimpse of the man now universally known as
"Father Abraham." As if to complete the comparison to another great
father of his people, Moses, a Michigan soldier in January spoke of
"Old Abe, who hands out the laws." The men felt so familiar with
their president now that they even created and shared mildly risqué
jokes at his expense. "Why is Mrs Lincoln like our Army Sutlers," one
soldier asked another, only to give the answer: "Because she *skins* Abra-
hams *privates.*"²

There was jubilation in the air even with the fighting not yet over.
On March 4, when Lincoln took his oath for the second time, soldiers
in the field held parties, some of them filling captured artillery to the
bursting point in order to destroy them at the same time that they
went off in celebration. "The lusty lungs of thousands of wildly exul-
tant men added to the din," said one of Sherman's men, and well they
should, for by now his army had reached Savannah and marched north,
isolating Charleston and threatening the rest of the Carolinas. Even
though Lee still held his works at Petersburg, Grant's ever-lengthening
line threatened to surround him at any time, cutting off all hope of escape. At Cheraw, South Carolina, soldiers broke into a planter's wine
cellar and held a merry party in Lincoln's honor. "All the soldiers are
going into ecstasies over it," one officer observed of inauguration day.
"I think the Army has far more confidence in the President than the
country at large." One sergeant sent the president the chevrons he
had gotten for re-enlisting as an inauguration gift, thinking he might
like them now that he, too, had been "re-enlisted." "U Air my Stile
of A man," he wrote. Another volunteer at Petersburg sent Lincoln one
of the ubiquitous *cartes de visite* in circulation and asked for his auto-
graph on it, "as you are the talles Father I ever had or ever expect to
have." He would prize it, he said, "as it comes from the Saviour of our
Country."³

There was still some road to go, of course, but the men in the ranks
were behind the president at every step. In December, he had issued
one more call for three hundred thousand men from the states, and
nothing but echoes of approval came from the ranks. That same

month, at last, the Lincolns also allowed their son Robert to don a uniform. Mary opposed it consistently, but in the end her husband reminded her, "Many a poor mother has given up all her sons, and our son is not more dear to us than the sons of other people are to their mothers." Lincoln even put into effect a program to offer Confederate prisoners of war a chance to obtain release if they entered the Union forces, took an oath of allegiance, and entered service on the northwestern or western frontier defending against native uprisings.[4]

Still, he remained vigilant in preventing abuse of the enlisted ranks. He defended a man who had been drafted after trying to enlist and being rejected on medical grounds. "I do not think a man offering himself a volunteer when he could receive a bounty & being rejected should afterwards be compelled to serve," he said in discharging the fellow. He allowed men who were in jail for minor crimes to be released and hired as substitutes, addressed inequities in the draft, especially when the quota applied to a particular community actually called for more men than lived there, and especially went after the practices of unscrupulous enlistment brokers who hoodwinked ignorant immigrants into the army without their knowing what was happening.[5]

And there were the same mercies to perform for the convicted and the condemned. On March 11, he issued a proclamation offering pardon to deserters who returned to their units before May 10—one of the ways he was trying to "bind up the nation's wounds," as he had said in his second inaugural. The sister of one deserter wrote to him immediately afterward in gratitude, addressing him as "you *our best of presidents*." Meanwhile, recipients of his previous mercy continued to fight and die. On April 1, the day before Grant finally broke through at Petersburg and put Lee to flight toward Appomattox, Private Roswell McIntyre of the 6th New York Cavalry was killed in action at the Battle of Five Forks. On his body his friends found the pardon the president had given him for desertion, providing he return to his regiment and serve out his time. By the day when McIntyre's time came up, Lincoln had intervened personally in more than sixteen hundred court-martial cases. Interestingly enough, despite the mythology already growing around his pardons for desertion, he actually stepped in just as often in cases of sleeping on duty, and even more in charges of insubordination involving disrespectful language to a superior. More than any other kind of offense, however, he intervened when men received harsh sentences for striking their superiors. He never lost the understanding of the independent nature of the common soldier, or of how passion and intemperance could lead a man to do something neither premeditated nor characteristic of him in normal times. He knew these men.[6]

There was a little more time now for participation in the philanthropic endeavors to aid the soldiers. On January 29, the Christian Commission held its anniversary meeting in the House of Representatives with Lincoln in attendance, and he agreed to appear at a Sanitary Fair in the Northwest later that spring, though it would be his first trip more than 150 miles from Washington since he took office.[7] But from the time of his election onward, and especially after his second inauguration, the principal thrust of the president's philanthropic efforts was more direct means of benefiting the soldiers, whom he could now see only months or even weeks away from marching home.

He set the tone in his inaugural when he spoke of caring "for him who shall have borne the battle, and for his widow, and his orphan." There were soldiers everywhere in the audience that day. They stood in groups immediately beneath the stand from which he spoke, and his words were a promise to them and hundreds of thousands like them. Perhaps he remembered reading, some forty years before in Weems's *Life of Washington,* about how discontent with an ungrateful Congress after the Revolution led one poor Continental soldier to ask his fellow volunteers, "After all, after wasting in her service the flower of your days—with bodies broken under arms, and bones filled with the pains and aches of a seven year's war, will you suffer yourselves to be sent home in rags to your families, to spend the sad remains of life in poverty and scorn?" According to Weems, there was talk of rebelling again, this time against Congress, before Washington quelled the discontent. There was a lesson there, though Lincoln scarcely needed to learn one in this regard. He intended that the nation should show every gratitude to the men who had kept it living.[8]

Indeed, if it had not been absent at a typesetter's, Lincoln would likely have given his own original of the address to the new National Soldiers Historical Association, which wanted to print a facsimile to include in a book memorializing the deeds of "the private soldiers who have fallen in this war for the life of the nation." Yet he had in mind much more than that. In March, Clara Barton approached him with a plan to launch a search for missing or unaccounted-for prisoners of war. When she set up her Office of Missing Soldiers on 7th Street, she did so with Lincoln's endorsement and his instructions to the commissioner of prisoner exchanges, General Ethan A. Hitchcock, to lend her assistance. He let the Sanitary Commission have the free use of a government lot in Springfield, Illinois, to build a lounge and sleeping rooms for soldiers, and turned his attention to the care of volunteers maimed during the war. Congress had approved payments to the disabled back in the summer of 1861, as well as to their widows. On July 14, 1862, Lincoln had approved an act that laid the groundwork for all future veterans' benefits, and since then continued signing legislation that increased the benefits, until by 1865 the expense ran into tens of millions of dollars. Now he approved legislation to commence institutional care, which would lead in two years to the establishment of the first four National Homes for Disabled Volunteer Soldiers.[9]

The president wanted to see something done for discharged soldiers as well. Obviously the government could not employ every volunteer going home from the army without a job, yet he repeatedly sought to find employment for them in one of the departments, and lent his support to the new Bureau for the Employment of Disabled and Discharged Soldiers headed by retired General Winfield Scott. "I shall at all times be ready to recognize the paramount claims of the soldiers of the nation," he said, "in the disposition of public trusts." He also made certain that Chase's replacement at Treasury, Hugh McCulloch, understood the necessity of having money ready to pay off the hundreds of thousands who would be discharged when the fighting ceased. In the end, every enlisted man would go home with about $250 in his pocket in combined pay and bounties.[10]

He tried to do something for those left behind, whose soldier boys would not be coming home. He apparently showed some interest in establishing a home for soldiers' orphans, and in his recent annual message reported diligent payment of pensions to soldier widows and orphans. Nor did he forget the widows and orphans of his black soldiers. Many marriages of Negro volunteers had taken place when they were still slaves, performed on the plantation without benefit of clergy, and holding no legal standing. Thus, by law, if the widow of a dead black soldier had never been legally married to him, she and her children were not entitled to any benefits. Lincoln addressed the inequity, holding that all slave marriages should be recognized as if legal "so that they can have the benefit of the provisions made the widows & orphans of white soldiers." His suggestion became Section 13 of House Resolution 406, providing equal treatment for widows and orphans white and black.[11]

Lincoln perhaps did the most with simple words, the kind that only he seemed able to muster to meet the hurts and touch the souls of the suffering. The War Department, possibly at his urging, sometimes referred especially hard or touching cases to him, and less than two weeks after his re-election the most heartbreaking of all landed on his desk. Lydia Bixby, a widow in Massachusetts, had given birth to five sons, and now every one of them had been killed in action. The loss was almost too overwhelming to contemplate, and yet seemingly it had happened. On November 21, 1864, the president took time out from dealing with the court-martial sentences, complaints over polling irregularities, and doling out the unending patronage to address to her one of his most perfect creations:

> I know how weak and fruitless must be any words of mine which shall attempt to beguile you from the grief of a loss so overwhelming. But I cannot refrain from tendering to you the consolation that may be found in the thanks of the Republic they died to save.
>
> I pray that our Heavenly Father may assuage the anguish of your bereavement, and leave you only the cherished memory of the loved and lost, and the solemn pride that must be yours, to have laid so costly a sacrifice upon the altar of Freedom.

The president would only have felt gladness if he later learned that the report had been in error, and that Mrs. Bixby had only two sons killed. Of the other three, one was captured, fate unknown, another deserted, and one served out his enlistment.[12] Far more important, however, is that the widow gave his letter to the Boston press for publication, and thereafter it appeared in newspapers throughout the Union, extending the sympathy and comfort he gave to one widow to tens of thousands of the bereaved everywhere. Along with newspaper editions of his Gettysburg Address, mothers everywhere clipped the Bixby letter from the pages and kept it in scrapbooks and albums along with photos of their departed and their president. Each could feel, quite rightly, that he had addressed the letter to her personally.

Never could he take his mind far from the living, however, the soldiers still in the field, and now evidently so near their long-sought goal. Sherman was marching at will through the Carolinas, pushing a Confederate army before him as he made his way toward Grant. Other Union armies farther to the west no longer faced serious opposition as exhaustion, casualties, and desertion gradually diminished Southern forces everywhere. Only Robert E. Lee and Richmond still held out.

By late March 1865, as the weather moderated and active campaigning could recommence, everyone knew that the final push would come soon, and Grant and Meade were too strong, and the once-invincible Lee now too weak. The president wanted to be there for the finish, to see his soldiers of the Army of the Potomac one more time, and to confer with his generals. On March 20, he boarded the *River Queen* and steamed down to Fort Monroe, and then up the James River to headquarters at City Point. With no fixed idea of what he would do or how long he would stay, he said he felt rather like a fellow who had built a log cabin with no idea of the timber required before he started, and no regret over how much he had used when finished. "I came down among you without any definite plans," he told one general, "and when I go home I shan't regret a moment I have spent with you."[13]

Lincoln lived aboard the *River Queen*, but spent virtually all his time with the soldiers. On March 23, with Mary and Tad at his side, he stood on the railroad platform at Humphrey's Station as several brigades marched past in review. Two days later, when fighting suddenly erupted on the line at Fort Stedman as a bold but desperate Confederate assault sought to disrupt Grant's supply lines and set up a Southern breakout, the president heard the firing and asked to be driven to the scene. From a hilltop he watched as the Confederate assault lost its momentum and Union counterattacks drove the attackers back to their works. Some soldiers saw Father Abraham there watching. "Oald Abe was there to see the fun," one said, and Lincoln himself regarded the fight as only a "little rumpus." He had joined Meade and his staff and was riding back when they came to a stream and saw two stragglers. The soldiers stood erect and presented arms, and Lincoln raised his hat in salute and rode past. "It seemed a reversal of things," said one of the soldiers, "for the head of the nation to pass in review before a couple of stragglers."[14]

In the next few days, the soldiers saw him often, sometimes conferring outdoors with Meade and Grant, other times watching them as they marched by. He reviewed a few of the new black regiments in the army one day and, perhaps pondering the Confederacy's recent decision to try to raise Negroes to fight for it, quipped to a bystander, "I wonder how Jeff would like to have such colored troops in his army!" Frequently when soldiers in the field saw him in the distance, they spontaneously began singing, "We are Coming Father Abraham."[15]

On March 26, Lincoln stood with Meade and others, the end of the war clearly on his mind. Already he was planning a celebration at Fort

Sumter, now once more in Union hands, for April 14, the fourth anniversary of its surrender.[16] Sherman was about to arrive in person to confer on future movements, which at this stage meant chiefly mopping up Lee's army. Meade tried to show the president a fresh dispatch with more good news, but Lincoln kept his gaze fixed on fifteen hundred newly captured Confederates being marched past to the rear. "*There* is the best despatch you can show me," Lincoln told him as he pointed at the prisoners. A member of Meade's staff witnessed the incident, and in confiding it to his diary left his impression of Lincoln on the edge of victory:

> The President is, I think, the ugliest man I ever put my eyes on; there is also an expression of plebian vulgarity in his face that is offensive (you recognize the recounter of coarse stories). On the other hand, he has the look of sense and wonderful shrewdness, while the heavy eyelids give him a mark almost of genius. He strikes me, too, as a very honest and kindly man; and, with all his vulgarity, I see no trace of low passions in his face. On the whole, he is such a mixture of all sorts, as only America brings forth. He is as much like a highly intellectual and benevolent Satyr as anything I can think of. I never wish to see him again, but, as humanity runs, I am well content to have him at the head of affairs.[17]

When he met with Grant and Sherman aboard the *River Queen*, they assured him that, even though the end was clearly in sight, there would still have to be more fighting. "Must more blood be shed?" he asked. "Cannot this last bloody battle be avoided?" He wanted no more men to die. Already he had an amnesty plan in mind: to grant free and liberal terms to Confederates, including even their leaders, in the hope that they would lay down their arms and not force him to keep fighting and his soldiers to keep dying. Demanding the utmost in retribution would only mean a battle to the bitterest end. "How many more lives of our citizen soldiers are the people willing to give up to insure the death penalty to Davis and his immediate coadjutors?" he asked Noah Brooks. He could probably remember from *The Life of Washington* how the great general looked "with a father's joy" on his men going home to their farms when their fighting ended, "with all their *little ones*, and flocks and herds, now no longer exposed to danger." He wanted to look on *his* children going home now.[18]

"I begin to feel I ought to be at home," Lincoln wired Stanton on March 30, and yet he was so close: "I dislike to leave without seeing nearer to the end." He decided to stay—and well that he did, for three days later, on April 2, the Confederates had evacuated their lines and Union troops at last marched into Richmond. The next day Lincoln went into Petersburg with the occupying soldiers, and on April 4 he set foot in the enemy capital itself. With an escort of six sailors and Tad by his side, he rode through the streets of Richmond, then accepted the protection of a squad of New York volunteers as he moved toward the Confederate executive mansion on East Clay Street. Weems had described Washington's triumphal entry into Philadelphia after his surprise victory at Trenton, and the president may have felt some of the same emotions, though there was little or no cheering from the civilians who watched his progress. But the blacks cheered him. "God has made you free," Lincoln told them; "you are now as free as I am, and if those that claim to be your superiors do not know that you are free, take the sword and bayonet and teach them that you are." As if to punctuate his meaning, small contingents of United States Colored Troops were in the city now, too, evidence of men who had fought to make themselves free.[19]

Grant and Meade were chasing Lee toward Appomattox, and the president would have liked to be with them, but he had stayed away from Washington as long as he dared. On April 8, he prepared to return, but before going he went to the military hospital at City Point. There were up to seven thousand sick and wounded, but so elated was the president at seeing victory over the next horizon that he insisted on shaking hands with every one of them, or at least trying. Despite warnings from the surgeons that he would exhaust himself, he went from cot to cot, taking each hand and pumping it up and down in a motion that witnesses thought reminiscent of sawing wood. "Are you well, sir?" he asked. "How do you do to-day?" "How are you sir?" He had at least a word or two for every man, and when one of them asked back, "Is this Father Abraham?" he said good-naturedly that indeed it was he. "The boys were pleased with it beyond measure," said one inmate. "Mr. Lincoln presides over millions of people, and each individual share of his attention must necessarily be very small, and yet he wouldn't slight the humblest of men." It was obvious that these soldiers admired and respected Lincoln, said a Vermont soldier, but there was more: "They love him." Moreover, Lincoln's affection for the soldiers was transparent, as was the delight he took in visiting with them in such happy circumstances. When Lincoln finished, he took an ax in his hands and actually did chop a little wood, just to show the surgeons that his grasp was not diminished by all those squeezes, and then—always a little vain about his strength and prowess with the ax—held it by the end of the handle and slowly raised it and his arm until both were perpendicular with his body. After he left, several soldiers tried the trick and could not do it. "We all wished that for many long years yet 'Father Abraham' might be spared to this nation, which he, humanly speaking, has saved," said one of them.[20]

The president arrived back in Washington the next evening, followed hard by the news that Lee had surrendered that morning. The war was not over, of course—there was still a Confederate army in North Carolina facing Sherman, and fragments elsewhere—but now it was obvious to all that the Confederacy was in total collapse and the affair could not last more than another few weeks, if that. Two days later, all Washington turned out to celebrate, and that evening thousands serenaded Lincoln at the White House, calling for him to speak. He did, chiefly about the future and his plans for reconstructing the Union, but he did not let the occasion pass without a tribute to "Gen. Grant, his skillful officers, and brave men," to whom, he said, all the credit belonged. That same day, an officer of one of the black regiments wrote him in the flush of victory, "Abraham Lincoln has proven himself to be a wise and good man."[21]

Unfortunately, that sentiment was not universal. Lincoln spent the next three days on the usual routine: appointments, a few pardons, and planning for the future. On April 14, he and Mary rode in their carriage down to the Navy Yard to the warship *Montauk*, where he spoke with some of the sailors, perhaps mindful that, in the overwhelming preoccupation with the land forces during the war, he had rarely had much opportunity to mix with their counterparts in the marine service. Back in his office, he faced more of the paperwork that had so dogged him, including some of his "leg cases." This very afternoon, there appeared on his desk the matter of Private Henry Broerman of the 74th Pennsylvania, who had a sick mother and a young wife and was serving five years for desertion; now his brother appealed for clemency. Perhaps Lincoln would deal with it tomorrow. Other soldier matters were on his mind today. Before finishing for the afternoon, he met with Secretary of the Treasury McCulloch, telling him, "We must look to you, Mr. Secretary, for money to pay off the soldiers."[22]

About eight o'clock that evening, Lincoln and Mary left to attend the theater on 10th Street to see a farce. Half an hour later, they arrived and went to a box immediately to stage left, the orchestra interrupting the performance, already under way, to play "Hail to the Chief" as he entered. The crowd cheered repeatedly, and the president acknowledged its greeting. As the door to the box closed behind him, he took his seat in a rocking chair, Mary at his side, and together they watched the balance of the first and second acts. Lincoln was surrounded by his soldiers now. Out in the audience he could see the heavy speckling of blue uniforms of officers and enlisted men. Sitting just the other side of Mary was Major Henry Rathbone, formerly on Burnside's staff and now in the adjutant general's office. Draped over the railing of his box was the flag of the United States Treasury Guards, a regiment composed of clerks who had volunteered for emergency duty. Next to it hung a framed portrait of Washington. During the interval after the second act, the orchestra played a new composition, "Honor to Our Soldiers." But none of them could save him, for outside his box the civilian guard on duty left his post, and another, quite unfriendly civilian approached. As the final act commenced, Lincoln's last words to a mortal man, if there were any, he spoke to Major Rathbone, a soldier.

An army surgeon was the first to reach the stricken president, and other soldiers helped to carry him out into the street and across to a boarding house, where he lay through the night; outside, mobs of outraged soldiers led some to fear that paroled Confederate soldiers in town, or even Southern sympathizers, might be attacked in retribution. "A bloody battle which would have shocked humanity was averted a thousand times that night by a miracle," thought one senator. But there was no miracle in the boarding house. The doctors draped a coverlet over him as his system fought its losing struggle with the ravages of a bullet. Beneath the coverlet, and next to his body, they placed a soldier's blanket. It was on him still when he died the next morning.[23]

The evening of April 15, the news began to hit the armies. Whippoorwills sounded in the treetops, reminiscent of the old Cherokee legends of the bird's song portending death. "What a death like Stillness came over the army that night not a stir in all the camp," recalled a man in the 148th Pennsylvania. "Seamed as if all our hardship and sufering had been for nothing." There was no drill, no dress parade that day. Regimental and company officers summoned the enlisted men to hear the news. "We moved away slowly to our quarters, as if each had lost a near and dear friend at home," a private wrote that night. "I always thought that he was most loved by all the Army," he went on. "What a hold Old Honest Abe Lincoln had on the hearts of the soldiers of the army could only be told by the way they showed their mourning for him."[24]

Over the next few days, the terrible news took time to settle into the soldiers' consciousness. "God have mercy on us," wailed an Illinois chaplain. "What is there man wont do?" In camp after camp, commanders ordered solemn "minute guns" fired at regular intervals throughout the day in reminder and mourning. Among other Illinois soldiers, a major was seen weeping as openly as a child; men in the ranks said they would gladly have yielded their lives in return for Lincoln's. In Sherman's army the news robbed the men of the joy they had felt at impending victory only hours before. "The whole army though flushed with victory is cast down with sorrow and gloom," an Illinois private wrote in his diary. "The camp is a mournful chapel." Others saw on the faces around them the evidence that "every man felt that he had lost a dear personal friend." Some brigades held mass meetings in memory of the president, and one soldier thought of three Confederate prisoners taken the day before the news arrived: had they been captured later, he reflected, they might not have been brought in alive.[25]

Out in the Far West, the news took longer to circulate, but came with no less stunning impact. At Pilot Knob, Missouri, men of the 7th Kansas Cavalry were shocked. "The nation has lost one whose place cannot be filled," said one of its sergeants. Way out on the Platte River, at Fort Cottonwood in the Nebraska Territory, the Unionist officers of the 3rd United States Volunteer Infantry, "Galvanized Yankees" formed from released Confederate prisoners, were saddened by the lamentable news. In United States Colored Troops regiments all across the map, the word hit with sledgehammer effect. "I cannot paint to you the grief and indignation," one USCT officer wrote on hearing. "With us of the U.S. Colored Army the death of Lincoln is indeed the loss of a friend. From him we received our commission—and toward him we have even looked as toward a Father." One black soldier recalled, "We have looked to him as our earthly Pilot to guide us." Another, though deeply saddened, said he would not weep: "I shed not a tear for him. He has done the work that was given him, and today sings the song of redeeming love."[26]

The sadness was nowhere greater than in Lincoln's own army, the Army of the Potomac. "I never saw so many sorry soldiers," a Pennsylvanian wrote home. In the camps of the Iron Brigade, whose men always enjoyed a mixed relationship with the president, the soldiers sat in silent clumps around their campfires. One officer thought that "they all seemed stupified by the terrible news." Elsewhere the soldiers reacted first with rage and then with numbness. Four days after Lincoln's death, as the minute guns went off and the flags drooped at half-mast, the men still struggled with the realization that he was dead. "All hearts are sad, and the grand old Army of the Potomac is in mourning for the nation's loss," said a Rhode Islander. "Lincoln was truly the soldiers' friend and will never be forgotten by them." Tears flowed everywhere. Many a man who once damned Lincoln as McClellan's enemy set aside or forgot old animosities in the grief of the moment. Men in the V Corps dipped their handkerchiefs in black ink to make mourning bands for their arms and to drape their regimental colors. "He was our best friend," sobbed a boy of the 48th Pennsylvania. "God bless him." Another Pennsylvania soldier reflected that on April 14 he, too, had attended the theater, in his case in Richmond. "It was the first night for me, the last for him," he told a friend on April 17. "But his deeds shall live. Thank God he lived to see his great principles established upon the track of a fleeing foe."[27]

An Illinois soldier stated what should have been the obvious when he wrote, "Not a word of disrespect for our honored dead, would a soldier tolerate from any one." Yet, amazingly, dozens of men in blue actually expressed satisfaction at Lincoln's death, reflecting no doubt bitterness at being drafted, anger over emancipation, or simply the foolish contrariness that sometimes impels men to resist cynically any tide of sympathy. "I am glad of it, god damn him," said an Indiana private; "he ought to have been killed long ago." An Oregon cavalryman exclaimed, "I'm glad the son of a bitch is dead"; a soldier at Fort Smith, Arkansas, said it was "the damndest best news he had heard for some time." Some rationalized their sentiments, saying that hundreds of thousands of soldiers had died, and "it is no worse for Lincoln to be killed than any other man." Others said it was a simple military act, entirely justified, just as if any soldier in blue had killed Jefferson Davis. A few simply sounded foolishly belligerent. "Old Abe is killed and I do not care a damn," said one quartermaster. "He was an abolitionist and he had been the cause of thousands of innocent men being killed." The racial resentment came out again when a Regular Army private said that he was glad, for he had seen Lincoln take off his hat to black soldiers. "The devil has been waiting to pick his bones for some time," sneered a New York cavalryman. Some boasted that with Lincoln dead they might take a hand at killing blacks now that Confederates were going out of season. "I don't think the news is sad—I am glad the President is killed," exclaimed a New York artilleryman. "Where art thou now, Father Abraham?"[28]

They should have known better: anyone expressing sentiments like those in the hearing of others soon found himself before a court-martial, sentenced to anything from thirty days at hard labor to ten years with a ball and chain. At least one man, Private Charles Hobson of the 2nd United States Veteran Reserve, was sentenced to be shot for his remarks, and spared only when his good past record and his having a family persuaded authorities to mitigate the sentence—just as the man he was happy to see dead would have done in his behalf.[29] Others were equally fortunate to escape the wrath of their fellow soldiers. The 85th New York satisfied itself with simply drumming out of camp one army nurse who expressed happiness at Lincoln's death. In the 17th Maine, with Grant, the soldiers dragged a man who said he approved of Lincoln's murder to a frog pond and there held him under the water until he was nearly dead. When he got away, covered in green slime, and complained to their colonel, the officer simply told him, "They served you right, only it is a d——d shame they didn't drown you!"[30]

It went much harder for Confederates who injudiciously expressed such sentiments. In the immediate aftermath, a majority of Union soldiers shared the view that Lincoln's assassin had at least the tacit approval of the Rebel authorities, if not in fact their actual involvement, and many would hold to that view for the rest of their lives. They felt intense bitterness, and an almost uncontrollable urge to take out their anger and frustration in vengeance. One captain said that, if the War Department issued "a proclamation of extermination with a call for Volunteers for the war," nine of ten Union soldiers would happily have enlisted for the work. Repeatedly, men in the Army of the Potomac echoed the Massachusetts soldier who wrote home, "It is well for the Rebel Army that they have surrendered for should we meet them now the *slaughter* would be *fearful*," and no mercy shown. Out on the front lines, some men swore that they would take at least one Confederate life apiece, making no distinction between killing a man in battle and wreaking vengeance on a helpless prisoner if need be. A wounded prisoner of war in one of the City Point hospitals unwisely showed his pleasure, and the other inmates, despite their wounds and infirmities, attacked and nearly killed him before being restrained by guards. In the Army of the James, angry soldiers attacked and beat several paroled Confederate enlisted men at random. "Revenge is the cry of all," said one of the men, and they took it at every opportunity. In the prison at Fort Delaware, Southern prisoners unwisely cheered at the news of the murder, and the commander immediately ordered his guards to shoot any who repeated the outburst. In occupied cities all across the South, citizens wisely held public meetings to pass resolutions condemning the assassination, hoping to forestall soldier retribution on themselves and their property. In South Carolina, some of the black regiments felt so inflamed that their commanders had to restrain them from burning and pillaging indiscriminately.[31]

Sherman's men gave even greater vent to their outrage, perhaps because they had always been more boisterous, more rugged than their eastern compatriots. "The army is crazy for vengeance," one Illinois infantryman wrote two days after Lincoln's death. They actually hoped that the Confederate army facing them would not surrender but try to fight on. "God pity this country if he retreats or fights us." Men in the 99th Ohio resolved not to take prisoners in the next battle if there was one. "Revenge will be taken and the soldiers are aroused to the highest pitch." One volunteer related, "I have heard only one sentiment expressed, & it seems to be universal throughout the army. Woe to the South if this Army is compelled to pass through it again." Some men said their only fear was the war might end before they had a chance to kill Confederates in retribution. "The battle cry will be 'Lincoln' and woe to the rebel that falls into our hands." Many swore that the blood of thousands could not compensate for the precious life extinguished. In Raleigh, North Carolina, General John Logan had to use the threat of their own artillery to contain two thousand soldiers who mobbed together intent on sacking the town in vengeance; for several days afterward, he kept guards on their camps. It was just as well, one of the enlisted men said, "for the boys would have shown no mercy."[32]

"Vengeance belongeth to God," one of Sherman's men wrote on April 19. "He will repay." But some of the anguished veterans felt no compunction about contributing a down payment. Given the opportunity, they showed no mercy. Stories circulated that soldiers in occupied Nashville killed civilians who publicly declared gladness at the president's death. In Washington, a soldier shot dead on the spot a man who said he was happy with the assassination, and down at City Point, when a Confederate prisoner said Lincoln should have been killed years before, volunteers took a rope and hanged him from an apple tree. In the prison at Fort Jefferson, another foolish Confederate found himself strung up by his thumbs so long that he died shortly after being cut down; a guard wrote, "I honestly confess that I have very little sympathy for him or every man who is punished for such expressions." Out in Missouri, the officers of the 7th Kansas met to decide what to do with yet another indiscreet prisoner of war. The vote came out twenty-five to five in favor of shooting him, but department headquarters refused to approve the sentence. When word came back to the Kansans, several of them took the offender and another guilty of the same offense out a few miles on a wood-gathering detail. When the detail returned, the soldiers reported that the two Confederates had been shot attempting to escape. Before long, Confederates themselves began to confess to the victors that the conquered South lost its best hope with the death of Lincoln.[33]

Soldiers found varying ways to cope with and try to understand what had happened, to find some meaning in the senseless murder. "I don't think we knew how much we did think of him until then," one of Sherman's privates reflected. Another decided that "Abe's heart was most too large." Others feared that the fault somehow was their own. "We had almost made Lincoln a god and now he has been taken from us," said one, speculating that the men had taken too much pride in the president, or he too much in himself, and this was the Almighty's punishment. Two men in a Connecticut regiment with Meade thought that God had taken Lincoln so that Americans would look not to this mortal man as their father, but to a supreme being instead. "He might have removed from us the Father of our Country that we might be induced to place our whole reliance on the God of our fathers, and not in man as perhaps has been done by too large a portion of our people," said one.[34]

However they interpreted the loss, they all felt it deeply. "No man, not even Grant himself, possesses the entire love of the army as did President Lincoln," said a Wisconsin soldier. "We mourn him not only as a President but as a man, for we had learned to love him." Thousands of soldiers passed by his casket as he lay in state in the White House, and thousands more would pay last respects as his remains were sent on a wide sweep across the North from city to city before finally coming to rest in Springfield. George F. Root composed a new funeral tribute to be played, titled "Farewell Father, Friend and

Guardian." Wherever he went, an honor guard of officers and enlisted men accompanied him. When, finally, his remains went into a temporary vault in Springfield, hundreds of soldiers swelled an audience otherwise composed of Lincoln's old neighbors and associates. They were all his friends now.[35]

Most felt that the president had been cheated. "President Lincoln was stricken down while in the height of glory, popularity and personal happiness," said a cavalryman. "His work was nearly completed, would to God he had been able to finish it and been spared to complete his remaining days in quiet and peace.—Enjoying the love and respect of the American people." His sudden disappearance from the scene caused considerable anxiety. "Things look darker to me than at any time since the issuing of the Emancipation Proclamation," one volunteer worried. Some feared that his death would cause the war to be prolonged, and a chaplain with the 2nd Colorado Cavalry feared that there would be blood up to their horses' bridles in retribution. The more conservative elements in the army expected that abolition could not last now, without Lincoln to keep the disparate elements of the Union together on the issue, and predicted internal strife at the least. In the immediate aftermath of the assassination, a group of Union officers formed a new organization, the Military Order of the Loyal Legion of the United States, its mission being to protect the country should anarchy or treason ensue.[36]

"Abraham Lincoln was killed," wrote soldier Wilbur Fisk, "but his spirit is still with us, and though dead, he yet speaketh." Indeed, the sentiments often took on a biblical tone as the soldiers quickly saw in retrospect more and more divine qualities in their martyred president. "They succeeded in killing the Son but the father liveth," said a Pennsylvania boy, comparing Lincoln to Christ. Lithographs appeared in the North showing Lincoln ascending through the clouds to heaven, where the welcoming arms of Washington awaited him. Surely a part of the soldiers' anger and disappointment came from the fact that they, like Lincoln, had been cheated of the opportunity to feel unalloyed joy at victory. "No Set of men in all Gods Creation has A write to Rejoice and Even Shout over the glad tidings of Peace more than the war worne Veteran," said one recruiter of black volunteers.

He who has with Musket and bayonet Waded through Snow, Rain, Hail, and Swamp, Amidst Rivers of Blood Living on Hard tack and Sowbelly with the Hevens for our dwelling place for the Space of four Long years far from our Homes and friends in the midst of Enemys Boath Male and female. Why should we not Rejoice at Peace and A Return to our Beautiful Homes and warm Harted friends far in the North. My Hart leaps for Joy while I write but Alass whare is our Great Leader President Lincoln.[37]

"It seemed as if we had lost a father," said many. Already they had started to speak in exaggeration. "Mr. Lincoln was different from everybody," said Fisk just a week after the slaying. "So sagacious, so straightforward in all that he did, so apt in all that he said, and withal so kind-hearted and honest." That would only be the beginning of the deification to follow, much of it at the hands of the soldiers themselves.[38]

However they dealt with the blow, the men in uniform had to accept that Father Abraham was gone and they must go on. The war was not yet over, but soon it would be. In late April and May, the remaining Confederate armies in the field surrendered one by one, and Jefferson Davis himself was captured on May 10. By June, resistance was virtually over everywhere, and all but a few of the civil leaders of the rebellion were imprisoned. At last it dawned on the soldiers that the long-awaited day was coming. Songwriter Thomas M. Towne caught the spirit of the moment:

The vacant fireside places
Have waited for them long;
The Love-light lacks their faces,
The chorus waits their song;
A shadowy fear has haunted
The long deserted room;
But now our prayers are granted,
Our boys are coming home! [39]

Even before the last Confederate soldiers furled their flags and surrendered their arms, Lincoln's soldiers began to look ahead. "There is no telling as yet what Uncle Sam is going to do with us," an Iowa man mused on June 10. The authorities had a lot of housecleaning to do. They must decide which regiments to keep in service awhile longer for the anticipated occupation of portions of the South and to guard the border with Mexico, where French adventurers seemed to pose a threat. Then there were volunteers who found that they liked the military as a profession and wanted to transfer to the Regular Army units, chiefly for service on the western frontiers. Even as McCulloch and the Treasury prepared for the issue of tens of millions of dollars in final pay and bounties, the military-justice branch started to deal with the thousands of men in prison or under sentences from courts-martial. On May 27, Stanton issued a general order discharging all but a few prisoners and remitting their remaining sentences. Some would not be released, however—chiefly those sentenced for capital crimes. At least forty-five more soldiers went to their deaths before firing squads now that Father Abraham was not there to shield them. All but four had been convicted of rape, murder, or mutiny, and eighteen of them came from black units, most of them convicted for joint crimes. The last to die met his end on June 8.[40]

Three days earlier, a Rhode Island volunteer reflected, "I was proud to be a Corporal and prouder still to be a soldier." Looking back on the past four years, he felt stunned. "I cannot realize that I have seen the beginning and the end of the great Civil War." That was the sentiment that Father Abraham had wanted all his boys to have, that feeling of accomplishing something, of taking part in a noble, unselfish enterprise and seeing it through to the end. That was what could give a young man the self-esteem to boost him on in life, and make him a credit to himself and his community. From the very beginning, he strove to get as many men as possible through their service honorably, to give each a chance to prove something to himself, and at the same time to do something for his country. Lincoln had helped to revolutionize the relationship of the citizen to the state, to implant in adult males, at least, a new sense of civic obligation, of a debt due for the benefits of democracy received. Thus his giving so many deserters and others a chance to redeem themselves, and his insistence on fair play for the soldiers in the ranks. He had helped to take the inadequate old militia tradition and recast it into something that could defend a major nation on the world stage. Without what he had done, the United States would not have been morally or militarily equipped to cope with the demands that the world would make upon it for the preservation of democracy in a century yet to come.

A part of the new compact that Father Abraham forged was the implicit understanding that the government would take care of the men who had defended it. Some, of course, were now beyond its help. More than three hundred thousand died on battlefields and in camps and hospitals all across the country, with tens of thousands more maimed through loss of limbs, eyes, or minds. The work that Lincoln began of caring for them continued after his death, and even as the armies began demobilizing. Institutional care for disabled soldiers, begun in 1865, continued at an accelerating pace, with new soldiers' homes opening regularly for almost seven decades after Appomattox. Pensions, too, commenced almost immediately after the end of the war. The Treasury paid some $15 million in 1866, but that grew almost exponentially. Within twenty years, veterans had received more than $700 million in total benefits; pensions alone totaled $174 million in the fiftieth-anniversary year of Gettysburg and Vicksburg. More than $5 billion had been paid out by 1917 and America's entry into World War I, and in another sixteen years, total benefits equaled double the actual cost of the war itself.[41]

Though he was beyond reach of those benefits himself, Lincoln in memory soon became drawn ever closer into the soldiers' orbit. When veterans' benevolent and fraternal organizations began forming in the 1880s, especially the Grand Army of the Republic, Lincoln invariably sat atop their stationery and on their forms and certificates. The Soldiers and Sailors Historical & Benevolent Society in Washington issued souvenir booklets in which soldiers could enter their details of service and family histories among pages filled with photographs of Lincoln and reproductions of the Gettysburg Address and second inaugural. Soldiers compiling scrapbooks of war mementos and memories inserted clippings about the president they had known and loved, including his favorite poem, "Why should spirit of mortal be proud." His face appeared on reunion ribbons and banners, and before long he became one of the primary tools of the veteran-dominated Republican Party in its almost unchallenged rule over national politics for the half-century after the war. When the so-called era of the bloody shirt appeared, the symbolic blood of a faceless three hundred thousand stained the fabric that Republicans waved to rally voters, yet the only visage they displayed was Father Abraham's. For all that Lincoln's memory was used by many to their own ends, however, for the men who had fought in his armies he remained something that politicians and demagogues could not take away. When William Powell published his massive history of the V Corps in 1895, he included five separate indexes. Entries for Lincoln were to be found listed in the index for Union soldiers. He had become one of them.[42]

Within weeks of Lincoln's death, the soldiers began remolding his memory, as well as their own recollections of him. One volunteer who had little good to say for him in life, now suddenly especially valued his commission as an officer, because it had been signed by Lincoln before his death. A host of enlisted men who voted for McClellan in 1864 would later, in memory, change their votes so as not to have been on the wrong side of the national issue. Entries critical of the president miraculously disappeared from many diaries, along with those covering visits to prostitutes and other matters considered unsavory. Letters home were sanitized of anti-Lincoln sentiments in some cases, and when men started writing memoirs, in the 1880s and later, some conveniently forgot hostility to Lincoln during the war in order to ride the national wave of memorializing. Soon anything associated with the martyred president took on a holiness, as in August 1865, when the historian of the Christian Commission spoke of the prayer with Lincoln in the East Room of the White House back in January as "the church of the nation consecrating the lamb for the nation's sacrifice." Memory is always forgiving and inventive, but never more so than where memoirists recalled Father Abraham, especially his acts of charity and clemency; some civilians, like Lucius Chittenden, provided whole imaginary episodes with extended conversation as if they came from genuine recollection.[43]

The soldiers fell subject to the same urges to exaggerate, though they were less inclined to outright invention. The overriding fact was the treasured memory of having seen Lincoln in the flesh. "The recollection of seeing Lincoln during the war is very precious to me," wrote New York veteran William A. Moore sometime after the war. The softening of memory started the very day Lincoln died. On April 15, 1865, Corporal Elisha Rhodes wrote that the soldiers had often seen Lincoln when he visited the army and always received him with cheers. That was true enough in the main, yet there had been times when some said the men cheered less enthusiastically. Within a few years, as soldiers began to edit their diaries from hindsight or write their memoirs, perceptions seemed to take a cast different from those contemporary accounts of events. A Maine soldier wrote, about the October 1862 review of the Army of the Potomac, that Lincoln "bore himself with a dignity that somehow made McClellan's urbane distinction less important," even though very few at the time thought the two compared quite that favorably to the president. Rhodes actually said at the time of the review that McClellan was underappreciated and unfairly treated. By 1885, he had done an about-face and asserted that Little Mac's manifest shortcomings were apparent all along, and that Lincoln was far the superior man and leader.[44]

Soon the hindsight came in an avalanche. Suddenly witnesses at those reviews had known all along how superior the president was to Little Mac, and accounts of the brief brush with Father Abraham became ever more effusive. "It was like an electric shock," one veteran recalled of seeing Lincoln after Antietam. "It flew from elbow to elbow, and with a loud cheer, every soldier gave vent to his suppressed feeling, making the welkin ring, and conveyed to him the fact that his smile had gone home and found a response." Now McClellan was gaudy and almost comical at the review, said another soldier, whereas "Mr. Lincoln seemed to tower as a giant." Another New York infantryman recalled of the review that "we all felt proud to know that we had been permitted to see and salute him who has proved to be the greatest citizen of modern times." In 1891, a Massachusetts volunteer looked back on that same October 1862 event and asserted, "Each soldier felt, after looking into his honest face, of doing his utmost to help lift the load that bore so heavily upon him."[45]

In one realm especially did they allow their memories and the romanticization to blend to create a new reality. "There is scarcely a hamlet in the loyal states that does not contain some witness of his clemency and lenity," a biographer of Lincoln wrote somewhat hyperbolically the very year of his death. Yet soon the well-known acts of pardon and suspension of sentences grew in legend. As Lincoln was compared to Jesus, so were his acts of clemency likened to the miracles of Christ, and one towered above them all in dominating and spreading the mythology—William Scott. Already *The Sleeping Sentinel* had sculpted the real story far out of shape, and now soldiers and civilians alike seized upon it as a vehicle for even more romanticizing. Chittenden, always unsparing in fictionalizing what he knew of Lincoln, celebrated the centenary of the president's birth by publishing a dramatically imaginative account that made himself and Lincoln the agents of Scott's salvation. In time, not only did Scott die at Lee's Mill with gratitude to Lincoln on his lips, but in his pocket would be found the pardon in the president's hand; later, the pardon was wrapped around a *carte de visite* of Lincoln himself, both pierced by the fatal bullet and stained with Scott's blood.[46]

Recollections of other soldier reprieves took on the attributes of the Scott case until they became confused. William A. Wheeler, vice-president under President Rutherford B. Hayes, recalled in 1885 that he had awakened Lincoln one night to get a soldier a stay of execution at the behest of the condemned's mother. "Now you just telegraph that mother that her boy is safe," Lincoln supposedly said, "and I will go home and go to bed." A few years later, Lamon took Wheeler's story, itself suspect, and changed it to fit the Scott mold even more closely. By 1916, soldier William Moore of the 82nd New York could give "from memory" a vivid account of the whole Scott affair. "I have seen this incident told in prose and poetry," he admitted, "but personally knew the facts," because his regiment and Scott's were in the same division. As a matter of fact, Moore's and Scott's regiments were not even in the same corps, let alone the same division; his supposed firsthand account was borrowed wholesale from what he had read, and also from a newer and even more powerful visual medium.[47]

Another feature of the Scott story illustrated a separate and rapidly expanding facet of the growing Lincoln myth among his old soldiers. Scott got his clemency *possibly* at Lincoln's intervention, and more likely from Little Mac himself. In any case, the official record reveals nothing about his mother. Yet, as soon as the story evolved, it was his mother who made her plea; soon thereafter, she became a widowed mother in the canon. Within a few decades of his death, almost all of Lincoln's acts of clemency came in popular mythology to result from the appeals of widowed mothers. Soon after the turn of the century, exaggerated recollections like Russell Conwell's had the president telling mothers that "he never did sign an order to shoot a boy under twenty years of age and that he never will." A 1918 recollection had him learning that a condemned deserter had left ranks to go home to see his dying mother, and as a result he stopped the execution and granted a reprieve, only to learn that the boy was subsequently killed in June 1864, a clear borrowing from the Scott story. Corollary to the pleas from mothers are those from sisters and sweethearts, and there, too, the exaggeration took firm hold. A letter written in 1863 by Lincoln asking an official to "hear this young lady" on an unspecified subject, by 1886 became a plea from her to pardon her brother from execution for sleeping on guard, yet another variant of Scott. Soldiers like Lieutenant Charles Woolsey of Hooker's staff even glorified themselves in later years merely for having been couriers who delivered Lincoln's messages of reprieve.[48]

In time, the Scott episode and the letter to the widow Bixby seemed somehow to come together in soldiers' imaginations, producing the very powerful image of a man of total compassion for women and mothers on the one hand, and for the condemned on the other. Again, the comparisons to Christ were hardly coincidental. There is no question that mercy was in Father Abraham's nature, nor is there any doubt that this attribute, perhaps above all others, is the one that most bound the soldiers to him, for it is the story they returned to again and again. The merciful Lincoln, the charitable Lincoln, was the man they knew and remembered, or *wanted* to remember.[49]

Starting in 1903, something else helped the aging veterans recall the man as they wanted to see him. Silent motion pictures were just a few years old when the first film devoted to Lincoln appeared. In all, perhaps a hundred silents would be made either about Lincoln or else including him as one of the protagonists. Their titles alone are eloquent of the kind of man that the veterans and their children wanted to see. In 1908 came *The Reprieve*. Two years later appeared *Abraham Lincoln's Clemency*, and the following year came *The Redemption of a Coward*. In short, in almost every film involving Lincoln, the pardoning of an innocent soldier wrongly convicted, or of the son of a widow sentenced merely for falling asleep on post, came to feature as a dramatic requirement. They were almost all variants of the Scott story, and all influential in shaping Lincoln's continuing myth. Most important of all, and borrowed directly from William Scott's experience, was an episode in D. W. Griffith's 1915 epic *The Birth of a Nation*. Griffith actually refers to Lincoln simply as "The Great Heart," a summation of the whole mythology around clemency. Significantly, when William Moore wrote his 1916 account of the Scott episode, he admitted that he had just seen Griffith's film, yet remained unaware of how it had influenced what he thought to be his own recollection of events he in all likelihood never actually witnessed.[50]

For generations after the war, until they themselves passed from the scene, the aging veterans carried with them their attachment to Father Abraham, often twisted, increasingly romanticized, and sometimes reduced to nothing more than senile fable. The important thing is not *what* they remembered that was accurate, but what they wanted to remember, and the fact that they clung so tenaciously to any recollection at all. They did not deify McClellan, or even Grant or Sherman. Only Lincoln called forth from them the imagination and the emotional energy that combined to build a legend. In his lifetime he had done what he could for them, and that they never forgot. In posterity they returned the favor by shaping a Father Abraham who could be a man for all time, a hero, a saint even, and yet always uniquely American in character. He got their best from them during the war, perhaps more than they knew they had. He helped them to grow up along with their country, to become men and citizens and soldiers. He gave them their memories, and they tried to protect and preserve his.

In October 1862, a schoolboy named William Paton called at the White House just to tell the president that he and his fellow students supported him. Lincoln patted him on the head. "You come of good people, you will soon be a grown man," he said. "Be a good man. Be a good American. Our country may have need of your services some day." At least that is what Paton remembered Lincoln saying, some fifty years later. Yet it was in character, even if the wording might not be precise. Another veteran declared in 1918, at the end of the world war overseas, "It is a splendid employment to be in the Army, or Navy of one's country!" The services were the strong arms of democracy, he said. "The wearer of the uniform ought to be honored by the people."[51]

Certainly that was how Lincoln felt. He honored the soldiers as they did honor to the Union, and it was no wonder that he took a place in their hearts and imaginations occupied by no other. "I count it one of the most precious privileges of my life that I once took in mine the hand of Abraham Lincoln," a Massachusetts chaplain wrote in 1918, "the *brotherly* hand . . . the *firm* hand . . . the *kindly* hand . . . the *tender* hand . . . the *strong* hand that struck the fetters from millions." With that hand in his grasp, the common soldier of the Union crossed borders of space and time, and even of the imagination. "Washington taught the world to know us, Lincoln taught us to know ourselves," said journalist Donn Piatt, himself a Union soldier. "The first won for us our independence, the last wrought out our manhood and self-respect."[52]

Forever after when American men and women donned uniforms to defend their nation or the civilization of which they were citizens, they answered in part the same call that Father Abraham had issued in his war, and out of a sense of duty and patriotism that he helped to instill not just in the young men of his time, but in their culture. Had they not come forward for him, and had he not been able to keep them coming and staying in the field, there might have been no United States to lead other nations in resisting the totalitarianism of the twentieth century. In fact, in many ways it was all the same fight, whether in 1861 or 1917 or 1941, and as millions left their hearths

to take their roads to war, echoes of an old soldier song marched with
them:

> *The Yankee boys have started out the Union for to save,*
> *And we're marching down to Washington to fight for Uncle Abe.*
> *Rip-rap, flip-flap,*
> *Strap your knapsack on your back,*
> *For we're going down to Washington to fight for Uncle Abe.*

NOTES

Introduction

1. Address to New Jersey Senate, February 21, 1861, in Roy P. Basler, ed., *The Collected Works of Abraham Lincoln* (New Brunswick, N.J., 1953–55), IV, p. 235 (hereafter cited as Basler).
2. Mason Locke Weems, *The Life of Washington*, ed. Marcus Cunliffe (Cambridge, Mass., 1962), pp. 93, 100–101.
3. Ibid., pp. 82–85.
4. Address, February 21, 1861, in Basler, IV, p. 236.
5. Weems, *Washington*, pp. 124, 182.
6. Ibid., pp. 38, 116, 119, 123, 141, 166.
7. Lincoln to the People of Sangamon County, March 9, 1832, in Basler, I, p. 8.
8. George B. Forgie, *Patricide in the House Divided: A Psychological Interpretation of Lincoln and His Age* (New York, 1979), pp. 15–19, 38. Forgie's is an insightful examination of the influence of patriarchal thinking on Lincoln's generation, though there are limitations to its usefulness, especially as it goes deeper into popular psychology. It is dangerous to put Lincoln and his contemporaries "on the couch," so to speak, since they cannot speak up and answer for themselves or say "nay."
9. Temperance Address, February 22, 1842, in Basler, I, p. 279.
10. Weems, *Washington*, p. 4.

Chapter 1. Common Men, Uncommon Crisis

1. Basler, I, p. 10.
2. William H. Herndon and Jesse Weik, *Herndon's Life of Lincoln* (New York, 1930), pp. 77–78. Though often challenged, Herndon's account is gaining credibility once more, and is in any case one of the very few knowledgeable sources for this period of Lincoln's life.

3. Ibid., pp. 77–78. Autobiography, June 1860, in Basler, IV, p. 64.

4. Herndon and Weik, *Lincoln*, p. 78.

5. Receipt, April 28, 1832, in Basler, I, p. 9.

6. Herndon and Weik, *Lincoln*, pp. 77–78.

7. Muster Roll, May 27, 1832, in Basler, I, pp. 10–13.

8. Michael Burlingame, ed., *An Oral History of Abraham Lincoln: John G. Nicolay's Interviews and Essays* (Carbondale, Ill., 1996), pp. 8, 133n.

9. Herndon and Weik, *Lincoln*, p. 80.

10. Speech, July 27, 1848, in Basler, I, pp. 509–10.

11. Herndon and Weik, *Lincoln*, p. 80.

12. Burlingame, ed., *Oral History*, pp. 8, 19.

13. George Harrison to Lincoln, May 29, 1860, in Burlingame, ed., *Oral History*, p. 100. Lincoln to Eli Blankenship, August 10, 1833, in Basler, I, p. 19.

14. Herndon and Weik, *Lincoln*, p. 79.

15. John Evangelist Walsh, *The Shadows Rise: Abraham Lincoln and the Ann Rutledge Legend* (Urbana, Ill., 1993), p. 90.

16. Ida M. Tarbell, *The Early Life of Abraham Lincoln* (New York, 1896), p. 142.

17. Herndon and Weik, *Lincoln*, p. 82.

18. Ibid.

19. Basler, I, p. 10n.

20. Harrison to Lincoln, May 29, 1860, in Burlingame, ed., *Oral History*, p. 100. Herndon and Weik, *Lincoln*, p. 83.

21. Burlingame, ed., *Oral History*, pp. 8, 133n.

22. Speech, July 27, 1848, in Basler, I, pp. 509–10. Herndon and Weik, *Lincoln*, p. 83.

23. Lyceum Speech, July 27, 1838, in Basler, I, pp. 112, 115.

24. Remarks on the Battle of New Orleans, January 8, 1841, in Basler, I, p. 226; Lincoln to the *Old Soldier*, February 28, 1840, pp. 204–5.

25. Lincoln to the *Old Soldier*, February 28, 1840, in Basler, I, pp. 204–5.

26. Lincoln to the editor of the *Sangamo Journal*, June 13, 1836, in Basler, I, p. 48; speech on the sub-treasury, December 26, 1839, p. 165; certification of service, 1832, VIII, p. 431.

27. Resolutions, April 5, 1847, in Basler, I, p. 393.

28. Speech in the House, January 12, 1848, in Basler, I, p. 441.

29. Lincoln to Herndon, February 1, 1848, in Basler, I, p. 447.

30. Speech in the House, July 27, 1848, in Basler, I, p. 514.

31. Autobiography, in Basler, IV, p. 66.

32. Lincoln to John Hardin, May 29, 1846, in Basler, I, p. 381; Lincoln to James K. Polk, December 8, 1847, p. 418; Lincoln to Andrew McClellan, February 4, 1848, pp. 448–49.

33. Lincoln to John McCalla, January 29, 1848, in Basler, I, p. 446; Remarks in the House, May 4, 1848, pp. 468–69; Lincoln to William Young, August 28, 1848, p. 519; Lincoln to Commissioner of Pensions, December 26,

1847, p. 422; Bill, January 17, 1848, p. 442; Lincoln to Young, February 17, 1848, p. 453; Remarks in the House, March 29, 1848, p. 460.

34. The text of the false oath is taken from Richard Allen Heckman, *Lincoln vs Douglas: The Great Debates Campaign* (Washington, D.C., 1967), pp. 112–13. Heckman does not appear to have realized that it was a parody.

35. Lincoln-Douglas debate, August 21, 1858, in Basler, III, pp. 6, 16–17.

36. Lincoln-Douglas debate, September 18, 1858, in Basler, III, pp. 182–83.

37. Ward Hill Lamon, *Recollections of Abraham Lincoln, 1847–1865* (Washington, D.C., 1911), p. 24. Lamon is not the most reliable of sources, being heavily influenced by hearsay and the growth of the Lincoln legend before he wrote his book.

38. An excellent analysis of Lincoln's nomination, and the most recent and insightful modern study of the man's life, is David Herbert Donald, *Lincoln* (New York, 1995), pp. 247–50.

39. Lincoln to David Hunter, October 26, 1860, in Basler, IV, p. 132.

40. Lincoln to Hunter, December 22, 1860, in Basler, IV, p. 159.

41. Lincoln to Francis P. Blair, December 21, 1860, in Basler, IV, p. 157; Lincoln to Lyman Trumbull, December 24, 1860, p. 162; Lincoln to Wool, January 14, 1861, p. 175.

42. Farewell Address, February 11, 1861, in Basler, IV, p. 191. There are at least three variants of this brief speech, the one quoted being regarded as perhaps the most authoritative.

43. Address, February 13, 1861, in Basler, IV, p. 204.

44. Lincoln Riflemen to Lincoln, February 4, 1861, in Harold Holzer, ed., *Dear Mr. Lincoln: Letters to the President* (New York, 1993), pp. 199–200. Speech, February 12, 1861, in Basler, IV, pp. 202–3.

45. Reply to Oliver Morton, February 11, 1861, in Basler, IV, p. 194; Remarks, February 14, 1861, p. 209; Speech, February 15, 1861, p. 215; Remarks, February 15, 1861, p. 217; Remarks, February 16, 1861, pp. 218–19.

46. Remarks, February 16, 1861, in Basler, IV, pp. 219–20; Remarks, February 19, 1861, p. 228–29. Weems, *Washington*, p. 182.

47. Charleston, South Carolina, *Daily Courier*, February 20, 1861. Lynda Laswell Crist and Mary Seaton Dix, eds., *The Papers of Jefferson Davis*, Vol. 7, *1861* (Baton Rouge, 1992), p. 48.

48. Address, February 21, 1861, in Basler, IV, pp. 235–36, 237; Speech in Independence Hall, February 22, 1861, pp. 240–41; Reply to Gov. Curtin, February 22, 1861, p. 243; Address to Pennsylvania General Assembly, February 22, 1861, p. 245.

49. Speech in Philadelphia, February 22, 1861, in Basler, IV, p. 240; First Inaugural, March 4, 1861, pp. 254, 271.

50. Weems, *Washington*, pp. 76–77.

51. Lincoln to Winfield Scott, March 9, 1861, in Basler, IV, p. 279; Lincoln to William H. Seward, March 15, 1861, p. 284; Memorandum on Fort

Sumter, March 18, 1861, pp. 288–89; Lincoln to Gideon Welles and Simon Cameron, March 29, 1861, p. 301. Don E. and Virginia Fehren-bacher, eds., *Recollected Words of Abraham Lincoln* (Stanford, Calif., 1996), p. 468.

52. Lincoln to Officers of the Army and Navy, April 1, 1861, in Basler, IV, p. 315; Lincoln to Welles, April 1, 1861, p. 318; Lincoln to Anderson, April 4, 1861, pp. 321–22; Lincoln to Curtin, April 8, 1861, p. 324.

53. Reply to Virginia Convention, April 13, 1861, in Basler, IV, p. 330; Proclamation, April 15, 1861, pp. 331–32.

54. Anonymous to Lincoln, April 10, 1861, in Holzer, ed., *Letters*, p. 47. The New Hampshire father is quoted in Donald, *Lincoln*, p. 297.

55. Reid C. Mitchell, "The Perseverance of the Soldiers," in Gabor S. Boritt, ed., *Why the Confederacy Lost* (New York, 1992), p. 115. Donald, *Lincoln*, p. 295.

56. Lincoln to William Dennison, April 15, 1861, in Basler, IV, p. 333.

57. Edgar Langsdorf, "Jim Lane and the Frontier Guard," *Kansas Historical Quarterly*, 9 (February 1940), pp. 243–45.

58. Fehrenbachers, eds., *Words*, p. 269.

59. Lincoln to Thomas Hicks and George Brown, April 20, 1861, in Basler, IV, p. 340; Reply to Baltimore Committee, April 22, 1861, pp. 341–42.

60. Malden, N.Y., *Malden City Press*, February 14, 1885.

61. Fehrenbachers, eds., *Words*, pp. 391–92. Lucius E. Chittenden, *Invisible Siege: The Journal of Lucius E. Chittenden, April 15, 1861–July 14, 1861* (San Diego, 1969), p. 8. Tyler Dennett, comp., *Lincoln and the Civil War in the Diaries and Letters of John Hay* (New York, 1939), p. 11. Donald, *Lincoln*, p. 298. Lucius E. Chittenden, *Recollections of President Lincoln and His Administration* (New York, 1891), pp. 129–30.

62. Chittenden, *Journal*, p. 14. Peter Burchard, *One Gallant Rush: Robert Gould Shaw and His Brave Black Regiment* (New York, 1965), pp. 34–35. Chittenden, *Recollections*, pp. 129–30. Russell Duncan, ed., *Blue-eyed Child of Fortune: The Civil War Letters of Colonel Robert Gould Shaw* (Athens, Ga., 1992), pp. 82, 88.

63. Lincoln to Timothy Munroe, April 27, 1861, in Basler, IV, p. 346; Remarks, May 2, 1861, pp. 352–53; Remarks, May 1, 1861, p. 352; Reply to the Frontier Guard, April 26, 1861, p. 345. Langsdorf, "Frontier Guard," pp. 243–45.

64. James A. Scrymser, *Personal Reminiscences* (n.p., 1915), pp. 17–18.

65. Duncan, ed., *Shaw*, p. 91.

66. Betsey Gates, ed., *The Colton Letters: Civil War Period, 1861–1865* (Scottsdale, Ariz., 1993), p. 31.

Chapter 2. *"A People's Contest"*

1. Proclamation, May 3, 1861, in Basler, IV, pp. 353–54.

2. Lawrence Delbert Cress, *Citizens in Arms: The Army and Militia in American Society to the War of 1812* (Chapel Hill, N.C., 1982), pp. 78–81, 86–87.

3. Ibid., pp. 90–92. The author has derived some very valuable insights into Knox and his attitudes from a paper titled "Between Myth and Reality: Citizenship and the Militia in Revolutionary America," delivered by Dr. Mark Thompson at a session on "The Soldier and the Citizen from Revolution to Roosevelt," at the November 7, 1997, session of the Southern Historical Association in Atlanta.

4. Ibid., pp. 116–20.

5. Edward M. Coffman, *The Old Army: A Portrait of the American Army in Peacetime, 1784–1898* (New York, 1986), pp. 6–7, 16–17.

6. Ibid., p. 38.

7. Ibid., p. 40. Cress, *Citizens in Arms,* pp. 172ff.

8. Draft of a Proposed Order, March 18, 1861, in Basler, IV, p. 291.

9. Lincoln to Charles S. Olden, May 4, 1861, in Basler, IV, p. 355; Lincoln to Hannibal Hamlin, May 6, 1861, pp. 357–58; Lincoln to Cameron, May 20, 1861, p. 374.

10. Chittenden, *Journal,* p. 47. Lincoln to Cameron, May 21, 26, 1861, in Basler, IV, pp. 380–81, 386; June 11, 13, 1861, pp. 402, 405; Endorsement, June 15, 1861, p. 408.

11. Lincoln to Carl Schurz, May 16, 1861, in Basler, IV, p. 371; Lincoln to Cameron, May 20, 1861, p. 374; June 12, 1861, p. 404. Fehrenbachers, eds., *Words,* p. 39.

12. Richard Nelson Current, *Lincoln's Loyalists: Union Soldiers from the Confederacy* (Boston, 1992), p. 5. Lincoln to Anderson, May 7, 1861, in Basler, IV, p. 359; Lincoln to Whom It May Concern, May 13, 1861, p. 368; Endorsement, June 8, 1861, p. 396; Lincoln to Cameron, July 20, 1861, p. 455.

13. Lincoln to Cameron, June 17, 22, 1861, in Basler, IV, pp. 410, 415; Endorsement, May 28, 1861, p. 388; Lincoln to Washington Bartlett, May 27, 1861, p. 386.

14. Lincoln to Lorenzo Thomas, May 30, July 19, 1861, pp. 390, 454; Lincoln to Cameron, May 13, 16, 1861, pp. 367, 370; July 18, 1861, p. 443; Lincoln to Morgan, May 20, 1861, p. 375.

15. Mitchell, "Perseverance," in Boritt, ed., *Why the Confederacy Lost,* p. 116, wonderfully encapsulates the sentiment of the early volunteers in saying that "the Union was a man's family writ large."

16. Chittenden, *Journal,* p. 65. Speech to the 7th Regiment, May 30, 1861, in Basler, IV, p. 390. Stephen W. Sears, ed., *For Country, Cause & Leader: The Civil War Journal of Charles B. Haydon* (New York, 1993), p. 23. Robert H. Rhodes, ed., *All for the Union: The Civil War Diary and Letters of Elisha Hunt Rhodes* (New York, 1991), pp. 20–21. Richard Moe, *The Last Full Measure: The Life and Death of the First Minnesota Volunteers* (New York, 1993), p. 36. Andrew McClintock to his sister, May 26, 1861, Frederick W. Chesson Collection, *Civil War Times Illustrated* Collection, United States Army Military

History Institute, Carlisle Barracks, Pa. (hereafter cited as *CWTI,* USAMHI).

17. Charles Perkins Diary, June 18, 19, 1861, *CWTI,* USAMHI. Fehrenbachers, eds., *Words,* p. 401. The Shaaber episode may be apocryphal.

18. Robert Colby to Lincoln, May 18, 1861, in Holzer, ed., *Letters,* p. 147.

19. Draft of a Proposed Order, March 18, 1861, in Basler, IV, p. 291; Lincoln to Ellsworth, April 15, 1861, p. 333.

20. Chittenden, *Journal,* pp. 57, 61. Lincoln to Ephraim D. and Phoebe Ellsworth, May 25, 1861, in Basler, IV, pp. 385–86; Lincoln to Cameron, June 17, 1861, p. 409.

21. Chittenden, *Journal,* p. 99.

22. Lincoln to Hiram Walbridge, November 18, 1861, in Basler, V, p. 27.

23. Daniel G. Crotty, *Four Years Campaigning in the Army of the Potomac* (Grand Rapids, Mich., 1874), p. 19. Chittenden, *Journal,* pp. 119, 121. Remarks, July 4, 1861, in Basler, IV, p. 441.

24. Message to Congress, July 4, 1861, in Basler, IV, pp. 420–21, 426, 437–39.

25. Chittenden, *Journal,* pp. 124–25. Lincoln to the Rev. B. O'Reilly, July 15, 1861, in Roy P. Basler, ed., *The Collected Works of Abraham Lincoln: Supplement, 1832–1865* (Westport, Conn., 1974), pp. 82–83 (hereafter cited as Basler, *Supplement*). John H. Burrill to his parents, July 5, 1861, John H. Burrill Papers, *CWTI,* USAMHI. Rhodes, ed., *All for the Union,* p. 22. Weems, *Washington,* p. 83.

26. Donald, *Lincoln,* p. 307. William C. Davis, *Battle at Bull Run* (New York, 1977), p. 252.

27. Charles Perkins Diary, July 23, 1861, *CWTI,* USAMHI. Robert Goldthwaite Carter, *Four Brothers in Blue* (Austin, Tex., 1978), pp. 15–16.

28. William T. Sherman, *Personal Memoirs of Gen. W. T. Sherman, by Himself* (New York, 1891), I, pp. 217–19.

29. George H. Otis, *The Second Wisconsin Infantry* (Dayton, Ohio, 1984), p. 40. John M. Carroll, ed., *A Few Memories of a Long Life* (Fairfield, Wash., 1988), p. 19. Remarks to the 69th New York, July 23, 1861, in Basler, IV, p. 458.

30. Michael E. Stevens, ed., *As if It Were Glory: Robert Beecham's Civil War from the Iron Brigade to the Black Regiments* (Madison, Wisc., 1997), p. 12.

31. Richard S. Skidmore, ed., *The Civil War Journal of Billy Davis* (Greencastle, Ind., 1989), p. 58. Memorandum, July 22, 1861, in Basler, IV, p. 456; Memoranda of Military Policy, July 23, 1861, p. 457.

32. Lincoln to Cameron, July 25, 1861, August 7, 1861, September 12, 1861, in Basler, IV, pp. 459, 475, 519; Lincoln to William Dennison, October 7, 1861, p. 550; Draft of Order, September 10, 1861, p. 515; Lincoln to Kentucky Delegation, July 29, 1861, p. 464; Lincoln to Francis P. Blair, August 21, 1861, p. 495; Lincoln to Scott, September 16, 1861, p. 525; Lincoln to

Gustave P. Koerner, August 8, 1861, p. 479; Lincoln to Cameron, December 27, 1861, V, p. 80.

33. Memorandum, April 25, 1861, in Basler, IV, p. 343; Lincoln to James Ripley, June 22, 1861, p. 415; Lincoln to Cameron, September 5, 1861, p. 509; Lincoln to Montgomery Meigs, August 27, 1861, p. 499. Alan D. Gaff, *On Many a Bloody Field: Four Years in the Iron Brigade* (Bloomington, Ind., 1996), p. 42. John Cranford to Lincoln, August 10, 1861, in Holzer, ed., *Letters*, p. 151. The standard work on Lincoln's involvement with arming and equipping the soldiers is Robert V. Bruce, *Lincoln and the Tools of War* (Indianapolis, 1956), a good book but now considerably dated.

34. Donald, *Lincoln*, p. 318. Crotty, *Four Years*, p. 28.

35. John D. McQuaide to Rebecca McQuaide, August 22, 1861, John D. McQuaide Papers, *CWTI*, USAMHI. Crotty, *Four Years*, p. 28.

36. Rufus R. Dawes, *Service with the Sixth Wisconsin Volunteers* (Marietta, Ohio, 1890), p. 19. Sears, ed., *For Country, Cause & Leader*, p. 77. LeRoy Crockett to Nellie, September 2, 1861, Charles and LeRoy Crockett Papers, Civil War Miscellaneous Collection (hereafter cited as CWMC), USAMHI.

37. Henry S. Hamilton, *Reminiscences of a Veteran* (Concord, N.H., 1897), p. 134. LeRoy Crockett to Nellie, September 21, 1861, Crockett Papers; John H. Boyer to Annie Eckert, September 17, 1861, John H. Boyer Papers; Samuel J. Alexander to Agnes Alexander, September 20, 1861, Samuel J. Alexander Papers; Amos Downing to P. Downing, October 20, 1861, Amos Downing Papers, CWMC, USAMHI. Lincoln to Scott, September 19, 1861, in Basler, IV, p. 528. Rhodes, ed., *All for the Union*, p. 46.

38. Boston *Journal*, November 19, 1892.

39. Dennett, comp., *John Hay*, p. 31.

40. John Berry Diary, November 20, 1861; Jacob Heffelfinger Diary, November 20, 1861, *CWTI*, USAMHI. Gardner Parker letter, November 28, 1861, in Eugene A. Nash, *A History of the Forty-fourth Regiment New York Volunteer Infantry* (Chicago, 1910), p. 312.

41. Heffelfinger Diary, November 20, 1861, *CWTI*; John H. Boyer to Abbie Eckert, November 24, 1861, Boyer Papers, CWMC, USAMHI. Parker letter, November 28, 1861, in Nash, *Forty-fourth New York*, p. 312. Sears, ed., *For Country, Cause & Leader*, pp. 129–30.

42. Samuel J. Alexander to Agnes Alexander, November 23, 1861, Alexander Papers, CWMC, USAMHI. Gaff, *Bloody Field*, p. 92.

43. Lincoln to Scott, September 17, 1861, in Basler, IV, p. 526; undated memorandum [December 25, 1861], V, p. 58. Charles Douglas Diary, November 12, 1861, CWMC, USAMHI. C. A. Stevens, *Berdan's United States Sharpshooters in the Army of the Potomac 1861–1865* (St. Paul, Minn., 1892), pp. 9–11.

44. Lincoln to John A. McClernand, November 10, 1861, in Basler, V, p. 20; Annual Message, December 3, 1861, pp. 40, 50.

45. Stevens, *Sharpshooters*, p. 11. Alexander to Agnes Alexander, November 25, 1861, Alexander Papers, CWMC, USAMHI.

Chapter 3. *The Year of McClellan*

1. Thomas Hodgkins to his brother, December 14, 1861, Thomas Hodgkins Papers, *CWTI*, USAMHI.
2. Suspension, November 11, 1861, in Basler, *Supplement*, p. 109. William H. Dunham to Dearest H., November 1, 1861, William H. Dunham Papers, CWMC; James Abraham to Jones and William Abraham, November 25, 1861, James Abraham Papers; Burrill to his parents, January 31, 1862, John H. Burrill Papers, *CWTI*, USAMHI.
3. Allan Nevins, ed., *A Diary of Battle: The Personal Journals of Colonel Charles S. Wainwright, 1861–1865* (New York, 1962), p. 10. David Ashley to his family, April 4, 1862, Ashley Family Papers, CWMC, USAMHI.
4. General War Order No. 1, January 27, 1862, in Basler, V, pp. 111–12; Special War Order No. 1, January 31, 1862, p. 115. Donald, *Lincoln*, p. 335.
5. Donald, *Lincoln*, p. 336. Rhodes, ed., *All for the Union*, p. 56.
6. Charles Crockett to Nellie, March 20, 1862, Charles and LeRoy Crockett Papers, CWMC, USAMHI. Moe, *Last Full Measure*, p. 128.
7. Crotty, *Four Years*, pp. 37–38. An example of this stationery will be found in Jacob Swartzlander to Hannah Delp, May 3, 1862, Hannah Delp Papers, CWMC, USAMHI.
8. Robert W. Daly, ed., *Aboard the USS "Monitor," 1862: The Letters of Acting Paymaster William Frederick Keeler, U.S. Navy* (Annapolis, Md., 1964), p. 107.
9. Stephen W. Sears, *To the Gates of Richmond: The Peninsula Campaign* (New York, 1992), p. 90. Georgeanna Woolsey Bacon and Eliza Woolsey Howland, comps., *Letters of a Family During the War for the Union, 1861–1865* (n.p., 1899), I, p. 356. Daly, ed., *Aboard the USS "Monitor,"* pp. 113, 115, 121.
10. Dawes, *Sixth Wisconsin*, p. 45. Skidmore, ed., *Billy Davis*, p. 134. Frederick Charles Decker, ed., *Yates Phalanx: The History of the Thirty-ninth Regiment, Illinois Volunteer Veteran Infantry* (Bowie, Md., 1994), p. 65. Otis, *Second Wisconsin*, p. 49.
11. James Abraham to Willie Abraham, June 2, 1862, Abraham Papers, *CWTI*, USAMHI.
12. Lincoln to McClellan, June 28, 1862, in Basler, V, p. 290; July 1, 1862, p. 298; Call for Troops, June 30, 1862, pp. 293–94.
13. Lincoln to McClellan, July 1, 1862, in Basler, V, p. 298; Lincoln to the Governors, July 3, 1862, p. 304; Speech, July 4, 1862, p. 306.
14. Lincoln to McClellan, July 5, 1862, in Basler, V, p. 307. James Abraham to William Abraham, July 5, 1862, Abraham Papers, *CWTI*, USAMHI.
15. Dennett, comp., *John Hay*, p. 176.

16. Carter, *Four Brothers*, p. 67. William H. Powell, *The Fifth Army Corps* (London, 1895), p. 181.

17. Carter, *Four Brothers*, p. 67. Evan R. Jones, *Four Years in the Army of the Potomac: A Soldier's Recollections* (London, 1882), p. 208. Oliver Wilcox Norton, *Army Letters 1861–1865* (Chicago, 1903), p. 101. Joseph D. Baker to his brother, n.d. [July 1862], Joseph D. Baker Papers, CWMC, USAMHI.

18. Donald, *Lincoln*, p. 359. Burrill to his parents, July 11, 1862, Burrill Papers, *CWTI*, USAMHI. Stephen W. Sears, ed., *The Civil War Papers of George B. Mc-Clellan: Selected Correspondence 1860–1865* (New York, 1989), p. 362.

19. Stephen W. Sears, *George B. McClellan: The Young Napoleon* (New York, 1988), p. 226. Charles A. Fuller, *Personal Recollections of the War of 1861* (Sherburne, N.Y., 1906), p. 46. See also Rhodes, ed., *All for the Union*, p. 74.

20. Nash, *Forty-fourth New York*, p. 91. Fuller, *Recollections*, p. 46. Jones, *Four Years*, p. 209.

21. Donald, *Lincoln*, p. 359. Daly, *Aboard the USS "Monitor,"* p. 189. Weems, *Washington*, p. 84. Gregory A. Coco, ed., *From Ball's Bluff to Gettysburg . . . and Beyond* (n.p., 1994), p. 116.

22. Fehrenbachers, eds., *Words*, p. 472. William Quentin Maxwell, *Lincoln's Fifth Wheel: The Political History of the United States Sanitary Commission* (New York, 1956), p. 159. Stephen W. Sears, *Landscape Turned Red: The Battle of Antietam* (Boston, 1983), pp. 37–38.

23. Lincoln to McClellan, July 13, 1862, in Basler, V, pp. 322–23.

24. Rogers W. Smith, *Civic Ideals: Conflicting Visions of Citizenship in U.S. History* (New Haven, Conn., 1997), p. 274.

25. Lincoln to Stanton, July 22, 1862, in Basler, V, p. 338; July 23, 1862, p. 339.

26. Lincoln to Agénor-Etienne de Gasparin, August 4, 1862, in Basler, V, p. 355. Lamon, *Recollections*, p. 245.

27. James Abraham to William Abraham, August 7, 1862, Abraham Papers; Burrill to his parents, August 12, 1862, *CWTI*, USAMHI.

28. For an excellent examination of Lincoln in mass-produced art, see Harold Holzer, Mark E. Neely, Jr., and Gabor S. Boritt, *The Lincoln Image: Abraham Lincoln and the Popular Print* (New York, 1984). The authoritative work on Lincoln in photographs is Charles Hamilton and Lloyd Ostendorf, *Lincoln in Photographs: An Album of Every Known Pose* (Dayton, Ohio, 1985). For the one possible Davis wartime photo, see William C. Davis, *"A Government of Our Own": The Making of the Confederacy* (New York, 1994), facing p. 119.

29. Kenneth A. Bernard, *Lincoln and the Music of the Civil War* (Caldwell, Idaho, 1966), pp. 74–77, 79–80. William Cullen Bryant was erroneously listed on the sheet music as author of the lyric.

30. "A Three Year Soldier," in James H. Montgomery Diary, n.d., CWMC, USAMHI.

31. Lincoln to Stanton, August 9, 1862, in Basler, V, p. 365; Lincoln to Andrew, August 12, 1862, pp. 367–68.

32. Samuel L. Condé to anonymous, August 15, 1862, Samuel L. Condé Papers, CWMC, USAMHI.

33. Fehrenbachers, *Words*, p. 472. Gideon Welles, *Diary of Gideon Welles* (Boston, 1909–11), I, pp. 113, 117.

34. Florence Cox, ed., *Kiss Josey for Me!* (Santa Ana, Calif., 1974), pp. 84–85. William E. Dunn to his sister, September 10, 1861, William E. Dunn Papers, *CWTI*; Boucher to Rachael Boucher, n.d. [September 1862], Boucher Family Papers, CWMC, USAMHI.

35. Amos S. Abbott Diary, August 31, 1862, CWMC, USAMHI. K. Jack Bauer, ed., *Soldiering: The Civil War Diary of Rice C. Bull, 123rd New York Volunteer Infantry* (San Rafael, Calif., 1977), p. 14.

36. Lincoln to Whom It May Concern, November 1, 1862, in Basler, V, pp. 484–85. Harry M. Kieffer, *The Recollections of A Drummer-Boy* (Boston, 1889), p. 48. William H. Martin to his wife, August 12, 1862, William H. Martin Papers, Harrisburg Civil War Round Table Collection, USAMHI. Beverly Hayes Kallgren and James L. Couthamel, eds., *"Dear Friend Anna": The Civil War Letters of a Common Soldier from Maine* (Orono, Me., 1992), p. 32.

37. Record of Dismissal of John J. Key, September 27, 1862, in Basler, V, pp. 442–43.

38. William A. Blair, ed., *A Politician Goes to War: The Civil War Letters of John White Geary* (University Park, Pa., 1995), pp. 58–59. Sears, *Antietam*, pp. 325, 339. John G. Nicolay and John Hay, eds., *Abraham Lincoln: A History* (New York, 1890), VI, p. 174.

39. William Marvel, *Burnside* (Chapel Hill, N.C., 1991), p. 151. Abner Hard, *History of the Eighth Cavalry Regiment, Illinois Volunteers* (Aurora, Ill., 1868), p. 198. Harold Adams Small, ed., *The Road to Richmond: The Civil War Memoirs of Major Abner R. Small* (Berkeley, Calif., 1939), pp. 50–51. Roderick M. Engert, ed., *Maine to the Wilderness: The Civil War Letters of Private William Lamson, 20th Maine Infantry* (Orange, Va., 1993), pp. 26–28.

40. Stevens, *Sharpshooters*, p. 211. Dawes, *Sixth Wisconsin*, p. 100. Carter, *Four Brothers*, pp. 121, 136.

41. Memorandum, September 12, 1864, in Basler, VII, p. 548. Nevins, ed., *Wainwright*, p. 110.

42. Memorandum, September 12, 1864, in Basler, VII, p. 548. Stephen Minot Weld, *War Diary and Letters of Stephen Minot Weld 1861–1865* (Boston, 1979), p. 83.

43. Thomas T. Ellis, *Leaves from the Diary of an Army Surgeon* (New York, 1863), p. 306. Nevins, ed., *Wainwright*, pp. 109–10.

44. Powell, *Fifth Corps*, p. 309.

45. Annette Tapert, ed., *The Brothers' War: Civil War Letters to Their Loved Ones from the Blue and Gray* (New York, 1988), p. 93. Dawes, *Sixth Wisconsin*, p. 100. Jonathan W. W. Boynton Memoir, CWMC, USAMHI. Arthur A. Kent,

ed., *Three Years with Company K* (Cranbury, N.J., 1976), p. 135. Gaff, *Bloody Field,* p. 197. Engert, ed., *Maine to the Wilderness,* p. 28.

46. Speech at Frederick, October 4, 1862, in Basler, V, p. 450. Donald L. Smith, *The Twenty-fourth Michigan* (Harrisburg, Pa., 1962), pp. 27–28.

47. John Cochrane, *The War for the Union: Memoir of Gen. John Cochrane* (n.p., 1875), p. 31.

48. Memorandum, November 1862, in Basler, V, p. 484; Lincoln to Thomas Henderson, December 20, 1862, VI, p. 12. Mary A. Livermore, *My Story of the War* (Hartford, Conn., 1888), pp. 241–42.

49. James M. McPherson, *Battle Cry of Freedom: The Civil War Era* (New York, 1988), pp. 561–62.

50. William E. Dunn to his sister, October 23, 1862, Dunn Papers, *CWTI;* William H. Dunham to William Odell, November 15, 1862, Dunham Papers; Enos R. Artman to Hannah Delp, June 25, 1862, Delp Papers, CWMC, USAMHI.

51. Henry Henney Diary, October 8–9, 1862, *CWTI,* USAMHI. Rufus Andrews, *"Kiss Each Other for Me": The Civil War Letters of Rufus Andrews 1861–1863* (Iron Mountain, Mich., 1979), pp. 36–37. Lee C. and Karen D. Drickamer, eds., *Fort Lyon to Harpers Ferry: The Civil War Letters and Newspaper Dispatches of Charles H. Moulton* (Shippensburg, Pa., 1987), p. 54.

52. William D. Kelley, *Lincoln and Stanton* (New York, 1885), p. 75.

53. Kevin E. O'Brien, ed., *My Life in the Irish Brigade* (Campbell, Calif., 1996), p. 13.

54. James C. and Eleanor A. Duram, eds., *Soldier of the Cross: The Civil War Diary and Correspondence of Rev. Andrew Jackson Hartsock* (Manhattan, Kans., 1979), pp. 23, 25. Lincoln to Halleck, November 5, 1862, in Basler, V, pp. 485–86.

55. James M. and Patricia R. McPherson, eds., *Lamson of the "Gettysburg"* (New York, 1997), p. 71. Memorandum, November 1862, in Basler, V, p. 484. James Magill to Henry Magill, January 27, 1863, James Magill Letters, CWMC, USAMHI. Moe, *Last Full Measure,* p. 204.

56. Ruth L. Silliker, ed., *The Rebel Yell & the Yankee Hurrah: The Civil War Journal of a Maine Volunteer* (Camden, Me., 1985), p. 50. Rhodes, ed., *All for the Union,* p. 88. Michael C. C. Adams, *Our Masters the Rebels: A Speculation on Union Military Failure in the East, 1861–1865* (Cambridge, Mass., 1978), pp. 110–20, gives the best overall account of the sentiment for an outright mutiny, and concludes rightly that it was confined to McClellan's top generals and an intimate circle of staff officers. Sears, *McClellan,* p. 342, also concluded that the only real demoralization was among some of the officers.

57. Sears, *Antietam,* pp. 37–38, 343–44. James P. Elliott Diary, November 10, 1862; Joseph Baker to Lizzie Baker, March 9, 1863, Baker Papers; John O'Connell Memoirs, CWMC, USAMHI. Sears, *McClellan,* p. 342. Silliker, ed., *Rebel Yell & Yankee Hurrah,* p. 50.

58. Moe, *Last Full Measure*, p. 204. Norton, *Army Letters*, p. 128. Durams, eds., *Soldier of the Cross*, p. 165. Charles Sterling Underhill, comp., *"Your Soldier Boy Samuel": Civil War Letters of Lieut. Samuel Edmund Nichols* (Buffalo, N.Y., 1929), pp. 46–48.

59. J. D. Bloodgood, *Personal Reminiscences of the War* (New York, 1893), p. 40. Nancy Niblack Baxter, *Gallant Fourteenth: The Story of an Indiana Civil War Regiment* (Traverse City, Ind., 1980), p. 112. Sears, *McClellan*, p. 342. Sears, ed., *For Country, Cause & Leader*, p. 288. John Chipman Gray and John Codman Ropes, *War Letters 1862–1865* (Boston, 1927), pp. 21–22.

60. Emery Edson Diary, November 11, 1862, CWMC, USAMHI. Sears, *McClellan*, p. 342. Sears, *Antietam*, pp. 343–44. John Gibbon, *Personal Recollections of the Civil War* (New York, 1928), pp. 96–99. Adams, *Our Masters the Rebels*, p. 120.

61. Drickamers, *Fort Lyon to Harpers Ferry*, p. 57. Liston Gray to his sister, November 14, 1862, Liston Gray Letter; Richard Packard to his mother, November 24, 1862, Richard Packard Letter, CWMC, USAMHI. Underhill, comp., *"Your Soldier Boy,"* p. 45. Fuller, *Recollections*, p. 75. John Berry Diary, November 10, 12, 1862, *CWTI*, USAMHI.

Chapter 4. The Price of Freedom

1. J. V. Boucher to Polly Boucher, December 7, 1861, Boucher Family Papers; William Dunham to ?, n.d. [November 1861], Dunham to Dear H., December 24, 1861, William H. Dunham Papers, CWMC, USAMHI. Jim Huffstodt, *Hard Dying Men* (Bowie, Md., 1994), p. 44. Wilbur Fisk, *Anti-Rebel: The Civil War Letters of Wilbur Fisk* (Croton-on-Hudson, N.Y., 1983), pp. 33–34. Weld, *War Diary*, p. 72.

2. Fehrenbachers, eds., *Words*, p. 434.

3. Cox, ed., *Kiss Josey*, p. 73. Richard P. Galloway, comp., *One Battle Too Many: The Writings of Simon Bolivar Hulbert, Private, Company E, 100th Regiment, New York State Volunteers, 1861–1864* (n.p., 1987), p. 53.

4. James Abraham to William Abraham, June 2, August 7, 1862, James Abraham Papers, *CWTI*, USAMHI. Coco, ed., *Ball's Bluff to Gettysburg*, p. 116.

5. Preliminary Emancipation Proclamation, September 22, 1862, in Basler, V, pp. 433–34.

6. Ellis, *Diary of an Army Surgeon*, p. 306. Donald, *Lincoln*, p. 385.

7. Moe, *Last Full Measure*, p. 194. Burrill to his parents, October 19, 1862, John H. Burrill Papers, *CWTI*, USAMHI. Gray and Ropes, *War Letters*, p. 6.

8. Henry Henney Diary, October 6, 1862, *CWTI*, USAMHI. Michael A. Mullins, *The Frémont Rifles: A History of the 37th Illinois Veteran Volunteer Infantry* (Wilmington, N.C., 1990), p. 137; Underhill, comp., *"Your Soldier Boy,"* p. 35.

9. Margery Greenleaf, ed., *Letters to Eliza from a Union Soldier, 1862–1865* (Chicago, 1969), p. 19. Norton, *Army Letters*, p. 128. Marlene C. Bumbera,

comp., *The Civil War Letters of Cpl. John H. Strathern* (Apollo, Pa., 1994), pp. 84, 86. Boucher to Rachael Boucher, September 29, 1862, Boucher Family Papers, CWMC, USAMHI.

10. Reply to Serenade, September 24, 1862, in Basler, V, p. 438. Greenleaf, ed., *Letters*, p. 17. Lydia P. Hecht, ed., *Echoes from the Letters of a Civil War Surgeon* (n.p., 1996), p. 280. John W. Rowell, *Yankee Artillerymen: Through the Civil War with Eli Lilly's Indiana Battery* (Knoxville, 1975), pp. 46–47. Annual Message to Congress, December 1, 1862, in Basler, V, p. 529.

11. Charles O. Varnam to his father, November 28, 1862, Charles O. Varnam Papers, CWMC, USAMHI.

12. Livermore, *My Story*, p. 561. New York *Times*, December 21, 1862. Duncan, ed., *Shaw*, pp. 270–71.

13. Congratulations, December 22, 1862, in Basler, VI, p. 13.

14. Gaff, *Bloody Field*, p. 212. Weld, *War Diary*, p. 155.

15. Stephen W. Sears, *Chancellorsville* (Boston, 1996), p. 14. Henney to ?, December 1862, Henney Diary, *CWTI*, USAMHI.

16. Washington *Star*, January 26, 1911. Frank Wilberforce to his father, January 23, 1863, Frank Wilberforce Papers; Allen Bevan to his sister, December 21, 1862, January 1, 1863, Allen Bevan Papers; Dexter Macomber to his brothers and sisters, December 17, 1862, Dexter Macomber Letter; Jacob F. Smith to My Dear Callie, February 5, 1863, Jacob F. Smith Letter, CWMC; Gillette to his parents, January 20, 1863, James Gillette Papers, *CWTI*, USAMHI.

17. Gillette to his parents, January 14, 1863, Gillette Papers; Henney Diary, December 31, 1862, *CWTI*, USAMHI.

18. Earl J. Hess, ed., *A German in the Yankee Fatherland: The Civil War Letters of Henry A. Kircher* (Kent, Ohio, 1983), p. 57. G. D. Stroud to Lincoln, October 29, 1862, in Holzer, ed., *Letters*, p. 163.

19. Henry Clay Trumbull, *War Memories of an Army Chaplain* (New York, 1989), pp. 110–11.

20. Burchard, *One Gallant Rush*, p. 67. Joseph T. Glatthaar, *Forged in Battle: The Civil War Alliance of Black Soldiers and White Officers* (New York, 1990), p. 28. Nevins, ed., *Wainwright*, p. 156. Gaff, *Bloody Field*, p. 215.

21. Baxter, *Gallant Fourteenth*, pp. 125–26. Nancy Niblack Baxter, ed., *Hoosier Farmboy in Lincoln's Army: The Civil War Letters of Pvt. John R. McClure* (Indianapolis, 1992), pp. 35–36. Dayton E. Flint to his father, January 17, 1863, Washington *Star*, January 26, 1911.

22. Huffstodt, *Hard Dying Men*, p. 125. File 111010, Jacob J. Crook; File 11185, W. B. Gillespie; File 1193, Charles I. Paul; File mm901, George D. Wiseburn; File 111359, Benjamin F. Sells, Records of General Courts Martial, Record Group 153, National Archives, Washington, D.C. (hereafter cited as RG 153, NA).

23. File 111010, Jacob J. Crook; File 11185, W. B. Gillespie; File 11552, I. C.

Fair; File mm744, Frank B. Smith; File 11811, Charles W. Mann; File mm369, Samuel Montgomery; File 11810, John Gibson, RG 153, NA.

24. Glatthaar, *Forged in Battle,* p. 28. Fehrenbachers, eds., *Words,* p. 429.

25. Charles W. Wills, *Army Life of an Illinois Soldier* (Washington, D.C., 1906), pp. 150–51. Letter of George S. Richardson, January 10, 1863, in Gordon C. Jones, ed., *"For My Country": The Richardson Letters, 1861–1865* (Wendell, N.C., 1984), n.p. Moe, *Last Full Measure,* p. 207. Sears, *McClellan,* p. 325. Baxter, *Gallant Fourteenth,* p. 127. Gaff, *Bloody Field,* p. 216. Henney Diary, December 1862, *CWTI,* USAMHI.

26. Van Willard Narrative, in possession of Steven S. Raub, Ardmore, Pennsylvania. Victor Hicken, *Illinois in the Civil War* (Urbana, Ill., 1966), p. 130.

27. Glatthaar, *Forged in Battle,* p. 28. Leslie Anders, *The Twenty-first Missouri: From Home Guard to Union Regiment* (Westport, Conn., 1975), p. 124. Letter of George S. Richardson, January 10, 1863, in Jones, ed., *"For My Country,"* n.p.

28. James Abraham to Mary Abraham, March 5, 1863, Abraham Papers; Burrill to his parents, January 1, 1863, Burrill Papers; A. Caldwell to ?, n.d., Caldwell Family Papers; Jacob Behm to Jacob Seiler, February 18, 1863, Jacob Behm Papers, *CWTI;* Boucher to Polly Boucher, January 2, 1863, Boucher Family Papers, CWMC, USAMHI. Wills, *Army Life,* p. 151. Reid C. Mitchell, "Perseverance," in Boritt, ed., *Why the Confederacy Lost,* pp. 116–17, makes the wonderful point that the soldiers saw emancipation as "the atomic bomb of the Civil War." For a good discussion of soldier feeling about emancipation, see James M. McPherson, *For Cause & Comrades: Why Men Fought in the Civil War* (New York, 1997), pp. 117–30.

29. Bruce Chadwick, ed., *Brother Against Brother: The Lost Civil War Diary of Lt. Edmund Halsey* (Secaucus, N.J., 1997), p. 74. Behm to Seiler, February 18, July 27, 1863, Behm Papers; Caldwell to his brother, January 11, 1863, Caldwell Family Papers, *CWTI,* USAMHI. Willard Narrative, December 17, 31, 1862.

30. Lincoln to John A. Dix, January 14, 1863, in Basler, VI, p. 56.

31. Anders, *Twenty-first Missouri,* p. 124. Abraham to Mary Abraham, March 5, 1863, Abraham Papers, *CWTI,* USAMHI. Glatthaar, *Forged in Battle,* p. 32. Kenneth W. Noe, ed., *A Southern Boy in Blue: The Memoir of Marcus Woodcock, 9th Kentucky Infantry (U.S.A.)* (Knoxville, 1996), p. 147. Wills, *Army Life,* p. 176.

32. Boucher to Polly Boucher, February 15, 1863, Boucher Family Papers; Henry Hoyt to William J. Hoyt, April 11, 1863, Henry Hoyt Papers, CWMC, USAMHI.

33. Wills, *Army Life,* pp. 152–53. Boucher to Mr. Sawyer, March 2, 1863, Boucher Family Papers, CWMC; Nelson Chapin to his wife, January 6, 1863, Nelson Chapin Papers, *CWTI,* USAMHI. Moe, *Last Full Measure,* p. 223. Current, *Loyalists,* pp. 67, 78.

34. Jonas Denton Elliott to his wife, March 8, 1863, Jonas Denton Elliott Papers; James Beard to Isaac Beard, January 28, 1863, James Beard Papers;

James Magill to his mother, February 1, 1863, James Magill Letters, CWMC, USAMHI.

Chapter 5. *The Friend of Friends*

1. Joseph Frederick Haas to Lincoln, February 20, 1864, Joseph F. Haas Letter, CWMC, USAMHI.

2. Endorsement, November 11, 1864, in Basler, VIII, p. 103; Lincoln to Joseph K. Barnes, February 25, August 16, 31, 1864, VII, pp. 203, 496, 526; December 19, 1864, VIII, p. 170; Lincoln to Henry Slocum, October 17, 1863, VI, p. 524; Lincoln to Stanton, May 29, 1862, V, p. 249. Memorandum, December 20, 1862, in Basler, *Supplement,* p. 167. Lincoln to William H. Hammond, September 18, 1862, in Basler, V, p. 429; Lincoln to U. S. Grant, July 27, 1864, VII, p. 465; Discharge, October 4, 1864, VIII, p. 36.

3. Lincoln to Scott, September 20, 1861, in Basler, IV, p. 529; Lincoln to Cameron, December 16, 1861, VIII, p. 482; Lincoln to Welles, n.d., VIII, p. 427. Memorandum, December 20, 1862, in Basler, *Supplement,* p. 167; Lincoln to Stanton, January 22, 1863, p. 175.

4. Lincoln to Quintin Campbell, June 28, 1862, in Basler, V, p. 288.

5. Lincoln to Stanton, April 7, 1862, in Basler, V, p. 183; October 15, 1863, VI, p. 516; Endorsement, January 3, 1863, VI, p. 35; Memorandum, September 27, 1864, VIII, p. 27; Endorsement, March 18, 1865, pp. 363–64. L. R. Dorsett to Lincoln, March 10, 1865, in Holzer, ed., *Letters,* p. 114.

6. Catherine Spielman to Lincoln, June 17, 1864, in Holzer, ed., *Letters,* p. 107. Lincoln to Dennison, February 6, 1865, in Basler, VIII, p. 261; Lincoln to Stanton, July 15, 1862, V, p. 326.

7. Fehrenbachers, eds., *Words,* p. 399.

8. Lincoln to George Gibson, September 5, 1861, in Basler, VIII, p. 476. David Humphrey Blair Diary, November 2, 1863, CWMC, USAMHI. Carter, *Four Brothers,* p. 169.

9. Lincoln to Montgomery Meigs, October 16, 17, 1863, in Basler, VI, pp. 519, 523; Lincoln to U. S. Grant, June 19, 1864, VII, p. 416; Lincoln to Esther Stockton, January 8, 1864, p. 117; Basler, *Supplement,* pp. 152–53; Lincoln to Nathaniel Banks, November 25, 1862, p. 165. Gray and Ropes, *War Letters,* p. 442. E. Harmon to Lincoln, January 19, 1863, in Holzer, ed., *Letters,* p. 186.

10. Lincoln to Timothy Andrews, November 9, 1864, in Basler, VIII, p. 97; Lincoln to Congress, January 17, 1863, VI, p. 60. Cox, ed., *Kiss Josey,* pp. 128–29.

11. Memorandum, September 5 and 18, 1863, in Basler, VI, p. 433; Lincoln to Cary H. Fry, August 12, 20, 1862, V, pp. 368–69, 385; Lincoln to Stanton, September 20, 1862, p. 431.

12. Lincoln to Hiram P. Barney, August 16, 1862, in Basler, V, pp. 377–78. O'Brien, ed., *Irish Brigade*, p. 217. Kenneth C. Turino, ed., *The Civil War Diary of Lieut. J. E. Hodgkins* (Camden, Me., 1994), p. 39. Merrill D. Peterson, *Lincoln in American Memory* (New York, 1994), pp. 105–6. Lamon, *Recollections*, pp. 103–4. Edward J. Hagerty, *Collis' Zouaves: The 114th Pennsylvania Volunteers in the Civil War* (Baton Rouge, 1997), p. 304.

13. Lincoln to Esther Stockton, January 8, 1864, in Basler, VII, p. 117; Lincoln to Henry Wilson, May 15, 1862, V, pp. 217–18; Lincoln to Ladies of Soldiers' Fair, December 19, 1864, VIII, p. 171; Speech at Union League Club, VII, p. 397; Lincoln to Sarah B. Meconkey, May 9, 1864, VII, p. 333; Reply to Philadelphia Delegation, January 24, 1865, VIII, p. 236.

14. James I. Robertson, Jr., *Soldiers Blue and Gray* (Columbia, S.C., 1988), p. 156.

15. Livermore, *My Story*, p. 129.

16. Order Establishing the Sanitary Commission, June 9, 1861, in Basler, *Supplement*, p. 76. Maxwell, *Fifth Wheel*, pp. 29, 178. Robert H. Bremner, *The Public Good: Philanthropy and Welfare in the Civil War Era* (New York, 1980), p. 39.

17. Lincoln to Scott, September 30, 1861, in Basler, IV, p. 543.

18. Maxwell, *Fifth Wheel*, p. 106. Chittenden, *Recollections*, pp. 156–57. Chittenden is the source for the confrontation story, and, like so much else in his book, it is certainly questionable or, if based on fact, probably heavily embellished, as are so many of his stories that can be checked.

19. Bremner, *Public Good*, pp. 50–51. David Gollaher, *Voice for the Mad: The Life of Dorothea Dix* (New York, 1995), p. 416.

20. Maxwell, *Fifth Wheel*, pp. 244–45.

21. Cordelia A. P. Harvey, "A Wisconsin Woman's Picture of President Lincoln," *Wisconsin Magazine of History*, I (1918), pp. 233–55 *passim*.

22. Alfred Mackay to Lincoln, April 6, 1864, in Holzer, ed., *Letters*, pp. 290–91. Address, April 18, 1864, in Basler, VII, p. 301; Lincoln to Mackay, May 20, 1864, p. 353; Endorsement, June 3, 1864, VIII, p. 595; Speech at Sanitary Fair, June 16, 1864, VII, p. 394; Speech, p. 397.

23. Lincoln to Sanitary Fair Ladies, October 26, 1863, in Basler, VI, p. 539; Lincoln to Mrs. Field, May 31, 1864, VII, p. 369; Lincoln to the New England Kitchen, March 2, 1864, p. 220. Livermore, *My Story*, pp. 430, 565. Lincoln to William B. Sprague, January 18, 1864, in Basler, *Supplement*, p. 219; Lincoln to Mrs. Augustus C. French, May 16, 1864, p. 242; Lincoln to Charles E. H. Richardson, May 21, 1864, p. 244. L. Montgomery Bond to Lincoln, May 10, 1864, in Holzer, ed., *Letters*, p. 104.

24. Both Maxwell, *Fifth Wheel*, p. 178, and Bremner, *Public Good*, pp. 63–64, conclude that Lincoln was not an especially warm supporter of the Sanitary Commission, but his public statements and private endorsements would seem to argue to the contrary.

25. Lincoln to Alexander H. Rice, November 8, 1864, in Holzer, ed., *Letters*, p.

222; Edward Everett to Lincoln, January 30, 1864, pp. 98–99. Lincoln to Everett, February 4, 1864, in Basler, VII, pp. 167–68.

26. Fehrenbachers, eds., *Words,* p. 196.

27. Sears, *Papers of McClellan,* pp. 290–91. Carl Sandburg, *Abraham Lincoln: The War Years* (New York, 1939), I, pp. 511–12. Sandburg is not always reliable, but in this instance cites the diary of Dr. Horace Green, who had the interview with Lincoln.

28. Lincoln to Director of Military Hospital, March 30, 1862, in Basler, *Supplement,* pp. 127–28; Memorandum, October 17, 1863, p. 206. Lincoln to Hammond, June 4, 1862, in Basler, V, p. 259; Lincoln to Whom It May Concern, n.d., VIII, p. 428; Lincoln to Ginery Twichell, September 5, 1862, V, pp. 406–7. Lemuel Moss, *Annals of the United States Christian Commission* (Philadelphia, 1868), p. 671.

29. Fehrenbachers, eds., *Words,* p. 106.

30. Ibid., pp. 73, 106. Chittenden, *Recollections,* pp. 327–29.

31. Michael Dougherty Diary, November 5, 1864, CWMC, USAMHI. G. Wayne Smith, *Nathan Goff, Jr.: A Biography* (Charleston, W. Va., 1959), pp. 48–49. William Marvel, *Andersonville: The Last Depot* (Chapel Hill, N.C., 1994), pp. 147, 149. James M. Wells, *"With Touch of Elbow" or Death Before Dishonor* (Philadelphia, 1909), pp. 178–79. Chittenden, *Recollections,* pp. 127–29.

32. Roger A. Fischer, "The Quality of Mercy: Lincoln's 'Gentle Legend' in American Popular Culture," in Linda Norbut Suits and George L. Painter, eds., *Abraham Lincoln and a Nation at War: Papers from the Ninth Annual Lincoln Colloquium* (Springfield, Ill., 1995), p. 60. Lincoln to the Sons of Temperance, September 29, 1863, in Basler, VI, p. 487; Lincoln to Stanton, September 30, 1863, p. 489.

33. Moss, *Christian Commission,* p. 94n. Lincoln to Butler, June 20, 1861, in Basler, IV, p. 413; Lincoln to John J. Hughes, October 21, 1861, p. 559; Lincoln to F. M. Magrath, October 30, 1861, V, pp. 8–9; Annual Message, December 3, 1861, p. 40; Lincoln to Hammond, July 3, 1862, VI, p. 313. William Wolf et al. to Lincoln, June 20, 1864, in Holzer, ed., *Letters,* p. 108.

34. Lincoln to People of Sangamon County, March 9, 1832, in Basler, I, p. 8; Approval, May 22, 1861, IV, p. 381.

35. Moss, *Christian Commission,* p. 248. Lincoln to George H. Stuart, December 12, 1861, in Basler, V, p. 67. Edward Smith, *Incidents of the United States Christian Commission* (Philadelphia, 1871), p. 54.

36. Fehrenbachers, eds., *Words,* p. 425. Gardiner H. Shattuck, Jr., *A Shield and Hiding Place: The Religious Life of the Civil War Armies* (Macon, Ga., 1987), p. 52. Lincoln to Arnold Fischel, December 14, 1861, in Basler, V, p. 69; Lincoln to Stanton, November 10, 1861, VIII, p. 102.

37. Fehrenbachers, eds., *Words,* p. 362. Order for Sabbath Observance, Novem-

ber 15, 1862, in Basler, V, pp. 497–98; Thanksgiving Proclamation, October 3, 1863, VI, p. 496.

38. Lincoln to Alexander Reed, February 22, 1863, in Basler, VI, p. 114. Moss, *Christian Commission*, p. 162. Stuart to Lincoln, January 24, 1865, in Holzer, ed., *Letters*, pp. 297–98.

39. Moss, *Christian Commission*, pp. 214–17, 528n. Reply to Christian Commission, January 27, 1865, in Basler, VIII, p. 242.

40. Moss, *Christian Commission*, pp. 216–17, 256.

41. As stated, there is no tally and no possible means for preparing one, but even if he saw only ten soldiers a week on average, it would come to about twenty-one hundred by the time of his death.

42. Fehrenbachers, eds., *Words*, p. 31.

43. Ibid., p. 466.

44. Ibid., p. 451. Recommendation, September 1, 1863, in Basler, VI, p. 426.

45. Lincoln to Cameron, August 8, 1861, in Basler, IV, p. 479; Memorandum, [March 1862], V, p. 139; Endorsement, November 1, 1864, VIII, p. 85; Endorsement, January 1, 1865, p. 194; Lincoln to Stanton, March 15, 1864, VII, p. 249; June 1864, p. 372. Fehrenbachers, eds., *Words*, pp. 21–22.

46. Endorsement, March 14, 1864, in Basler, VII, p. 245. Fehrenbachers, eds., *Words*, pp. 31, 294.

47. Lincoln to Stanton, September 2, 1863, in Basler, VI, p. 429; October 16, 1863, p. 520. Burlingame, ed., *Oral History*, pp. 81–82.

48. Francis Donaldson to Jacob Donaldson, March 3, 1864, Francis Donaldson Papers, Civil War Library and Museum, Philadelphia.

49. Fehrenbachers, eds., *Words*, pp. 165–66.

50. Holzer, ed., *Letters*, p. 3. Charles Wesley Belknap Diary, November 26, 1862, CWMC, USAMHI. Moe, *Last Full Measure*, p. 209.

51. Holzer, ed., *Letters*, p. 3.

52. John P. Nourse Memoir, n.d., in possession of Joseph W. Goodell, Brea, Calif.

Chapter 6. Promises Kept

1. Fehrenbachers, eds., *Words*, pp. 428–29.

2. Noah Brooks, *Washington D.C. in Lincoln's Time* (Chicago, 1971, reprint), p. 77.

3. Remarks, May 22, 1863, in Basler, VI, pp. 226–27. Brooks, *Washington*, p. 258.

4. McPherson, *For Cause & Comrades*, offers an excellent discussion of soldier motivation, and refers to what kept the men going after the initial wave of enthusiasm as "sustaining motivation."

5. Lincoln to Joseph Hooker, April 3, 1863, in Basler, VI, p. 161. Rhodes, ed., *All for the Union*, p. 102.

6. Bacon and Howland, comps., *Letters,* II, pp. 518–19.

7. Allen Bevan to his sister, April 10, 1863, Allen Bevan Papers, CWMC, US-AMHI. Memorandum, April 6, 1863, in Basler, VI, p. 164.

8. Norton, *Army Letters,* p. 148. Robert W. Elmer Diary, April 8, 1863, CWMC; John Berry Diary, April 7, 1863, *CWTI,* USAMHI. Richard W. Musgrave, *Autobiography of Capt. Richard W. Musgrave* (n.p., 1921), p. 60. Carter, *Four Brothers,* p. 235. Silliker, ed., *Rebel Yell & Yankee Hurrah,* p. 75.

9. Frank L. Byrne and Andrew T. Weaver, eds., *Haskell of Gettysburg: His Life and Civil War Papers* (Madison, Wisc., 1970), pp. 57–58. Carter, *Four Brothers,* pp. 235–36.

10. Fisk, *Letters,* p. 64. Charles Perkins Diary, April 7, 1863, *CWTI,* USAMHI. Baxter, *Gallant Fourteenth,* p. 134. Weld, *War Diary,* p. 169. Durams, eds., *Soldier of the Cross,* p. 89.

11. Russell White, ed., *The Civil War Diary of Wyman S. White* (Hamet, Calif., 1979), p. 72. Sears, *Chancellorsville,* p. 115. Brooks, *Washington,* pp. 54–55. Weld, *War Diary,* p. 171. Bauer, ed., *Soldiering,* p. 33.

12. Moe, *Last Full Measure,* p. 229. Van Willard Narrative. Gaff, *Bloody Field,* p. 232. Dawes, *Sixth Wisconsin,* pp. 131–132n. Stevens, *As if It Were Glory,* pp. 12–13; Silliker, ed., *Rebel Yell & Yankee Hurrah,* p. 75. James M. Greiner, Janet L. Coryell, and James R. Smither, eds., *A Surgeon's Civil War: The Letters & Diary of Daniel M. Holt, M.D.* (Kent, Ohio, 1994), p. 87.

13. Alonzo Keeler Diary, April 10, 1863; Charles S. Bourneman Diary, April 11, 1863; Leander Davis to his wife, April 10, 1863, Leander Davis Papers; Magill to his sister, April 10, 1863, James Magill Letters, CWMC; Henry Henney Diary, April 10, 1863, *CWTI,* USAMHI. John M. Priest, ed., *John T. McMahon's Diary of the 136th New York 1861–1864* (Shippensburg, Pa., 1993), p. 46. W. W. Wallace, *Reminiscences* (n.p., 1915), pp. 38–39.

14. Brooks, *Washington,* pp. 54–55. Hagerty, *Collis' Zouaves,* p. 177. Milo M. Quaife, ed., *From the Cannon's Mouth: The Civil War Letters of General Alpheus S. Williams* (Detroit, 1959), p. 176.

15. Brooks, *Washington,* pp. 54–55. Clarence H. Bell to Licetta Bell, April 8, 1863, Clarence H. Bell Papers, CWMC, USAMHI. Silliker, ed., *Rebel Yell & Yankee Hurrah,* p. 75.

16. Fisk, *Letters,* pp. 69–70.

17. Memorandum, April 6–10, 1863, in Basler, VI, pp. 164–65. Sears, *Chancellorsville,* p. 129. Bacon and Howland, comps., *Letters,* II, p. 517. Fehrenbachers, eds., *Words,* p. 416.

18. Weld, *War Diary,* p. 193. John McCowan to Lizzie McCowan, May 29, 1863, John McCowan Letters, CWMC, USAMHI.

19. Proclamation, July 15, 1863, in Basler, VI, pp. 277–78. John J. Pullen, *A Shower of Stars: The Medal of Honor and the 27th Maine* (Philadelphia, 1966), pp. 67–68, 71–72. Weld, *War Diary,* p. 217.

20. Weld, *War Diary,* p. 228. Announcement, July 4, 1863, in Basler, VI, p. 314.

21. Response to Serenade, July 7, 1863, in Basler, VI, p. 320; Proclamation, July 15, 1863, p. 332.

22. Lincoln to James C. Conkling, August 26, 1863, in Basler, VI, pp. 409–10.

23. Adrian Cook, *The Armies of the Streets: The New York Draft Riots of 1863* (Lexington, Ky., 1974), p. 52.

24. Van Willard Narrative, July 1863. Smith, *Civic Ideals*, p. 274.

25. Lincoln to Joel Parker, July 25, 1863, in Basler, VI, p. 347; Lincoln to Horatio Seymour, August 7, 1863, p. 369; Opinion on the Draft, September 14, 1863, pp. 445–48.

26. Burrill to his parents, September 13, 1863, John H. Burrill Papers, *CWTI;* John P. Campbell to his father, August 25, 1863, John P. Campbell Papers; Charles E. Stevens to Friend Cone, October 29, 1863, Charles E. Stevens Papers, CWMC, USAMHI. Nash, *History of the Forty-fourth New York*, p. 169.

27. Memorandum, October 31, 1863, in Basler, VI, pp. 551–52; Order on the Draft, November 1, 1863, pp. 553–54.

28. Proclamation, October 17, 1863, in Basler, VI, p. 523.

29. Order, February 1, 1864, in Basler, VII, p. 164; Draft Order, p. 245. Samuel J. Marks to Carrie Powers, February 4, 1864, Samuel J. Marks Papers, CWMC, USAMHI. Margaret Probst Roth, ed., *Well Mary: Civil War Letters of a Wisconsin Volunteer* (Madison, Wisc., 1960), pp. 92–93.

30. Lincoln to Congress, January 5, 1864, in Basler, VII, pp. 101–8. Mitchell, "Perseverance," in Boritt, ed., *Why the Confederacy Lost*, pp. 117–18. Reid Mitchell, *Civil War Soldiers* (New York, 1988), p. 182. Fuller, *Recollections*, p. 107.

31. Welles, *Diary*, I, pp. 439–40. A. S. Lewis, ed., *My Dear Parents: The Civil War Seen by an English Union Soldier* (New York, 1982), p. 33.

32. Fehrenbachers, eds., *Words*, pp. 171, 195, 279.

33. Priest, ed., *McMahon's Diary*, p. 66. Fehrenbachers, eds., *Words*, pp. 125–26.

34. David Wills to Lincoln, November 2, 1863, in Holzer, ed., *Letters*, p. 287.

35. Lincoln to Stanton, November 17, 1863, in Basler, VII, p. 16.

36. Philip B. Kunhardt, Jr., *A New Birth of Freedom: Lincoln at Gettysburg* (Boston, 1983), pp. 115, 118. Bernard, *Lincoln and the Music*, pp. 81–82.

37. Herndon and Weik, *Lincoln*, p. 83.

38. Kunhardt, *New Birth*, pp. 156ff.

39. Gettysburg Address, November 19, 1863, in Basler, VII, pp. 17–18.

40. Fisk, *Letters*, p. 19.

41. Lincoln to Meade, November 20, 1863, in Basler, VII, p. 25. Laurence M. Hauptman, *The Iroquois in the Civil War* (Syracuse, N.Y., 1993), p. 109.

42. Lincoln to George Opdyke et al., December 2, 1863, in Basler, VII, p. 32.

43. Remarks, August 4, 1862, in Basler, V, p. 357.

44. Smith, *Civic Ideals*, p. 143.

45. Fehrenbachers, eds., *Words*, p. 435. Lincoln to Johnson, March 26, 1863, in Basler, VI, pp. 149–50.

46. Dudley T. Cornish, *The Sable Arm: Black Troops in the Union Army, 1861–1865*

(Lawrence, Kans., 1956), p. 91. Friedrich A. Braeutigam Diary, January 3, 1863, CWMC, USAMHI. New York *Anglo-African,* January 3, 10, 1863.

47. Philip S. Foner, ed., *The Life and Writings of Frederick Douglass* (New York, 1950–75), III, p. 335. Current, *Loyalists,* pp. 196–97. Memorandum, January 6, 1863, in Basler, VI, p. 41. Fehrenbachers, eds., *Words,* p. 187.

48. Fehrenbachers, eds., *Words,* pp. 144–45. Benjamin F. Butler, *Butler's Book* (Boston, 1892), pp. 577–78. Lincoln to Sumner, June 1, 1863, in Basler, VI, p. 243; Remarks, May 30, 1863, p. 239.

49. Donald Yacovone, ed., *A Voice of Thunder: The Civil War Letters of George E. Stephens* (Urbana, Ill., 1997), p. 324.

50. Lincoln to Conkling, August 26, 1863, in Basler, VI, pp. 409–10.

51. Glenn W. Sunderland, *Five Days to Glory* (New York, 1970), pp. 85–86.

52. Lincoln to Whom It May Concern, August 21, 1863, in Basler, VI, p. 401.

53. Ira Berlin et al., eds., *Free at Last: A Documentary History of Slavery, Freedom, and the Civil War* (New York, 1992), pp. 450–51. Order of Retaliation, July 30, 1863, in Basler, VI, p. 357.

54. Chicago *Tribune,* September 16, 1863. New York *Times,* September 9, 1863.

55. Address at Sanitary Fair, April 18, 1864, in Basler, VII, p. 301; Lincoln to Cabinet, May 3, 1864, p. 328; Lincoln to Stanton, May 17, 1864, p. 345.

56. Lincoln to Stanton, February 1865, in Basler, VIII, p. 268; Lincoln to Stanton, February 7, 1865, p. 266. John Hope Franklin, ed., *The Diary of James T. Ayers, Civil War Recruiter* (Springfield, Ill., 1947), p. 5.

57. Yacovone, ed., *Voice of Thunder,* p. 58. Foner, ed., *Douglass,* III, p. 335. James H. Gooding to Lincoln, September 28, 1863, in Holzer, ed., *Letters,* pp. 259–61.

58. Yacovone, ed., *Voice of Thunder,* pp. 72–75, 320. Ella Lonn, *Desertion During the Civil War* (Washington, D.C., 1928), p. 150. Andrew to James B. Congdon, December 20, 1863, in Virginia M. Adams, ed., *On the Altar of Freedom: A Black Soldier's Civil War Letters from the Front* (Amherst, Mass., 1991), p. 123. Gooding to Lincoln, September 28, 1863, in Holzer, ed., *Letters,* pp. 259–61.

59. Lincoln to Bates, June 24, 1864, in Basler, VII, pp. 404–6; Lincoln to Stanton, July 14, 1864, p. 440. Yacovone, ed., *Voice of Thunder,* pp. 77ff.

60. Lincoln to Stanton, February 8, 1865, in Basler, VIII, p. 272; Message to Congress, December 8, 1863, VII, p. 50; Lincoln to Charles D. Robinson, August 17, 1864, p. 500; Lincoln to Isaac M. Schermerhorn, September 12, 1864, VIII, p. 2.

61. Lincoln to James S. Wadsworth, n.d. [January 1864], in Basler, VII, p. 101. Fehrenbachers, eds., *Words,* p. 187. The comment in the Fehrenbachers' book comes from an 1867 recollection of something said by Lincoln in February 1864. Though they regard it as rather inventive, and therefore of questionable reliability, it so closely mirrors Lincoln's letter to Wadsworth that it seems entitled to credence, at least for sentiment, though it should be noted that some question the Wadsworth letter, too.

62. Marion G. Phillips and Valeria Phillips Parsegian, eds., *Richard and Rhoda: Letters from the Civil War* (Rhinebeck, N.Y., 1981), p. 4. Warren Wilkinson, *Mother May You Never See the Sights I Have Seen: The Fifty-seventh Massachusetts Veteran Volunteers in the Army of the Potomac 1864–1865* (New York, 1990), p. 48. Weld, *War Diary*, p. 284. Stephen B. Oates, *A Woman of Valor: Clara Barton and the Civil War* (New York, 1994), p. 222.

Chapter 7. *The Quality of Mercy*

1. Van Willard Narrative, December 29, 1862. Peterson's *Lincoln in American Memory*, p. 104, very briefly makes this same point about Lincoln's understanding of the common folk.
2. Lincoln to Cameron, August 10, 1861, in Basler, IV, p. 480.
3. Lincoln to Bates, July 29, 1862, in Basler, V, p. 347; Lincoln to Stanton, December 26, 1862, VI, p. 20; September 1, 1863, pp. 426–27; March 1, 1864, VII, p. 217. File 1112, R. W. Shenk, RG 153, NA. Pardon, October 22, 1863, in Basler, *Supplement*, p. 206.
4. Lincoln to Holt, August 4, 1864, in Basler, VII, p. 479; February 10, 1864, p. 175. File 11541, Edward Young, RG 153, NA.
5. File 111635, J. K. Herbert, RG 153, NA. Lincoln to Holt, February 23, 1865, in Basler, VIII, p. 313; Lincoln to Seth Eastman, November 24, 1863, VII, p. 29; Memorandum, January 20, 1864, p. 139; Order, September 18, 1863, VI, pp. 463–64.
6. Lincoln to Schofield, August 22, 1863, in Basler, VI, p. 402; Petition, May 28, 1861, IV, p. 389; Lincoln to John F. Miller, August 20, 1864, VII, p. 509; Lincoln to Caleb Carlton, November 5, 1864, VIII, p. 91; Lincoln to John P. Gray, April 25, 1864, VII, p. 313; Memorandum, September 23, 1864, VIII, p. 19; Lincoln to Holt, March 7, 1864, VII, p. 227; July 1864, p. 447; Lincoln to Butler, December 21, 1863, p. 82; Lincoln to Johnson, August 18, 1864, p. 502.
7. New York *Tribune*, September 9–10, 1861. Fischer, "Quality of Mercy," pp. 56–57. William Scott's court-martial file is number 00209, RG 153, NA. It is brief and shows no involvement by Lincoln at all. He never saw Scott or wrote anything to or about him that is on record. The file is now full of letters from writers who over the years asked the War Department to send transcripts of the case, and the original documents are almost worn to fragments, so that the file can only be viewed under supervision as of this writing. George B. McClellan, *McClellan's Own Story* (New York, 1887), p. 91, publishes an edited extract from a September 8, 1861, letter in which the general recounts Lincoln's visit and request for a pardon. Scott is not specifically mentioned, but the coincidence seems too great at this stage of the war for the request to be on behalf of anyone else.

8. James E. Murdoch, ed., *Patriotism in Poetry and Prose* (Philadelphia, 1866), pp. 103–7. Fischer, "Quality of Mercy," pp. 55–56. Francis De Haas Janvier, *The Sleeping Sentinel* (Philadelphia, 1863), pp. 1ff.

9. Lincoln to Sumner, May 21, 1862, in Basler, V, p. 228; Lincoln to George H. Thomas, April 26, 1864, VII, p. 316.

10. John Eaton with Ethel Osgood Mason, *Grant, Lincoln and the Freedmen* (New York, 1907), pp. 91, 180.

11. Lincoln to Holt, July 21, 1863, in Basler, VI, p. 340; Lincoln to Stanton, October 22, 1863, p. 532; Lincoln to Bates, June 4, 1862, V, p. 258; Lincoln to Holt, July 9, 1864, VII, p. 436. Parris Griffith to Lincoln, April 4, 1863, File mm189, Thomas M. Griffith, RG 153, NA.

12. Joshua Painter to Lincoln, February 1865, File 113108, File 112815, Augustus Lochbeller, RG 153, NA. Lincoln to Holt, July 20, 1863, in Basler, VI, p. 337; January 23, 1865, VIII, p. 233; December 5, 1864, p. 133; Lincoln to Bates, September 14, 1864, p. 5. Fischer, "Quality of Mercy," p. 57.

13. File 111075, Bernard McCloy, RG 153, NA. Order, October 25, 1862, in Basler, V, p. 476; Commutation, April 28, 1863, VI, p. 189; Lincoln to Oliver Morton, July 18, 1863, p. 337. Fehrenbachers, eds., *Words*, p. 394.

14. Fehrenbachers, eds., *Words*, pp. 50, 137. Helen Nicolay, *Personal Traits of Abraham Lincoln* (New York, 1912), p. 281. Holt told substantially the same story of Lincoln's Irishman account in an 1875 interview with John Nicolay, which is surely the source of the version in Helen Nicolay's book. (Burlingame, ed., *Oral History*, pp. 68–69.)

15. Fehrenbachers, eds., *Words*, pp. 259, 457. Lincoln to Holt, June 23, 1863, in Basler, VI, p. 292; June 24, 1863, p. 293; August 24, 1864, VII, p. 516. File kk371, Charles Arthur, RG 163, NA.

16. Lincoln to Cameron, November 2, 1861, in Basler, V, p. 11.

17. Fort Riley, Kansas, *Soldier's Letter*, December 27, 1864.

18. Numerous examples of such pardons are to be found in Basler, some of them being in VII, pp. 89, 130, 137, 175, 309, 321; VIII, pp. 112, 176, 315.

19. Endorsement, November 7, 1864, in Basler, VIII, p. 94; Lincoln to Stanton, January 28, 1864, VII, p. 158; Lincoln to Butler, December 30, 1863, p. 98. Butler to Lincoln, December 30, 1863, in Holzer, ed., *Lincoln*, p. 95.

20. Endorsement, January 7, 1865, in Basler, VIII, p. 203; Endorsement, February 18, 1865, p. 306; Endorsement, March 20, 1865, p. 366; Lincoln to Holt, February 10, 1864, VII, p. 176.

21. Endorsement, April 1, 1864, in Basler, VII, p. 277; Lincoln to Holt, February 8, 1864, p. 173; Lincoln to Meade, April 17, 1864, p. 301; June 6, 1864, p. 378; Endorsement, April 20, 1864, p. 305; Lincoln to Robert Tyler, July 25, 1864, p. 460.

22. Examples of these commutations and pardons are very numerous. See, e.g.,

Basler, VII, pp. 60, 323, 520; VIII, pp. 36, 167, 219, 229, 233, 238, 252–53, 269, 273, 305, 405.

23. Fehrenbachers, eds., *Words,* p. 126. Lincoln to Holt, July 18, 1863, in Basler, VI, p. 335.

24. Basler, VII, p. 198n.

25. Burlingame, ed., *Oral History,* pp. 68–69, 150n. Edward D. Neill, "Reminiscences of the Last Year of President Lincoln's Life," in Minnesota Commandery, Military Order of the Loyal Legion of the United States, *Glimpses of the Nation's Struggle* (St. Paul, Minn., 1887), I, p. 35. Order, February 26, 1864, in Basler, VII, p. 208. Fischer, "Quality of Mercy," p. 57. Fehrenbachers, eds., *Words,* p. 457.

26. Nathaniel West to Lincoln, June 13, 1863, File mm333, Samuel Crumb, RG 153, NA. Endorsement, January 7, 1864, in Basler, VII, p. 111. Holzer, ed., *Letters,* pp. 71–72. Fischer, "Quality of Mercy," p. 58. Fehrenbachers, eds., *Words,* pp. 409, 441.

27. Lonn, *Desertion,* pp. 152, 233–35. These averages are based on tallies compiled by Thomas and Beverly Lowry, and used with their gracious cooperation.

28. Lonn, *Desertion,* p. 150. The calculation that one-third of all courts-martial were for desertion comes from Thomas and Beverly Lowry, whose work in 42,671 cases to date shows 14,146 to be for desertion.

29. Oliver Sepp to Lincoln, February 6, 1864, File 111677, Hiram Oakley; Henry Snyder to Lincoln, March 1, 1865, File 111766, Henry Snyder; Mary E. Hopkins to Lincoln, April 1, 1865, File 112793, Frederick Hopkins; Martin Zurman to Lincoln, December 16, 1864, File 112656, Martin Zurman, RG 153, NA.

30. Fehrenbachers, eds., *Words,* pp. 113, 428.

31. Butler, *Butler's Book,* pp. 296, 579–80. Fehrenbachers, eds., *Words,* p. 73. Lincoln to Butler, December 10, 1863, in Basler, VII, p. 59; February 26, 1864, p. 206; Lincoln to Holt, July 24, 1863, VI, p. 347. Jessie A. Marshall, ed., *Private and Official Correspondence of General Benjamin F. Butler During the Period of the Civil War* (Norwood, Mass., 1917), III, pp. 396–97. Lamon, *Recollections,* pp. 102–3.

32. Richard Nelson Current, *The Lincoln Nobody Knows* (New York, 1958), pp. 174–75, is perceptive on Lincoln's political use of clemency. The statements on proportions of total cases, and Lincoln's interventions state by state, are drawn from tallies of their findings furnished by Thomas and Beverly Lowry, and represent just under half of the total of all courts-martial. A base of forty-two thousand is included; it is unlikely that the raw proportions will be much different when the total of over a hundred thousand are examined.

33. Fehrenbachers, eds., *Words,* pp. 162, 302, 357, 498. Burlingame, ed., *Oral History,* p. 53.

34. Peterson, *Lincoln in American Memory*, p. 108. Fehrenbachers, eds., *Words*, p. 132. Livermore, *My Story*, p. 573. Allan Nevins, ed., *Diary of the Civil War 1860–1865: George Templeton Strong* (New York, 1962), p. 205. Dennett, comp., *Hay*, pp. 68–69.

35. Coffman, *Old Army*, pp. 16–17.

36. Proclamation, March 10, 1863, in Basler, VI, pp. 132–33. Gaff, *Bloody Field*, p. 227. Sears, *Chancellorsville*, pp. 70–71.

37. Lincoln to George Stoneman, August 1863, in Basler, VI, p. 360; Lincoln to John Sedgwick, January 26, 1864, VII, p. 152; General Orders No. 76, February 26, 1864, p. 208. George R. Agassiz, ed., *Meade's Headquarters 1863–1865: Letters of Colonel Theodore Lyman from the Wilderness to Appomattox* (Boston, 1922), p. 117. Nevins, ed., *Wainwright*, p. 431.

38. Lincoln to Rosecrans, December 8, 1864, in Basler, VIII, p. 159; Lincoln to Meade, September 11, 1863, VI, p. 441.

39. Lincoln to Thomas Daines, September 23, 1863, in Basler, VI, p. 475; Lincoln to Hooker, June 4, 1863, p. 248; Lincoln to Holt, June 16, 1863, p. 280; Lincoln to Meade, August 21, 1863, p. 400; September 21, 1863, p. 472. File aa529, Richard Hembree; File 112922, Rudolph Schmidhauser; George Hutchinson to Lincoln, October 11, 1863, File mm524, George Hutchinson, RG 153, NA.

40. Benjamin F. Hall to Lincoln, October 6, 1864, File 112626, Benjamin F. Hall; File mm107, Charles N. Heath; John Johnson to Lincoln, August 13, 1864, File 111623, John Johnson, RG 153, NA. Robert I. Alotta, *Civil War Justice: Union Army Executions Under Lincoln* (Shippensburg, Pa., 1989), pp. 192ff. Of twenty-two men known to have been executed for rape during the war, half were black soldiers, almost all killed after Lincoln's assassination.

41. Fehrenbachers, eds., *Words*, pp. 141–42. Emmy Advena to Lincoln, January 27, 1865, File 111584, Joseph Advena; Cora Boyce to Lincoln, November 12, 1863, File mm1168, Charles H. Boyce, RG 153, NA. Endorsement, September 14, 1864, in Basler, VII, p. 5; Order, May 2, 1864, p. 328; Lincoln to Albert Hobbs, November 1, 1864, VIII, p. 86; Lincoln to Grant, January 26, 1865, p. 239.

42. Polly Kellison to William Kellison, December 2, 1862, File mm573, William Kellison; Mrs. Charles Heath to Lincoln, December 22, 1864, File mm107, Charles N. Heath; Mrs. H. J. Higgins to Lincoln, November 25, 1864, File 112685, W. F. Higgins; Narcises Bartley to Lincoln, November 16, 1864, File 111439, William Bartley, RG 153, NA.

43. Fehrenbachers, eds., *Words*, pp. 2, 141–42, 497. Russell H. Conwell, *Why Lincoln Laughed* (New York, 1922), p. 33.

44. A. Reed to Lincoln, February 26, 1865, File 113108, Joshua Painter; A. Curtis to Seth Williams, August 24, 1863, File mm769, Eugene Sullivan, RG 153, NA.

45. Numerous examples of such suspensions will be found in Basler, as, for instance, VII, pp. 166, 510, 515;VIII, pp. 215, 218, 411.
46. Lincoln to Stanton, August 12, 1863, in Basler, VI, p. 384.
47. Mary Milo to Lincoln, October 8, 1864, File 112049, John Milo; Jane Fisk to Lincoln, December 12, 1864, File 112794, James M. Fisk; Elizabeth Hawkins to Lincoln, July 27, 1864, File 11675, Patrick G. Hawkins, RG 153, NA.
48. Lincoln to Grant, February 9, 1865, in Basler, VIII, p. 274; Note, n.d., p. 590; Lincoln to E. O. C. Ord, January 19, 1865, p. 224; Lincoln to Butler, December 29, 1864, p. 189; Memorandum, April 10, 1862, V, p. 185. Fehrenbachers, eds., Words, p. 303.
49. Memorandum, November 16, 1863, in Basler, VII, p. 14; Lincoln to Meade, December 2, 1863, p. 31; November 3, 1863, VI, p. 561; Lincoln to Bates, July 2, 1862, V, p. 300; June 26, 1862, p. 285; Order, November 8, 1862, p. 491; Endorsement, January 7, 1864, VII, p. 111. Lamon, Recollections, pp. 87–88.
50. Lincoln to Dix, June 4, 1864, in Basler, VII, p. 375; Lincoln to Holt, April 11, 1864, p. 294; Lincoln to John Clark, January 19, 1864, p. 137; Lincoln to Stephen Cabot, February 12, 1864, p. 180; Lincoln to Butler, January 26, 1864, p. 151; Lincoln to John F. Miller, January 25, 1865, VIII, pp. 237–38; Lincoln to Meade, December 29, 1863, VII, p. 96; Lincoln to Meade, September 24, 1863, VI, p. 478; October 8, 1863, p. 506; Lincoln to Herman Kretz, September 22, 1863, pp. 473–74; Lincoln to George F. Shepley, February 1, 1865, VIII, p. 255.
51. Osgood V. Tracy to his mother, October 9, 1863, Osgood V. Tracy Letters in possession of Sarah B. Winch, Needham, Mass. Lincoln to Meade, October 29, 1863, in Basler, VI, p. 548; Lincoln to Grant, January 6, 1865, VIII, p. 203.
52. Fehrenbachers, eds., Words, pp. 19, 415.
53. Lincoln to Meade, November 20, 1863, in Basler, VII, p. 25. The War Department's *official* list of soldiers executed during the war was published as *List of U.S. Soldiers Executed by United States Military Authorities During the Late War* in an 1885 Adjutant General's Report, and is published as an appendix in Alotta, *Civil War Justice,* pp. 191–201. The research of the Lowrys indicates that at least one hundred executions are not included in the report, yet they have not to date found record of a single officer who was executed.
54. For an excellent discussion of officer courts-martial through case histories, see Thomas P. Lowry, *Tarnished Eagles: The Courts-Martial of Fifty Union Colonels and Lieutenant-Colonels* (Harrisburg, Pa., 1997).
55. Fehrenbachers, eds., Words, p. 501.
56. Adams, *Our Masters the Rebels,* p. 121. Duncan, ed., *Shaw,* p. 258. Lincoln to Grant, January 24, 1865, in Basler, VIII, p. 235; Lincoln to Butler, April 12,

1864, VII, p. 297; Lincoln to Cabot, April 21, 1864, p. 306; Lincoln to Meade, August 27, 1863, VI, p. 414; Lincoln to Adoniram Warner, December 22, 1864, VIII, p. 177; Lincoln to John P. Slough, September 8, 1864, VII, p. 544; Lincoln to Meade, April 25, 1864, p. 314; Lincoln to John G. Foster, October 17, 1863, VI, p. 522. Fischer, "Quality of Mercy," pp. 58–59. Peterson, *Lincoln in American Memory*, pp. 106–7. Burlingame, ed., *Oral History*, p. 150n. Jonathan T. Dorris, "President Lincoln's Clemency," *Journal of the Illinois State Historical Society*, 20 (January 1928), p. 553. The official government tally of executions as stated in the report reprinted in Alotta and also in the Dorris article is 267, of which 141 were for desertion.

57. Lincoln to Stephen Burbridge, February 2, 1865, in Basler, VIII, p. 256; Lincoln to Rosecrans, September 13, 1864, p. 4; Order, August 30, 1864, VII, p. 524; Lincoln to Stanton, February 5, 1864, p. 169. Fehrenbachers, eds., *Words*, pp. 81, 171, 336.

58. Fehrenbachers, eds., *Words*, p. 171.

Chapter 8. Vox Militum

1. A presidential election had been held in 1812, during the second war with Britain, but that was two decades before the commencement of *popular* elections.

2. Burrill to his parents, December 28, 1863, John H. Burrill Papers, *CWTI*; David Blair to Lizzie Blair, March 2, 1864, David Humphrey Blair Diary and Letters; J. A. Moore to R. A. Moore, April 26, 1864, Moore Family Papers; CWMC, USAMHI. Sunderland, *Five Days to Glory*, p. 133. Gaff, *Bloody Field*, p. 229. Julia A. Drake, ed., *The Mail Goes Through, or the Civil War Letters of George Drake* (San Angelo, Tex., 1964), p. 71. Larry H. Whiteaker and W. Calvin Dickinson, eds., *Civil War Letters of the Tenure Family, Rockland County, N.Y., 1862–1865* (New York, 1990), p. 62.

3. Remarks, March 18, 1864, in Basler, VII, p. 254; Response to Serenade, May 9, 1864, p. 334; Response to Serenade, June 9, 1864, p. 384; Remarks, June 11, 1864, p. 388.

4. Speech, June 16, 1864, in Basler, VII, p. 398; Speech at Sanitary Fair, June 16, 1864, p. 394.

5. Carter, *Four Brothers*, p. 427. Agassiz, ed., *Meade's Headquarters*, p. 154. Paul M. Angle, ed., *Three Years in the Army of the Cumberland: The Letters and Diary of Major James A. Connolly* (New York, 1969), p. 217. Barry Popchock, ed., *Soldier Boy: The Civil War Letters of Charles O. Musser, 29th Iowa* (Iowa City, 1995), p. 137.

6. Sunderland, *Five Days to Glory*, p. 147. Lincoln to Dennison, June 17, 1864, in Basler, VII, p. 411.

7. Donald, *Lincoln*, p. 513.

8. Horace Porter, *Campaigning with Grant* (Bloomington, Ind., 1961, reprint), pp. 216–24.

9. Ibid., pp. 218–19. Dana, *Recollections*, p. 225. Donald, *Lincoln*, pp. 515–16. Decker, ed., *Yates Phalanx*, p. 160. Fehrenbachers, eds., *Words*, p. 73. McPhersons, eds., *Lamson*, p. 183.

10. Concord, New Hampshire, *Veteran's Advocate*, June 15, 1886. Dennett, comp., *Hay*, p. 208.

11. Frank Wilkeson, *Recollections of a Private Soldier in the Army of the Potomac* (New York, 1887), pp. 231ff. Greiner, Coryell, and Smither, eds., *Surgeon's Civil War*, p. 220. Concord, New Hampshire, *Veteran's Advocate*, June 15, 1886. A. B. Beamish, "The Battle of Fort Stevens," July 10, 1886, CWMC, USAMHI. Rhodes, ed., *All for the Union*, p. 170.

12. Chalmers to his sister, August 10, 1864, Morris W. Chalmers Papers; John P. Campbell to his sister, August 16, 1864, John P. Campbell Papers, CWMC, USAMHI. Frank L. Byrne, ed., *The View from Headquarters: Civil War Letters of Harvey Reid* (Madison, Wisc., 1965), pp. 178–79.

13. Joseph M. Overfield, ed., *The Civil War Letters of Private George Parks, Company C, 24th New York Cavalry Volunteers* (Buffalo, N.Y., 1992), p. 33.

14. Gray and Ropes, *War Letters*, p. 376. Byrne, ed., *View from Headquarters*, p. 181.

15. Weld, *War Diary*, p. 368. Washington *Star*, March 30, 1911. Carter, *Four Brothers*, p. 480. Robert G. Athearn, ed., *Soldier in the West: The Civil War Letters of Alfred Lacey Hough* (Philadelphia, 1957), p. 218. Wills, *Army Life*, p. 296.

16. Sears, *McClellan*, p. 379. McPherson, *For Cause & Comrades*, p. 177. Angle, ed., *Three Years*, pp. 262–63. Joseph T. Glatthaar, *The March to the Sea and Beyond: Sherman's Troops in the Savannah and Carolinas Campaigns* (New York, 1985), p. 46. David E. Long, *The Jewel of Liberty: Abraham Lincoln's Re-election and the End of Slavery* (Harrisburg, Pa., 1994), p. 224.

17. McPherson, *For Cause & Comrades*, p. 177. Drake, ed., *Mail Goes Through*, p. 113. John P. Campbell to his father, September 11, 1864, Campbell Papers, CWMC, USAMHI. Long, *Jewel of Liberty*, p. 224. Sunderland, *Five Days to Glory*, p. 160.

18. Agassiz, ed., *Meade's Headquarters*, p. 204. Interview, August 19, 1864, in Basler, VII, p. 506; Memorandum, August 23, 1864, p. 514.

19. Speech to 148th Ohio, August 31, 1864, in Basler, VII, p. 528; Speech to 164th Ohio, August 18, 1864, pp. 504–5; Speech to 166th Ohio, August 22, 1864, p. 512.

20. Robert W. McBride, *Personal Recollections of Abraham Lincoln* (Indianapolis, 1926), p. 55. Fehrenbachers, eds., *Words*, pp. 339–40, 414.

21. Order, September 3, 1864, Order of Thanks, September 3, 1864, in Basler, VII, p. 532; Proclamation, September 3, 1864, p. 533.

22. Long, *Jewel of Liberty*, p. 216. Chapin to his wife, March 6, 1864, Nelson Chapin Papers, *CWTI*, USAMHI. Noe, ed., *Southern Boy in Blue*, p. 272.

23. Arnold Gates, ed., *The Rough Side of War: The Civil War Journal of Chesley A. Mosman* (Garden City, N.Y., 1987), p. 213. McPherson, *For Cause & Comrades*, p.

176. J. Henry Blakeman to his mother, October 6, 1864, J. Henry Blakeman Papers; Magill to his mother, February 16, 1863, James Magill Letters; D. M. Garland to his wife, October 31, 1864, D. M. Garland Papers, CWMC, USAMHI.

24. Charles Chapin Diary, November 7, 1864, CWMC, USAMHI. Fisk, *Letters*, pp. 264–65.

25. Noe, ed., *Southern Boy in Blue*, pp. 272–73.

26. Nicholas DeGraff Memoir, *CWTI*, USAMHI. Trumbull, *Memoirs*, pp. 35–36. Hambleton Tapp and James C. Klotter, eds., *The Union, the Civil War, and John W. Tuttle* (Frankfort, Ky., 1980), p. 228. United States War Department, *List of Synonyms of Organizations in the Volunteer Service of the United States* (Washington, D.C., 1885; republished in vol. II of William F. Amman, ed., *Personnel of the Civil War* [New York, 1961]), pp. 127, 320, 322. Drickamers, eds., *Fort Lyon to Harpers Ferry*, p. 116. Sunderland, *Five Days to Glory*, p. 182.

27. McPherson, *For Cause & Comrades*, p. 129. Overfield, ed., *George Parks*, p. 41. Hodgkins to his mother, November 9, 1862, Thomas Hodgkins Papers, *CWTI*; Chalmers to his sister, September 26, 1864, Chalmers Papers, CWMC, USAMHI. Gray and Ropes, *War Letters*, pp. 376–77. Randall C. Jimerson, *The Private Civil War: Popular Thought During the Sectional Conflict* (Baton Rouge, 1988), p. 44.

28. Hicken, *Illinois*, p. 132. Jacob Behm to Jacob Seiler, February 1, 1864, Jacob Behm Papers, *CWTI*, USAMHI.

29. John Gourilie to his brother, September 23, 1864, John Gourilie Papers, CWMC, USAMHI. Glatthaar, *March to the Sea*, pp. 46–47, 50. McPherson, *For Cause & Comrades*, p. 176. Fisk, *Letters*, p. 207. Athearn, ed., *Soldier in the West*, pp. 208–9. Underhill, comp., *"Your Soldier Boy Samuel,"* pp. 118–19. Greiner, Coryell, and Smither, *Surgeon's Civil War*, p. 245.

30. Jack C. Davis, ed., *Dear Wife: Letters of A Civil War Soldier* (Louisville, Ky., 1991), pp. 29–30. Agassiz, ed., *Meade's Headquarters*, pp. 247–48. Oliver B. Fluke to George Hartman, September 23, 1864, Oliver B. Fluke Letter; Chalmers to his sister, October 27, 1864, Chalmers Papers, CWMC, USAMHI. Nevins, ed., *Wainwright*, p. 476. Glatthaar, *March to the Sea*, pp. 48–49. Overfield, ed., *George Parks*, p. 43.

31. Marks to Carrie Powers, October 1, 1864, Samuel J. Marks Papers; J. S. Graham to Ellen Lee, October 24, 1864, J. S. Graham Papers, CWMC, USAMHI. Drake, ed., *Mail Goes Through*, p. 115. Bacon and Howland, comps., *Letters*, pp. 626–27. Albert O. Marshall, *Army Life: From A Soldier's Journal* (Joliet, Ill., 1884), p. 403.

32. Leander Davis to his wife, October 21, 1864, Leander Davis Papers; John P. Campbell to his father, October 4, 1864, Campbell Papers; Gourilie to his brother, November 3, 1864, Gourilie Papers, CWMC, USAMHI. Whiteaker and Dickinson, *Tenure Family*, p. 76. H. Draper Hunt, ed., *Dearest*

Father: The Civil War Letters of Lt. Frank Dickerson (Unity, Me., 1992), p. 122. Glatthaar, *March to the Sea*, p. 46. Francis B. Carpenter, *Six Months at the White House with Abraham Lincoln* (New York, 1867), p. 231.

33. Leander Davis to his wife, September 29, 1864, Davis Papers, CWMC, Henry Henney Diary, October 13, 1864, *CWTI*, USAMHI. Davis, ed., *Dear Wife*, p. 33.

34. William H. Martin to his wife, October 30, 1864, William H. Martin Papers, Harrisburg Civil War Round Table Collection, USAMHI. Mitchell, *Civil War Soldiers*, p. 188.

35. Long, *Jewel of Liberty*, p. 217. New York *World*, October 14, 1864.

36. William Hesseltine, *Lincoln and the War Governors* (New York, 1948), pp. 334–35. Ida M. Tarbell, *A Reporter for Lincoln: The Story of Henry E. Wing, Soldier and Newspaperman* (New York, 1929), pp. 70–71.

37. Lincoln to Sherman, September 19, 1864, in Basler, VIII, p. 11; Lincoln to Morton, October 13, 1864, p. 46; Lincoln to Rosecrans, September 26, 1864, p. 24. Nicolay and Hay, *Lincoln*, IX, pp. 370–71.

38. Alexander K. McClure, *Abraham Lincoln and Men of War-Times* (Philadelphia, 1892), pp. 202–3.

39. Response to Serenade, October 19, 1864, in Basler, VIII, p. 53; Response to Serenade, October 21, 1864, p. 58; Speech to 189th New York, October 24, 1864, p. 75; Speech, October 31, 1864, p. 84. Fehrenbachers, eds., *Words*, p. 51.

40. Sears, ed., *Papers of McClellan*, pp. 609–12. Lincoln to Augustus Bradford, November 2, 1863, in Basler, VI, p. 557; Memorandum, September 12, 1864, VII, p. 548. Decker, ed., *Yates Phalanx*, p. 181.

41. Kieffer, *Drummer-Boy*, p. 48. Bernard, *Lincoln and the Music*, p. 196n. Washington M. Grimes to Lincoln, August 26, 1864, in Holzer, ed., *Letters*, pp. 218–19. Franklin, ed., *Civil War Recruiter*, p. 115. New York *Times*, October 2, 1864.

42. Popchock, ed., *Soldier Boy*, p. 157. Dale E. Floyd, ed., *"Dear Friends at Home": The Letters and Diary of Thomas James Owen, Fiftieth New York Volunteer Engineer Regiment, During the Civil War* (Washington, D.C., 1985), p. 57. Roth, ed., *Well Mary*, p. 92. Franklin, ed., *Civil War Recruiter*, p. 53.

43. Overfield, ed., *George Parks*, p. 36. Jones, ed., *"For My Country,"* p. 169. Hicken, *Illinois*, p. 263. Sunderland, *Five Days to Glory*, pp. 11, 33, 88. Decker, ed., *Yates Phalanx*, p. 172. Angle, ed., *Three Years*, p. 217.

44. Popchock, ed., *Soldier Boy*, p. 146. Charles Maxim to Marcus Maxim, September 11, 1864, Charles Maxim Papers; Garland to his wife, October 31, 1864, Garland Papers; John McCowan to Lizzie McCowan, October 25, 1864, John McCowan Letters; David Blair to Lizzie Blair, October 17, 1864, Blair Diary and Letters; Amos Breneman to My dear friend, October 25, 1864, Amos Breneman Papers, CWMC, USAMHI. Jones, ed., *"For My Country,"* p.

170. Long, *Jewel of Liberty*, p. 225. Blair, ed., *Politician Goes to War*, p. 210. Horatio Dana Chapman, *Civil War Diary: Diary of a Forty-Niner* (Hartford, Conn., 1929), p. 98. W. Springer Menge and J. August Shimrak, eds., *The Civil War Notebook of Daniel Chisholm* (New York, 1989), p. 43.

45. Raymond G. Barber and Gary E. Swinson, eds., *The Civil War Letters of Charles Barber, Private, 104th New York Volunteer Infantry* (Torrance, Calif., 1991), p. 196. Josiah Henry Benton, *Voting in the Field: A Forgotten Chapter of the Civil War* (Boston, 1915), pp. 15ff. Theodore Skinner to friends at home, October 15, 29, 1864, Theodore Skinner Papers; William A. Moore Memoirs; Frank Wilberforce to his father, October 31, 1864, Frank Wilberforce Papers, CWMC, USAMHI. Lincoln to Welles, October 10, 1864, in Basler, VIII, p. 43. Hunt, ed., *Dearest Father*, p. 123. Vivian C. Hopkins, ed., "Soldier of the 92nd Illinois: Letters of William H. Brown and his Fiancee, Emma Jane Frazey," *Bulletin of the New York Public Library*, 73 (February 1969), p. 8.

46. Glatthaar, *March to the Sea*, pp. 49, 207. Agassiz, ed., *Meade's Headquarters*, p. 245. Jones, ed., *"For My Country,"* p. 166. Leander Davis to Susie, November 2, 1864, Davis Papers; William B. Gates to Cyrus Keffer, September 14, 1864, William B. Gates Letter, CWMC, USAMHI.

47. Charles A. Dana, *Recollections of the Civil War* (New York, 1898), pp. 260–61. Lincoln to Stanton, November 3, 1864, in Basler, VIII, p. 89. Athearn, ed., *Soldier in the West*, pp. 211–12. Benjamin Hall to Lincoln, October 6, 1864, File 112626, Benjamin F. Hall; File 112923, John M. Thompson; File 113144, John Lynch, RG 153, NA. Brooks, *Washington*, p. 196. The conclusion about sentences for deserters claiming they left to vote is drawn from a number of such cases examined by Thomas and Beverly Lowry.

48. David Blair to Samuel Blair, November 7, 1864, Blair Diary and Letters; William Cox to his brother, November 6–7, 1864, William F. Cox Papers, CWMC, USAMHI. Jones, ed., *"For My Country,"* p. 171. Menge and Shimrak, eds., *Chisholm*, p. 138. Carter, *Four Brothers*, p. 480. Roth, ed., *Well Mary*, p. 95. Tapert, ed., *Brothers' War*, p. 224.

49. Joseph Smith Graham to Ellen Lee, November 7, 1864, Graham Papers; John W. Bates Diary, November 8, 1864; Skinner to friends at home, November 9, 1864, Skinner Papers; Orville Upton to Mrs. Frank Mudgett, November 12, 1864, Orville Upton Letter, CWMC, USAMHI.

50. Stephen H. Smith Diary, November 8, 1864, CWMC, USAMHI. Stephen E. Ambrose, ed., *A Wisconsin Boy in Dixie: Civil War Letters of James K. Newton* (Madison, Wisc., 1961), p. 127. Harold D. Brinkman, ed., *Dear Companion: The Civil War Letters of Silas I. Shearer* (Ames, Iowa, 1995), p. 110. Popchock, ed., *Soldier Boy*, pp. 160–61.

51. Glatthaar, *March to the Sea*, p. 47. George Bargus Diary, November 8, 1864; Lyman Daniel Ames Diary, November 8, 1864, *CWTI*; Ephraim F. Brower Diary, November 8, 1864; Brigham Foster to his wife, November 9, 1864,

Brigham Foster Papers; David Blair to Lizzie Blair, March 14, 1864, Blair Diary and Letters, CWMC, USAMHI. Angle, ed., *Three Years*, p. 292. Drake, ed., *Mail Goes Through*, p. 122. Huffstodt, *Hard Dying Men*, p. 234. B. F. McGee, *History of the 72d Indiana Volunteer Infantry of the Mounted Lightning Brigade* (LaFayette, Ind., 1882), p. 384. Noe, ed., *Southern Boy in Blue*, pp. 272–73. Parole of Frank Wolford, July 1864, in Basler, VII, p. 446. Robert A. and Gloria S. Driver, eds., *Letters Home: The Personal Side of the American Civil War* (Roseburg, Oreg., 1992), p. 85.

52. Davis, ed., *Dear Wife*, p. 59. James W. Davis Diary, November 8, 1864; Simon Bennage Diary, November 8, 1864, CWMC; Christian Getz to unknown, n.d. [November 1864], Fulton-Lenz Papers, *CWTI*, USAMHI. McPhersons, eds., *Lamson of the "Gettysburg,"* p. 209.

53. Small, ed., *Road to Richmond*, p. 267. Arthur B. Wyman Diary, November 9, 1864; Arthur B. Wyman Papers; Charles Chapin Diary, November 8, 1864, CWMC, USAMHI. Turino, ed., *Hodgkins*, p. 109. Weld, *War Diary*, p. 385. Wayne Mahood, ed., *Charlie Mosher's Civil War: From Fair Oaks to Andersonville with the Plymouth Pilgrims (85th N.Y. Infantry)* (Hightstown, N.J., 1994), p. 270.

54. Fisk, *Letters*, pp. 273, 276, 277. Allan Baker Diary, November 8, 1864, CWMC, USAMHI.

55. Long, *Jewel of Liberty*, p. 229. Joseph Smith Graham to Ellen Lee, November 7, 1864, Graham Papers; William F. Buker Diary, November 8, 1864, CWMC, USAMHI. Menge and Shimrak, eds., *Chisholm*, p. 48.

56. Kallgren and Couthamel, eds., *"Dear Friend Anna,"* p. 107. Smith, *Twenty-fourth Michigan*, p. 231. Gaff, *Bloody Field*, p. 390. Blakeman to his mother, October 21, November 8, 1864, Blakeman Papers; Graham to Ellen Lee, November 7, 1864, Graham Papers; Samuel A. Beddall Diary, November 8, 1864, CWMC, USAMHI. Kermit Molyneux Bird, ed., *Quill of the Wild Goose: Civil War Letters and Diaries of Private Joel Molyneux, 141st P.V.* (Shippensburg, Pa., 1996), p. 242. Charles A. Humphreys, *Field, Camp, Hospital and Prison in the Civil War, 1863–1865* (New York, 1918), pp. 416–17. Nevins, ed., *Wainwright*, p. 480. United States War Department, *War of the Rebellion: Official Records of the Union and Confederate Armies* (Washington, D.C., 1880–1901), ser. I, vol. 42, prt. 3, pp. 565–66, 568, 570, 574.

57. Silliker, ed., *Rebel Yell & Yankee Hurrah*, p. 218. Jimerson, *Private Civil War*, p. 223; Kallgren and Couthamel, eds., *"Dear Friend Anna,"* p. 107.

58. Brooks, *Washington*, p. 196. Dana, *Recollections*, pp. 261–62. Lincoln to Managing Committee, November 8, 1864, in Basler, VIII, p. 95. James W. Davis Diary, November 11, 1864; Wilberforce to his father, November 18, 1864, Wilberforce Papers, CWMC, USAMHI. Rhodes, ed., *All for the Union*, p. 196. James M. McPherson, *Ordeal by Fire: The Civil War and Reconstruction* (New York, 1982), p. 458.

59. McPherson, *For Cause & Comrades*, pp. 176–77. Glatthaar, *March to the Sea*, p. 47. Sears, *McClellan*, pp. 385–86.
60. Long, *Jewel of Liberty*, p. 285. Harold Hyman, "Election of 1864," in Arthur M. Schlesinger, Jr., ed., *History of American Presidential Elections 1789–1968* (New York, 1971), II, p. 1244. The analysis of the impact of the soldier vote here is not taken from these sources, but built upon information that they provide.
61. Glatthaar, *March to the Sea*, p. 48.
62. Response to Serenade, December 6, 1864, in Basler, VIII, p. 154; Response to Serenade, November 10, 1864, p. 101; Henry Hoffman to Lincoln, November 10, 1864, p. 100n; Message to Congress, December 6, 1864, p. 150.
63. Burlingame, ed., *Oral History*, p. 83. Lincoln to Holt, February 27, 1865, in Basler, VIII, p. 321. Richard Harwell and Philip N. Racine, eds., *The Fiery Trail: A Union Officer's Account of Sherman's Last Campaigns* (Knoxville, 1986), p. 44. Silliker, ed., *Rebel Yell & Yankee Hurrah*, p. 219. J. H. Mechling to Owen Sturdevant, November 25, 1864, Ann Sturdevant Collection, CWMC, US-AMHI. Franklin, ed., *Civil War Recruiter*, p. 63.
64. McPherson, *For Cause & Comrades*, p. 146. Wilberforce to his father, November 11, 1864, Wilberforce Papers; John McCowan to his father, December 29, 1864, McCowan Letters; Blakeman to his mother, n.d. [November 1864], Blakeman Papers, CWMC, USAMHI.
65. Floyd, ed., *"Dear Friends,"* p. 62. Agassiz, ed., *Meade's Headquarters*, p. 259. Athearn, ed., *Soldier in the West*, pp. 230–31.
66. Reid Mitchell, in *The Vacant Chair: The Northern Soldier Leaves Home* (New York, 1993), pp. 43–52, is one of the few historians to devote any discussion (and that brief) to the development and idea of Lincoln as Father Abraham and the nature of the spiritual bond between Lincoln and the soldiers. It is Kunhardt, in *New Birth of Freedom*, p. 101, who says that Lincoln disliked being called Father Abraham, but he offers no authority for the statement; it would have been in character for Lincoln to prefer not to be so nicknamed, however.
67. Sunderland, *Five Days to Glory*, p. 193. McPhersons, eds., *Lamson of the "Gettysburg,"* p. 209. Mitchell, *Vacant Chair*, p. 52. Glatthaar, *Forged in Battle*, pp. 208–9.
68. Carter, *Four Brothers*, p. 498. Glatthaar, *March to the Sea*, p. 51.

Chapter 9. "Where Are You Now, Father Abraham?"

1. Washington *Star*, April 13, 1911.
2. Fehrenbachers, eds., *Words*, p. 369. McPherson, *For Cause & Comrades*, p. 178. Drivers, eds., *Letters Home*, p. 95. Albert H. McGeehan, ed., *My Country and*

Cross: The Civil War Letters of John Anthony Wilterdink, Company I, 25th Michigan Infantry (Dallas, 1982), p. 77. Oscar Cram to Ellen Cram, February 18, 1865, Oscar Cram Papers, CWMC, USAMHI.

3. F. Y. Hedley, *Marching Through Georgia* (Chicago, 1884), p. 398. George W. Nichols, *The Story of the Great March* (New York, 1865), p. 202. Harwell and Racine, eds., *Fiery Trail,* p. 167. William Johnson to Lincoln, March 3, 1865, in Holzer, ed., *Letters,* p. 232; H. C. Beemer to Lincoln, March 23, 1865, p. 113.

4. Proclamation, December 19, 1864, in Basler, VIII, p. 171; Lincoln to Grant, September 22, 1864, p. 17; Lincoln to Stanton, September 20, 1864, p. 14. Roth, ed., *Well Mary,* p. 110. Fehrenbachers, eds., *Words,* pp. 234, 274. Current, *Loyalists,* pp. 124–25.

5. Endorsement, October 29, 1864, in Basler, VIII, p. 80; Lincoln to Stanton, December 14, 1864, p. 168; Order, January 9, 1865, p. 206; Memorandum, January 22, 1865, p. 231. File 112683, Julius Crone; File 113133, Frederick Schlag; File mm2060, Justus Ohage, RG 153, NA.

6. Proclamation, March 11, 1865, in Basler, VIII, pp. 349–50. Mary Matthews to Lincoln, March 18, 1865, File mm1970, Henry Dickenson, RG 153, NA. Fischer, "Quality of Mercy," p. 61. The statements about the variety of cases in which Lincoln intervened are based on the findings of the Lowrys, who have to date examined 42,942 courts-martial, something less than half of the total, and found 792 cases in which Lincoln took a personal interest; thus sixteen hundred or more out of over a hundred thousand seems a reasonable estimate.

7. Smith, *Incidents,* pp. 89–90. Livermore, *My Story,* pp. 580–81.

8. Second Inaugural, March 4, 1865, in Basler, VIII, p. 333. Weems, *Washington,* pp. 117–18.

9. John D. Caldwell to Lincoln, March 16, 1865, in Holzer, ed., *Letters,* p. 115. Oates, *A Woman of Valor,* p. 304. Lincoln to Friends of Missing Persons, n.d. [March 1865], in Basler, VIII, p. 423; Lincoln to Richard Yates, February 3, 1864, VII, p. 167. Bremner, *Public Good,* pp. 145–46.

10. Recommendation, December 9, 1864, in Basler, VIII, p. 160; Lincoln to Scott, March 1, 1865, p. 327. Bremner, *Public Good,* p. 147.

11. Fehrenbachers, eds., *Words,* p. 339. Annual Message, December 6, 1864, in Basler, VIII, p. 147. Lincoln to Sumner, May 19, 1864, in Basler, *Supplement,* p. 243.

12. Lincoln to Lydia Bixby, November 21, 1864, in Basler, VIII, pp. 116–17.

13. Fehrenbachers, eds., *Words,* pp. 22, 115. Stephen B. Oates, *With Malice Toward None: The Life of Abraham Lincoln* (New York, 1977), pp. 417–20, is good for Lincoln's last visit to the army.

14. Jones, *Four Years,* pp. 208–9; Menge and Shimrak, eds., *Chisholm,* p. 70. Simon Crandall to Cynthia Crandall, March 26, 1865, Crandall Family Pa-

pers, CWMC, USAMHI. Wilkinson, *Fifty-seventh Massachusetts*, p. 337. Robert E. McBride, *In the Ranks from the Wilderness to Appomattox Court-House* (Cincinnati, 1881), p. 163.

15. Rhodes, ed., *All for the Union*, p. 222. Gibbon, *Personal Recollections*, p. 291. Bernard, *Lincoln and the Music*, p. 83.
16. Lincoln to Stanton, March 26, 1865, in Basler, VIII, p. 375.
17. Agassiz, ed., *Meade's Headquarters*, pp. 324–25.
18. Sherman, *Memoirs*, II, p. 327. Fehrenbachers, eds., *Words*, p. 57. Weems, *Washington*, p. 123.
19. Lincoln to Stanton, March 30, 1865, in Basler, VIII, p. 377. Donald, *Lincoln*, pp. 576–77. Weems, *Washington*, p. 85. Fehrenbachers, eds., *Words*, p. 257.
20. Fehrenbachers, eds., *Words*, p. 396. Fisk, *Letters*, pp. 322–23. Donald, *Lincoln*, p. 575.
21. Last Public Address, April 11, 1865, in Basler, VIII, p. 400. Phillips and Parsegian, eds., *Richard and Rhoda*, p. 65.
22. Donald, *Lincoln*, p. 593. Lewis Broerman to Lincoln, March 24, 1865, File mm1636, Henry Broerman, RG 153, NA. Fehrenbachers, eds., *Words*, p. 320. The Broerman case was referred to Lincoln by Holt on April 13, meaning it should have been in the president's office the next day.
23. Thomas Reed Turner, *Beware the People Weeping: Public Opinion and the Assassination of Abraham Lincoln* (Baton Rouge, 1982), pp. 26–27. Donald, *Lincoln*, p. 598.
24. Henry C. Campbell Memoir, CWMC, USAMHI. Menge and Shimrak, eds., *Chisholm*, pp. 81–82.
25. Hicken, *Illinois*, p. 366. Harwell and Racine, eds., *Fiery Trail*, p. 211. Thomas Finley Diary, April 18–19, 1865, CWMC, USAMHI. Byrne, ed., *View from Headquarters*, p. 243. Hard, *Eighth Illinois*, p. 321.
26. Stephen Z. Starr, *Jennison's Jayhawkers: A Civil War Cavalry Regiment and Its Commander* (Baton Rouge, 1973), p. 375. James A. P. Fancher Diary, April 16, 1865, CWMC, USAMHI. Glatthaar, *Forged in Battle*, p. 209.
27. William Dunlap to his sister, April 20, 1865, William Dunlap Papers; Marks to Carrie Marks, April 16, 1865, Samuel J. Marks Papers; Samuel A. Beddall Diary, April 17, 1865; John P. Barbor to Friend Agie, April 17, 1865, John P. Barbor Papers, CWMC, USAMHI. Gaff, *Bloody Field*, p. 418. Rhodes, ed., *All for the Union*, p. 232. Powell, *Fifth Corps*, p. 870.
28. Hard, *Eighth Illinois*, p. 321. File mm2531, John W. Nash; File mm2226, John McCarty; File mm2240, Amos Polson; File mm2384, William Hall; File mm2870, Richard McDermott; File mm1936, Elijah Chapman; File mm2384, William Robinson; File mm2190, Barney Lowrie, RG 153, NA.
29. File mm2304, Charles B. Hobson, RG 153, NA.
30. Mahood, ed., *Mosher's Civil War*, p. 292. Silliker, ed. *Rebel Yell & Yankee Hurrah*, p. 269.

31. Mitchell, *Civil War Soldiers*, p. 200. Wilkinson, *Fifty-seventh Massachusetts*, p. 352. Fisk, *Letters*, p. 323. Edward G. Longacre, *Army of Amateurs: General Benjamin F. Butler and the Army of the James, 1863–1865* (Harrisburg, Pa., 1997), pp. 312–13. Michael Davis, *The Image of Lincoln in the South* (Knoxville, 1971), pp. 99–101. John P. Nourse Memoir.

32. Wills, *Army Life*, p. 371. Drivers, eds., *Letters Home*, p. 102. Mitchell, *Civil War Soldiers*, pp. 198–201. Glatthaar, *March to the Sea*, pp. 176–77.

33. Lyman Daniel Ames Diary, April 19, 1865, *CWTI*. David E. Gingrich to ?, April 30, 1865, David E. Gingrich Papers, CWMC, USAMHI. Mitchell, *Civil War Soldiers*, pp. 198–99. Turner, *Beware the People*, pp. 49–50; Overfield, ed., *George Parks*, p. 70. Starr, *Jennison's Jayhawkers*, p. 357.

34. Glatthaar, *March to the Sea*, pp. 51, 178. Mitchell, *Civil War Soldiers*, pp. 199–200. Mitchell, *Vacant Chair*, p. 120.

35. Ambrose, ed., *Wisconsin Boy*, p. 152. Bernard, *Lincoln and the Music*, p. 309.

36. Wilberforce to his father, April 16, 1865, Frank Wilberforce Papers; Oscar Cram to Ellen Cram, April 17, 1865, Oscar Cram Papers, CWMC, USAMHI. Gray and Ropes, *War Letters*, pp. 471–72. Fort Riley, Kansas, Soldier's Letter, May 27, 1865.

37. Fisk, *Letters*, p. 327. David E. Gingrich to ?, April 30, 1865, Gingrich Papers, CWMC, USAMHI. Franklin, ed., *Civil War Recruiter*, p. 98.

38. Fisk, *Letters*, p. 323.

39. Willard A. and Porter W. Heaps, *The Singing Sixties: The Spirit of Civil War Days Drawn from the Music of the Times* (Norman, Okla., 1960), p. 368.

40. Jones, ed., *"For My Country,"* p. 179. Alotta, *Justice*, pp. 208–9.

41. Rhodes, ed., *All for the Union*, p. 242. Bremner, *Public Good*, pp. 145–46.

42. "Lincoln's Favorite Poem," William H. Bartlett Papers, CWMC, USAMHI. Powell, *Fifth Corps*, p. 888.

43. Gray and Ropes, *War Letters*, p. 482. Moss, *Christian Commission*, p. 216.

44. William A. Moore Memoirs, CWMC, USAMHI. Rhodes, ed., *All for the Union*, pp. 84, 231. Small, ed., *Road to Richmond*, pp. 50–51.

45. Carter, *Four Brothers*, p. 121. Dawes, *Sixth Wisconsin*, p. 100. Jonathan W. W. Boynton Memoir, CWMC, USAMHI. Kent, ed., *Company K*, p. 135.

46. Frank Crosby, *Life of Abraham Lincoln* (Philadelphia, 1865), p. 389. Chittenden, *Recollections*, pp. 268–83. Lucius E. Chittenden, *The Sleeping Sentinel: The True Story* (New York, 1909), *passim*. Fischer, "Quality of Mercy," pp. 55–57.

47. Fehrenbachers, eds., *Words*, p. 487. Lamon, *Recollections*, pp. 86–87. William A. Moore Memoirs, CWMC, USAMHI.

48. Conwell, *Why Lincoln Laughed*, p. 33. Fehrenbachers, eds., *Words*, p. 507. Lincoln to Francis E. Spinner, September 22, 1863, in Basler, *Supplement*, pp. 202–4n. Bacon and Howland, comps., *Letters*, II, p. 506.

49. A good look at this "gentle legend" of Lincoln will be found in Peterson, *Lincoln in American Memory*, pp. 103ff., and in Fischer, "Quality of Mercy."

50. Michael Davis, *The Image of Lincoln in the South* (Knoxville, 1971), pp. 149–50. Fischer, "Quality of Mercy," pp. 62–65. Moore Memoirs, CWMC, US-AMHI.

51. Fehrenbachers, eds., *Words,* p. 353. Fuller, *Recollections,* pp. 107–8.

52. Humphreys, *Field, Camp, Hospital and Prison,* pp. 295–96. Allen Thorndike Rice, *Reminiscences of Abraham Lincoln* (New York, 1885), p. 500.

BIBLIOGRAPHY

In all the vast Lincoln literature, the growth of the image of him as Father Abraham, and the spiritual bond between him and the Union soldier, have not been fully explored previously, though touched upon briefly in a number of recent works, most notably in two by Reid Mitchell, *Civil War Soldiers* and *The Vacant Chair: The Northern Soldier Leaves Home.* Randall C. Jimerson attempts to delve into soldier motivation in *The Private Civil War: Popular Thought During the Sectional Conflict* with some success, though offering little on Lincoln. James M. McPherson's path-breaking *For Cause & Comrades: Why Men Fought in the Civil War* presents an excellent investigation into soldier motives and political awareness, with Lincoln always in the background. George B. Forgie, *Patricide in the House Divided: A Psychological Interpretation of Lincoln and His Age* develops the familial metaphor to the greatest extent, but goes somewhat overboard in the process.

Though several works on the life of the common soldiers have much to offer, none of them actually address the relationship between Lincoln and his soldiers. Most useful is James I. Robertson, Jr.'s recent *Soldiers Blue and Gray,* which considerably updates the older classic by Bell I. Wiley, *The Life of Billy Yank.* For a look at the Union veteran and Civil War posterity, Larry M. Logue's *To Appomattox and Beyond: The Civil War Soldier in War and Peace* is enlightening. Merrill D. Peterson's *Lincoln in American Memory* is excellent on the development of Lincoln mythology and American fascination with him, but does not address the subject with specific relation to soldier attitudes toward Father Abraham during or after the war. Several of the innumerable Lincoln biographies have bits to contribute, though, again, none really focus on the Lincoln-soldier relationship to any depth. Most useful and satisfying are Stephen B. Oates's *With Malice Toward None: The Life of Abraham Lincoln,* and David Donald's recent *Lincoln.*

PRIMARY SOURCES

Manuscripts

Civil War Library and Museum, Philadelphia, Pa.
  Francis Donaldson Papers
Joseph W. Goodell, Brea, Calif.
  John P. Nourse Memoir
Robert Grunwell, Lynchburg, Va.
  Albert B. Grunwell Diary
National Archives, Washington, D.C.
  Records of General Courts Martial, Record Group 153
Steven S. Raab, Ardmore, Pa.
  Van Willard Narrative
United States Army Military History Institute, Carlisle Barracks, Pa.
  Civil War Miscellaneous Collection
    Amos S. Abbott Diary
    John Quincy Adams Diary
    Samuel J. Alexander Papers
    Ashley Family Papers
    Allan Baker Diary
    Joseph D. Baker Papers
    John P. Barbor Papers
    William H. Bartlett Papers
    John W. Bates Diary
    A. B. Beamish, "The Battle of Fort Stevens"
    James Beard Papers
    Samuel A. Beddall Diary
    Charles Wesley Belknap Diary
    Clarence H. Bell Papers
    Simon Bennage Diary
    Allen Bevan Papers
    David Humphrey Blair Diary and Letters
    J. Henry Blakeman Papers
    Boucher Family Papers
    Charles S. Bourneman Diary
    John H. Boyer Papers
    Jonathan W. W. Boynton Memoir
    Friedrich A. Braeutigam Diary

Amos Breneman Papers
Ephraim F. Brower Diary
William F. Buker Diary
Henry C. Campbell Memoir
John P. Campbell Papers
Morris W. Chalmers Papers
Charles Chapin Diary
Samuel L. Condé Papers
Harrison H. Comings Reminiscences
William F. Cox Papers
Oscar Cram Papers
Crandall Family Papers
Charles and LeRoy Crockett Papers
James W. Davis Diary
Leander Davis Papers
Hannah Delp Papers
Michael Dougherty Diary
Charles Douglas Diary
Amos Downing Papers
William H. Dunham Papers
William Dunlap Papers
Emery Edson Diary
James P. Elliott Diary
Jonas Denton Elliott Papers
Robert W. Elmer Diary
James A. P. Fancher Diary
Thomas Finley Diary
Oliver B. Fluke Letter
Brigham Foster Papers
Peter Gamache Memoir
D. M. Garland Papers
William B. Gates Letter
David E. Gingrich Papers
John Gourilie Papers
J. S. Graham Papers
Liston Gray Letter
Joseph F. Haas Letter
David Herman Diary
Henry Hoyt Papers
Alonzo Keeler Diary
Dexter Macomber Letter
James Magill Letters
Samuel J. Marks Papers

Charles Maxim Papers
John McCowan Letters
James H. Montgomery Diary
William A. Moore Memoirs
John O'Connell Memoirs
Richard Packard Letter
William B. Rhodes Diary
Theodore Skinner Papers
Jacob F. Smith Letter
Stephen H. Smith Diary
Daniel Sober Diary
Charles E. Stevens Papers
Ann Sturdivant Collection
Orville Upton Letter
Charles O. Varnum Papers
Frank Wilberforce Papers
Isaac Williams Papers
Arthur B. Wyman Papers

Civil War Times Illustrated Collection
James Abraham Papers
Lyman Daniel Ames Diary
George Bargus Diary
Jacob Behm Papers
John Berry Diary
John H. Burrill Papers
Caldwell Family Papers
Nelson Chapin Papers
Frederick W. Chesson Collection
Nicholas DeGraff Memoir
Eleazor B. Doane Papers
William E. Dunn Papers
Fulton-Lenz Papers
James Gillette Papers
Jacob Heffelfinger Diary
Henry Henney Diary
Thomas Hodgkins Papers
John D. McQuaide Papers
Charles Perkins Diary

Harrisburg Civil War Round Table Collection
William H. Martin Papers

Moore Family Papers

Sarah B. Winch, Needham, Mass.

Osgood V. Tracy Letters

Newspapers

Boston *Journal,* 1892.
Charleston, South Carolina, *Daily Courier,* 1861.
Chicago *Tribune,* 1863.
Concord, New Hampshire, *Veteran's Advocate,* 1886.
Fort Riley, Kansas, *Soldier's Letter,* 1865.
Kansas City, Missouri, *Soldier's Letter,* 1864.
Malden, New York, *Malden City Press,* 1885.
New York *Anglo-African,* 1863.
New York *Times,* 1862, 1863.
New York *Tribune,* 1861.
New York *World,* 1864.
Washington *Star,* 1911.

Published Letters, Diaries, and Memoirs

Adams, Virginia M., ed. *On the Altar of Freedom: A Black Soldier's Civil War Letters from the Front.* Amherst, Mass., 1991.
Agassiz, George R., ed. *Meade's Headquarters 1863–1865: Letters of Colonel Theodore Lyman from the Wilderness to Appomattox.* Boston, 1922.
Ambrose, Stephen E., ed. *A Wisconsin Boy in Dixie: Civil War Letters of James K. Newton.* Madison, Wisc., 1961.
Andrews, Rufus. *"Kiss Each Other for Me": The Civil War Letters of Rufus Andrews 1861–1863.* Iron Mountain, Mich., 1979.
Angle, Paul M., ed. *Three Years in the Army of the Cumberland: The Letters and Diary of Major James A. Connolly.* New York, 1969.
Athearn, Robert G., ed. *Soldier in the West: The Civil War Letters of Alfred Lacey Hough.* Philadelphia, 1957.
Bacon, Georgeanna Woolsey, and Eliza Woolsey Howland, comps. *Letters of a Family During the War for the Union, 1861–1865.* 2 vols. N.p., 1899.
Barber, Raymond G., and Gary E. Swinson, eds. *The Civil War Letters of Charles Barber, Private, 104th New York Volunteer Infantry.* Torrance, Calif., 1991.
Basler, Roy P., ed. *The Collected Works of Abraham Lincoln.* 9 vols. New Brunswick, N.J., 1953–55.
———. *The Collected Works of Abraham Lincoln: Supplement, 1832–1865.* Westport, Conn., 1974.
Bassett, Morton H., ed. *From Bull Run to Bristow Station.* St. Paul, Minn., 1962.
Bates, David Homer. *Lincoln in the Telegraph Office.* New York, 1907.

Bauer, K. Jack, ed. *Soldiering: The Civil War Diary of Rice C. Bull, 123rd New York Volunteer Infantry.* San Rafael, Calif., 1977.

Baxter, Nancy Niblack, ed. *Hoosier Farmboy in Lincoln's Army: The Civil War Letters of Pvt. John R. McClure.* Indianapolis, 1992.

Berlin, Ira., et al., eds. *Free at Last: A Documentary History of Slavery, Freedom, and the Civil War.* New York, 1992.

Bird, Kermit Molyneux, ed. *Quill of the Wild Goose: Civil War Letters and Diaries of Private Joel Molyneux, 141st P.V.* Shippensburg, Pa., 1996.

Blair, William A., ed. *A Politician Goes to War: The Civil War Letters of John White Geary.* University Park, Pa., 1995.

Bloodgood, J. D. *Personal Reminiscences of the War.* New York, 1893.

Brinkman, Harold D., ed. *Dear Companion: The Civil War Letters of Silas I. Shearer.* Ames, Iowa, 1995.

Brooks, Noah. *Washington, D.C. in Lincoln's Time.* Chicago, 1971 (reprint).

Bumbera, Marlene C., comp. *The Civil War Letters of Cpl. John H. Strathern.* Apollo, Pa., 1994.

Burlingame, Michael, ed. *An Oral History of Abraham Lincoln: John G. Nicolay's Interviews and Essays.* Carbondale, Ill., 1996.

Butler, Benjamin F. *Butler's Book.* Boston, 1892.

Byrne, Frank L., ed. *The View from Headquarters: Civil War Letters of Harvey Reid.* Madison, Wisc., 1965.

——, and Andrew T. Weaver, eds. *Haskell of Gettysburg: His Life and Civil War Papers.* Madison, Wisc., 1970.

Carpenter, Francis B. *Six Months at the White House with Abraham Lincoln.* New York, 1867.

Carroll, John M. *A Few Memories of a Long Life.* Fairfield, Wash., 1988.

Carter, Robert Goldthwaite. *Four Brothers in Blue.* Austin, Tex., 1978.

Chadwick, Bruce, ed. *Brother Against Brother: The Lost Civil War Diary of Lt. Edmund Halsey.* Secaucus, N.J., 1997.

Chapman, Horatio Dana. *Civil War Diary: Diary of a Forty-Niner.* Hartford, Conn., 1929.

Chittenden, Lucius E. *Invisible Siege: The Journal of Lucius E. Chittenden, April 15, 1861–July 14, 1861.* San Diego, 1969.

——. *Recollections of President Lincoln and His Administration.* New York, 1891.

——. *The Sleeping Sentinel: The True Story.* New York, 1909.

Cochrane, John. *The War for the Union: Memoir of Gen. John Cochrane.* N.p., 1875.

Coco, Gregory A., ed. *From Ball's Bluff to Gettysburg ... and Beyond.* N.p., 1994.

Cox, Florence, ed. *Kiss Josey for Me!* Santa Ana, Calif., 1974.

Crist, Lynda Laswell, and Mary Seaton Dix, eds. *The Papers of Jefferson Davis.* Vol. 7, 1861. Baton Rouge, 1992.

Crotty, Daniel G. *Four Years Campaigning in the Army of the Potomac.* Grand Rapids, Mich., 1874.

Daly, Robert W., ed. *Aboard the USS "Monitor," 1862: The Letters of Acting Paymaster William Frederick Keeler, U.S. Navy.* Annapolis, Md., 1964.

Dana, Charles A. *Recollections of the Civil War.* New York, 1898.

Davis, Jack C., ed. *Dear Wife: Letters of a Civil War Soldier.* Louisville, 1991.

Dawes, Rufus R. *Service with the Sixth Wisconsin Volunteers.* Marietta, Ohio, 1890.

Dennett, Tyler, comp. *Lincoln and the Civil War in the Diaries and Letters of John Hay.* New York, 1939.

Drake, Julia A., ed. *The Mail Goes Through, or the Civil War Letters of George Drake.* San Angelo, Tex., 1964.

Drickamer, Lee C. and Karen D., eds. *Fort Lyon to Harpers Ferry: The Civil War Letters and Newspaper Dispatches of Charles H. Moulton.* Shippensburg, Pa., 1987.

Driver, Robert A. and Gloria S., eds. *Letters Home: The Personal Side of the American Civil War.* Roseburg, Oreg., 1992.

Duncan, Russell, ed. *Blue-eyed Child of Fortune: The Civil War Letters of Colonel Robert Gould Shaw.* Athens, Ga., 1992.

Duram, James C. and Eleanor A., eds. *Soldier of the Cross: The Civil War Diary and Correspondence of Rev. Andrew Jackson Hartsock.* Manhattan, Kans., 1979.

Ellis, Thomas T. *Leaves from the Diary of an Army Surgeon.* New York, 1863.

Engert, Roderick M., ed. *Maine to the Wilderness: The Civil War Letters of Private William Lamson, 20th Maine Infantry.* Orange, Va., 1993.

Fehrenbacher, Don E. and Virginia, eds. *Recollected Words of Abraham Lincoln.* Stanford, Calif., 1996.

Fisk, Wilbur. *Anti-Rebel: The Civil War Letters of Wilbur Fisk.* Croton-on-Hudson, N.Y., 1983.

Floyd, Dale E., ed. *"Dear Friends at Home": The Letters and Diary of Thomas James Owen, Fiftieth New York Volunteer Engineer Regiment, During the Civil War.* Washington, D.C., 1985.

Foner, Philip S., ed. *The Life and Writings of Frederick Douglass.* 5 vols. New York, 1950–75.

Franklin, John Hope, ed. *The Diary of James T. Ayers, Civil War Recruiter.* Springfield, Ill., 1947.

Fuller, Charles A. *Personal Recollections of the War of 1861.* Sherburne, N.Y., 1906.

Galloway, Richard P., comp. *One Battle Too Many: The Writings of Simon Bolivar Hulbert, Private, Company E, 100th Regiment, New York State Volunteers, 1861–1864.* N.p., 1987.

Gates, Arnold, ed. *The Rough Side of War: The Civil War Journal of Chesley A. Mosman.* Garden City, N.Y., 1987.

Gates, Betsey, ed. *The Colton Letters: Civil War Period, 1861–1865.* Scottsdale, Ariz., 1993.

Gibbon, John. *Personal Recollections of the Civil War.* New York, 1928.

Gray, John Chipman, and John Codman Ropes. *War Letters 1862–1865.* Boston, 1927.

Greenleaf, Margery, ed. *Letters to Eliza from a Union Soldier, 1862–1865.* Chicago, 1969.

Greiner, James M., Janet L. Coryell, and James R. Smither, eds. *A Surgeon's Civil War: The Letters & Diary of Daniel M. Holt, M.D.* Kent, Ohio, 1994.

Hamilton, Henry S. *Reminiscences of a Veteran.* Concord, N.H., 1897.

Harwell, Richard, and Philip N. Racine, eds. *The Fiery Trail: A Union Officer's Account of Sherman's Last Campaigns.* Knoxville, 1986.

Hecht, Lydia P., ed. *Echoes from the Letters of a Civil War Surgeon.* N.p., 1996.

Hedley, F. Y. *Marching Through Georgia.* Chicago, 1884.

Herndon, William H., and Jesse Weik. *Herndon's Life of Lincoln.* New York, 1930.

Hess, Earl J., ed. *A German in the Yankee Fatherland: The Civil War Letters of Henry A. Kircher.* Kent, Ohio, 1983.

Hoerner, George M., Jr., ed. *Chattanooga, Savannah and Alexandria: The Diary of One of Sherman's Soldiers.* Easton, Pa., 1988.

Holzer, Harold, ed. *Dear Mr. Lincoln: Letters to the President.* New York, 1993.

Howe, Mark DeWolfe, ed. *Home Letters of General Sherman.* New York, 1909.

Humphreys, Charles A. *Field, Camp, Hospital and Prison in the Civil War, 1863–1865.* New York, 1918.

Hunt, H. Draper, ed. *Dearest Father: The Civil War Letters of Lt. Frank Dickerson.* Unity, Me., 1992.

Jones, Evan R. *Four Years in the Army of the Potomac: A Soldier's Recollections.* London, 1882.

Jones, Gordon C., ed. *"For My Country": The Richardson Letters, 1861–1865.* Wendell, N.C., 1984.

Kallgren, Beverly Hayes, and James L. Couthamel, eds. *"Dear Friend Anna": The Civil War Letters of a Common Soldier from Maine.* Orono, Me., 1992.

Kent, Arthur A., ed. *Three Years with Company K.* Cranbury, N.J., 1976.

Kieffer, Harry M. *The Recollections of a Drummer-Boy.* Boston, 1889.

Lamon, Ward Hill. *Recollections of Abraham Lincoln, 1847–1865.* Washington, D.C., 1911.

Lewis, A. S., ed. *My Dear Parents: The Civil War Seen by an English Union Soldier.* New York, 1982.

Livermore, Mary A. *My Story of the War.* Hartford, Conn., 1888.

Mahood, Wayne, ed. *Charlie Mosher's Civil War: From Fair Oaks to Andersonville with the Plymouth Pilgrims (85th N.Y. Infantry).* Hightstown, N.J., 1994.

Marshall, Albert O. *Army Life: From a Soldier's Journal.* Joliet, Ill., 1884.

Marshall, Jessie A., ed. *Private and Official Correspondence of General Benjamin F. Butler During the Period of the Civil War.* 5 vols. Norwood, Mass., 1917.

McBride, Robert E. *In the Ranks from the Wilderness to Appomattox Court-House.* Cincinnati, 1881.

McBride, Robert W. *Personal Recollections of Abraham Lincoln.* Indianapolis, 1926.

McClellan, George B. *McClellan's Own Story.* New York, 1887.

McClure, Alexander K. *Abraham Lincoln and Men of War-Times.* Philadelphia, 1892.

McGeehan, Albert H., ed. *My Country and Cross: The Civil War Letters of John Anthony Wilterdink, Company I, 25th Michigan Infantry.* Dallas, 1982.

McPherson, James M. and Patricia R., eds. *Lamson of the "Gettysburg."* New York, 1997.

Menge, W. Springer, and J. August Shimrak, eds. *The Civil War Notebook of Daniel Chisholm.* New York, 1989.

Minnesota Commandery, Military Order of the Loyal Legion of the United States. *Glimpses of the Nation's Struggle.* 6 vols. St. Paul, Minn., 1887.

Moss, Lemuel. *Annals of the United States Christian Commission.* Philadelphia, 1868.

Musgrave, Richard W. *Autobiography of Capt. Richard W. Musgrave.* N.p., 1921.

Nevins, Allan, ed. *A Diary of Battle: The Personal Journals of Colonel Charles S. Wainwright, 1861–1865.* New York, 1962.

————, ed. *Diary of the Civil War 1860–1865: George Templeton Strong.* New York, 1962.

Nichols, George W. *The Story of the Great March.* New York, 1865.

Nicolay, Helen. *Personal Traits of Abraham Lincoln.* New York, 1912.

Noe, Kenneth W., ed. *A Southern Boy in Blue: The Memoir of Marcus Woodcock, 9th Kentucky Infantry (U.S.A.).* Knoxville, 1996.

Norton, Oliver Wilcox. *Army Letters 1861–1865.* Chicago, 1903.

O'Brien, Kevin E., ed. *My Life in the Irish Brigade.* Campbell, Calif., 1996.

Overfield, Joseph M., ed. *The Civil War Letters of Private George Parks, Company C, 24th New York Cavalry Volunteers.* Buffalo, N.Y., 1992.

Palladino, Anita, ed. *Diary of a Yankee Engineer: The Civil War Story of John H. Westervelt, Engineer, 1st New York Volunteer Engineer Corps.* New York, 1997.

Phillips, Marion G., and Valeria Phillips Parsegian, eds. *Richard and Rhoda: Letters from the Civil War.* Rhinebeck, N.Y., 1981.

Popchock, Barry, ed. *Soldier Boy: The Civil War Letters of Charles O. Musser, 29th Iowa.* Iowa City, 1995.

Porter, Horace. *Campaigning With Grant.* Bloomington, Ind., 1961.

Priest, John M., ed. *John T. McMahon's Diary of the 136th New York 1861–1864.* Shippensburg, Pa., 1993.

Quaife, Milo M., ed. *From the Cannon's Mouth: The Civil War Letters of General Alpheus S. Williams.* Detroit, 1959.

Rhodes, Robert H., ed. *All for the Union: The Civil War Diary and Letters of Elisha Hunt Rhodes.* New York, 1991.

Rice, Allen Thorndike. *Reminiscences of Abraham Lincoln.* New York, 1885.

Roth, Margaret Probst, ed. *Well Mary: Civil War Letters of a Wisconsin Volunteer.* Madison, Wisc., 1960.

Scrymser, James A. *Personal Reminiscences.* N.p., 1915.

Sears, Stephen W., ed. *The Civil War Papers of George B. McClellan: Selected Correspondence 1860–1865.* New York, 1989.

————, ed. *For Country, Cause & Leader: The Civil War Journal of Charles B. Haydon.* New York, 1993.

Sherman, William T. *Memoirs of General William T. Sherman, by Himself.* 2 vols. New York, 1891.

Silliker, Ruth L., ed. *The Rebel Yell & the Yankee Hurrah: The Civil War Journal of a Maine Volunteer.* Camden, Me., 1985.

Skidmore, Richard S., ed. *The Civil War Journal of Billy Davis.* Greencastle, Ind., 1989.

Small, Harold Adams, ed. *The Road to Richmond: The Civil War Memoirs of Major Abner R. Small.* Berkeley, Calif., 1939.

Smith, Edward. *Incidents of the United States Christian Commission.* Philadelphia, 1871.

Sterling, Ada, ed. *A Belle of the Fifties: Memoirs of Mrs. Clay of Alabama.* New York, 1905.

Stevens, C. A. *Berdan's United States Sharpshooters in the Army of the Potomac 1861–1865.* St. Paul, Minn., 1892.

Stevens, Michael E., ed. *As if It Were Glory: Robert Beecham's Civil War from the Iron Brigade to the Black Regiments.* Madison, Wisc., 1997.

Tapert, Annette, ed. *The Brothers' War: Civil War Letters to Their Loved Ones from the Blue and Gray.* New York, 1988.

Tapp, Hambleton, and James C. Klotter, eds. *The Union, the Civil War, and John W. Tuttle.* Frankfort, Ky., 1980.

Trumbull, Henry Clay. *War Memories of an Army Chaplain.* New York, 1989.

Turino, Kenneth C., ed. *The Civil War Diary of Lieut. J. E. Hodgkins.* Camden, Me., 1994.

Underhill, Charles Sterling, comp. *"Your Soldier Boy Samuel": Civil War Letters of Lieut. Samuel Edmund Nichols.* Buffalo, N.Y., 1929.

Wallace, W. W. *Reminiscences.* N.p., 1915.

Weld, Stephen Minot. *War Diary and Letters of Stephen Minot Weld 1861–1865.* Boston, 1979.

Welles, Gideon. *Diary of Gideon Welles.* 3 vols. Boston, 1909–11.

Wells, James M. *"With Touch of Elbow" or Death Before Dishonor.* Philadelphia, 1909.

White, Russell, ed. *The Civil War Diary of Wyman S. White.* Hamet, Calif., 1979.

Whiteaker, Larry H., and W. Calvin Dickinson, eds. *Civil War Letters of the Tenure Family, Rockland County, N.Y., 1862–1865.* New York, 1990.

Wilkeson, Frank. *Recollections of a Private Soldier in the Army of the Potomac.* New York, 1887.

Wills, Charles W. *Army Life of an Illinois Soldier.* Washington, D.C., 1906.

Yacovone, Donald, ed. *A Voice of Thunder: The Civil War Letters of George E. Stephens.* Urbana, Ill., 1997.

Official Publications

United States War Department. *List of Synonyms of Organizations in the Volunteer Service of the United States.* Washington, D.C., 1885. Reprinted as vol. II of William F. Amman, ed., *Personnel of the Civil War* (New York, 1961).

———. *War of the Rebellion: Official Records of the Union and Confederate Armies.* 128 vols. Washington, D.C., 1880–1901.

Articles

Harvey, Cordelia A. P. "A Wisconsin Woman's Picture of President Lincoln." *Wisconsin Magazine of History,* I (1918), pp. 233–55.

Hopkins, Vivian C., ed. "Soldier of the 92nd Illinois: Letters of William H. Brown and His Fiancee, Emma Jane Frazey." *Bulletin of the New York Public Library,* 73 (February 1969), pp. 114–36.

SECONDARY SOURCES

Regimental Histories

Anders, Leslie. *The Twenty-first Missouri: From Home Guard to Union Regiment.* Westport, Conn., 1975.

Baxter, Nancy Niblack. *Gallant Fourteenth: The Story of an Indiana Civil War Regiment.* Traverse City, Ind., 1980.

Burchard, Peter. *One Gallant Rush: Robert Gould Shaw and His Brave Black Regiment.* New York, 1965.

Decker, Frederick Charles, ed. *Yates Phalanx: The History of the Thirty-ninth Regiment, Illinois Volunteer Veteran Infantry.* Bowie, Md., 1994.

Gaff, Alan D. *On Many a Bloody Field: Four Years in the Iron Brigade.* Bloomington, Ind., 1996.

Hagerty, Edward J. *Collis' Zouaves: The 114th Pennsylvania Volunteers in the Civil War.* Baton Rouge, 1997.

Hard, Abner. *History of the Eighth Cavalry Regiment, Illinois Volunteers.* Aurora, Ill., 1868.

Huffstodt, Jim. *Hard Dying Men.* Bowie, Md., 1994.

McGee, B. F. *History of the 72d Indiana Volunteer Infantry of the Mounted Lightning Brigade.* LaFayette, Ind., 1882.

Moe, Richard. *The Last Full Measure: The Life and Death of the First Minnesota Volunteers.* New York, 1993.

Mullins, Michael A. *The Frémont Rifles: A History of the 37th Illinois Veteran Volunteer Infantry.* Wilmington, N.C., 1990.

Nash, Eugene A. *A History of the Forty-fourth Regiment New York Volunteer Infantry.* Chicago, 1910.

Otis, George H. *The Second Wisconsin Infantry.* Dayton, Ohio, 1984.

Powell, William H. *The Fifth Army Corps.* London, 1895.

Pullen, John J. *A Shower of Stars: The Medal of Honor and the 27th Maine.* Philadelphia, 1966.

Rowell, John W. *Yankee Artillerymen: Through the Civil War with Eli Lilly's Indiana Battery.* Knoxville, 1975.

Smith, Donald L. *The Twenty-fourth Michigan.* Harrisburg, Pa., 1962.

Starr, Stephen Z. *Jennison's Jayhawkers: A Civil War Cavalry Regiment and Its Commander.* Baton Rouge, 1973.

Sunderland, Glenn W. *Five Days to Glory.* New York, 1970.

Wilkinson, Warren. *Mother May You Never See the Sights I Have Seen: The Fifty-seventh Massachusetts Veteran Volunteers in the Army of the Potomac 1864–1865.* New York, 1990.

Biographies, Monographs, and Special Studies

Adams, Michael C. C. *Our Masters the Rebels: A Speculation on Union Military Failure in the East, 1861–1865.* Cambridge, Mass., 1978.

Alotta, Robert I. *Civil War Justice: Union Army Executions Under Lincoln.* Shippensburg, Pa., 1989.

Benton, Josiah Henry. *Voting in the Field: A Forgotten Chapter of the Civil War.* Boston, 1915.

Bernard, Kenneth A. *Lincoln and the Music of the Civil War.* Caldwell, Idaho, 1966.

Boritt, Gabor S., ed. *Why the Confederacy Lost.* New York, 1992.

Bremner, Robert H. *The Public Good: Philanthropy and Welfare in the Civil War Era.* New York, 1980.

Bruce, Robert V. *Lincoln and the Tools of War.* Indianapolis, 1956.

Coffman, Edward M. *The Old Army: A Portrait of the American Army in Peacetime, 1784–1898.* New York, 1986.

Conwell, Russell H. *Why Lincoln Laughed.* New York, 1922.

Cook, Adrian. *The Armies of the Streets: The New York Draft Riots of 1863.* Lexington, Ky., 1974.

Cornish, Dudley T. *The Sable Arm: Black Troops in the Union Army, 1861–1865.* Lawrence, Kans., 1956.

Cramer, John Henry. *Lincoln Under Enemy Fire: A Complete Account of His Experiences During Early's Attack on Washington.* Baton Rouge, 1948.

Cress, Lawrence Delbert. *Citizens in Arms: The Army and Militia in American Society to the War of 1812.* Chapel Hill, N.C., 1982.

Crosby, Frank. *Life of Abraham Lincoln.* Philadelphia, 1865.

Current, Richard Nelson. *The Lincoln Nobody Knows.* New York, 1958.

————. *Lincoln's Loyalists: Union Soldiers from the Confederacy.* Boston, 1992.

Davis, Michael. *The Image of Lincoln in the South.* Knoxville, 1971.

Davis, William C. *Battle at Bull Run.* New York, 1977.

————. *"A Government of Our Own": The Making of the Confederacy.* New York, 1994.

Donald, David Herbert. *Lincoln.* New York, 1995.

Eaton, John, with Ethel Osgood Mason. *Grant, Lincoln and the Freedmen.* New York, 1907.

Forgie, George B. *Patricide in the House Divided: A Psychological Interpretation of Lincoln and His Age.* New York, 1979.

Glatthaar, Joseph T. *Forged in Battle: The Civil War Alliance of Black Soldiers and White Officers.* New York, 1990.

———. *The March to the Sea and Beyond: Sherman's Troops in the Savannah and Carolinas Campaigns.* New York, 1985.

Gollaher, David. *Voice for the Mad: The Life of Dorothea Dix.* New York, 1995.

Hamilton, Charles, and Lloyd Ostendorf. *Lincoln in Photographs: An Album of Every Known Pose.* Dayton, Ohio, 1985.

Hauptman, Laurence M. *The Iroquois in the Civil War.* Syracuse, N.Y., 1993.

Heaps, Willard A. and Porter W. *The Singing Sixties: The Spirit of Civil War Days Drawn from the Music of the Times.* Norman, Okla., 1960.

Heckman, Richard Allen. *Lincoln vs Douglas: The Great Debates Campaign.* Washington, D.C., 1967.

Hess, Earl J. *Liberty, Virtue, and Progress: Northerners and Their War for the Union.* New York, 1988.

Hesseltine, William. *Lincoln and the War Governors.* New York, 1948.

Hicken, Victor. *Illinois in the Civil War.* Urbana, Ill., 1966.

Holzer, Harold, Mark E. Neely, Jr., and Gabor S. Boritt. *The Lincoln Image: Abraham Lincoln and the Popular Print.* New York, 1984.

Janvier, Francis De Haas. *The Sleeping Sentinel.* Philadelphia, 1863.

Jimerson, Randall C. *The Private Civil War: Popular Thought During the Sectional Conflict.* Baton Rouge, 1988.

Kelley, William D. *Lincoln and Stanton.* New York, 1885.

Kunhardt, Philip B., Jr. *A New Birth of Freedom: Lincoln at Gettysburg.* Boston, 1983.

Logue, Larry M. *To Appomattox and Beyond: The Civil War Soldier in War and Peace.* New York, 1996.

Long, David E. *The Jewel of Liberty: Abraham Lincoln's Re-election and the End of Slavery.* Harrisburg, Pa., 1994.

Longacre, Edward G. *Army of Amateurs: General Benjamin F. Butler and the Army of the James, 1863–1865.* Harrisburg, Pa., 1997.

Lonn, Ella. *Desertion During the Civil War.* Washington, D.C., 1928.

Lowry, Thomas P. *Tarnished Eagles: The Courts-Martial of Fifty Union Colonels and Lieutenant-Colonels.* Harrisburg, Pa., 1997.

Marvel, William. *Andersonville: The Last Depot.* Chapel Hill, N.C., 1994.

———. *Burnside.* Chapel Hill, N.C., 1991.

Maxwell, William Quentin. *Lincoln's Fifth Wheel: The Political History of the United States Sanitary Commission.* New York, 1956.

McConnell, Stuart. *Glorious Contentment: The Grand Army of the Republic, 1865–1900.* Chapel Hill, N.C., 1992.

McPherson, James M. *Battle Cry of Freedom: The Civil War Era.* New York, 1988.

———. *For Cause & Comrades: Why Men Fought in the Civil War.* New York, 1997.

———. *Ordeal by Fire: The Civil War and Reconstruction.* New York, 1982.

Mitchell, Reid. *Civil War Soldiers.* New York, 1988.

———. *The Vacant Chair: The Northern Soldier Leaves Home.* New York, 1993.

Murdoch, James E., ed. *Patriotism in Poetry and Prose.* Philadelphia, 1866.

Murdock, Eugene Converse. *Patriotism Limited, 1862–1865: The Civil War Draft and the Bounty System.* Kent, Ohio, 1967.

Nicolay, John G., and John Hay. *Abraham Lincoln: A History.* 10 vols. New York, 1890.

Oates, Stephen B. *A Woman of Valor: Clara Barton and the Civil War.* New York, 1994.

————. *With Malice Toward None: The Life of Abraham Lincoln.* New York, 1977.

Peterson, Merrill D. *Lincoln in American Memory.* New York, 1994.

Robertson, James I., Jr. *Soldiers Blue and Gray.* Columbia, S.C., 1988.

Sandburg, Carl. *Abraham Lincoln: The War Years.* 4 vols. New York, 1939.

Schlesinger, Arthur M., Jr., ed. *History of American Presidential Elections, 1789–1968.* 4 vols. New York, 1971.

Sears, Stephen W. *Chancellorsville.* Boston, 1996.

————. *George B. McClellan: The Young Napoleon.* New York, 1988.

————. *Landscape Turned Red: The Battle of Antietam.* Boston, 1983.

————. *To the Gates of Richmond: The Peninsula Campaign.* New York, 1992.

Shattuck, Gardiner H., Jr. *A Shield and Hiding Place: The Religious Life of the Civil War Armies.* Macon, Ga., 1987.

Sigelschiffer, Saul. *The American Conscience: The Drama of the Lincoln-Douglas Debates.* New York, 1973.

Smith, G. Wayne. *Nathan Goff, Jr.: A Biography.* Charleston, W.Va., 1959.

Smith, Rogers W. *Civic Ideals: Conflicting Visions of Citizenship in U.S. History.* New Haven, Conn., 1997.

Strozier, Charles B. *Lincoln's Quest for Union: Public and Private Meanings.* New York, 1982.

Tarbell, Ida M. *The Early Life of Abraham Lincoln.* New York, 1896.

Turner, Thomas Reed. *Beware the People Weeping: Public Opinion and the Assassination of Abraham Lincoln.* Baton Rouge, 1982.

Walsh, John Evangelist. *The Shadows Rise: Abraham Lincoln and the Ann Rutledge Legend.* Urbana, Ill., 1993.

Waugh, Jack C. *Reelecting Lincoln: The Presidential Election of 1864.* New York, 1998.

Weems, Mason Locke. *The Life of Washington.* Edited by Marcus Cunliffe. Cambridge, Mass., 1962. First published as book in 1809.

Articles

Dorris, Jonathan T. "President Lincoln's Clemency." *Journal of the Illinois State Historical Society,* 20 (January 1928), pp. 547–68.

Fischer, Roger A. "The Quality of Mercy: Lincoln's 'Gentle Legend' in American Popular Culture." In Linda Norbut Suits and George L. Painter, eds., *Abraham Lincoln and a Nation at War: Papers from the Ninth Annual Lincoln Colloquium* (Springfield, Ill., 1995), pp. 55–68.

Langsdorf, Edgar. "Jim Lane and the Frontier Guard." *Kansas Historical Quarterly,* 9 (February 1940), pp. 243–78.

Thompson, Mark. "Between Myth and Reality: Citizenship and the Militia in Revolutionary America." Paper presented at the Southern Historical Association meeting in Atlanta, Ga., November 7, 1997.

Winther, Oscar O. "The Soldier Vote in the Election of 1864." *New York History,* 25 (October 1944), pp. 440–58.

INDEX